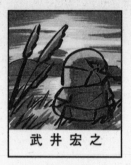

武井宏之

A lot of stuff happens. Or not.

—*Hiroyuki Takei*

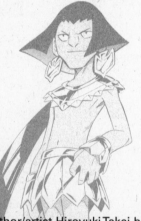

Unconventional author/artist Hiroyuki Takei began his career by winning the coveted Hop Step Award (for new manga artists) and the Osamu Tezuka Award (named after the famous artist of the same name). After working as an assistant to famed artist Nobuhiro Watsuki, Takei debuted in **Weekly Shonen Jump** in 1997 with **Butsu Zone**, an action series based on Buddhist mythology. His multicultural adventure manga **Shaman King**, which debuted in 1998, became a hit and was adapted into an anime TV series. His new series **Ultimo** (*Karakuri Dōji Ultimo*) is currently being serialized in the U.S. in **SHONEN JUMP**. Takei lists Osamu Tezuka, American comics and robot anime among his many influences.

SHAMAN KING VOL. 28
SHONEN JUMP Manga Edition

STORY AND ART BY
HIROYUKI TAKEI

English Adaptation/Lance Caselman
Translation/Lillian Olsen
Touch-up Art & Lettering/John Hunt
Design/Nozomi Akashi
Editor/Eric Searleman

VP, Production/Alvin Lu
VP, Sales & Product Marketing/Gonzalo Ferreyra
VP, Creative/Linda Espinosa
Publisher/Hyoe Narita

Printed in the U.S.A.

Published by VIZ Media, LLC
P.O. Box 77010
San Francisco, CA 94107

10 9 8 7 6 5 4 3 2 1
First printing, May 2010

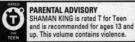

THE WORLD'S
MOST POPULAR MANGA

www.viz.com

www.shonenjump.com

SHONEN JUMP MANGA

Shaman King

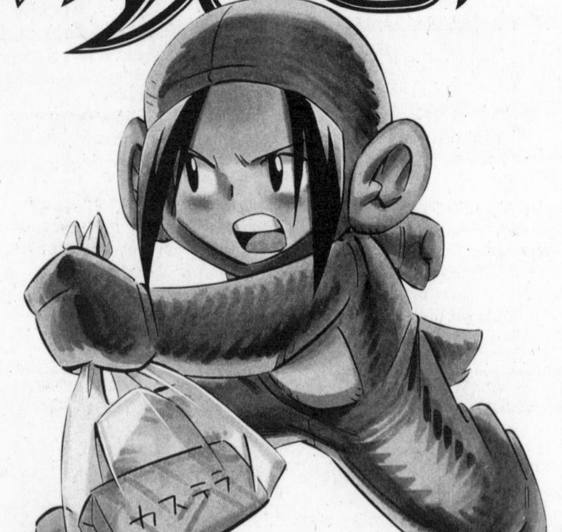
カステラ

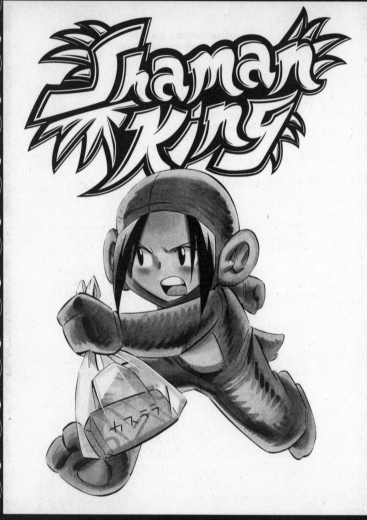

VOL. 28

A GOOD WOMAN

STORY AND ART BY
HIROYUKI TAKEI

CHARACTERS

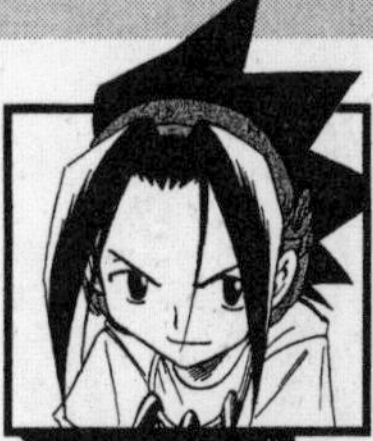

Yoh Asakura
Outwardly carefree and easygoing, Yoh bears a great responsibility as heir to a long line of Japanese shamans.

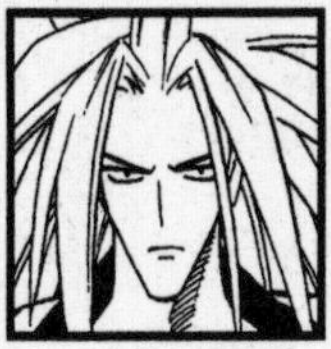

Amidamaru
"The Fiend" Amidamaru was, in life, a samurai of such skill and ferocity that he was a veritable one-man army. Now he is Yoh's loyal, and formidable, spirit ally.

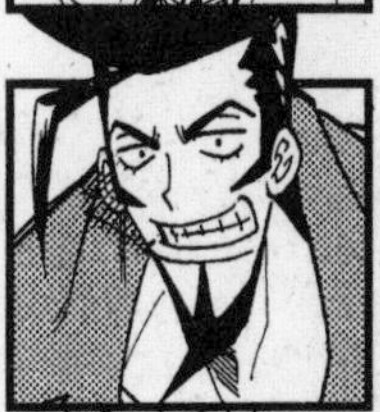

"Wooden Sword" Ryu
On a quest to find his Happy Place. Along the way, he became a shaman.

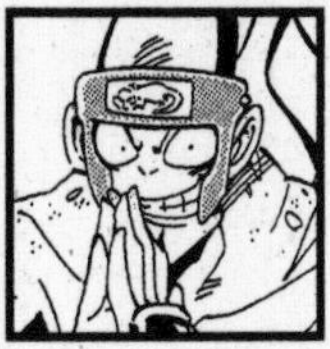

Tokagero
The ghost of a bandit slain by Amidamaru. He is now Ryu's spirit ally.

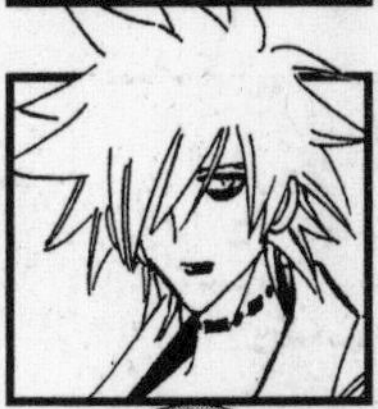

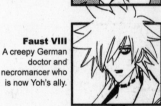

Faust VIII
A creepy German doctor and necromancer who is now Yoh's ally.

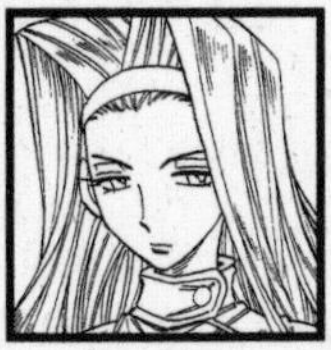

Eliza
Faust's late wife.

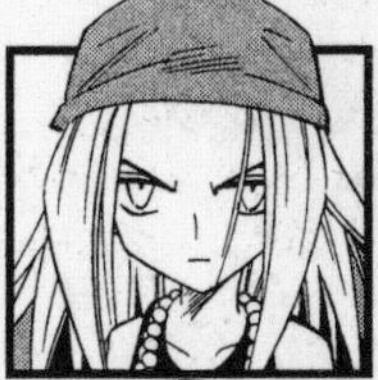

Anna Kyoyama
Yoh's butt-kicking fiancée. Anna is an itako, a traditional Japanese village shaman.

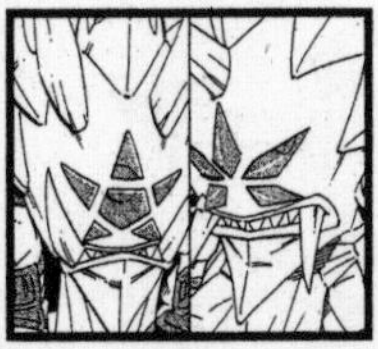

Zenki & Goki
Spirits who formerly served Hao but now serve Anna.

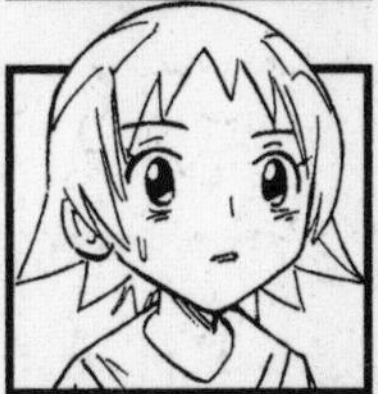

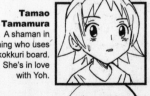

Tamao Tamamura
A shaman in training who uses a kokkuri board. She's in love with Yoh.

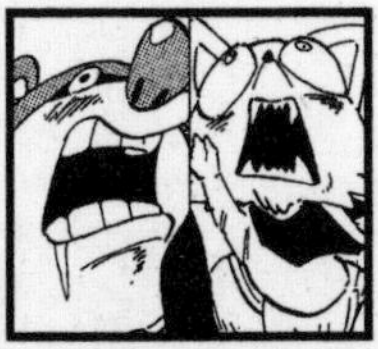

Ponchi & Konchi
Tamao's spirit allies. Not known for their genteel ways.

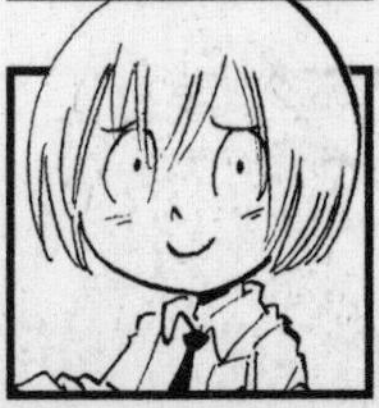

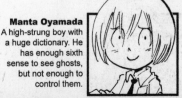

Manta Oyamada
A high-strung boy with a huge dictionary. He has enough sixth sense to see ghosts, but not enough to control them.

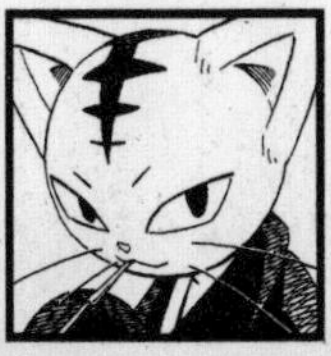

Matamune
A split-tailed cat who helped Yoh save Anna from her own powers.

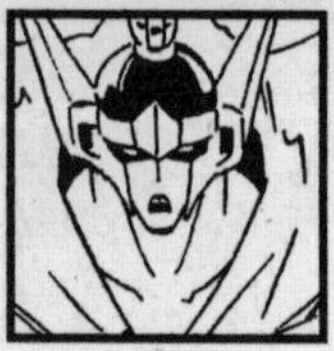

Bason
Ren's spirit ally is the ghost of a fearsome warlord from ancient China.

Tao Ren
A powerful shaman and the scion of the ruthless Tao Family.

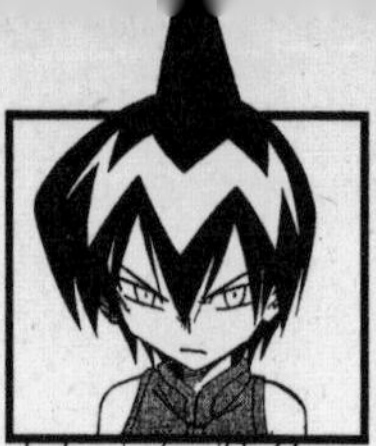

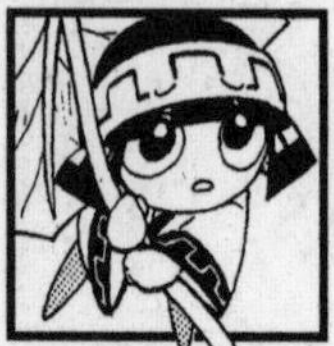

Kororo
Horohoro's spirit ally is one of the little nature spirits that the Ainu call Koropokkur.

Horohoro
An Ainu shaman whose Over Soul looks like a snowboard.

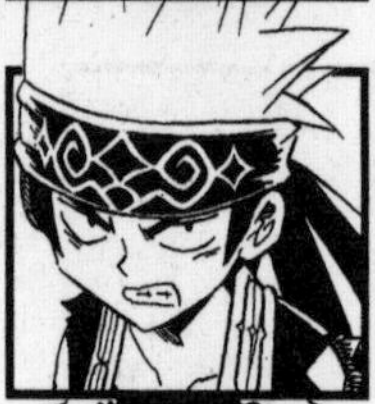

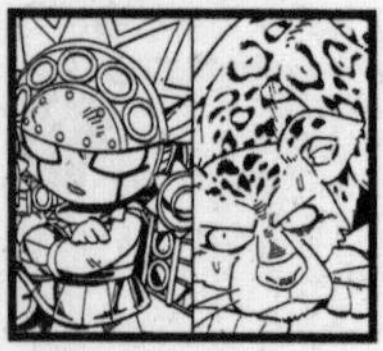

Mic & Pascual Abaj
Joco's jaguar spirit ally and the ghost of an Indio shaman.

Joco
A shaman who uses humor as a weapon. Or tries to.

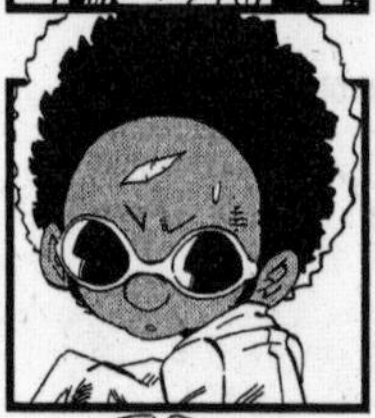

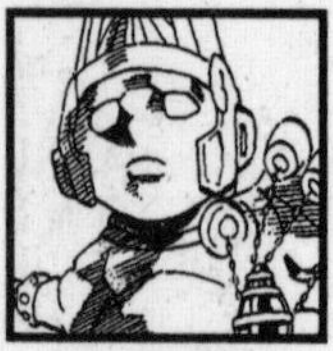

Shamash
Jeanne's spirit ally, a Babylonian god.

Jeanne, the Iron Maiden
The nominal leader of the X-LAWS. Spends most of her time in a medieval torture cabinet.

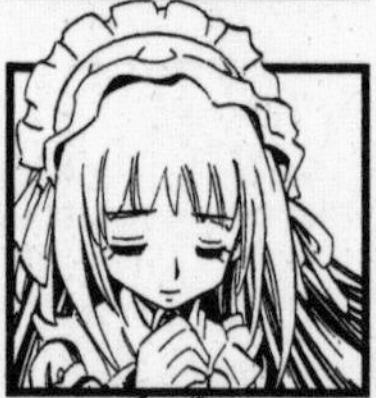

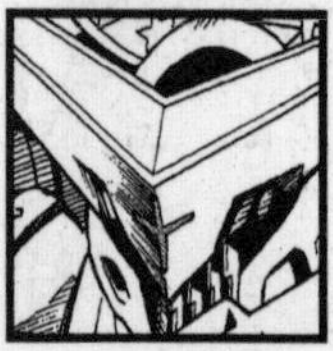

Michael
Marco's Archangel.

Marco
The true leader of the X-LAWS.

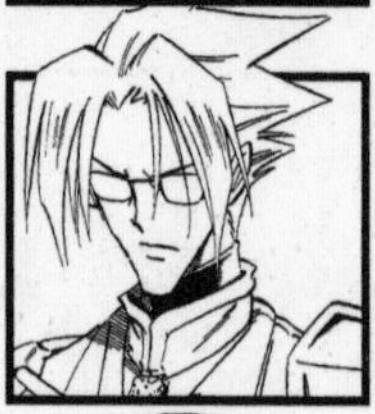

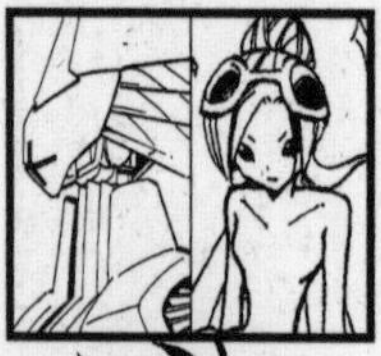

Morphea & Zeruel
Lyserg's poppy fairy and his new Angel.

Lyserg
A young shaman with a vendetta against Hao.

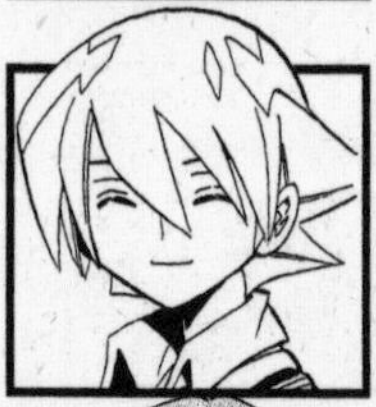

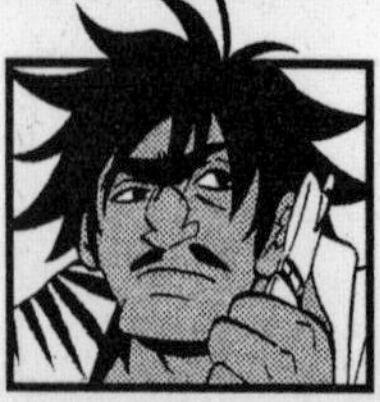

Kadu
A member of Gandala with Ragaraja.

Sati
The leader of Gandala. She brought Ryu and Joco back from the dead.

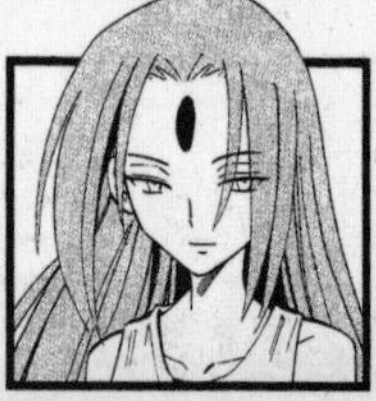

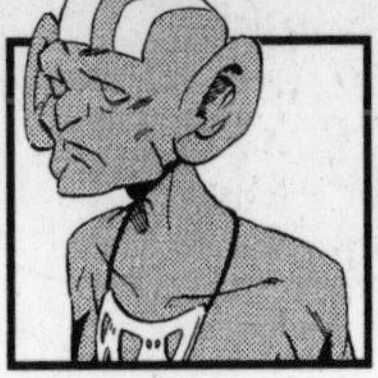

Yainage
A member of Gandala with Kundali.

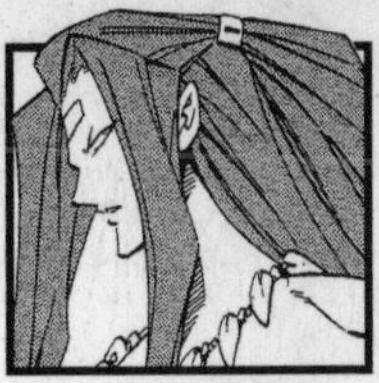

Jackson
A member of Gandala with Acala.

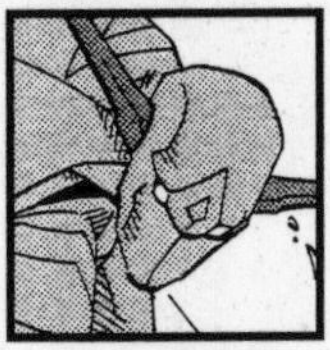

Spirit of Fire
One of the five High Spirits that belonged to the Patch.

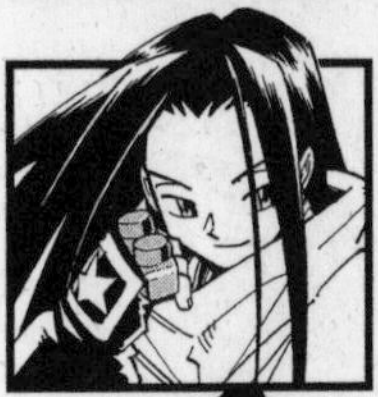

Hao
An enigmatic figure who calls himself the "Future King."

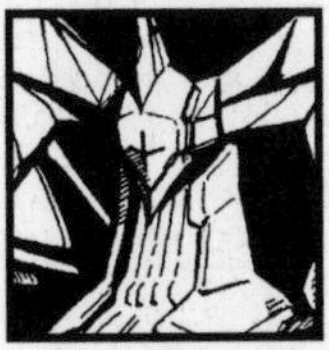

Lucifer
The first Angel, controlled by Luchist.

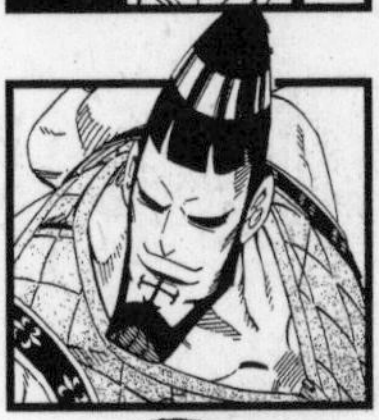

Luchist
The founder of the X-LAWS who now wants to destroy them for his master, Hao.

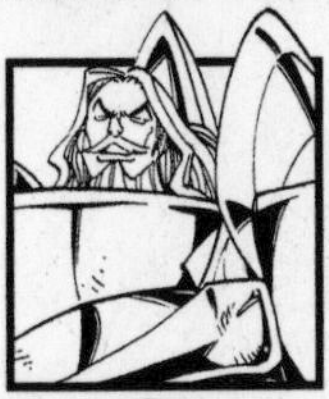

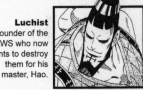

Ashcroft
Canna's spirit, an aged knight who seems chivalrous but actually has a foul mouth and a worse temper.

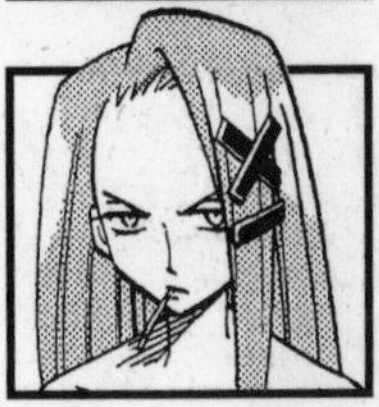

Canna Bismarck
A member of Hana-gumi, one of Hao's teams.

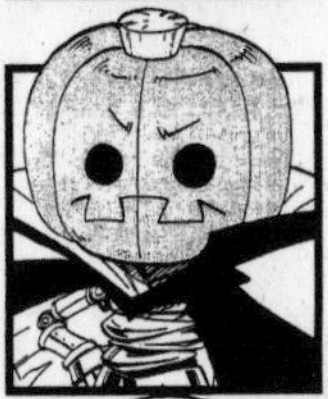

Jack
Mattie's pumpkin doll, which uses knives as weapons.

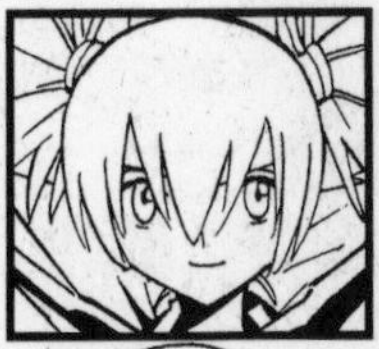

Mathilda
Nicknamed "Mattie," she's a druid with Hana-gumi.

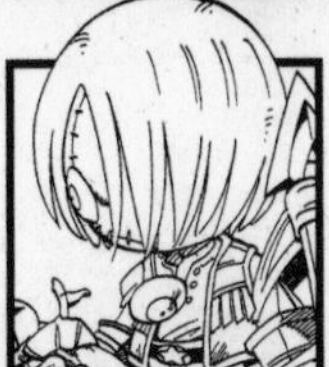

Chuck
Marie's cowboy gunslinger doll.

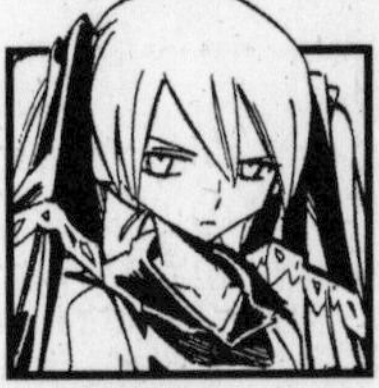

Marion Fauna
Nicknamed "Marie," she's a quiet doll-master with Hana-gumi.

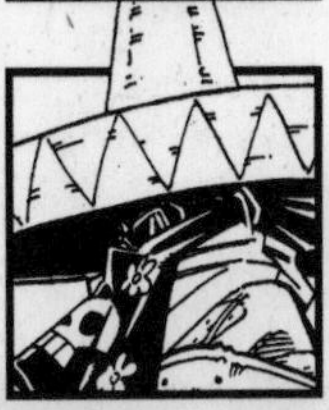

Peyote
Formerly with Tsuchi-gumi. He was defeated by Team Ren but continues to work for Hao.

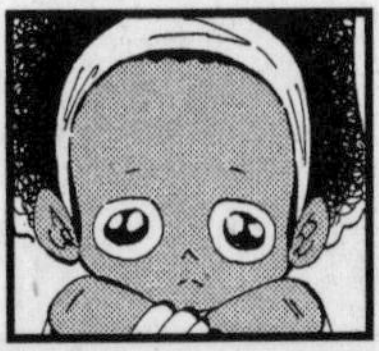

Opacho
Hao's devoted minion who has the power to see the future.

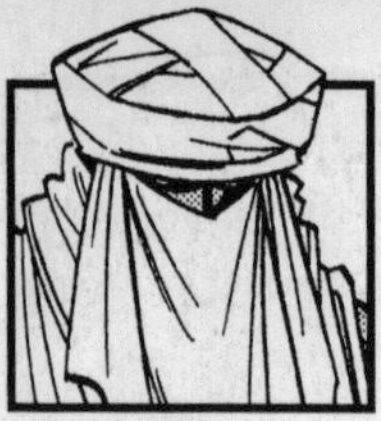

Turbine
A minion of Hao's who hides his face behind a turban and a veil.

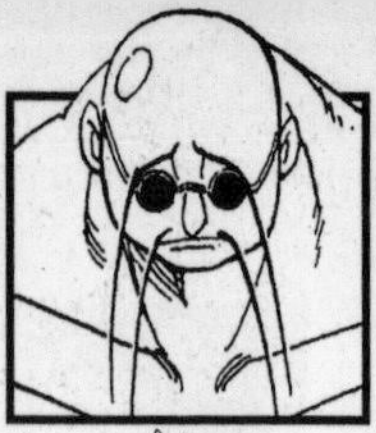

Zang Ching
A minion of Hao's whose spirit ally is a panda ghost called Xiong Xiong.

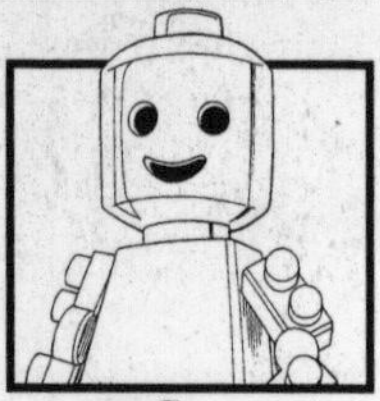

Blocken
A minion of Hao's whose body is made of toy building blocks.

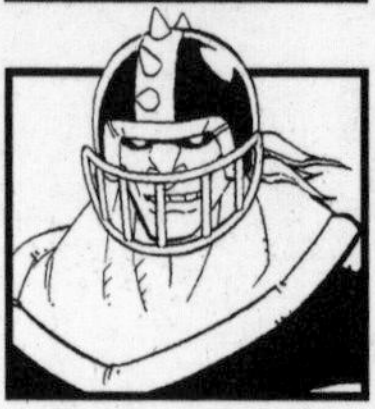

Big Guy Bill
Hao's minion, a football player whose spirit allies are his 21 former teammates.

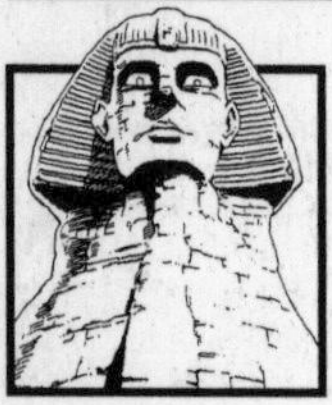

Sphinx
Anahol's flying spirit ally.

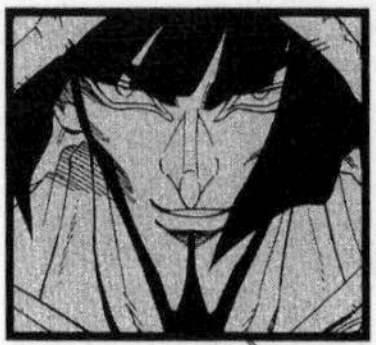

Anahol
A minion of Hao's whose brother, Anatel, was killed by the X-LAWS.

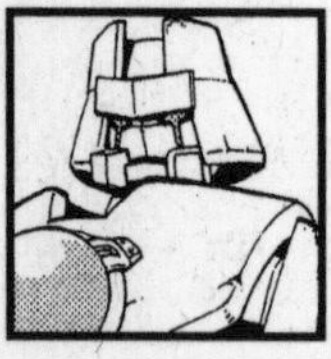

Golem
A robotic creature constructed by Dr. Munzer, Salerm and Ludsev's father.

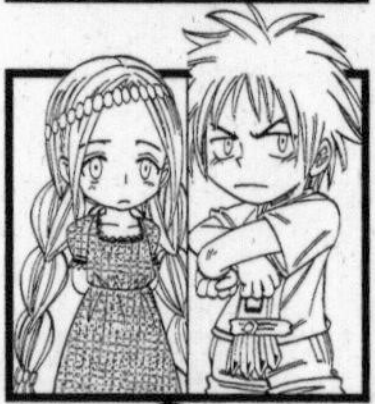

Salerm & Ludsev
A brother and sister who own the Golem.

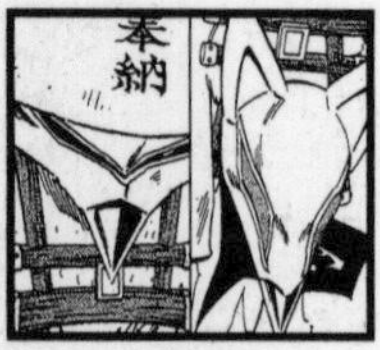

Shigaraki & Imari
Mickey's shape-shifting mountain spirit allies whom he also used for transportation.

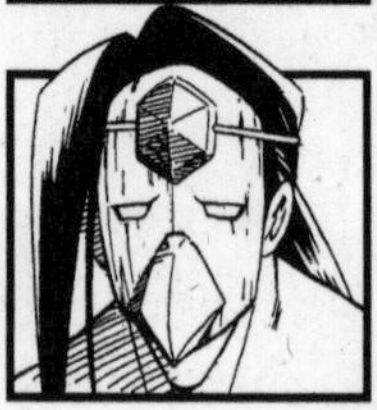

Mickey Asakura
Yoh's father. He wears a tengu mask.

THE STORY THUS FAR

Yoh Asakura not only sees dead people, he talks and fights with them too. That's because Yoh is a shaman, a traditional holy man able to interact with the spirit world. Yoh is now a competitor in the Shaman Fight, a tournament held every 500 years to decide who will become the Shaman King and shape humanity's future.

Hao continues to attack the other teams inside and outside of the official tournament. Meanwhile, Sati hatches a plan to use "five warriors" to defeat Hao, but it requires that Yoh, Ren, Horohoro, Joco and Lyserg to do some extra training—in Hell! But when Sati and Lady Jeanne are killed by Hao's minions, who will bring the warriors back again?!

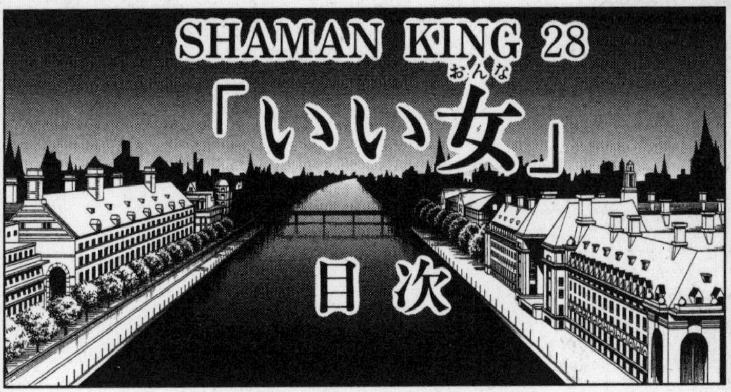
SHAMAN KING 28
「いい女」
目次

VOL. 28
A GOOD WOMAN

CONTENTS

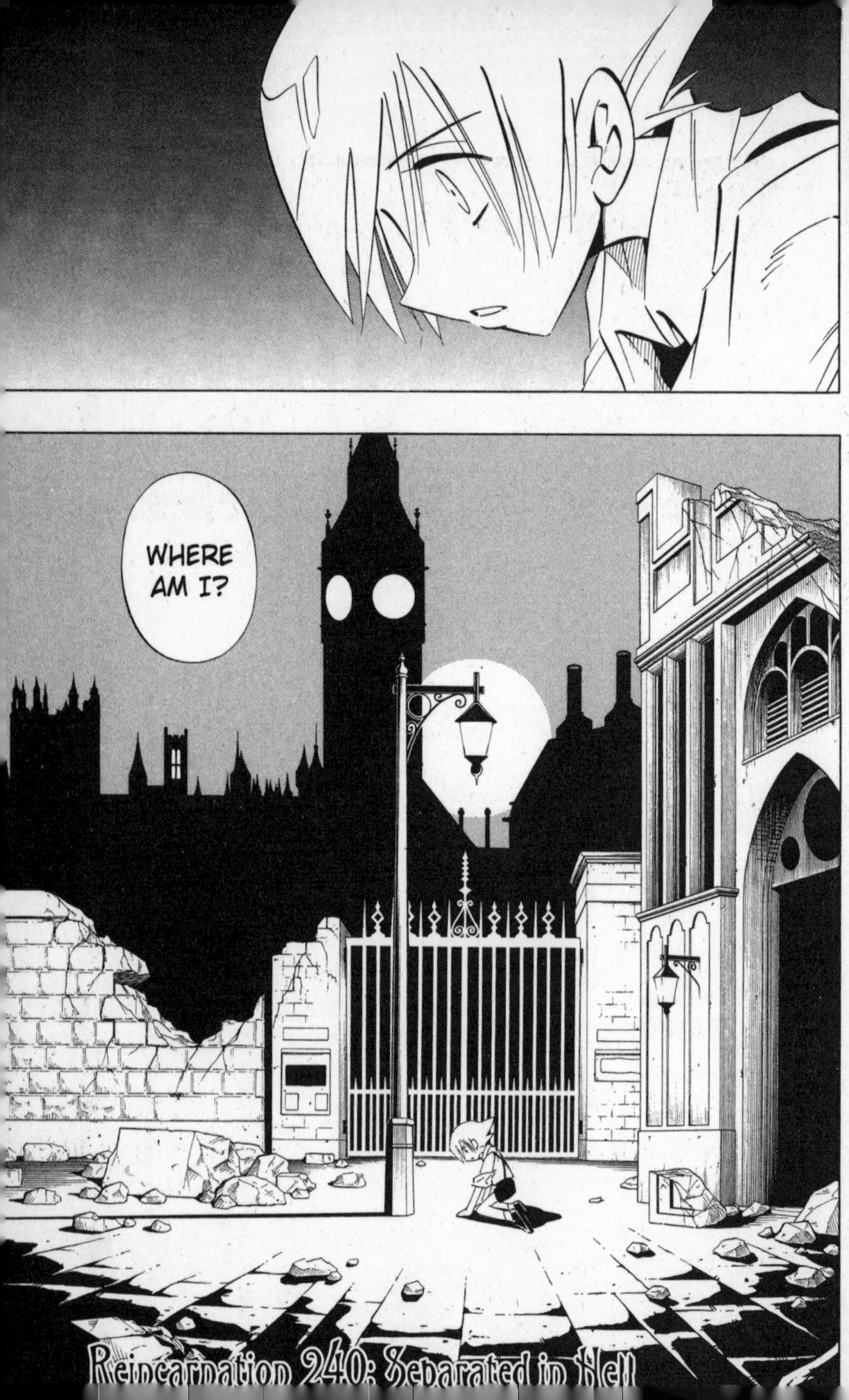
WHERE AM I?
Reincarnation 240: Separated in Hell

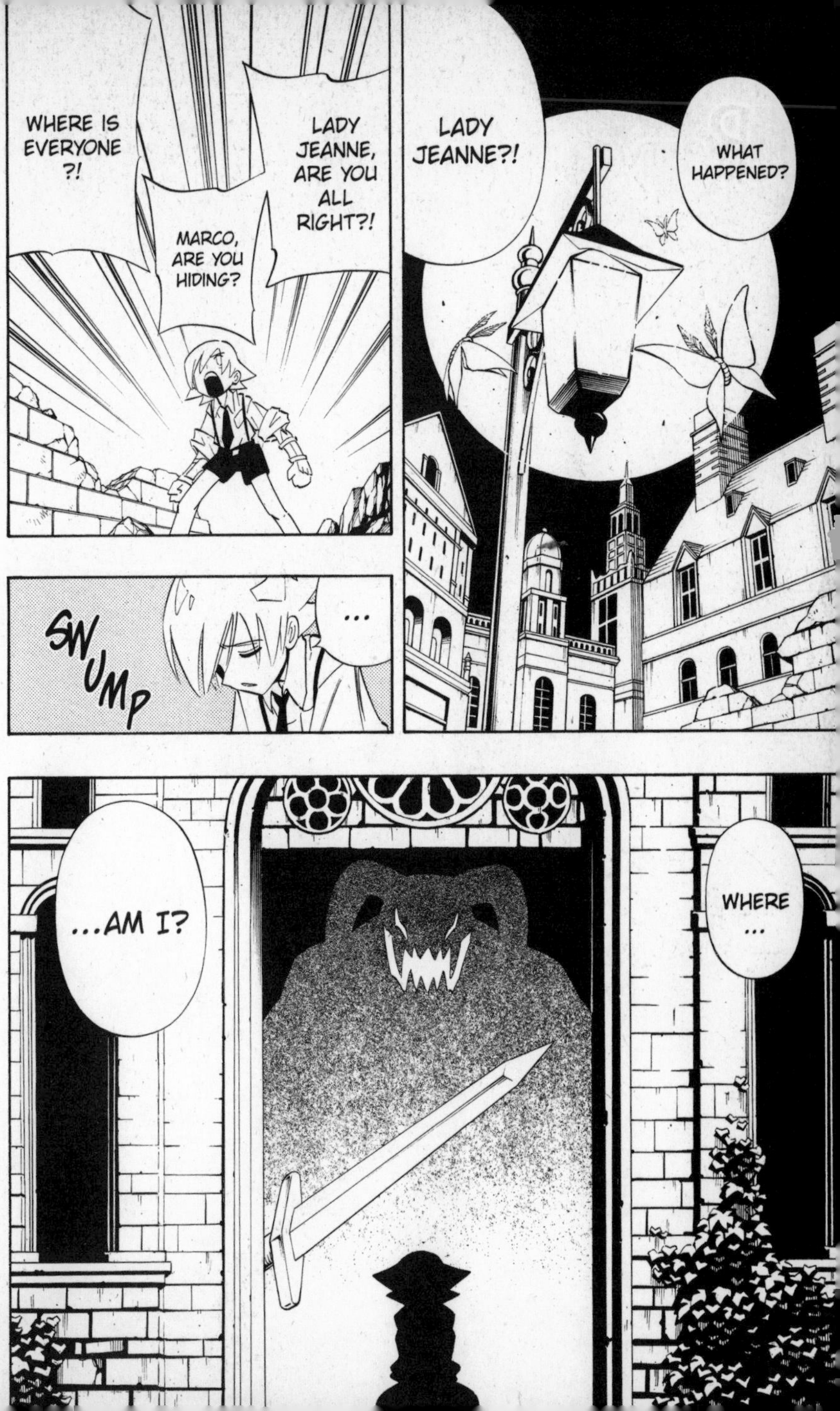
WHAT HAPPENED?
LADY JEANNE?!
LADY JEANNE, ARE YOU ALL RIGHT?!
WHERE IS EVERYONE ?!
MARCO, ARE YOU HIDING?
...
SWUMP
WHERE ...
...AM I?

Reincarnation 240: Separated in Hell

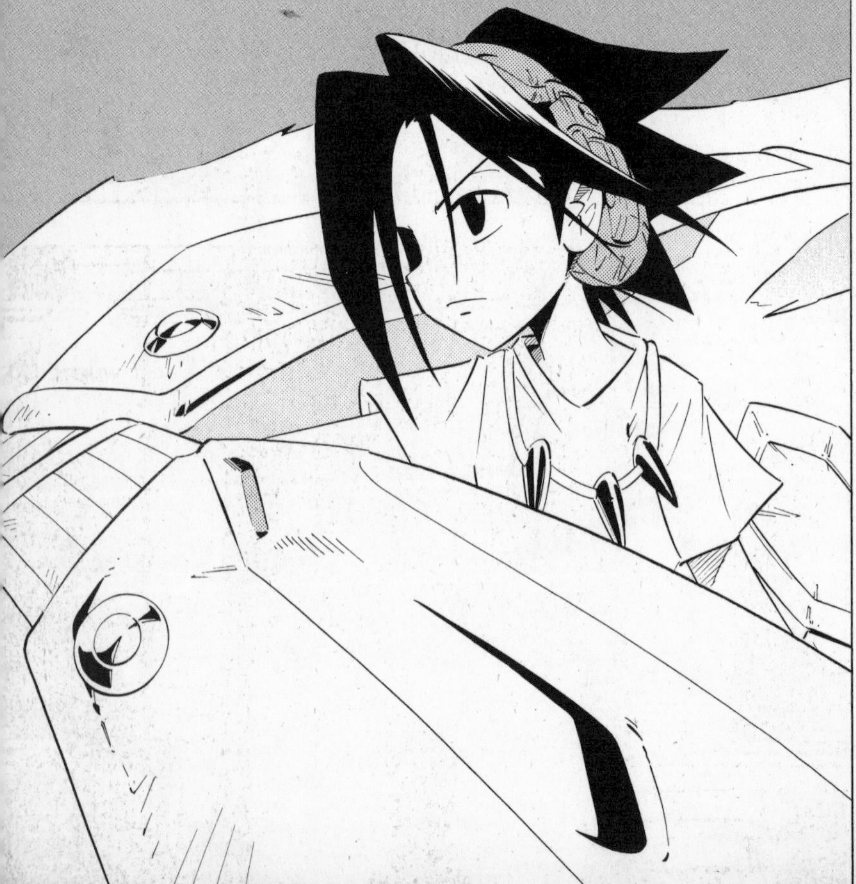

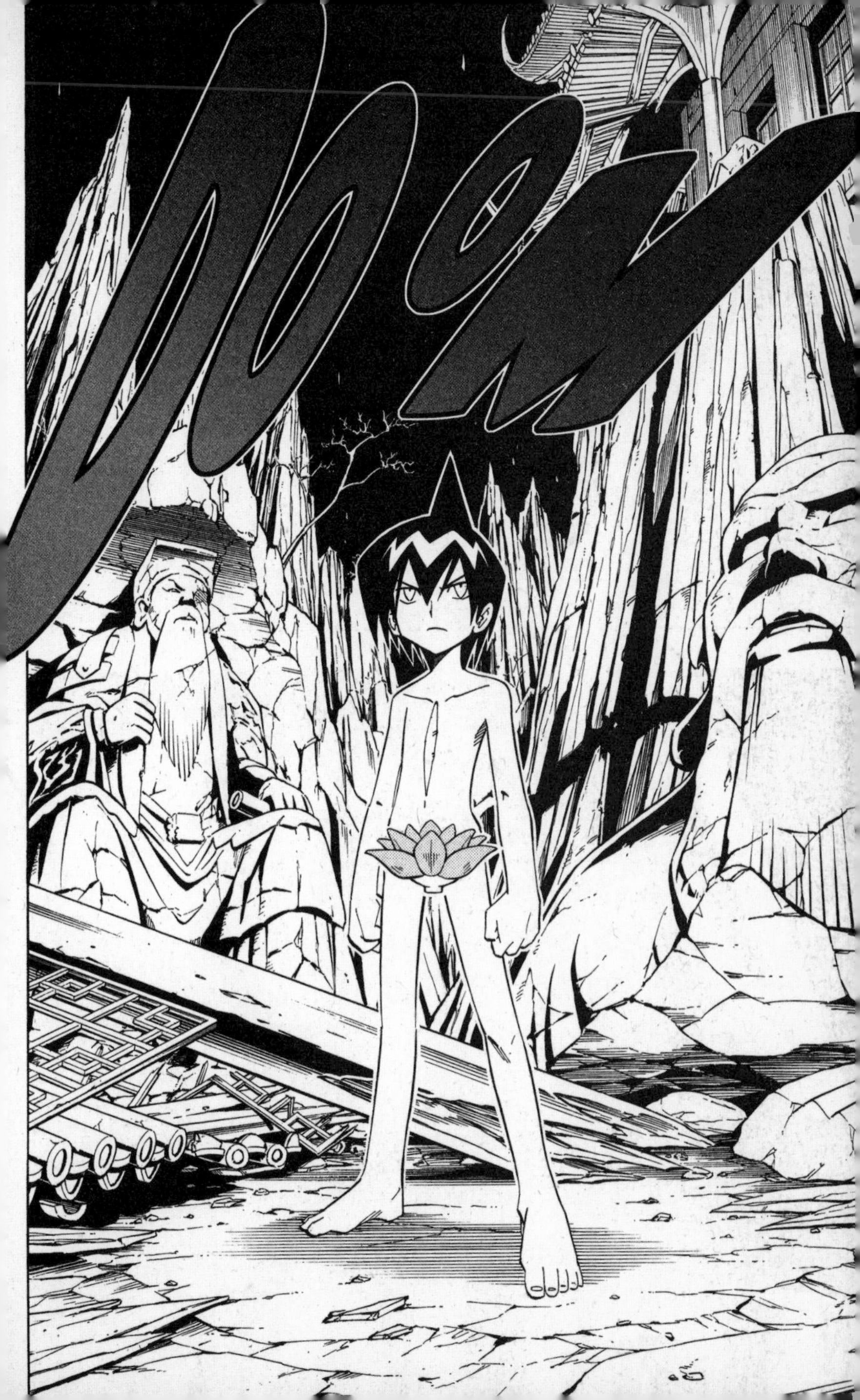

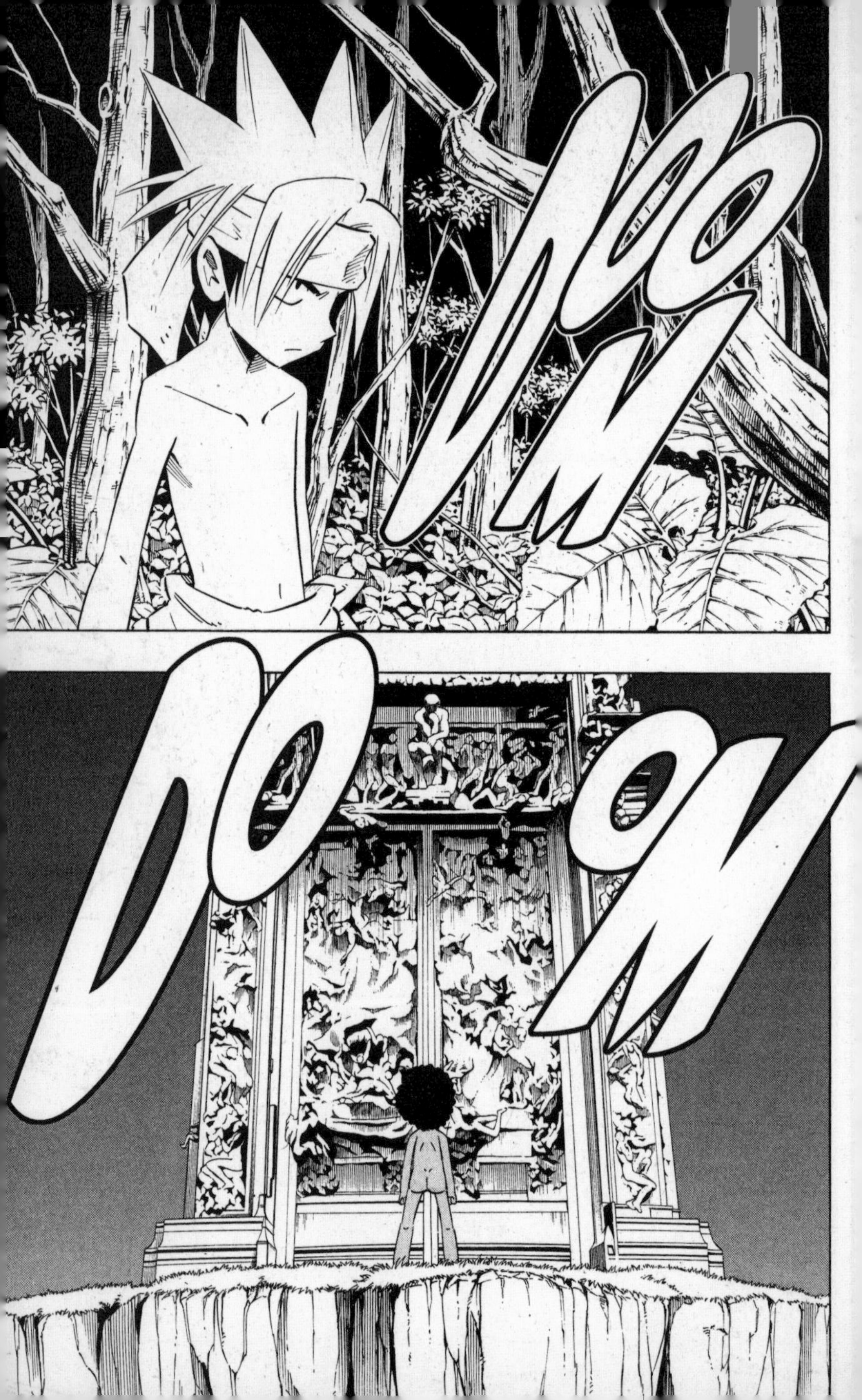

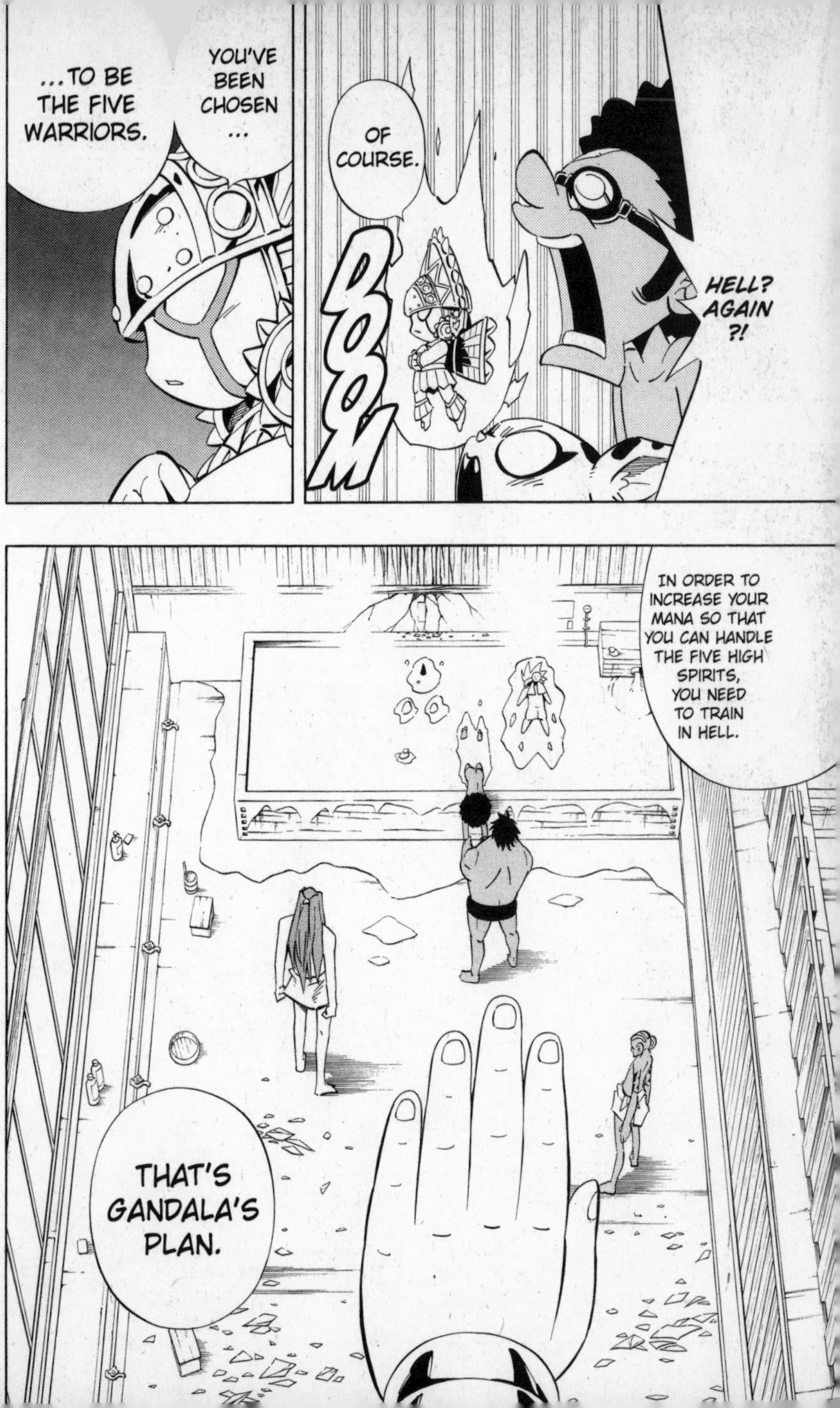
HELL? AGAIN ?!
OF COURSE.
DOOM
YOU'VE BEEN CHOSEN ...
...TO BE THE FIVE WARRIORS.
IN ORDER TO INCREASE YOUR MANA SO THAT YOU CAN HANDLE THE FIVE HIGH SPIRITS, YOU NEED TO TRAIN IN HELL.
THAT'S GANDALA'S PLAN.

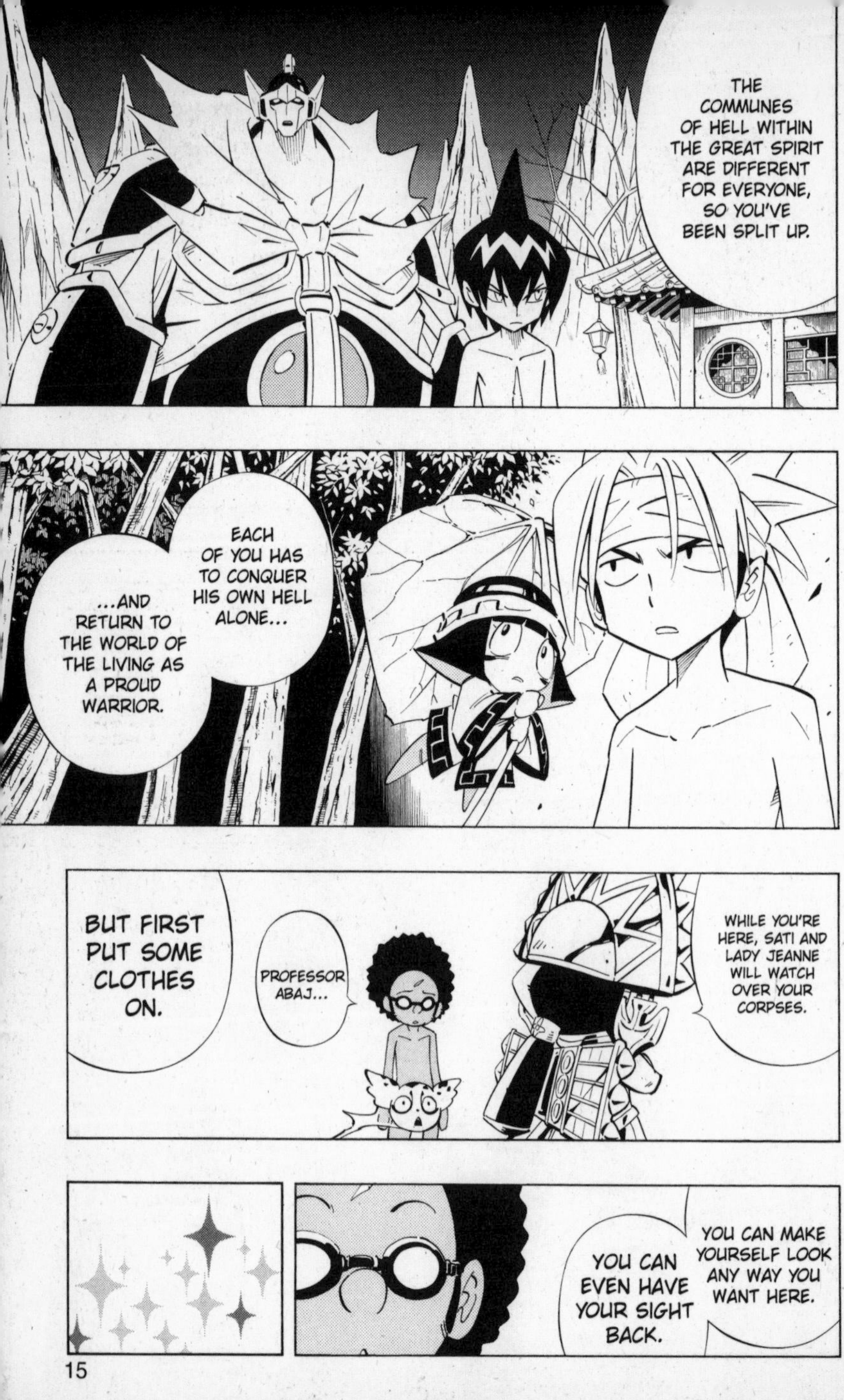
THE COMMUNES OF HELL WITHIN THE GREAT SPIRIT ARE DIFFERENT FOR EVERYONE, SO YOU'VE BEEN SPLIT UP.
EACH OF YOU HAS TO CONQUER HIS OWN HELL ALONE...
...AND RETURN TO THE WORLD OF THE LIVING AS A PROUD WARRIOR.
WHILE YOU'RE HERE, SATI AND LADY JEANNE WILL WATCH OVER YOUR CORPSES.
PROFESSOR ABAJ...
BUT FIRST PUT SOME CLOTHES ON.
YOU CAN MAKE YOURSELF LOOK ANY WAY YOU WANT HERE.
YOU CAN EVEN HAVE YOUR SIGHT BACK.

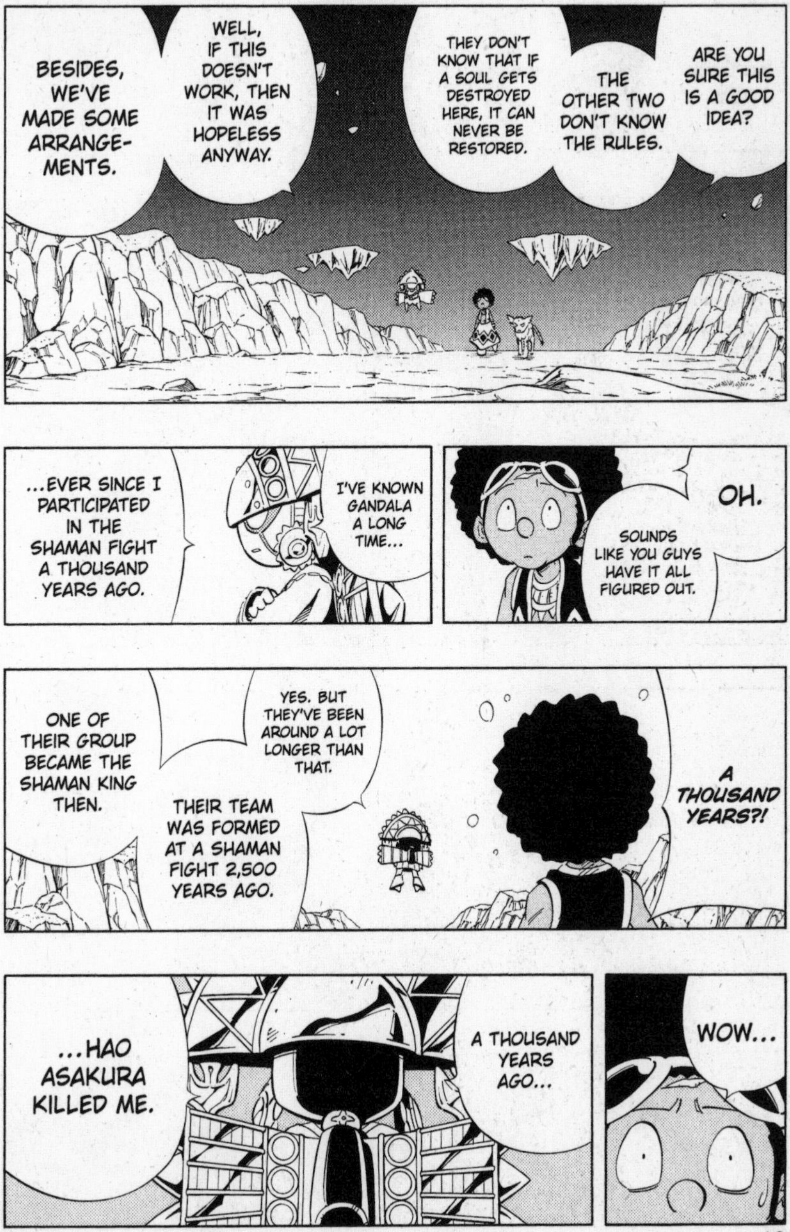
ARE YOU SURE THIS IS A GOOD IDEA?
THE OTHER TWO DON'T KNOW THE RULES.
THEY DON'T KNOW THAT IF A SOUL GETS DESTROYED HERE, IT CAN NEVER BE RESTORED.
WELL, IF THIS DOESN'T WORK, THEN IT WAS HOPELESS ANYWAY.
BESIDES, WE'VE MADE SOME ARRANGE-MENTS.
OH.
SOUNDS LIKE YOU GUYS HAVE IT ALL FIGURED OUT.
I'VE KNOWN GANDALA A LONG TIME...
...EVER SINCE I PARTICIPATED IN THE SHAMAN FIGHT A THOUSAND YEARS AGO.
A THOUSAND YEARS?!
YES. BUT THEY'VE BEEN AROUND A LOT LONGER THAN THAT.
THEIR TEAM WAS FORMED AT A SHAMAN FIGHT 2,500 YEARS AGO.
ONE OF THEIR GROUP BECAME THE SHAMAN KING THEN.
WOW...
A THOUSAND YEARS AGO...
...HAO ASAKURA KILLED ME.

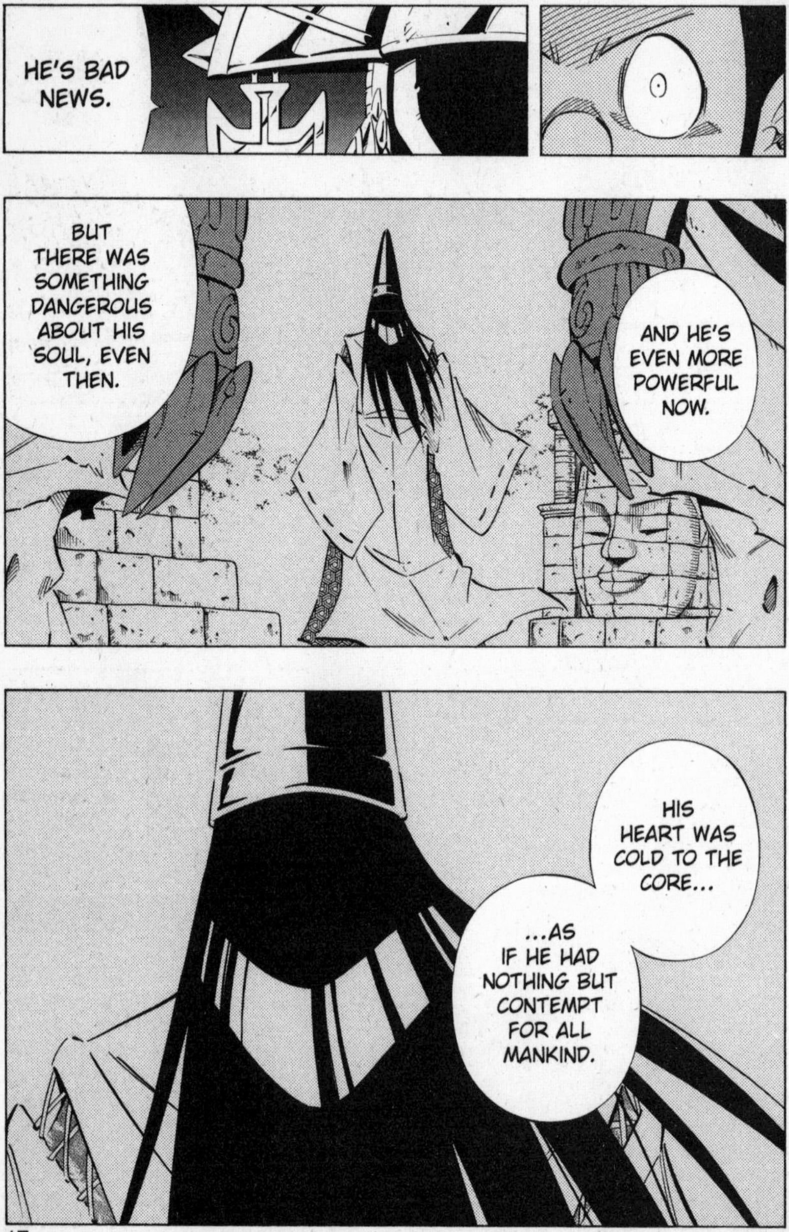
HE'S BAD NEWS.
BUT THERE WAS SOMETHING DANGEROUS ABOUT HIS SOUL, EVEN THEN.
AND HE'S EVEN MORE POWERFUL NOW.
HIS HEART WAS COLD TO THE CORE...
...AS IF HE HAD NOTHING BUT CONTEMPT FOR ALL MANKIND.

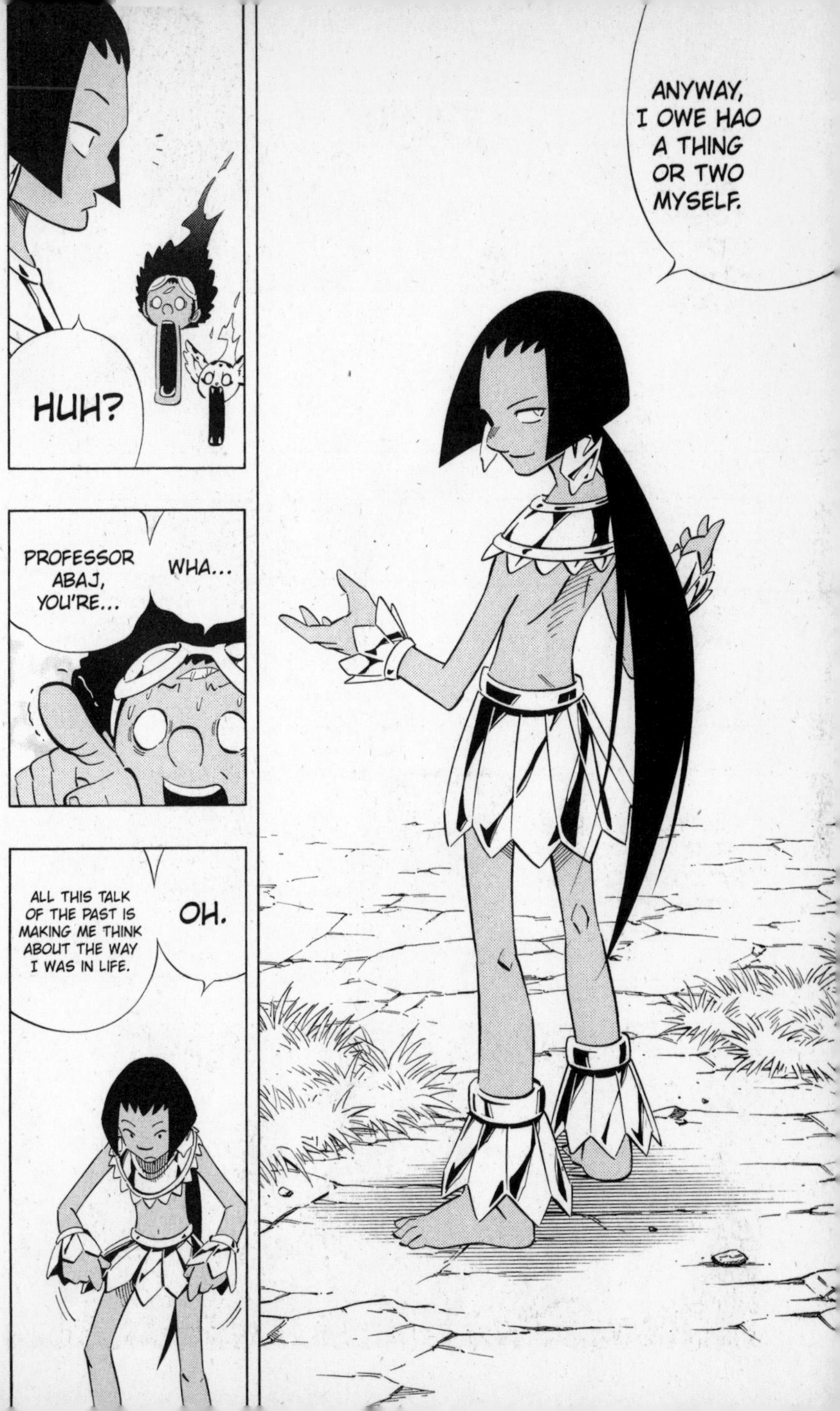
ANYWAY, I OWE HAO A THING OR TWO MYSELF.
HUH?
WHA...
PROFESSOR ABAJ, YOU'RE...
OH.
ALL THIS TALK OF THE PAST IS MAKING ME THINK ABOUT THE WAY I WAS IN LIFE.

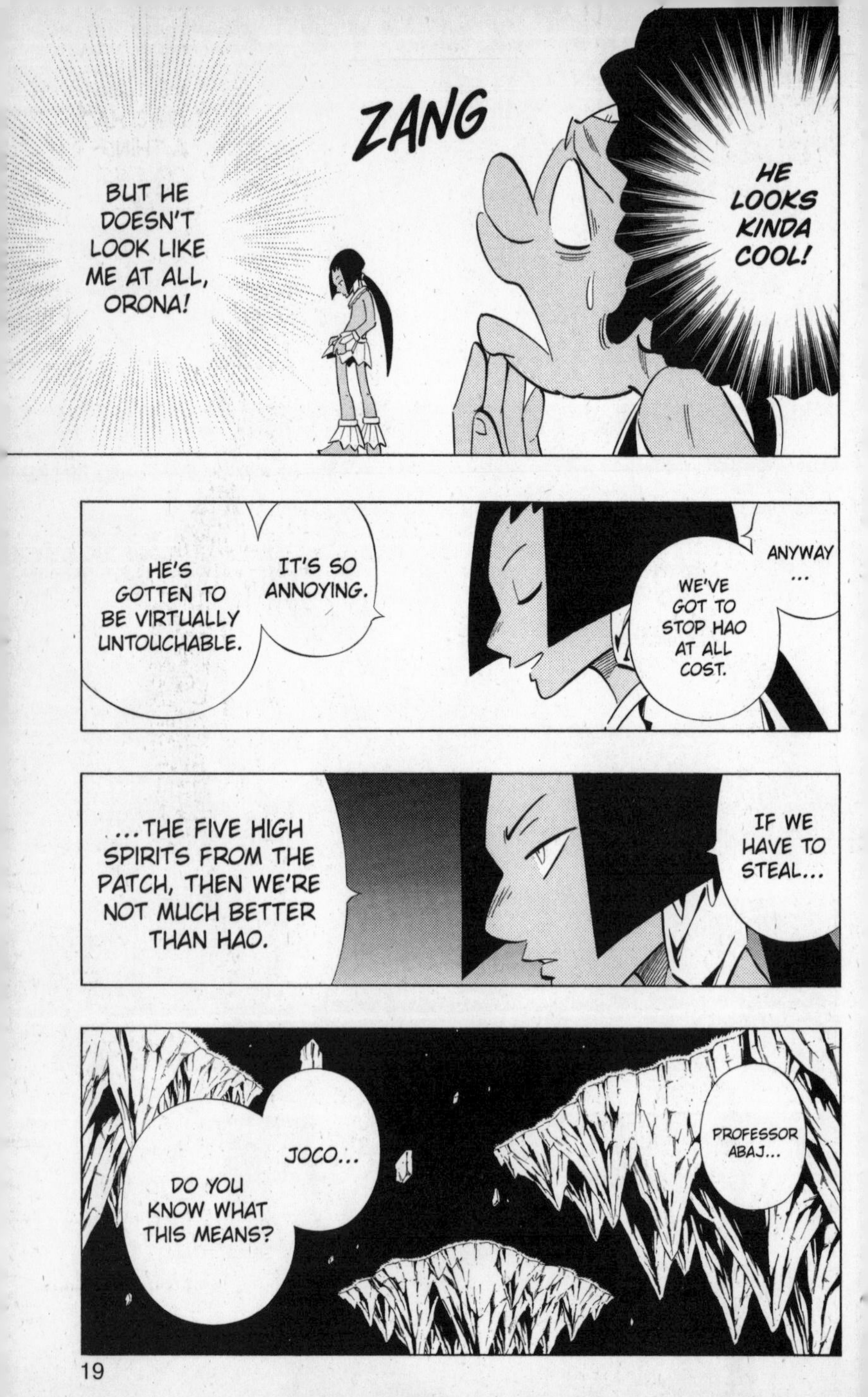
HE LOOKS KINDA COOL!
ZANG
BUT HE DOESN'T LOOK LIKE ME AT ALL, ORONA!
ANYWAY ...
WE'VE GOT TO STOP HAO AT ALL COST.
IT'S SO ANNOYING.
HE'S GOTTEN TO BE VIRTUALLY UNTOUCHABLE.
IF WE HAVE TO STEAL...
...THE FIVE HIGH SPIRITS FROM THE PATCH, THEN WE'RE NOT MUCH BETTER THAN HAO.
PROFESSOR ABAJ...
JOCO...
DO YOU KNOW WHAT THIS MEANS?

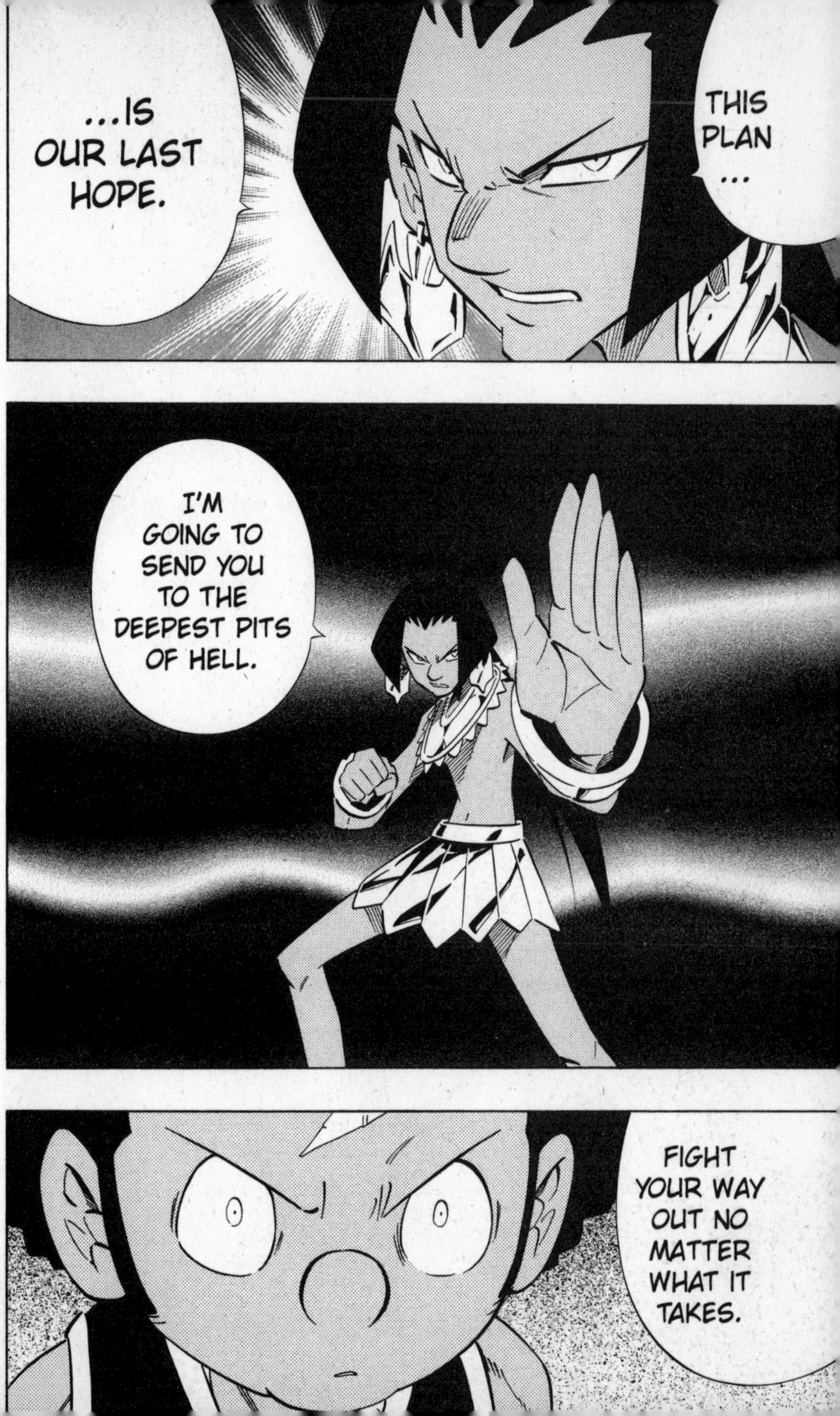
THIS PLAN ...
...IS OUR LAST HOPE.
I'M GOING TO SEND YOU TO THE DEEPEST PITS OF HELL.
FIGHT YOUR WAY OUT NO MATTER WHAT IT TAKES.

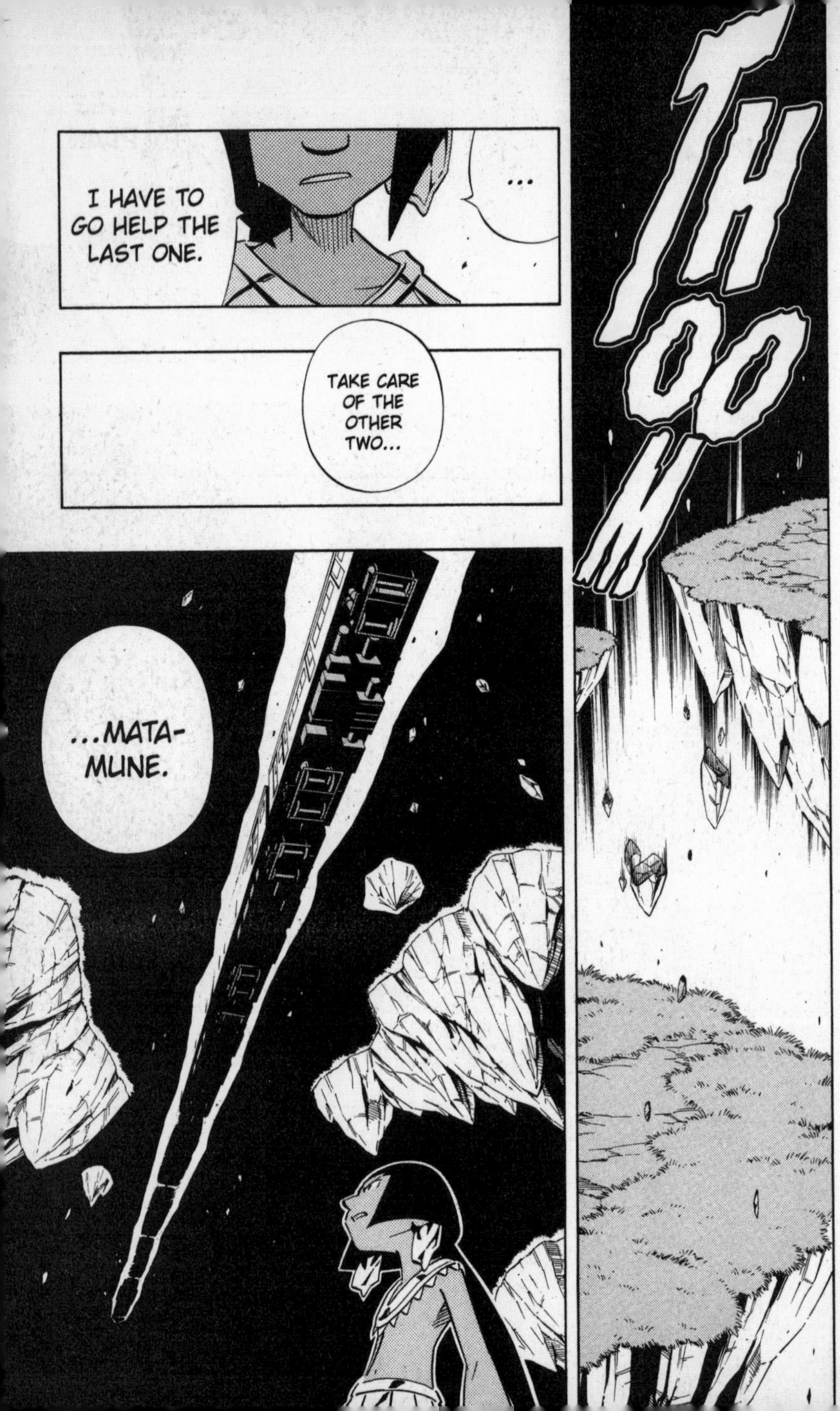
THOOM
...
I HAVE TO GO HELP THE LAST ONE.
TAKE CARE OF THE OTHER TWO...
...MATA-MUNE.

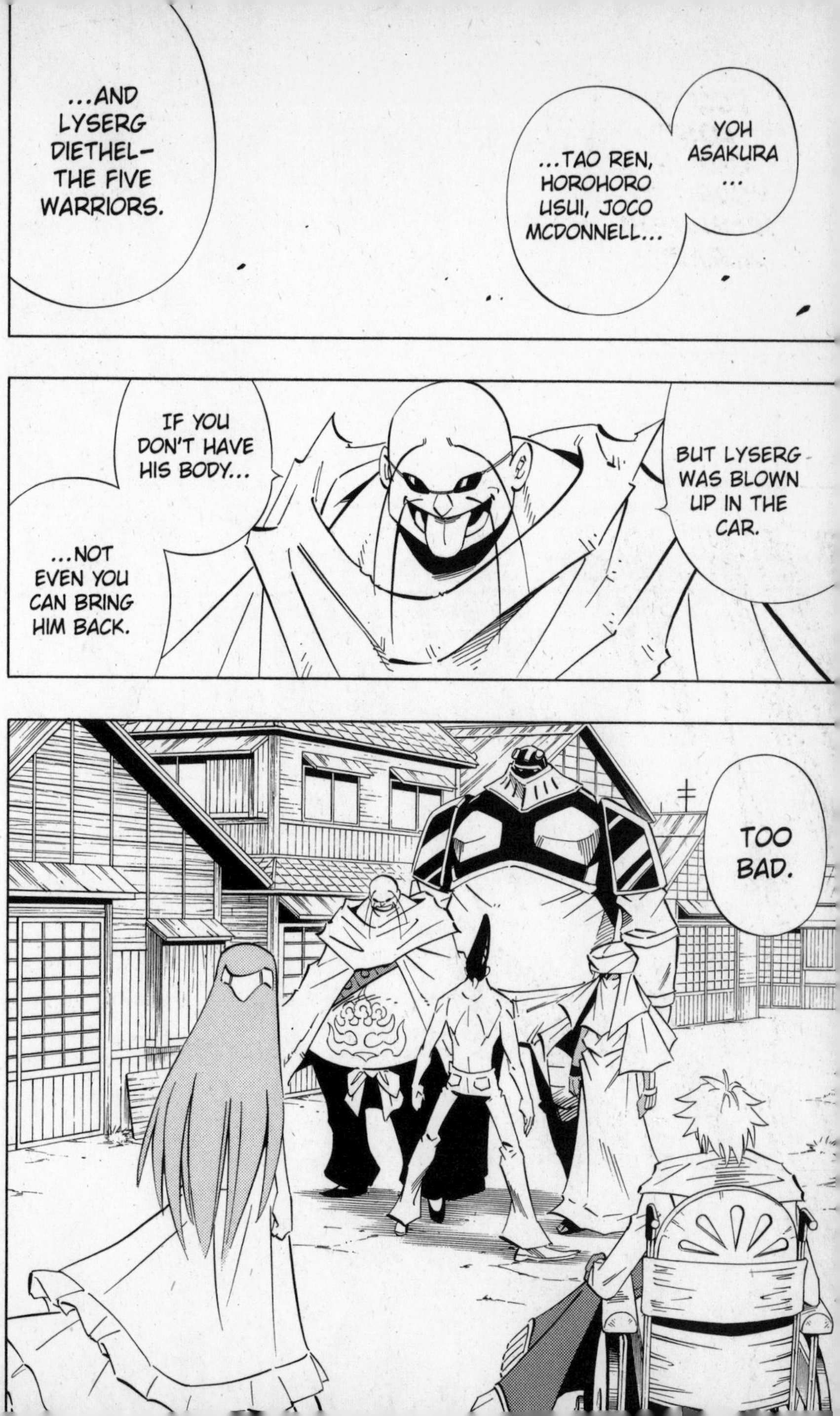
YOH ASAKURA ...
...TAO REN, HOROHORO USUI, JOCO MCDONNELL...
...AND LYSERG DIETHEL— THE FIVE WARRIORS.
BUT LYSERG WAS BLOWN UP IN THE CAR.
IF YOU DON'T HAVE HIS BODY...
...NOT EVEN YOU CAN BRING HIM BACK.
TOO BAD.

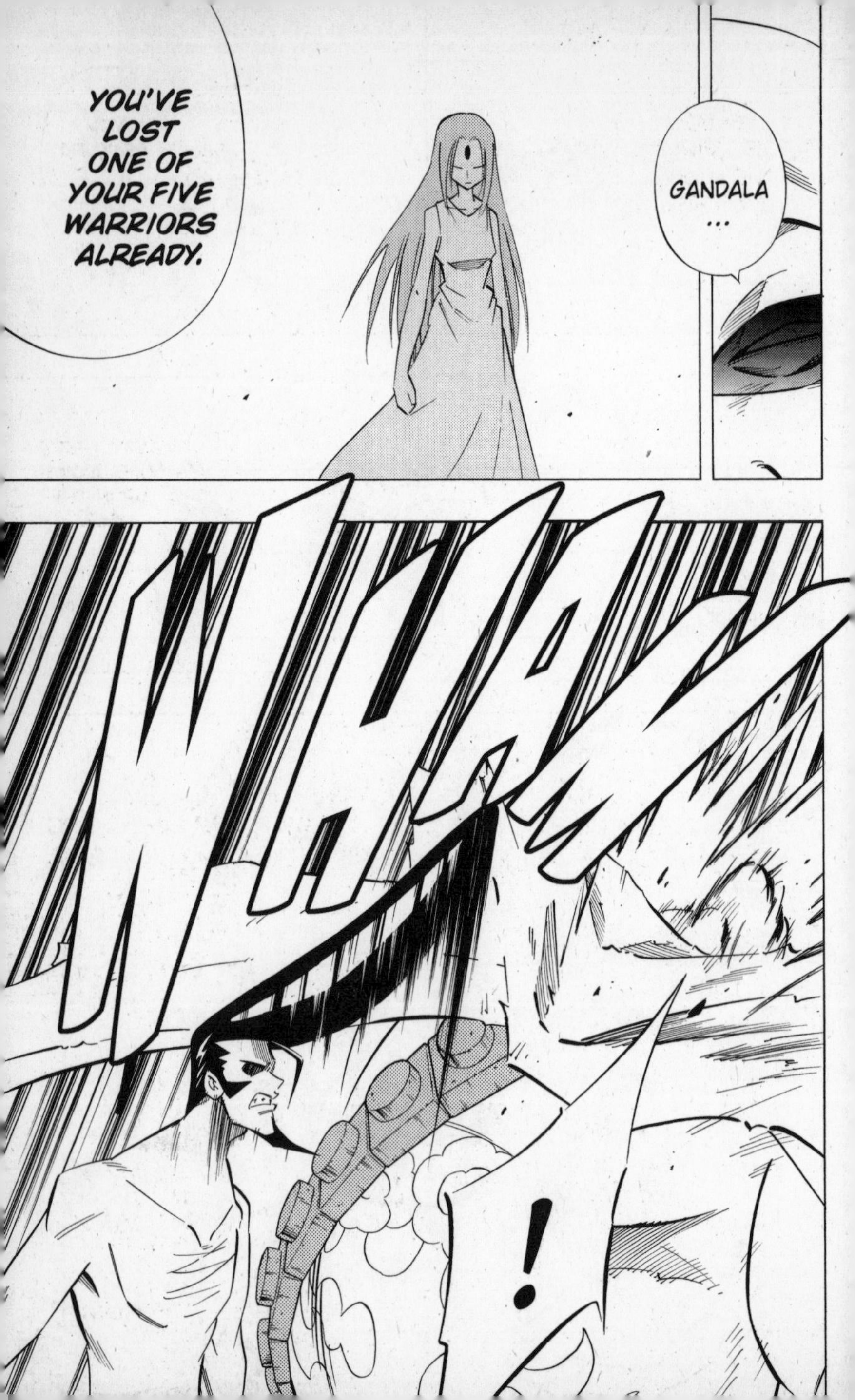
GANDALA ...
YOU'VE LOST ONE OF YOUR FIVE WARRIORS ALREADY.
!

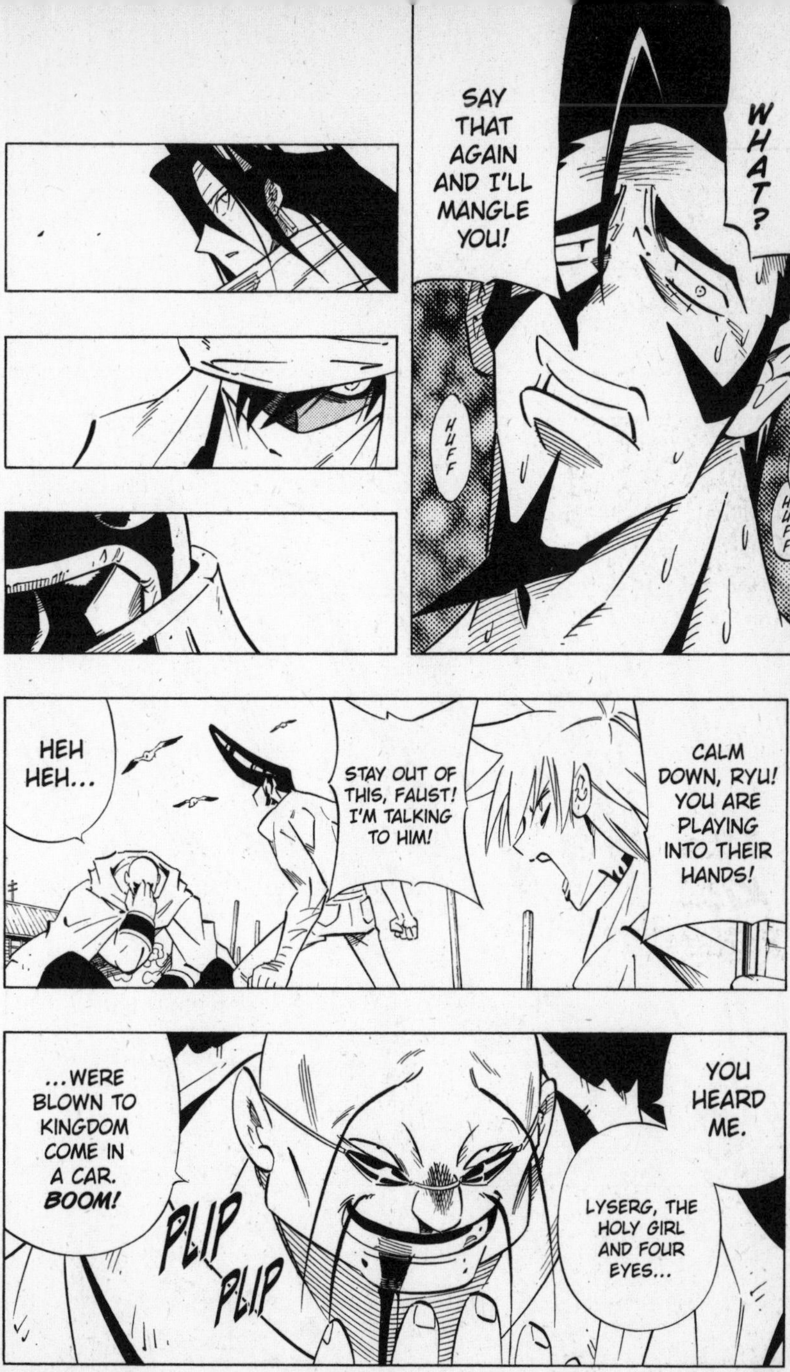
WHAT?
SAY THAT AGAIN AND I'LL MANGLE YOU!
HUFF
HUFF
HUFF
CALM DOWN, RYU! YOU ARE PLAYING INTO THEIR HANDS!
STAY OUT OF THIS, FAUST! I'M TALKING TO HIM!
HEH HEH...
YOU HEARD ME.
LYSERG, THE HOLY GIRL AND FOUR EYES...
...WERE BLOWN TO KINGDOM COME IN A CAR. BOOM!
PLIP
PLIP

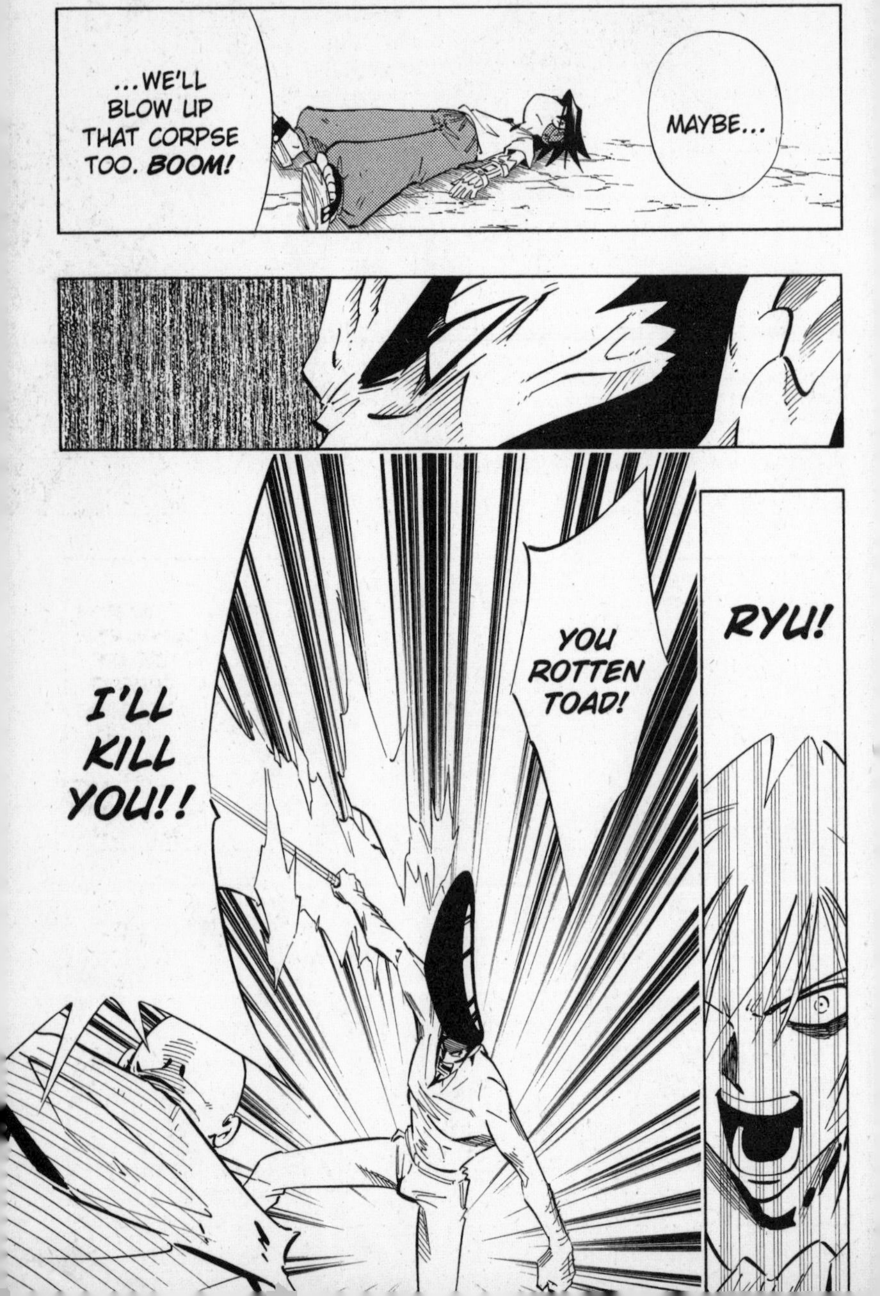
MAYBE...
...WE'LL BLOW UP THAT CORPSE TOO. BOOM!
RYU!
YOU ROTTEN TOAD!
I'LL KILL YOU!!

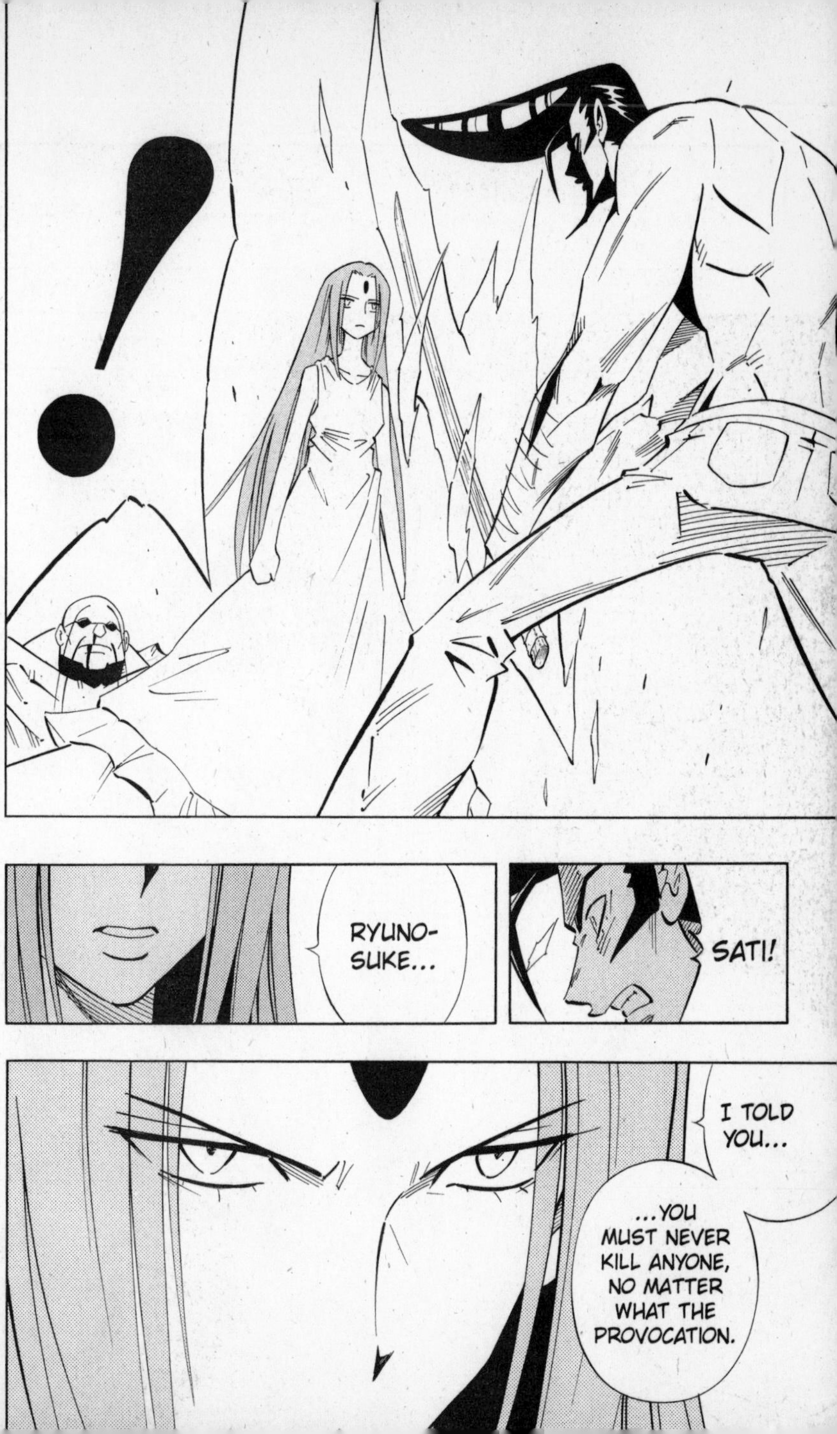
SATI!
RYUNO-SUKE...
I TOLD YOU...
...YOU MUST NEVER KILL ANYONE, NO MATTER WHAT THE PROVOCATION.

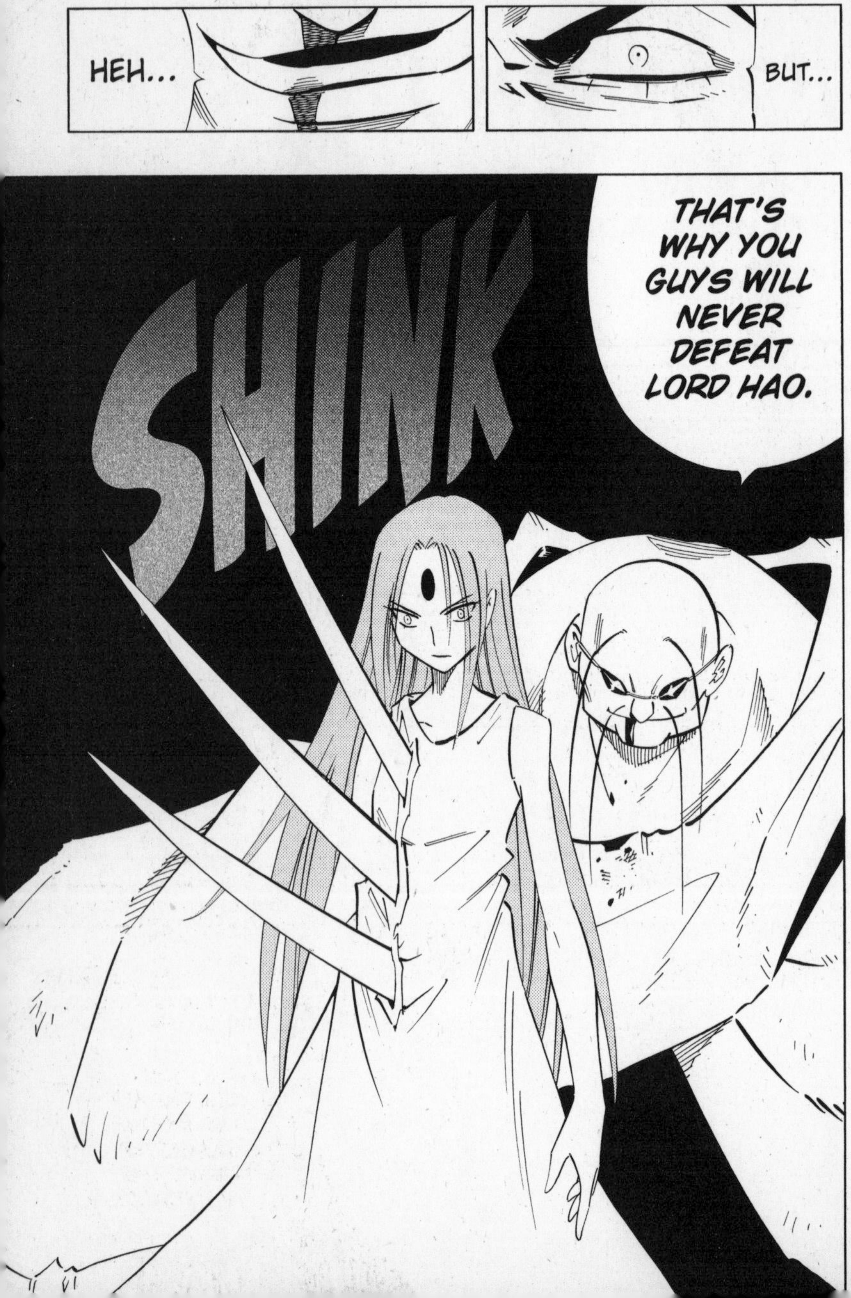
BUT...
HEH...
THAT'S WHY YOU GUYS WILL NEVER DEFEAT LORD HAO.
SHINK

SHAMAN KING CHARACTER FILE No.142

パスカル・アバフ
（人間時）

Pascual Abaj

(HUMAN FORM)

2001
(JAN)

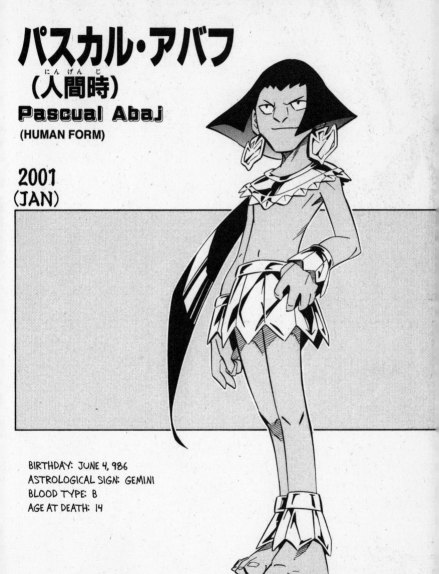

BIRTHDAY: JUNE 4, 986
ASTROLOGICAL SIGN: GEMINI
BLOOD TYPE: B
AGE AT DEATH: 14

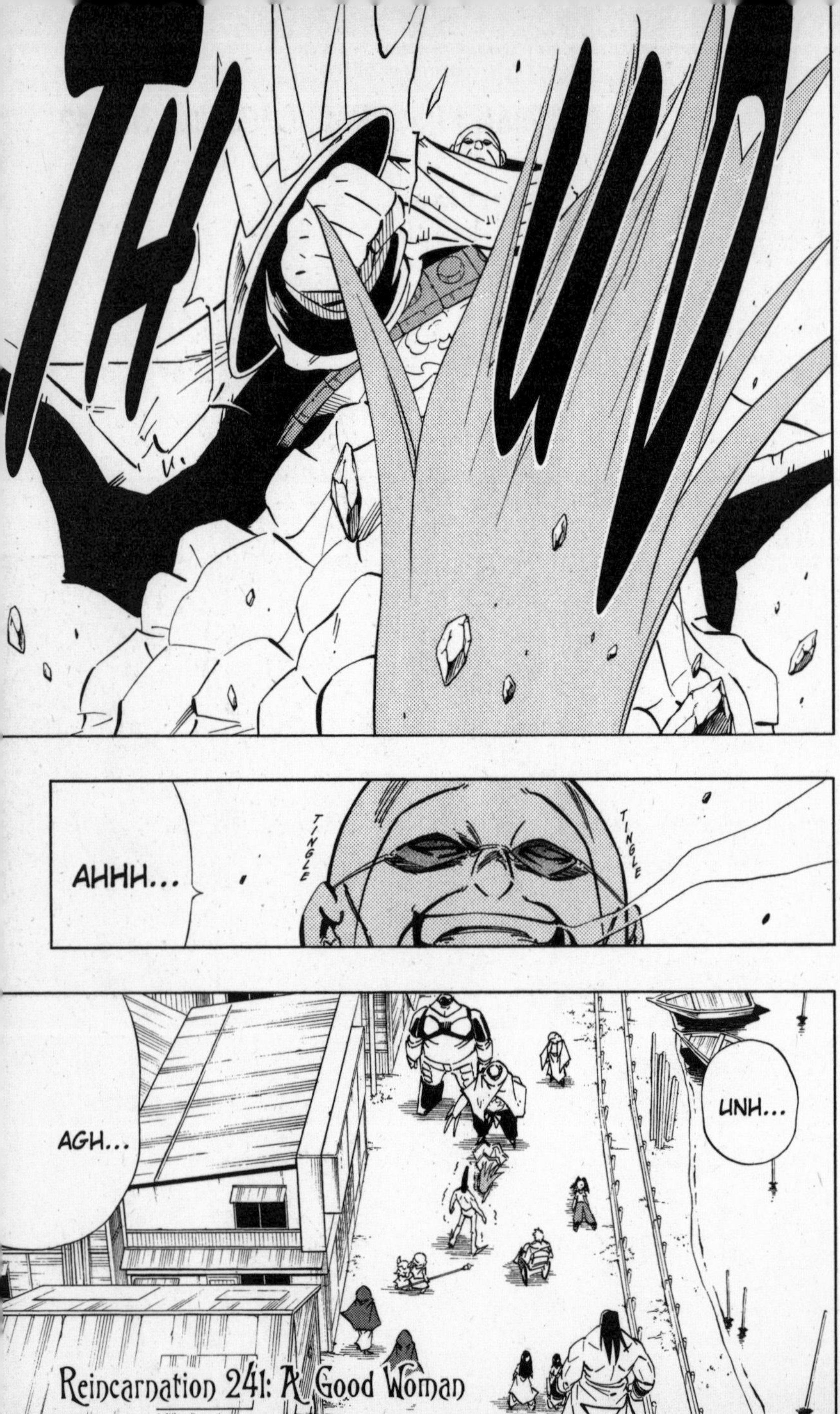
THUD
TINGLE
TINGLE
AHHH...
UNH...
AGH...

Reincarnation 241: A Good Woman

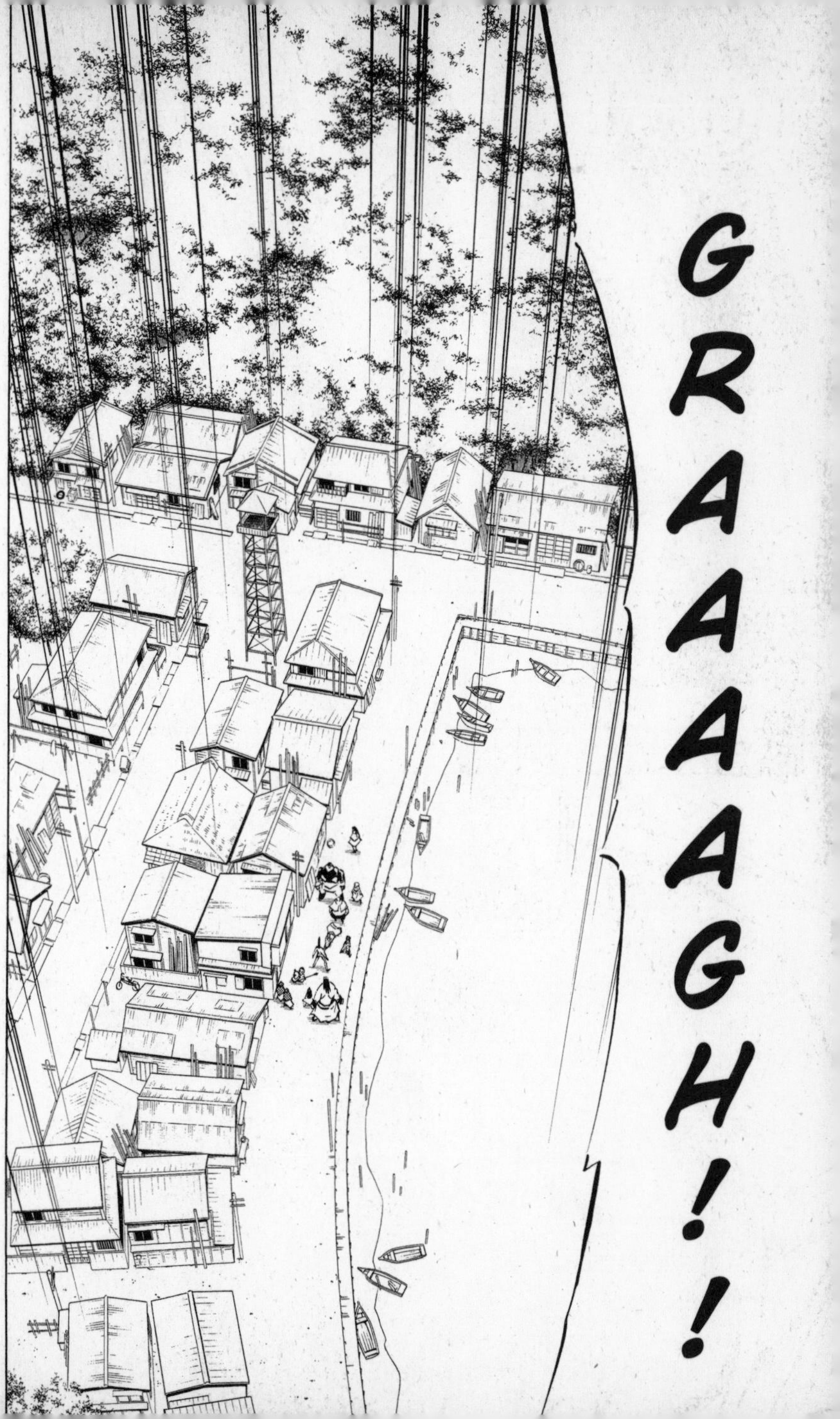
GRAAAAGH!!

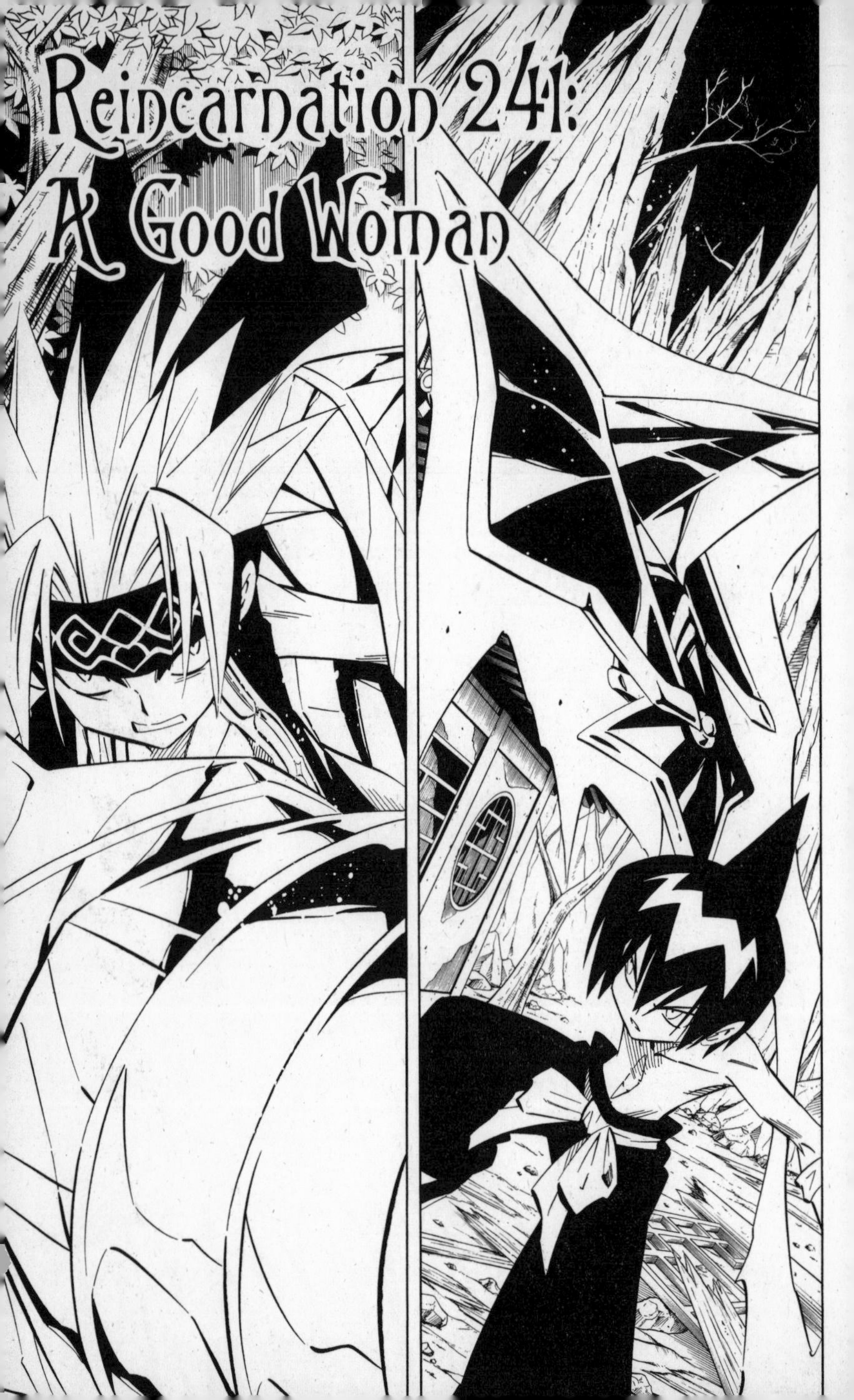
Reincarnation 241:
A Good Woman

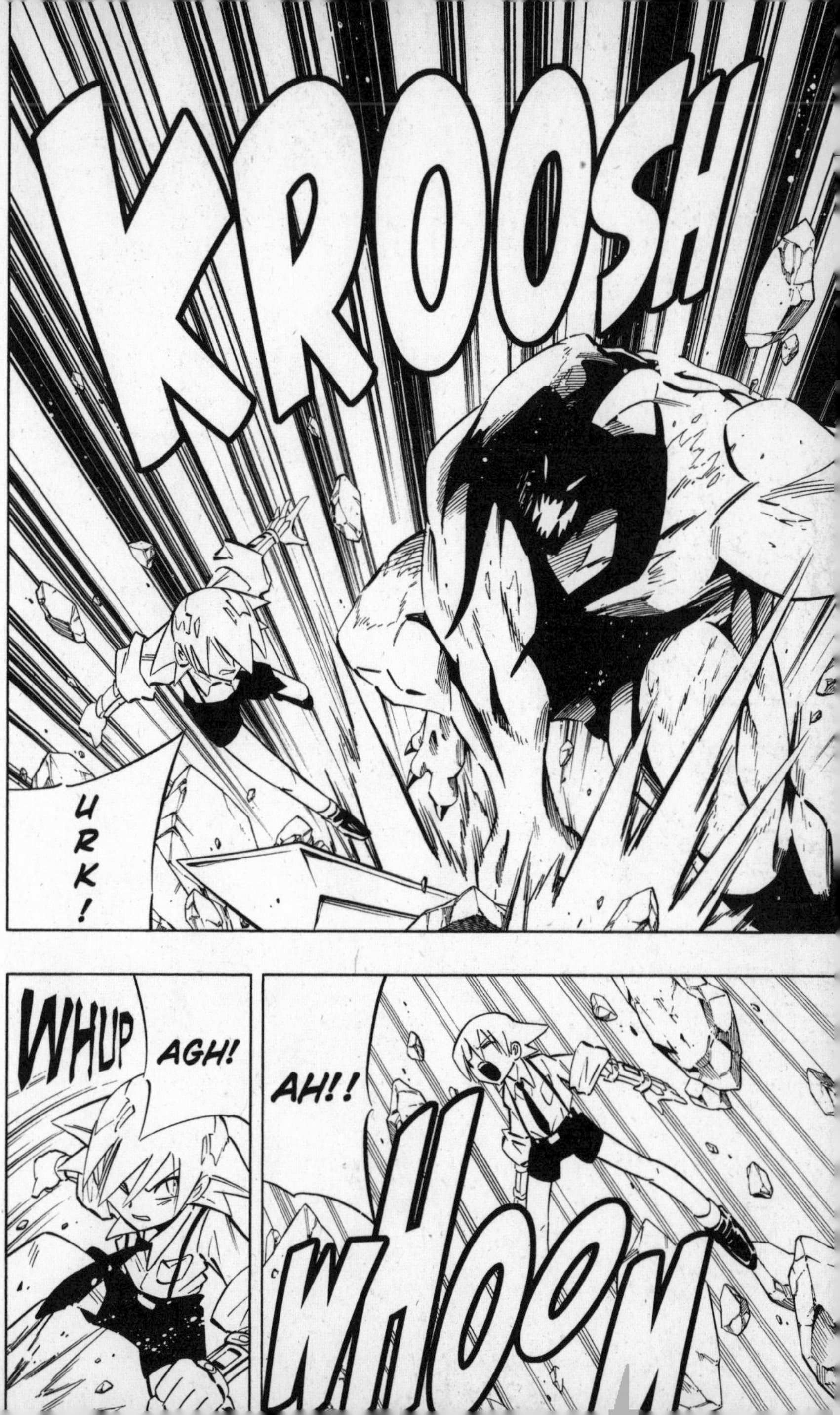
KROOSH
URK!
AH!!
WHOOM
WHUP
AGH!

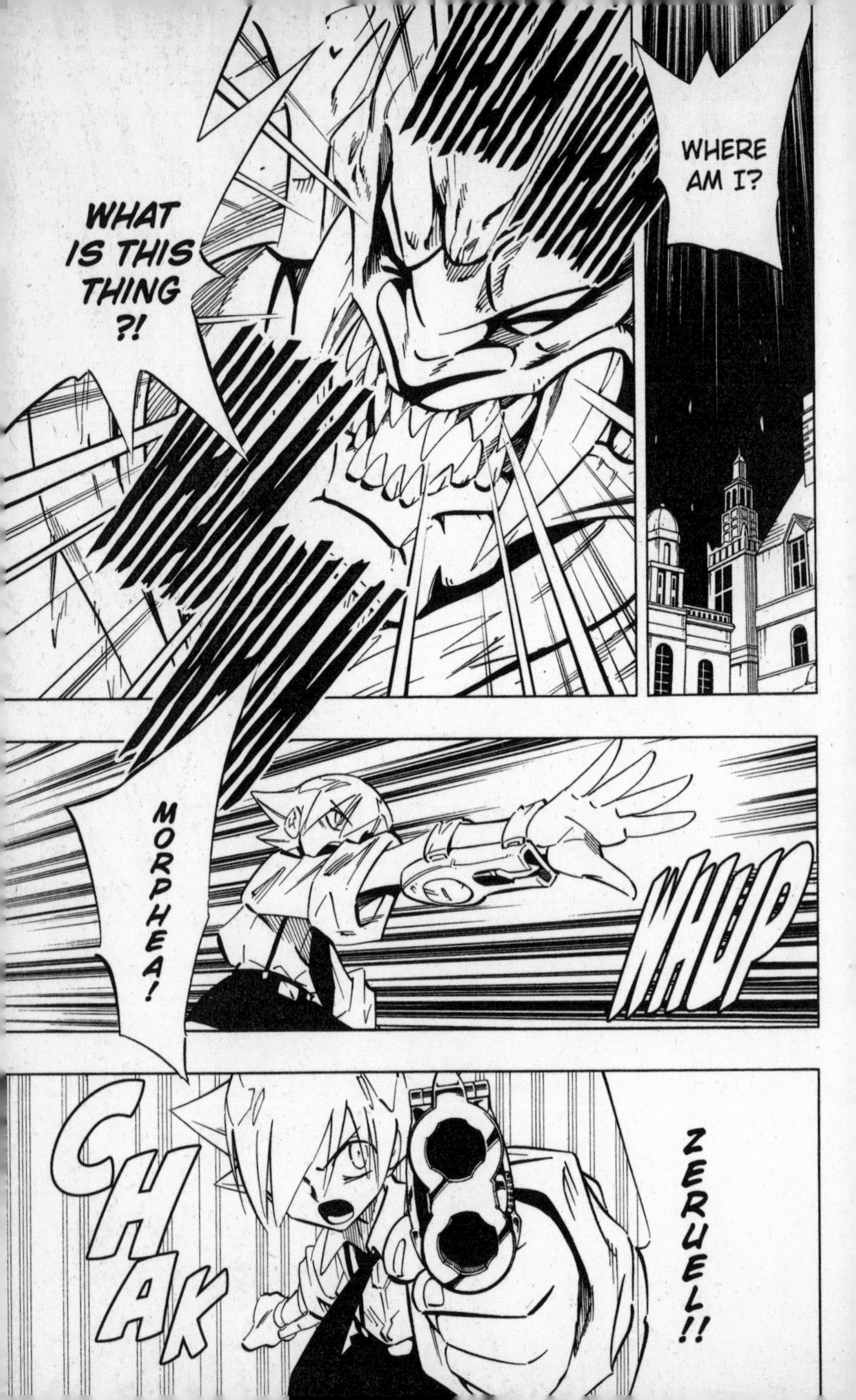
WHERE AM I?
WHAT IS THIS THING?!
WHUP
MORPHEA!
ZERUEL!!
CHAK

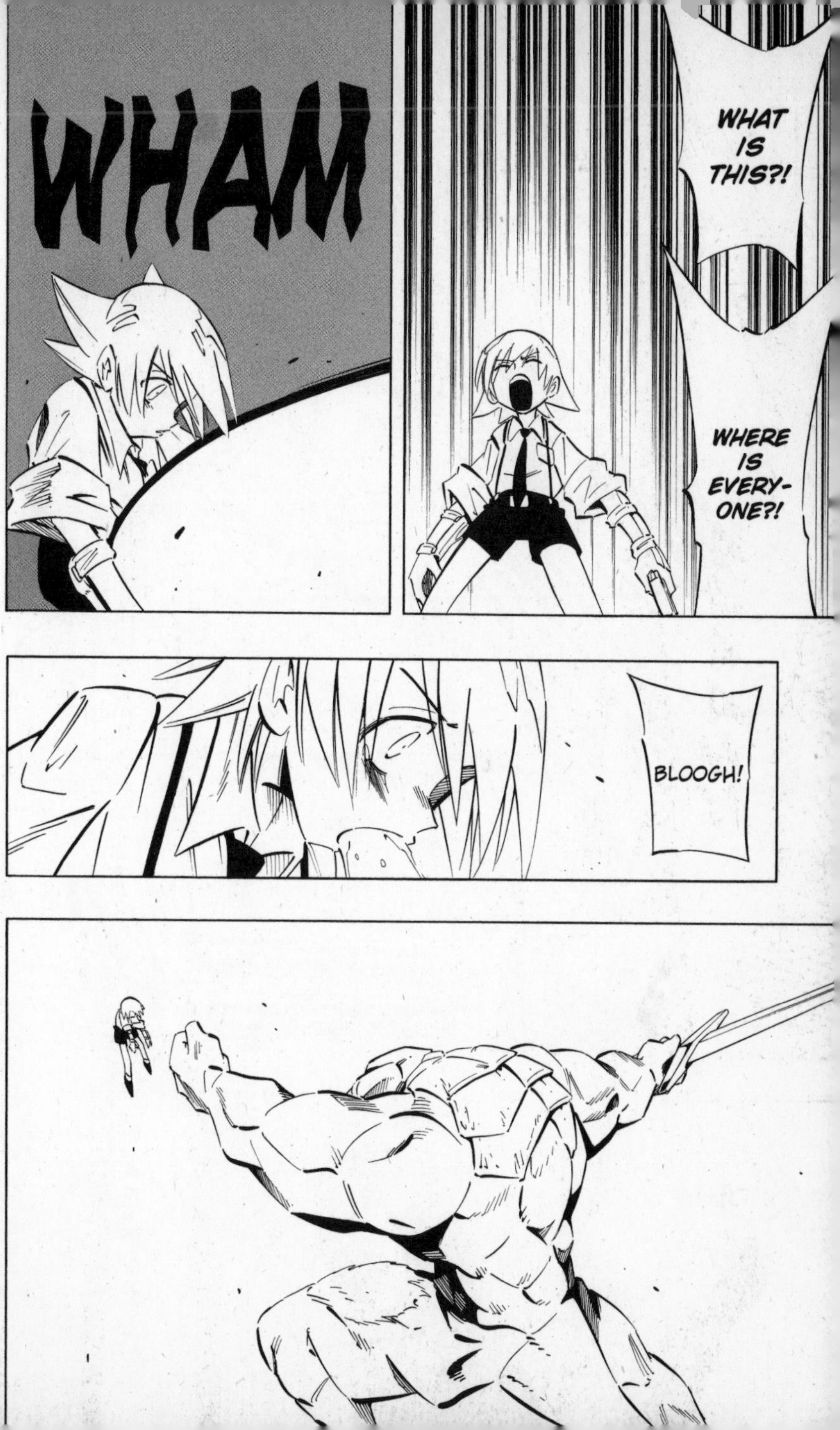
WHAT IS THIS?!
WHERE IS EVERYONE?!
WHAM
BLOOGH!

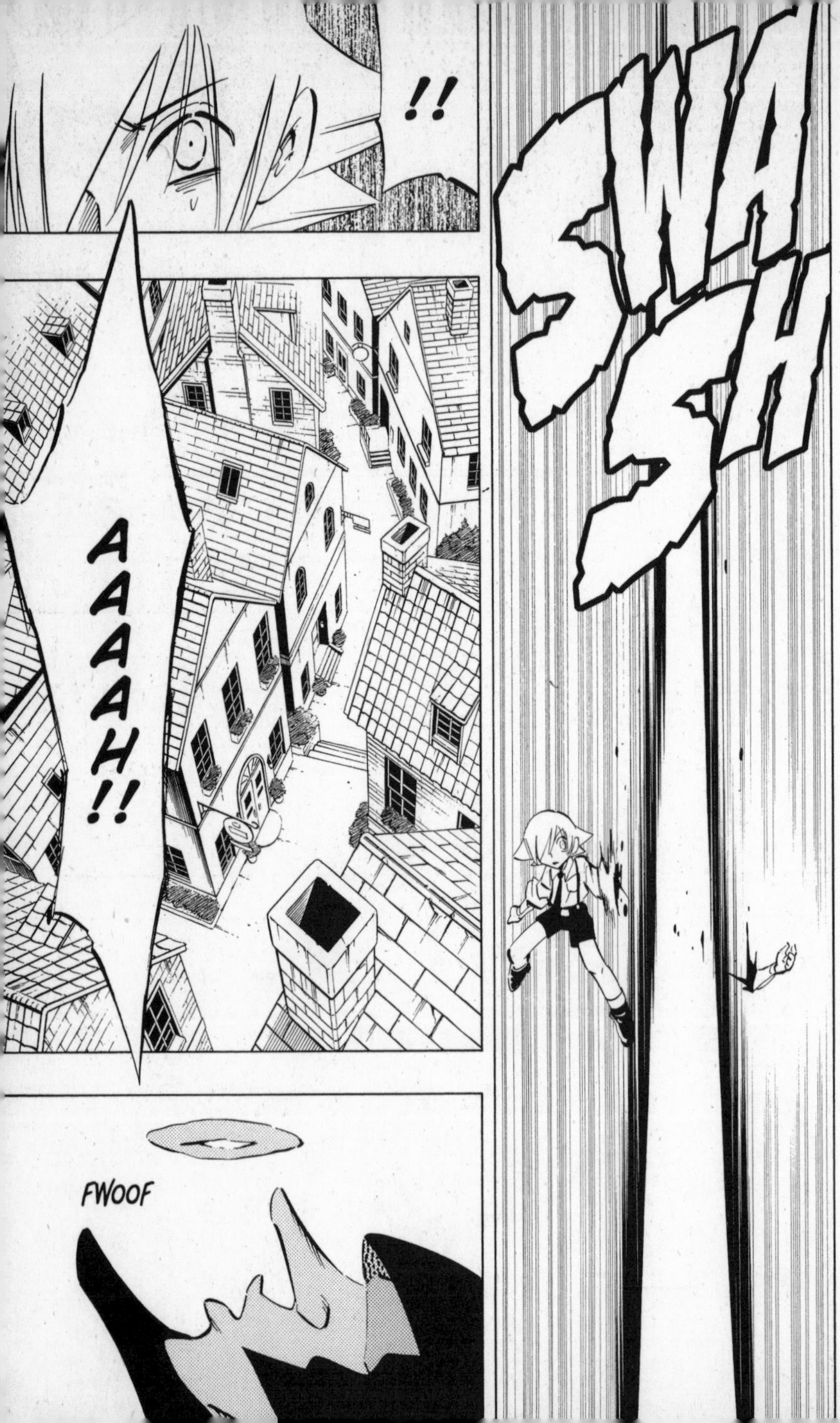
SWASH
!!
AAAAAH!!
FWOOF

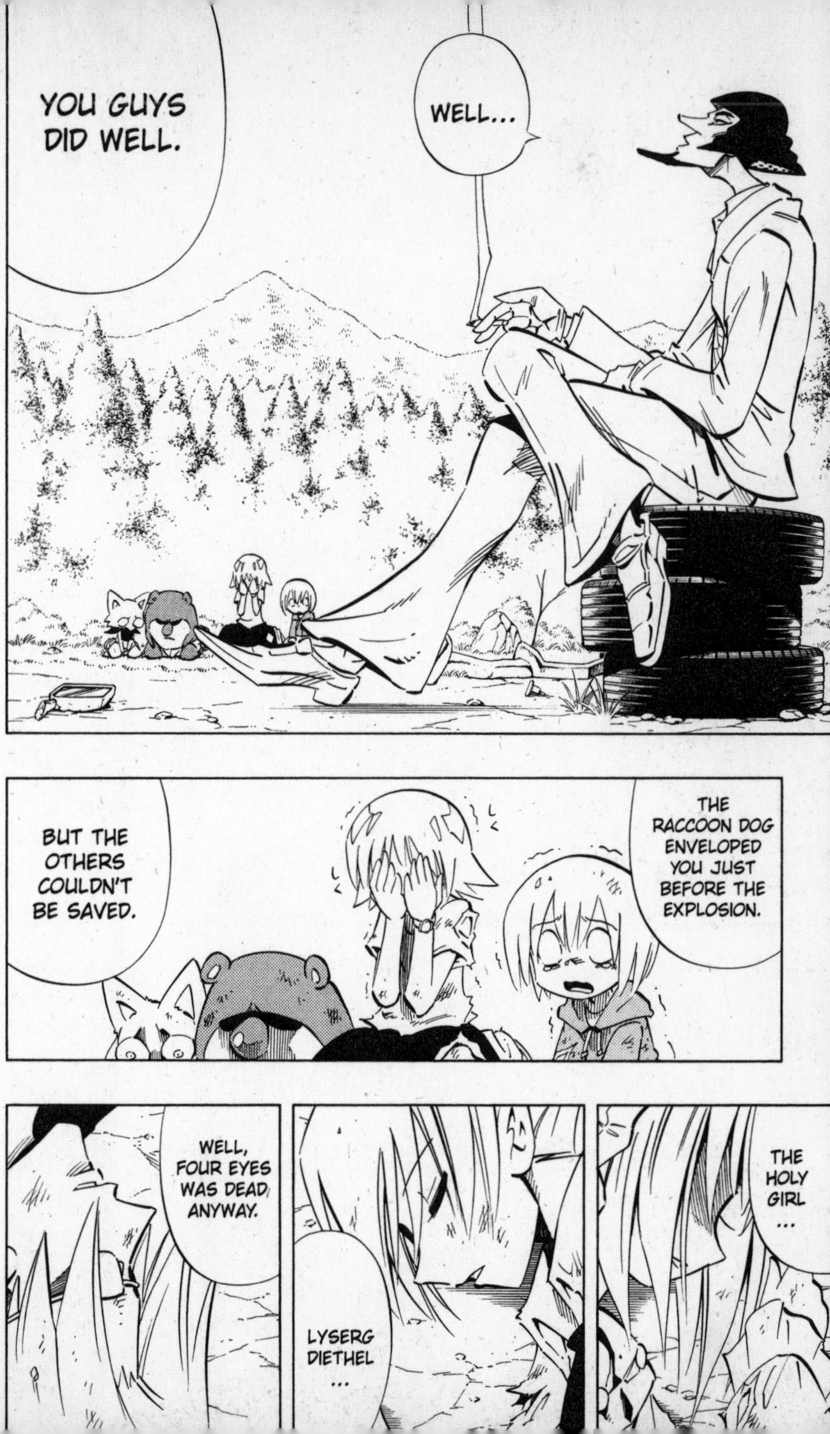
WELL...
YOU GUYS DID WELL.
THE RACCOON DOG ENVELOPED YOU JUST BEFORE THE EXPLOSION.
BUT THE OTHERS COULDN'T BE SAVED.
THE HOLY GIRL...
LYSERG DIETHEL...
WELL, FOUR EYES WAS DEAD ANYWAY.

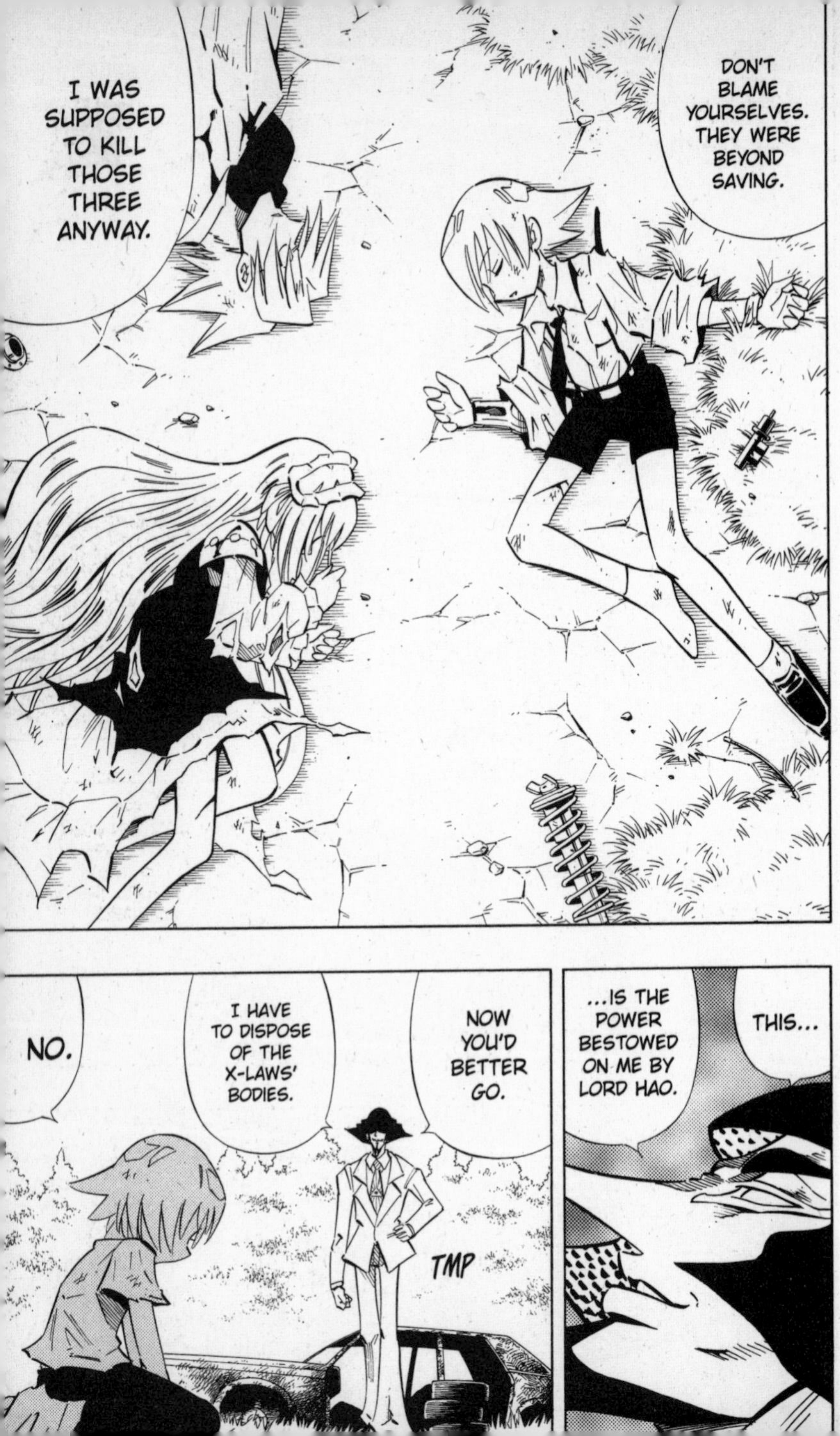
DON'T BLAME YOURSELVES. THEY WERE BEYOND SAVING.
I WAS SUPPOSED TO KILL THOSE THREE ANYWAY.
THIS...
...IS THE POWER BESTOWED ON ME BY LORD HAO.
NOW YOU'D BETTER GO.
I HAVE TO DISPOSE OF THE X-LAWS' BODIES.
TMP
NO.

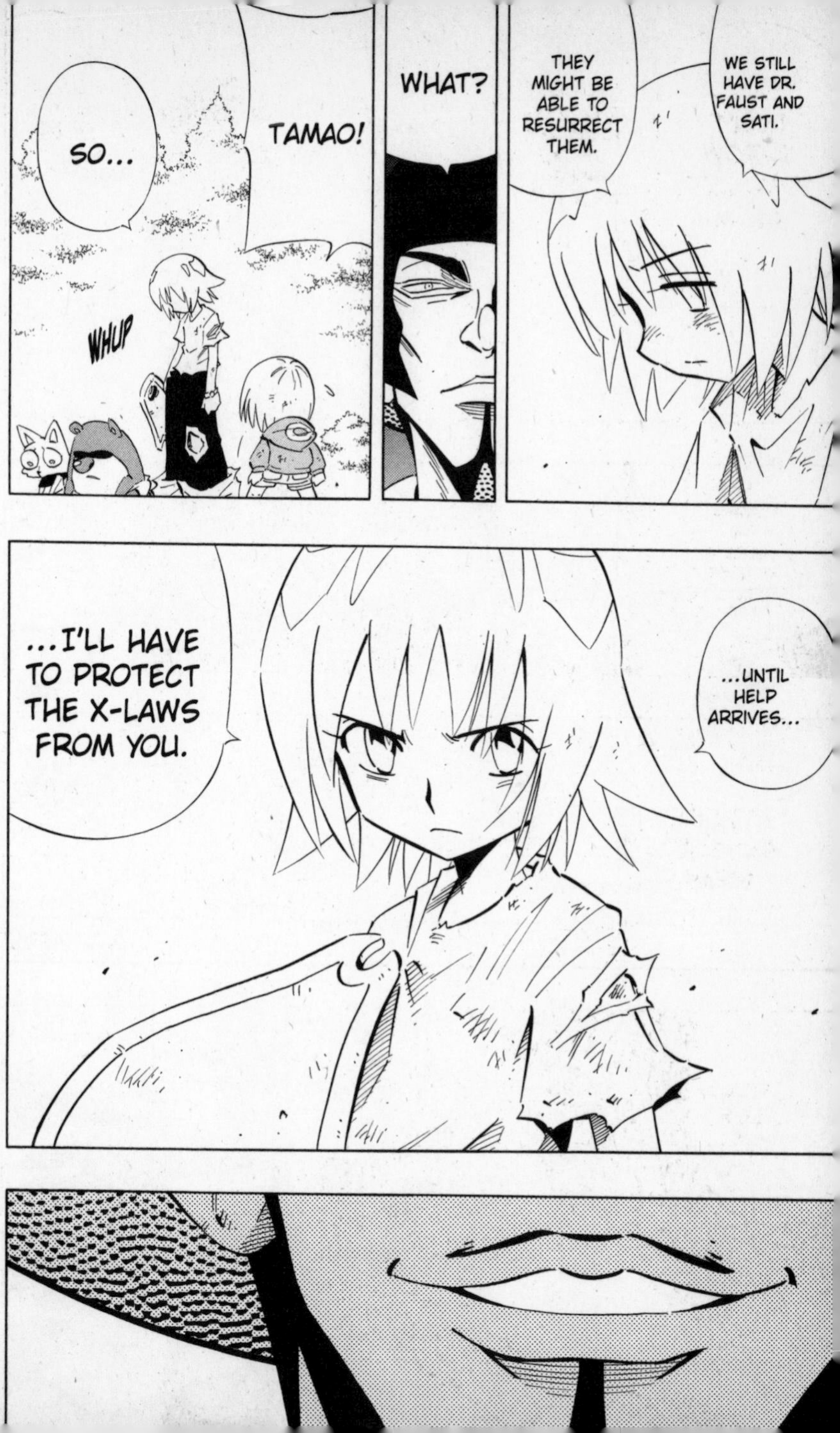
WE STILL HAVE DR. FAUST AND SATI.
THEY MIGHT BE ABLE TO RESURRECT THEM.
WHAT?
TAMAO!
SO...
WHUP
...UNTIL HELP ARRIVES...
...I'LL HAVE TO PROTECT THE X-LAWS FROM YOU.

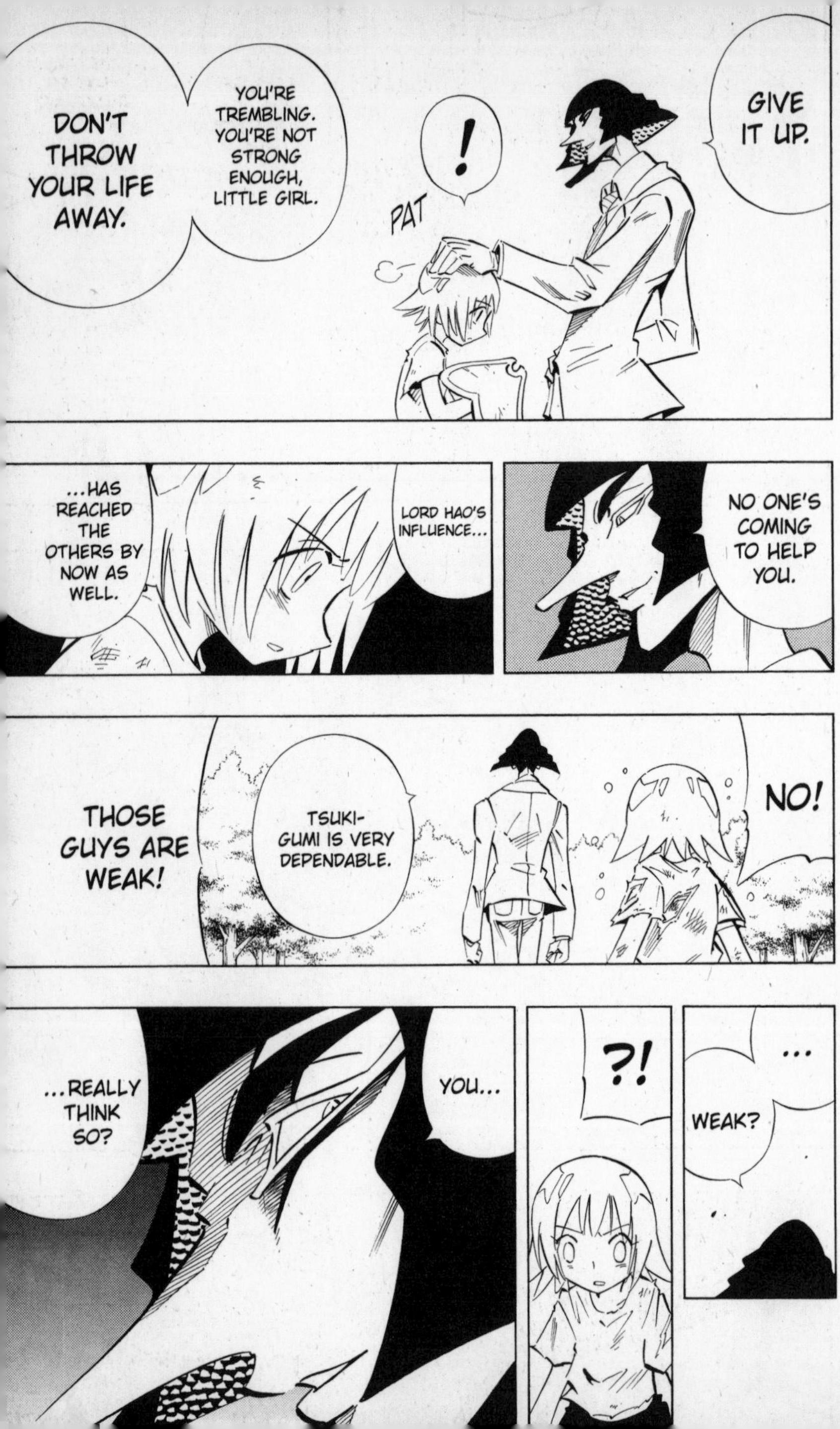
GIVE IT UP.
!
YOU'RE TREMBLING. YOU'RE NOT STRONG ENOUGH, LITTLE GIRL.
DON'T THROW YOUR LIFE AWAY.
PAT
NO ONE'S COMING TO HELP YOU.
LORD HAO'S INFLUENCE...
...HAS REACHED THE OTHERS BY NOW AS WELL.
NO!
TSUKI-GUMI IS VERY DEPENDABLE.
THOSE GUYS ARE WEAK!
...
WEAK?
?!
YOU...
...REALLY THINK SO?

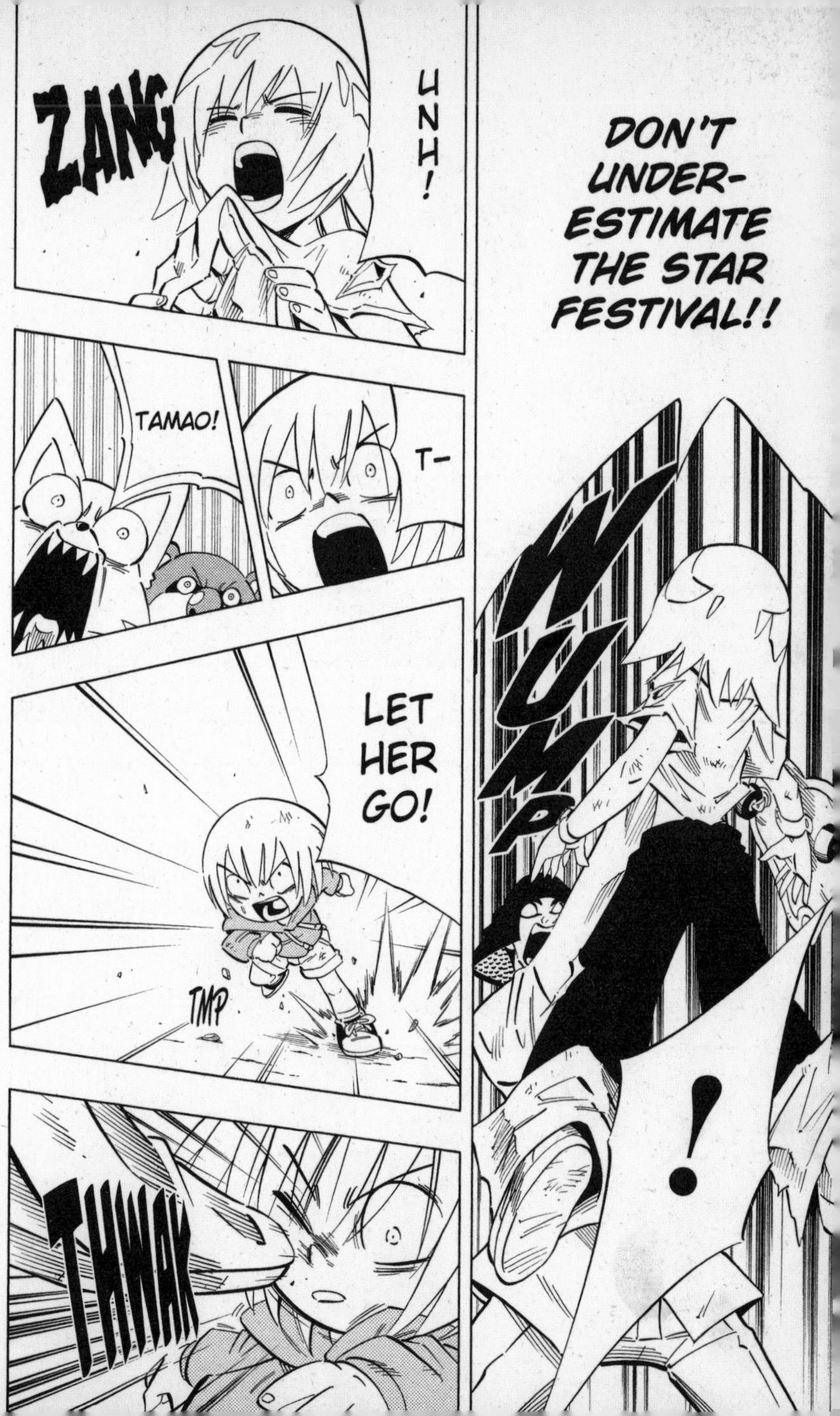
ZANG
UNH!
TAMAO!
T-
LET HER GO!
TMP
THWAK
DON'T UNDER-ESTIMATE THE STAR FESTIVAL!!
WUMP
!

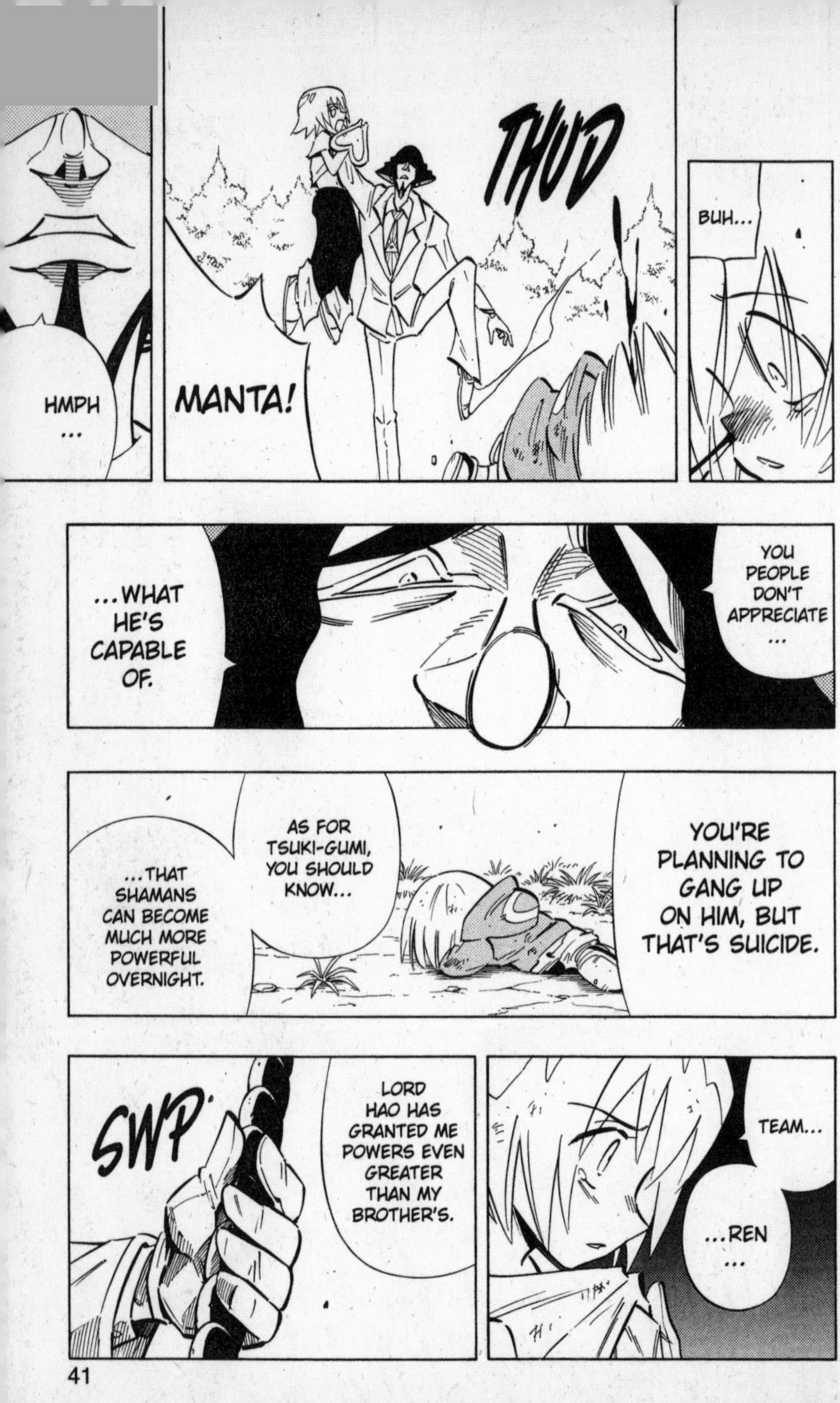
BUH...
THUD
MANTA!
HMPH ...
YOU PEOPLE DON'T APPRECIATE ...
...WHAT HE'S CAPABLE OF.
YOU'RE PLANNING TO GANG UP ON HIM, BUT THAT'S SUICIDE.
AS FOR TSUKI-GUMI, YOU SHOULD KNOW...
...THAT SHAMANS CAN BECOME MUCH MORE POWERFUL OVERNIGHT.
TEAM...
...REN ...
LORD HAO HAS GRANTED ME POWERS EVEN GREATER THAN MY BROTHER'S.
SWP

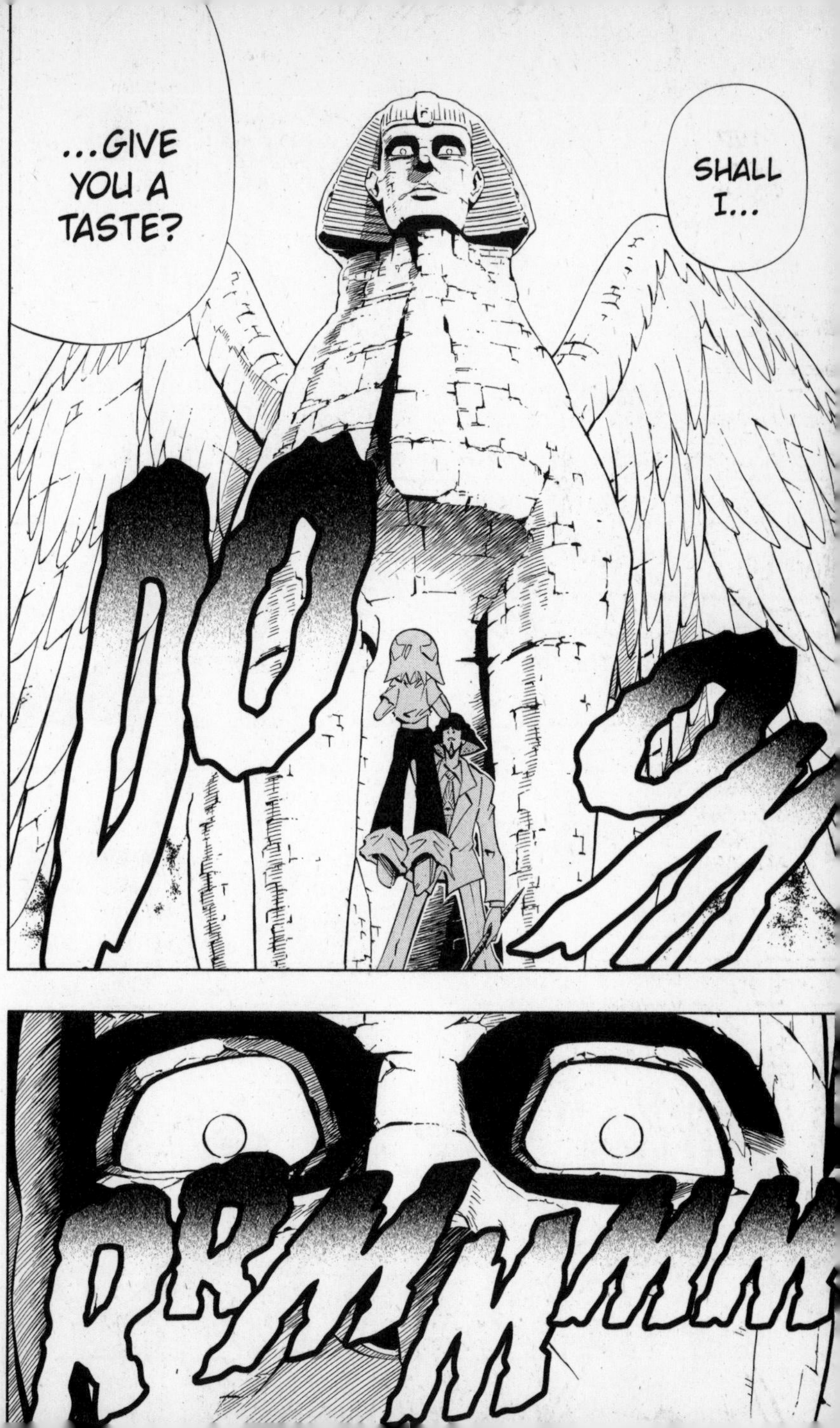
SHALL I...
...GIVE YOU A TASTE?

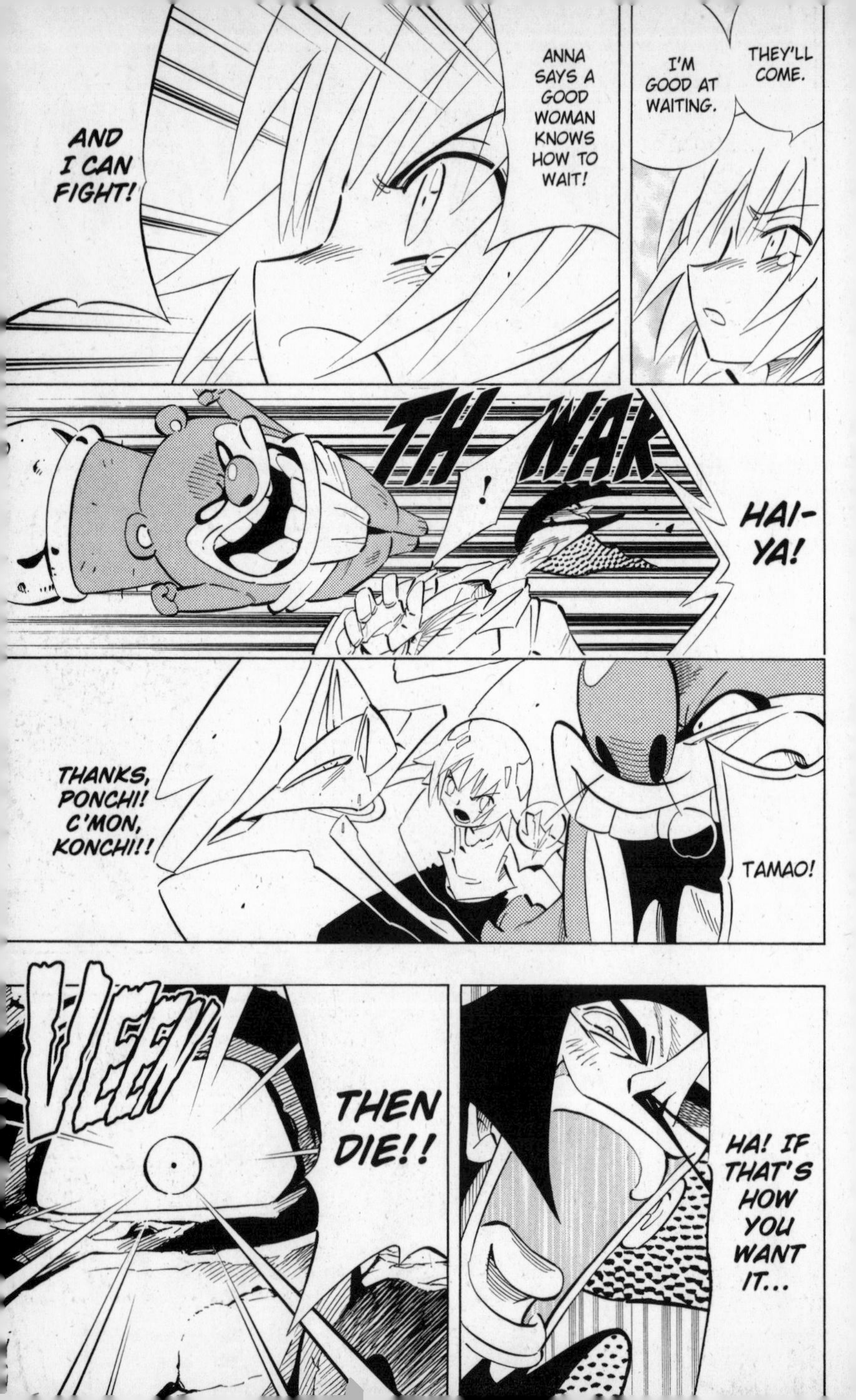
THEY'LL COME.
I'M GOOD AT WAITING.
ANNA SAYS A GOOD WOMAN KNOWS HOW TO WAIT!
AND I CAN FIGHT!
HAI-YA!
TH WAK
!
TAMAO!
THANKS, PONCHI! C'MON, KONCHI!!
HA! IF THAT'S HOW YOU WANT IT...
THEN DIE!!

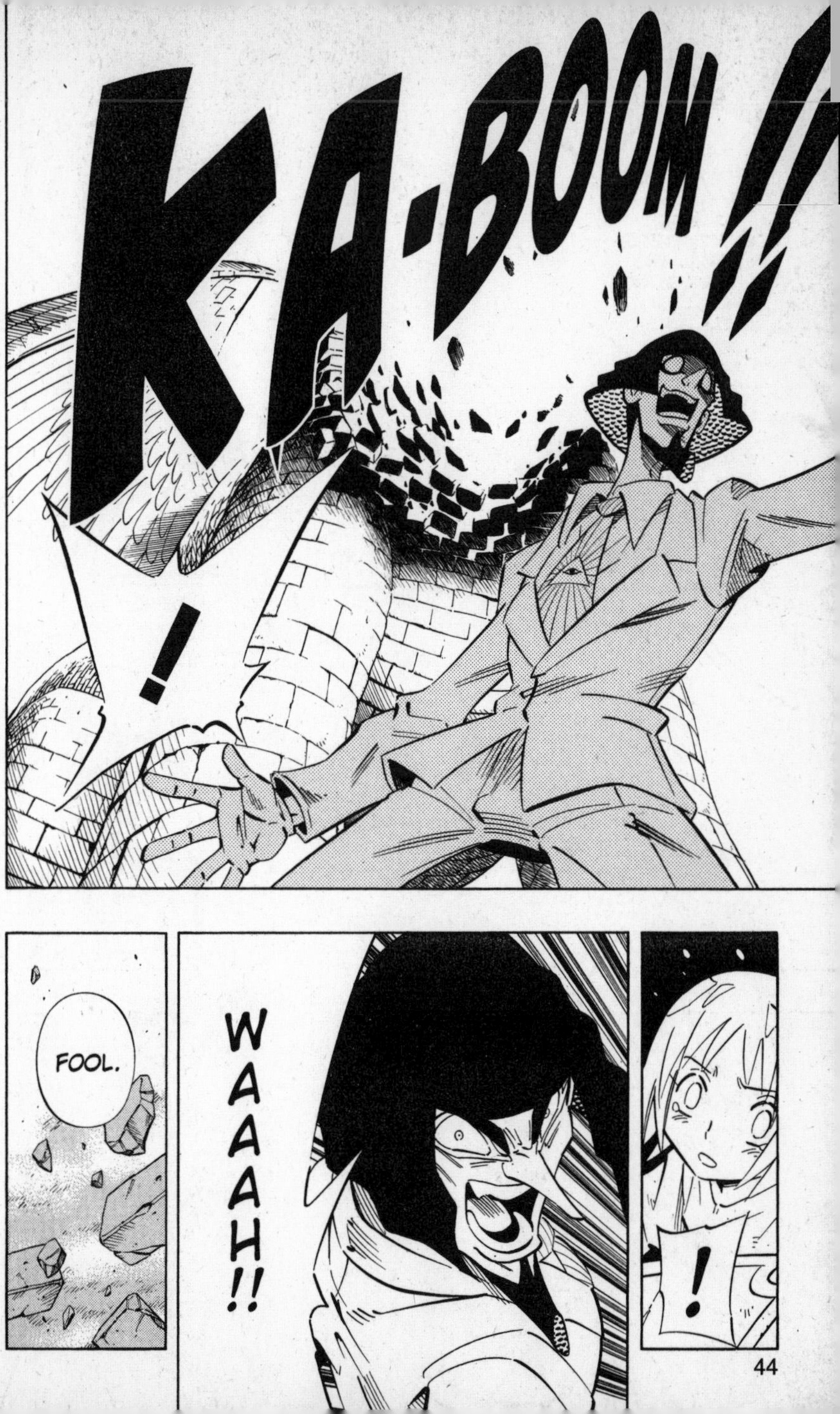
KA-BOOM!!
!
!
WAAAAH!!
FOOL.

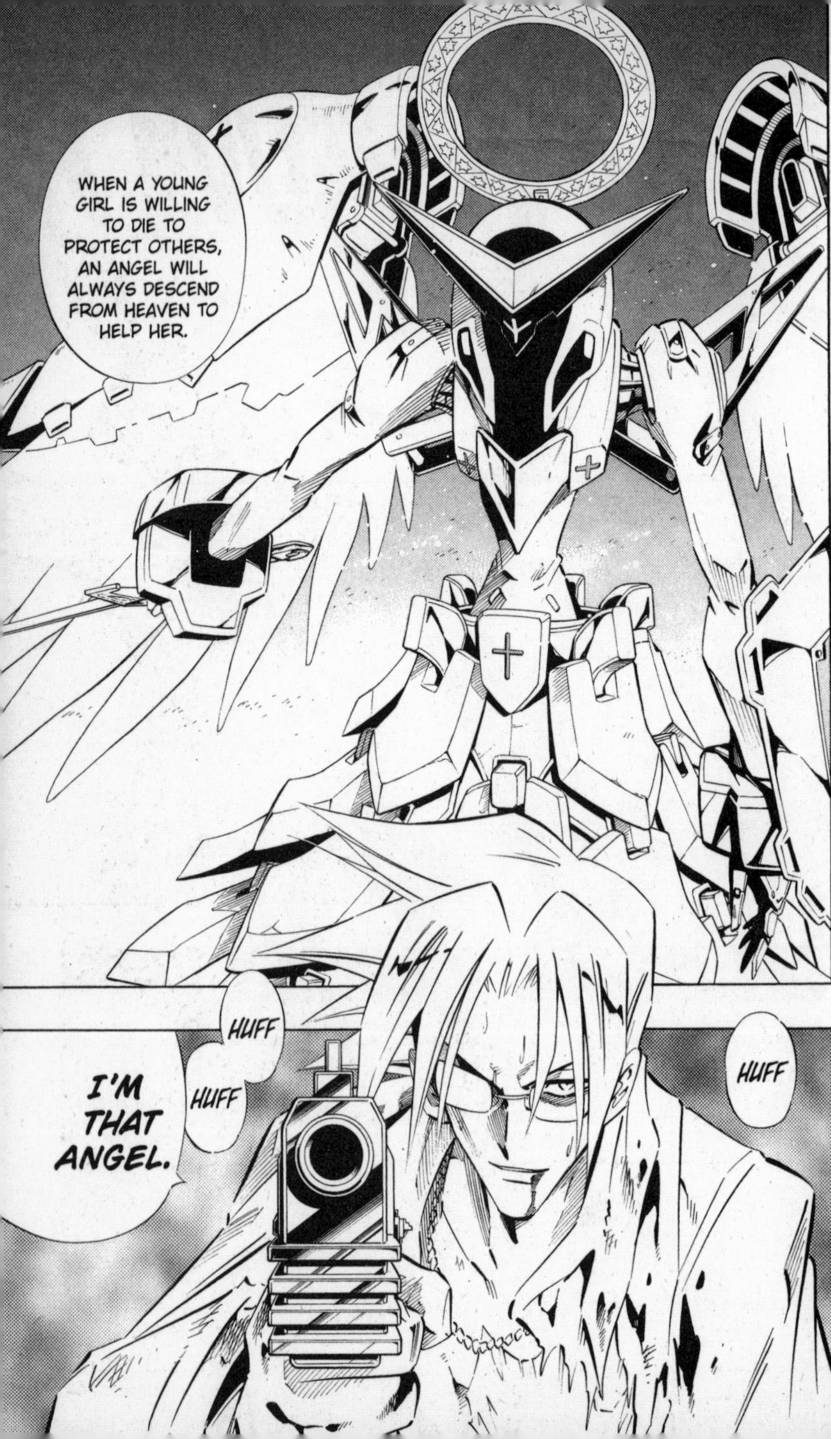
WHEN A YOUNG GIRL IS WILLING TO DIE TO PROTECT OTHERS, AN ANGEL WILL ALWAYS DESCEND FROM HEAVEN TO HELP HER.
HUFF
HUFF
HUFF
I'M THAT ANGEL.

SHAMAN KING CHARACTER FILE No.143

アナホル
ANAHOL

2001
(JAN)

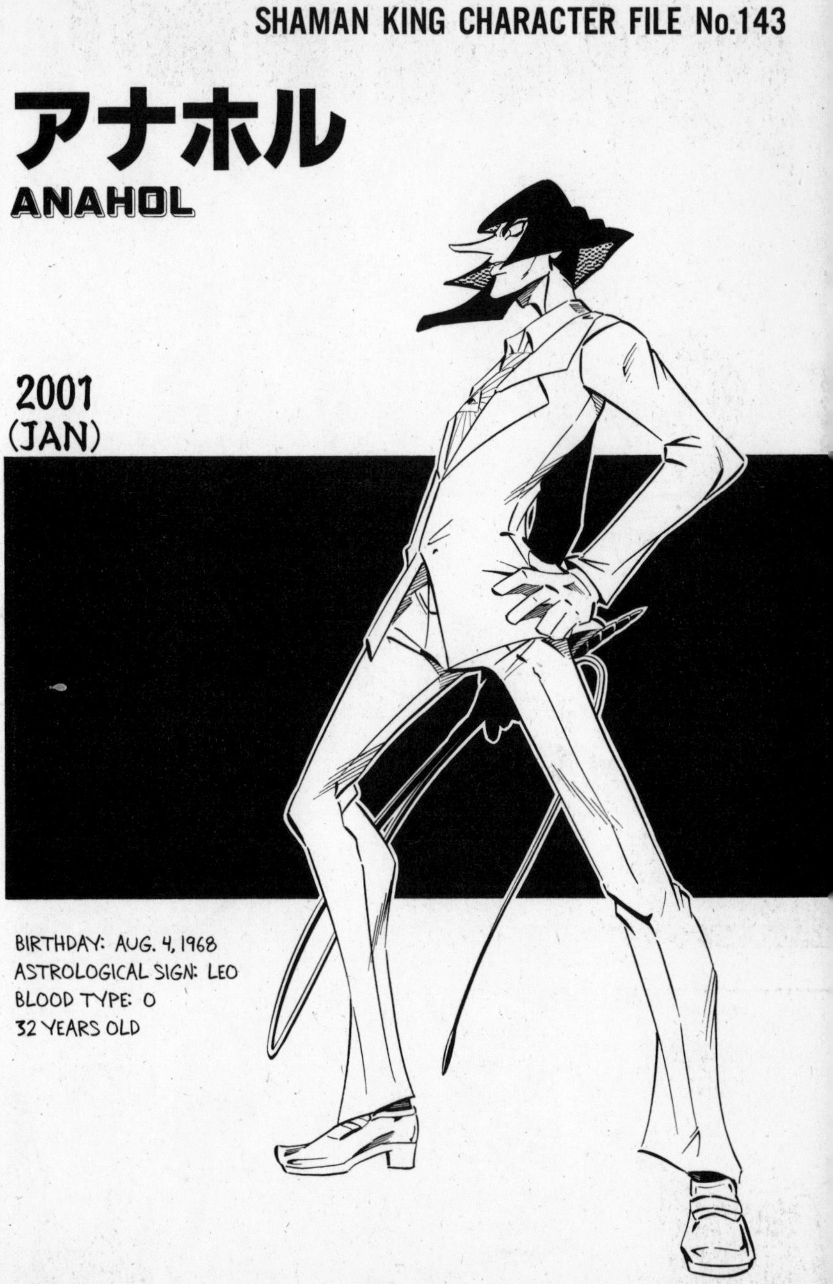

BIRTHDAY: AUG. 4, 1968
ASTROLOGICAL SIGN: LEO
BLOOD TYPE: O
32 YEARS OLD

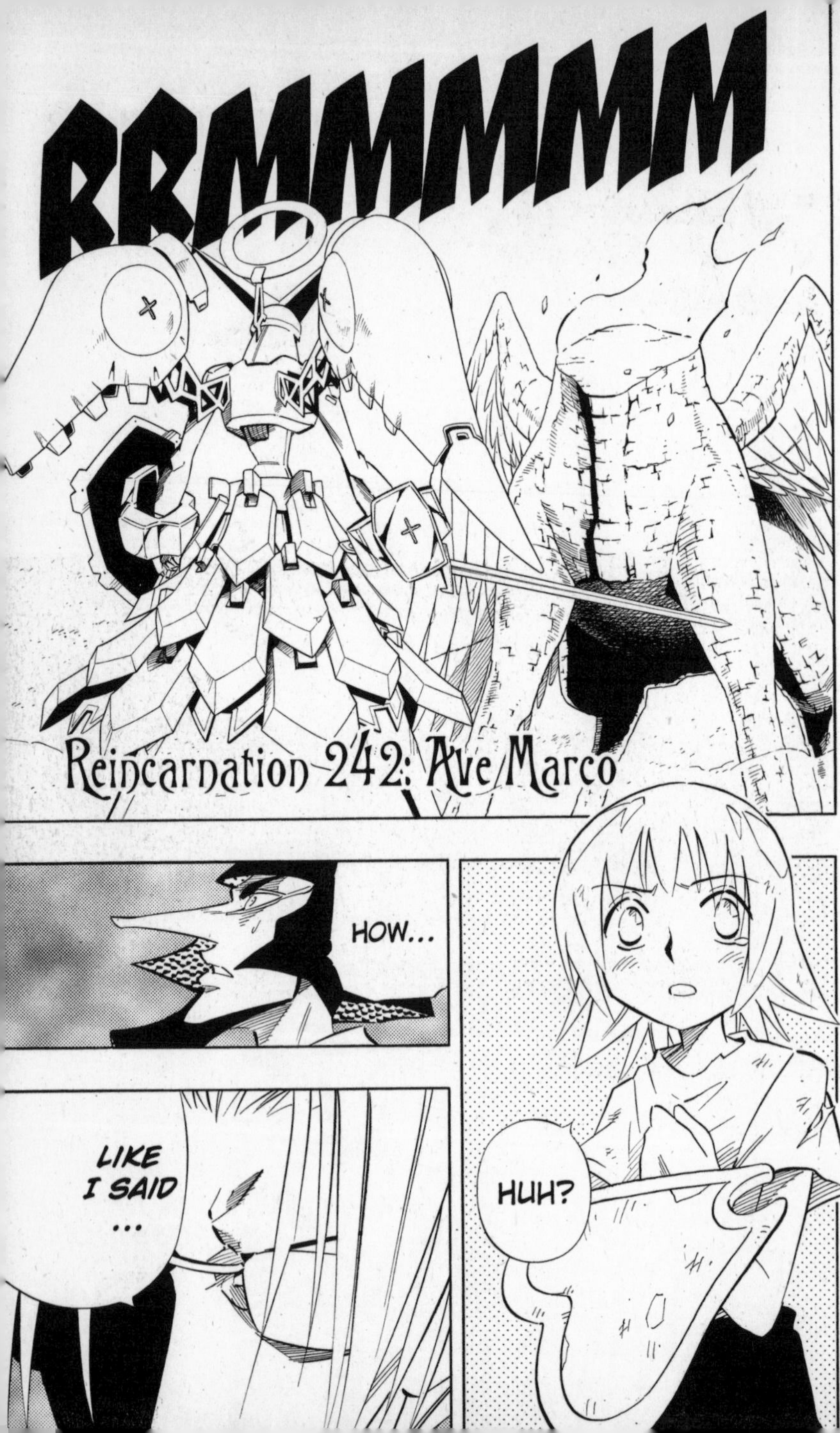
RBMMMMMM
Reincarnation 242: Ave Marco
HUH?
HOW...
LIKE I SAID ...

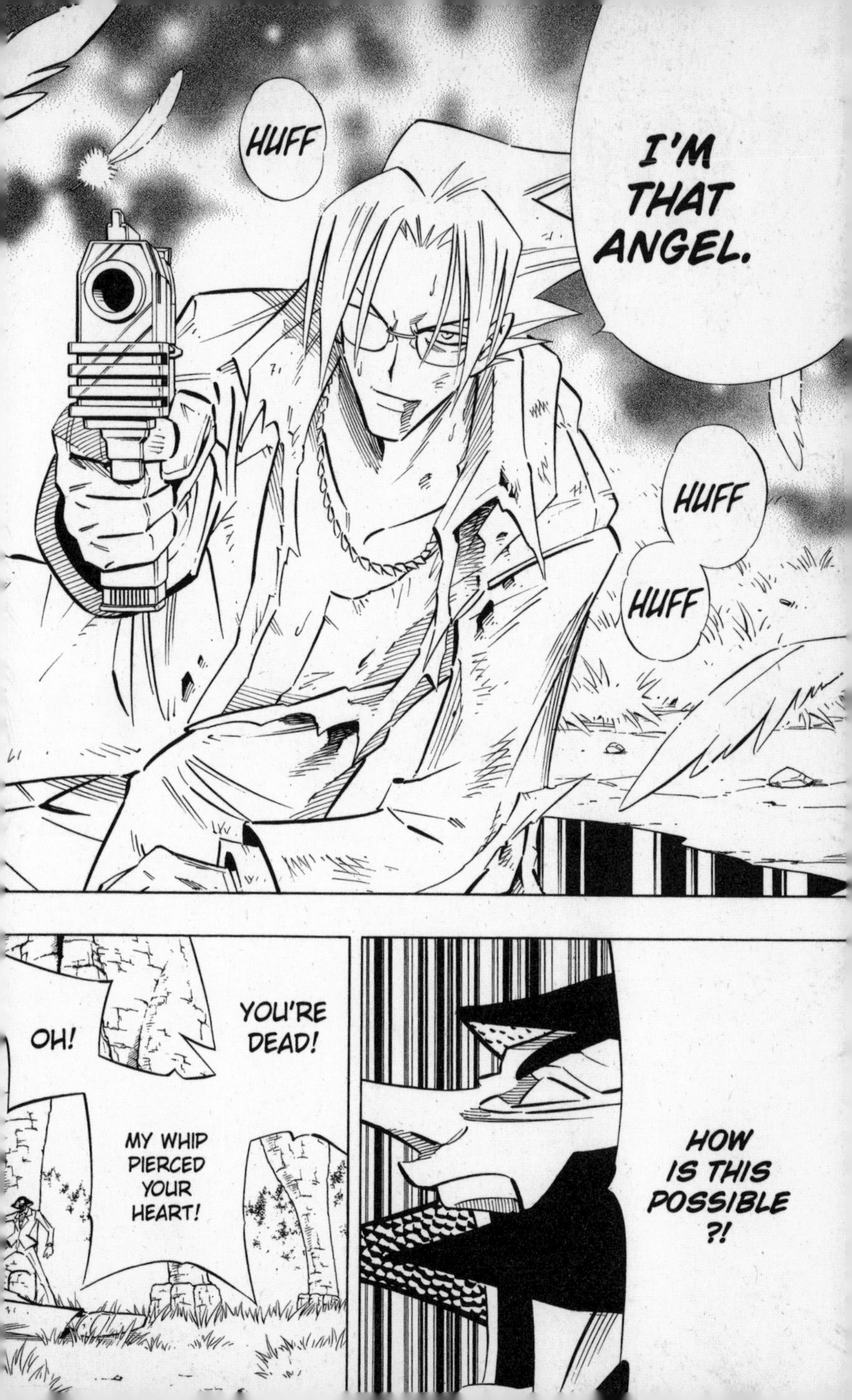
I'M THAT ANGEL.
HUFF
HUFF
HUFF
HOW IS THIS POSSIBLE ?!
YOU'RE DEAD!
OH!
MY WHIP PIERCED YOUR HEART!

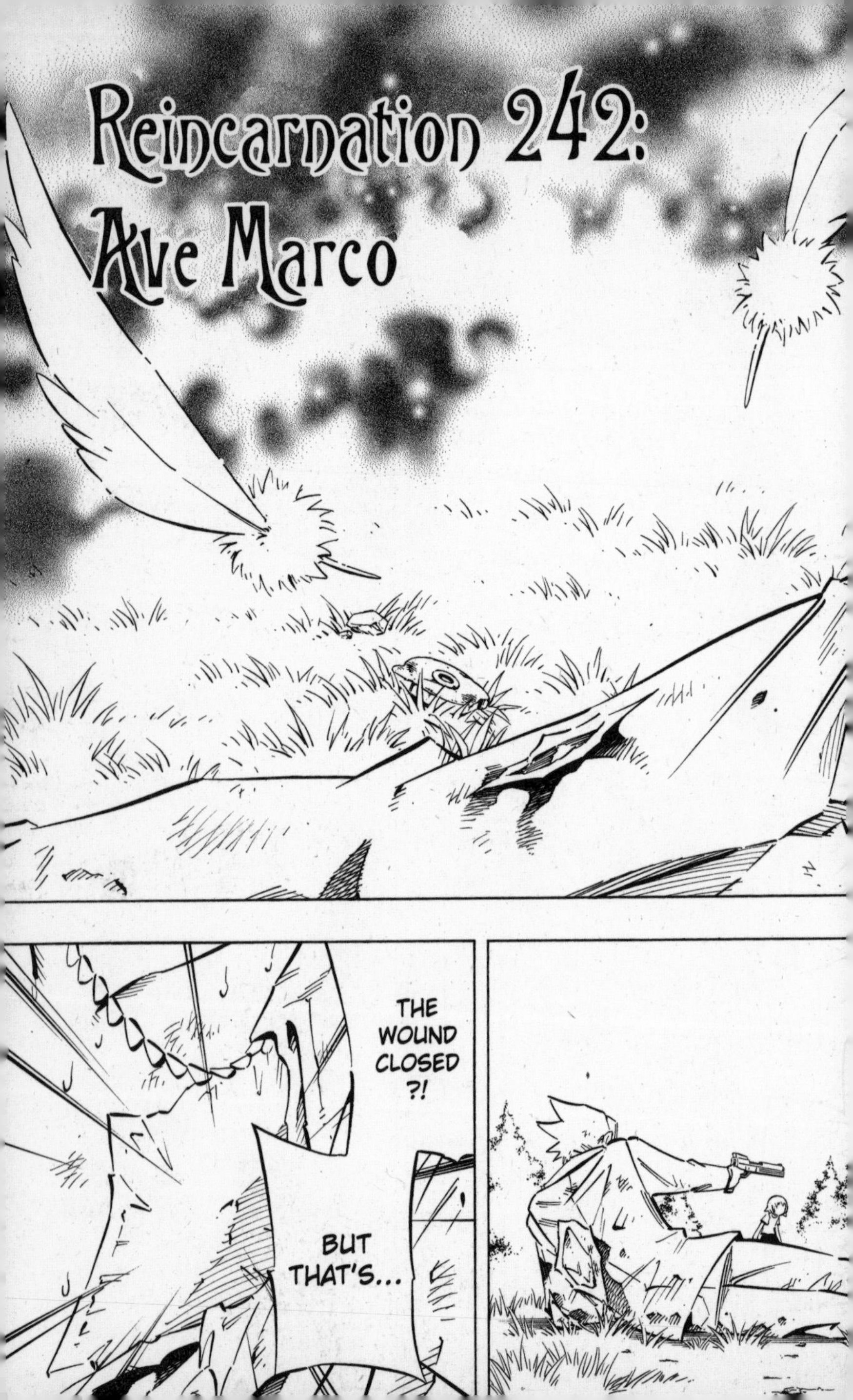
Reincarnation 242:
Ave Marco
THE WOUND CLOSED ?!
BUT THAT'S...

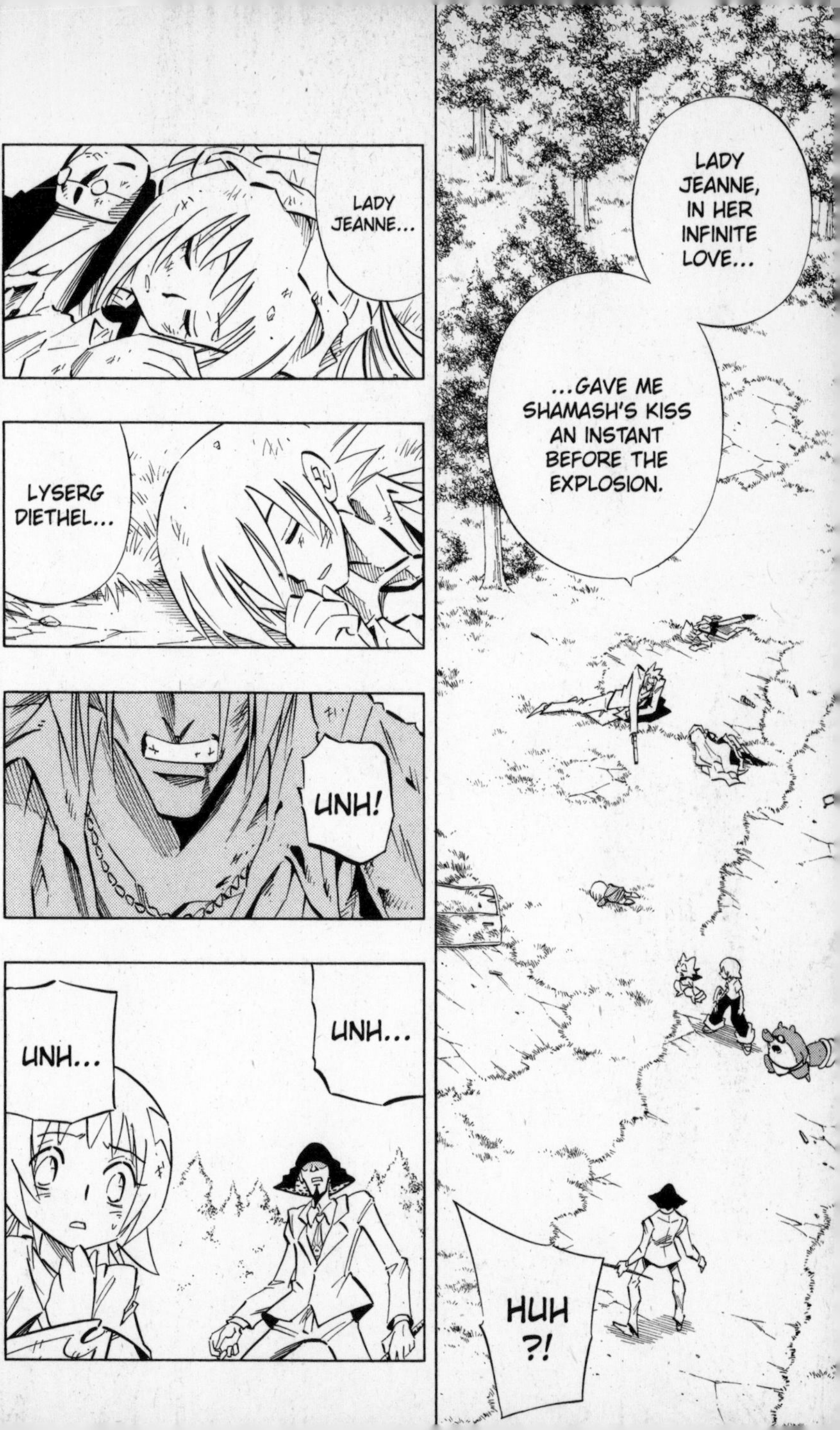
LADY JEANNE, IN HER INFINITE LOVE...
...GAVE ME SHAMASH'S KISS AN INSTANT BEFORE THE EXPLOSION.
HUH ?!
LADY JEANNE...
LYSERG DIETHEL...
UNH!
UNH...
UNH...

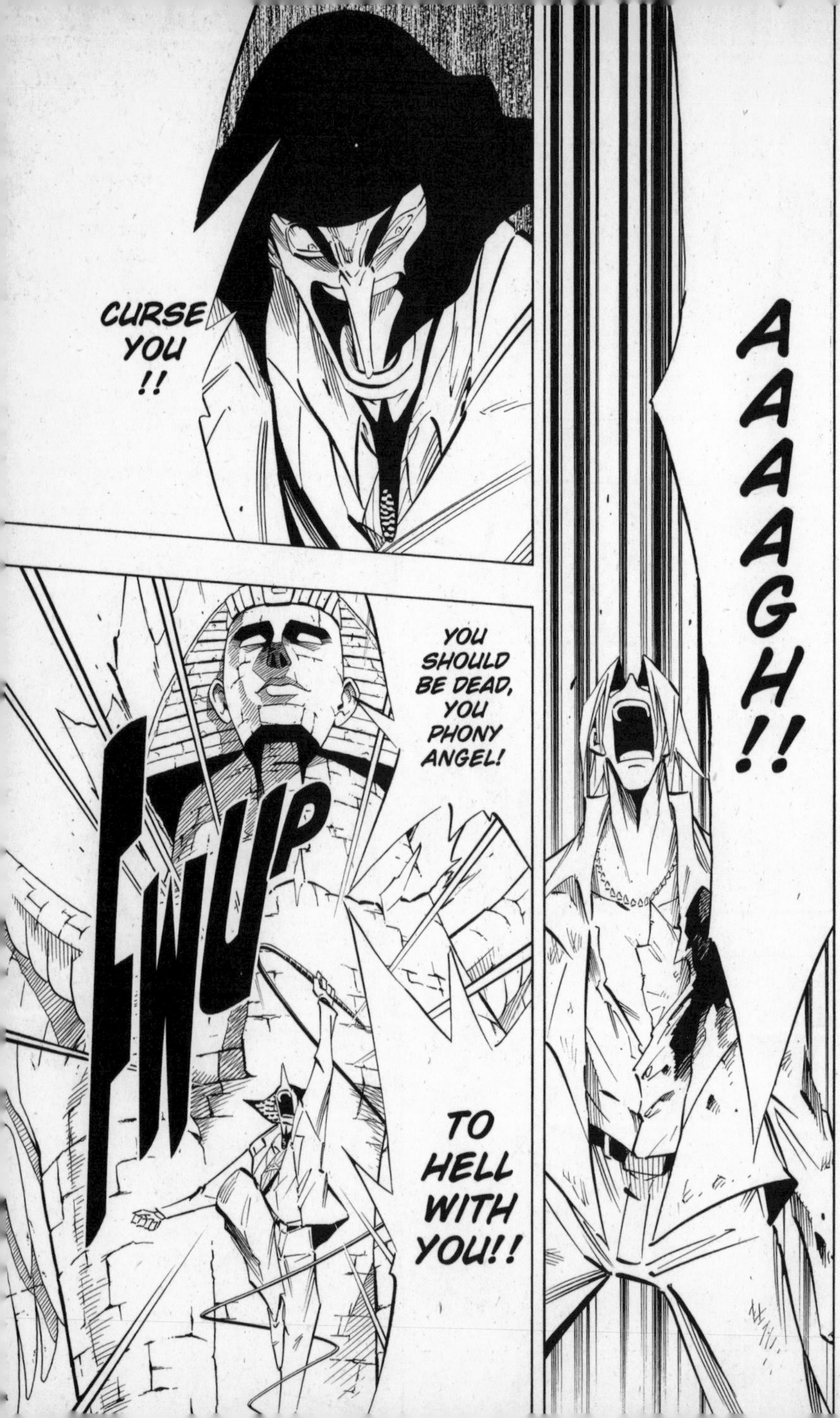
AAAAGH!!
CURSE YOU !!
YOU SHOULD BE DEAD, YOU PHONY ANGEL!
FWUP
TO HELL WITH YOU!!

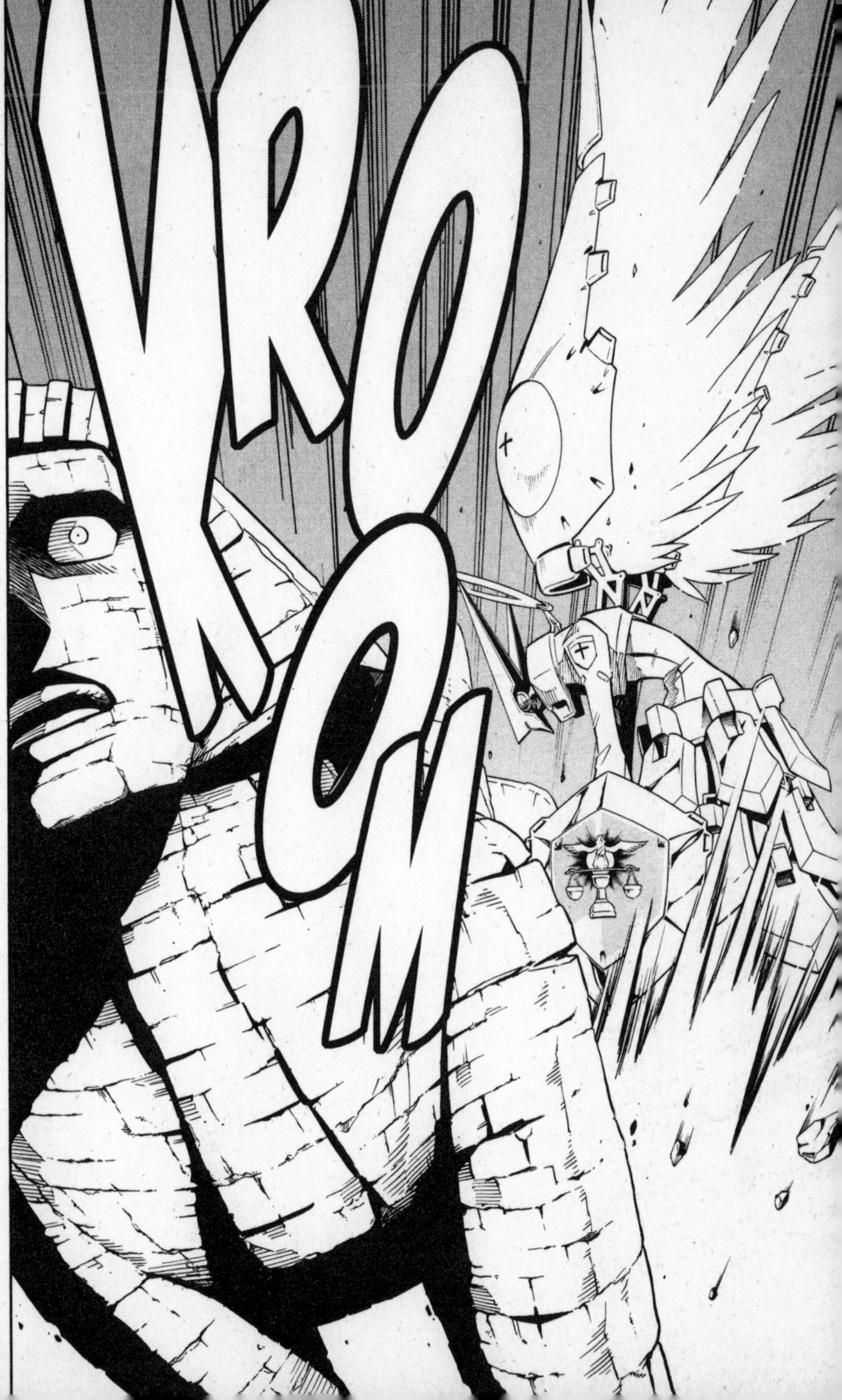
VROOOM

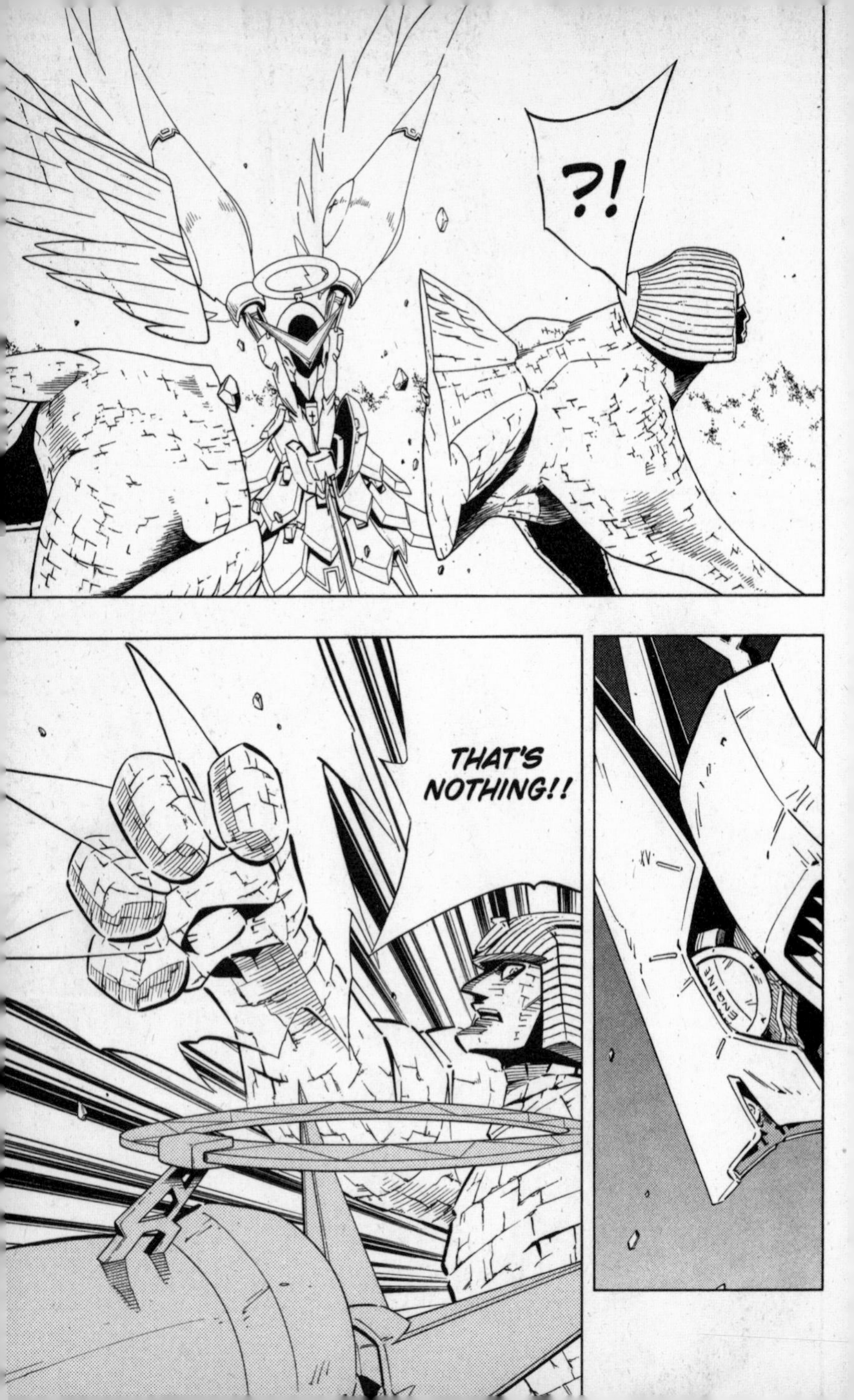
?!
THAT'S NOTHING!!
ENGINE

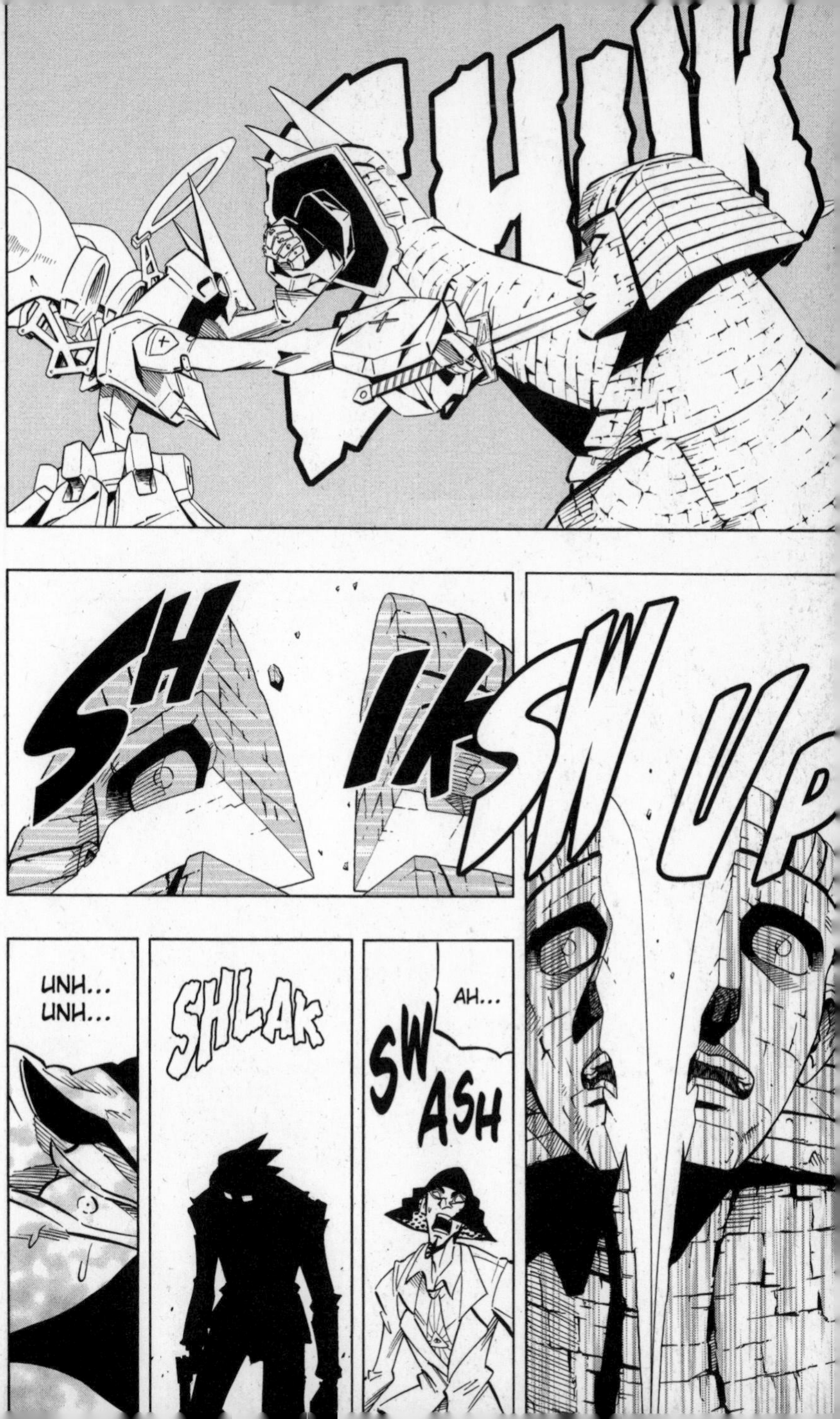
SHUK
SHUP
SHIK
AH...
SWASH
SHLAK
UNH...
UNH...

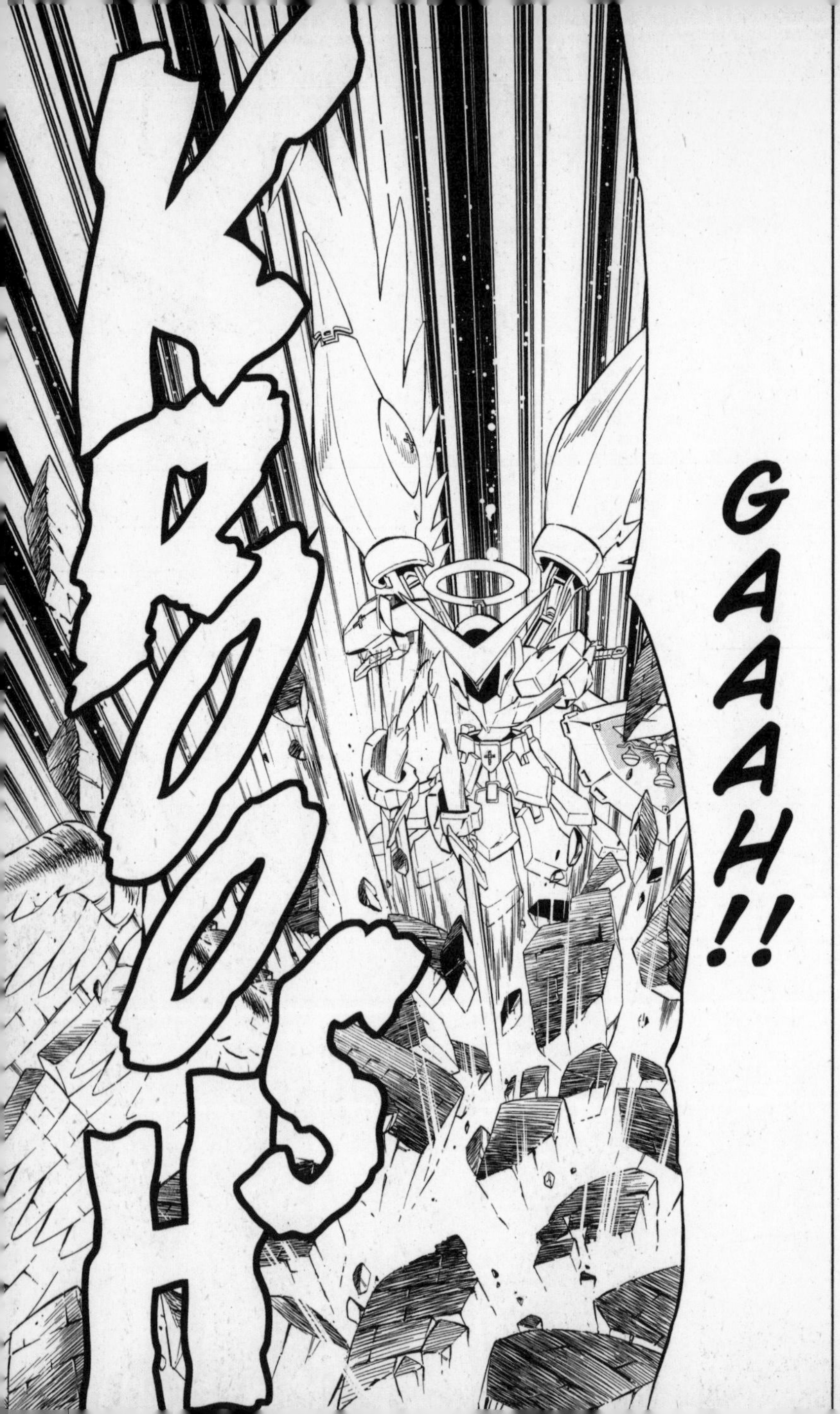
GAAAH!!

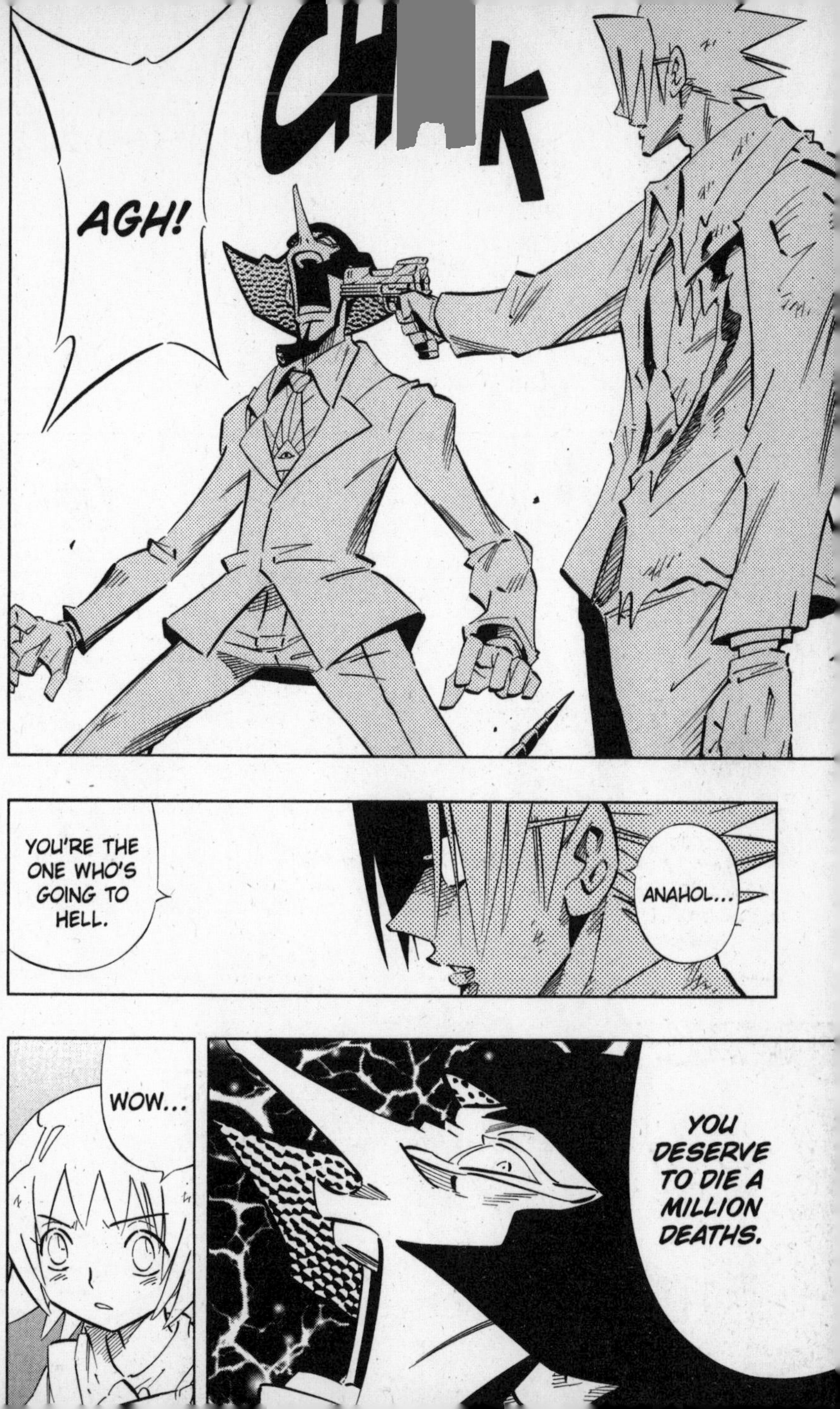
AGH!
ANAHOL...
YOU'RE THE ONE WHO'S GOING TO HELL.
YOU DESERVE TO DIE A MILLION DEATHS.
WOW...

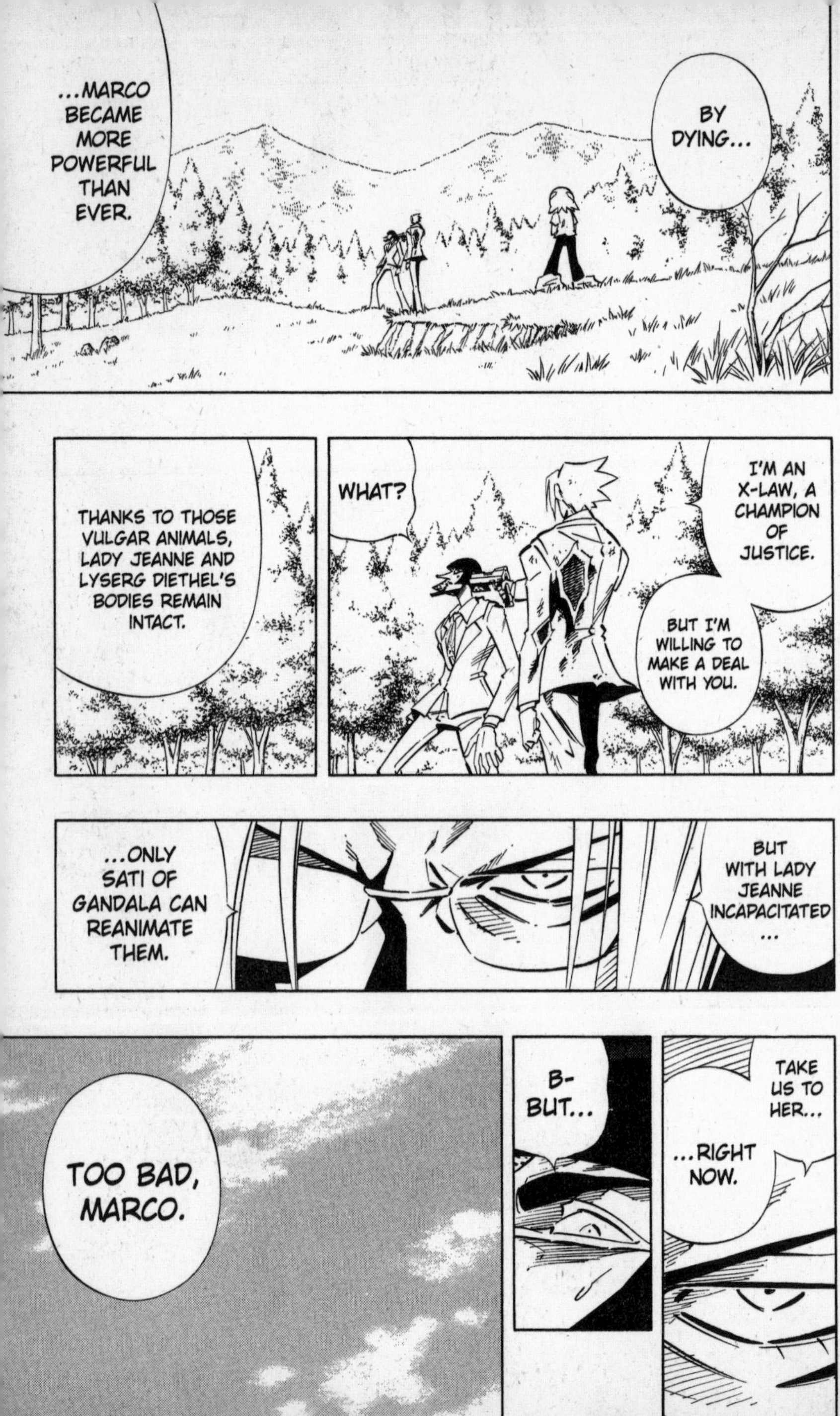
BY DYING...
...MARCO BECAME MORE POWERFUL THAN EVER.
I'M AN X-LAW, A CHAMPION OF JUSTICE.
BUT I'M WILLING TO MAKE A DEAL WITH YOU.
WHAT?
THANKS TO THOSE VULGAR ANIMALS, LADY JEANNE AND LYSERG DIETHEL'S BODIES REMAIN INTACT.
BUT WITH LADY JEANNE INCAPACITATED...
...ONLY SATI OF GANDALA CAN REANIMATE THEM.
TAKE US TO HER...
...RIGHT NOW.
B-BUT...
TOO BAD, MARCO.

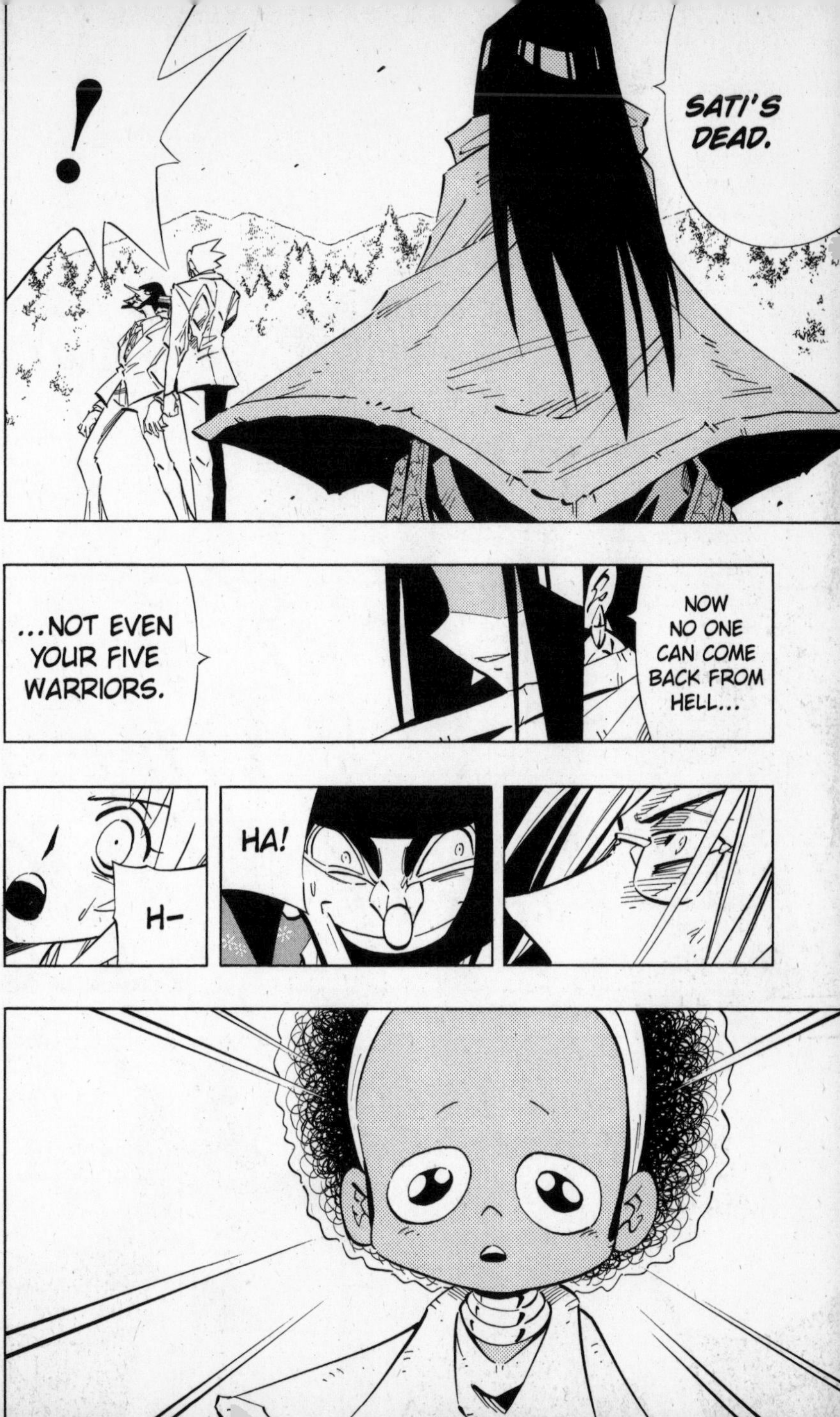
SATI'S DEAD.
!
NOW NO ONE CAN COME BACK FROM HELL...
...NOT EVEN YOUR FIVE WARRIORS.
HA!
H-

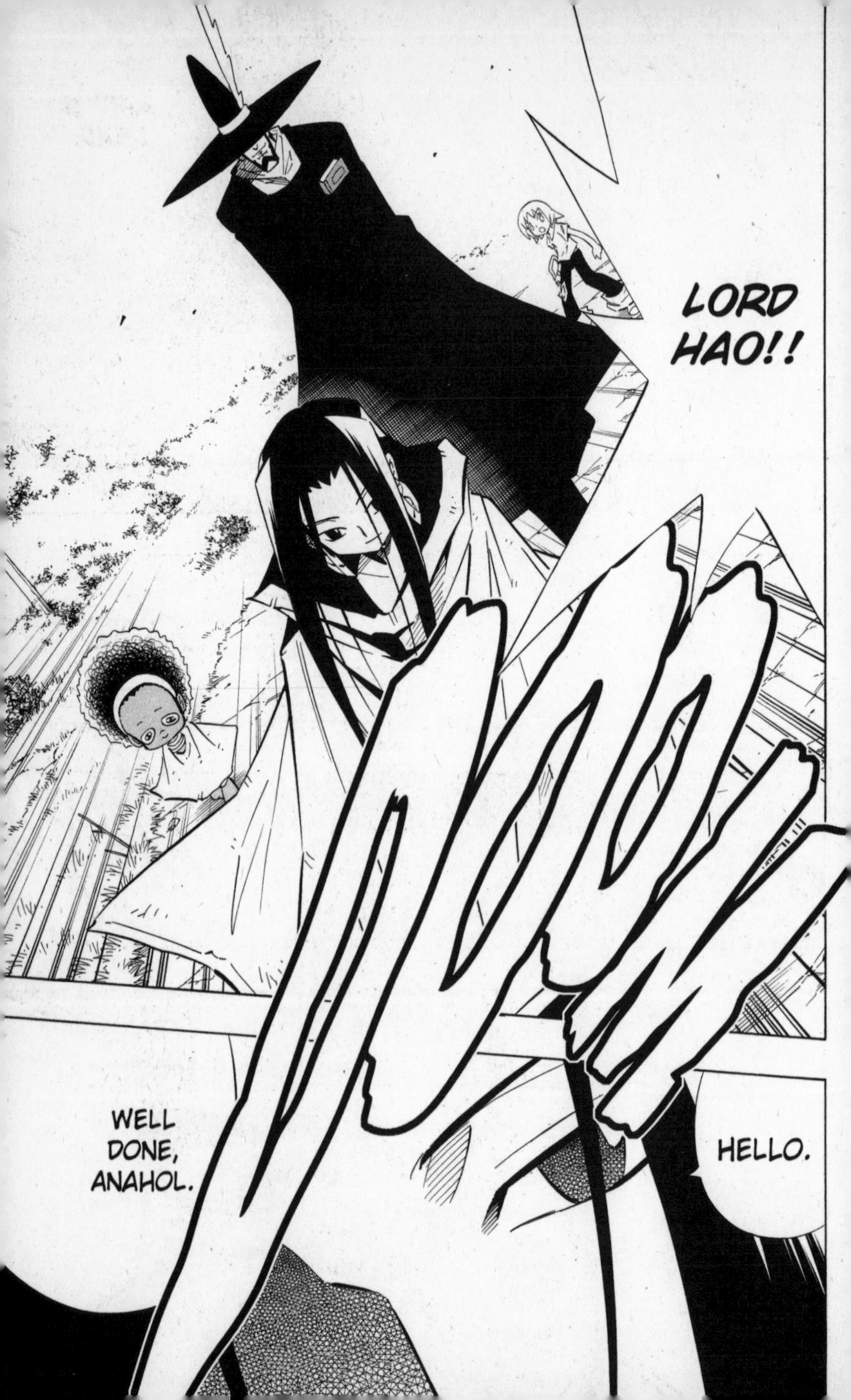
LORD HAO!!
HELLO.
WELL DONE, ANAHOL.

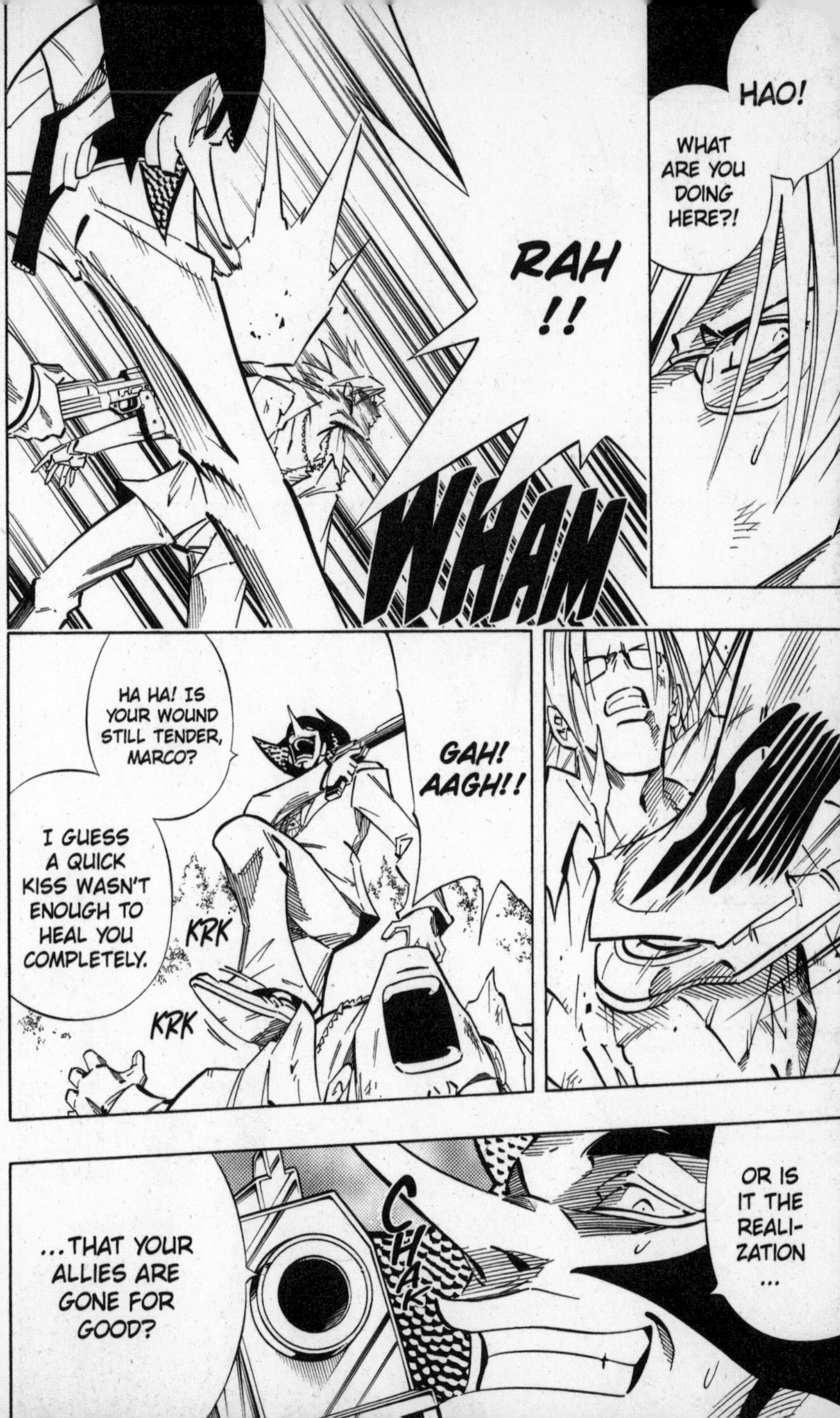
HAO!
WHAT ARE YOU DOING HERE?!
RAH!!
WHAM
HA HA! IS YOUR WOUND STILL TENDER, MARCO?
I GUESS A QUICK KISS WASN'T ENOUGH TO HEAL YOU COMPLETELY.
GAH! AAGH!!
KRK
KRK
OR IS IT THE REALI-ZATION...
CHAK
...THAT YOUR ALLIES ARE GONE FOR GOOD?

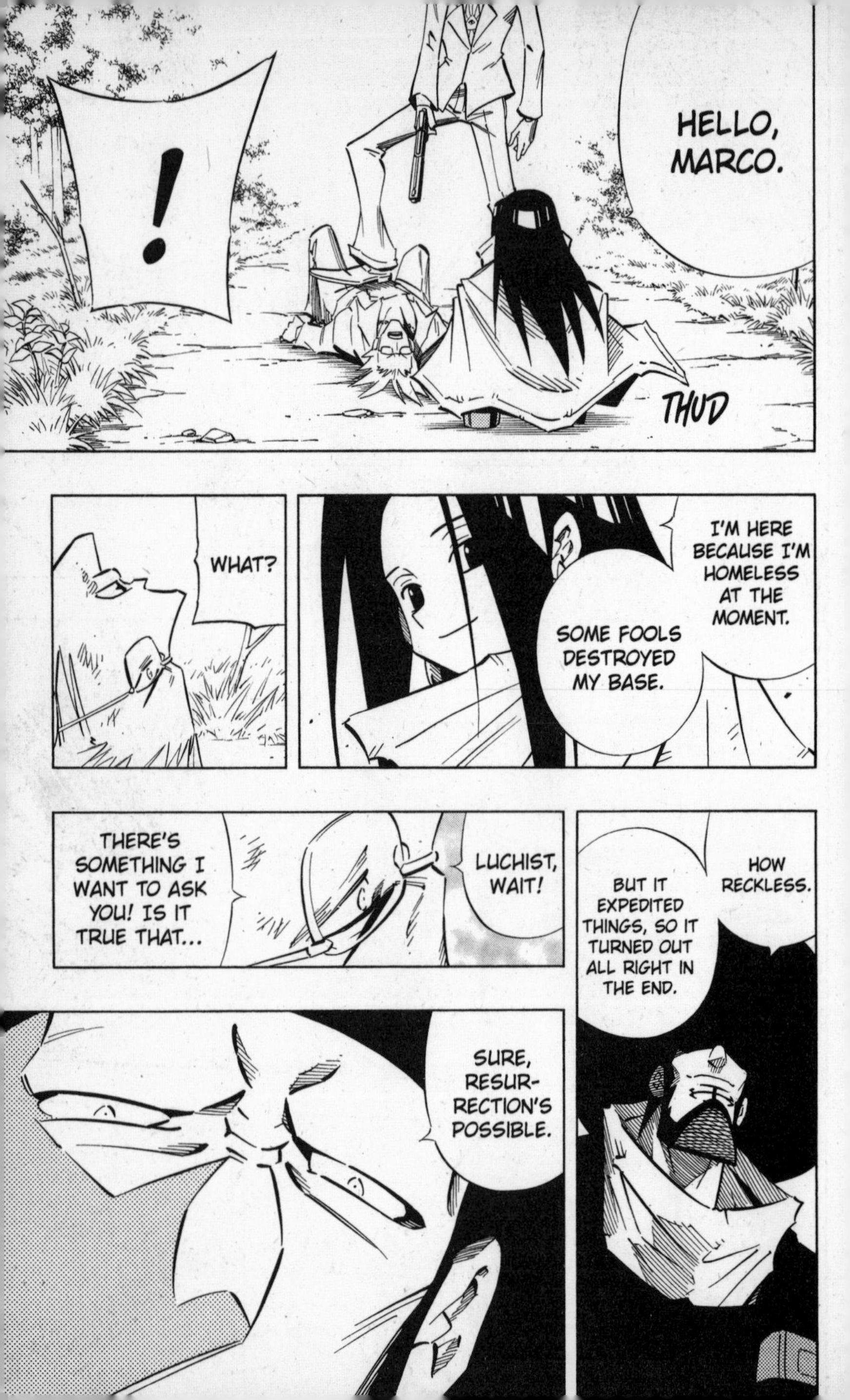
HELLO, MARCO.
THUD
!
I'M HERE BECAUSE I'M HOMELESS AT THE MOMENT.
SOME FOOLS DESTROYED MY BASE.
WHAT?
HOW RECKLESS.
BUT IT EXPEDITED THINGS, SO IT TURNED OUT ALL RIGHT IN THE END.
LUCHIST, WAIT!
THERE'S SOMETHING I WANT TO ASK YOU! IS IT TRUE THAT...
SURE, RESURRECTION'S POSSIBLE.

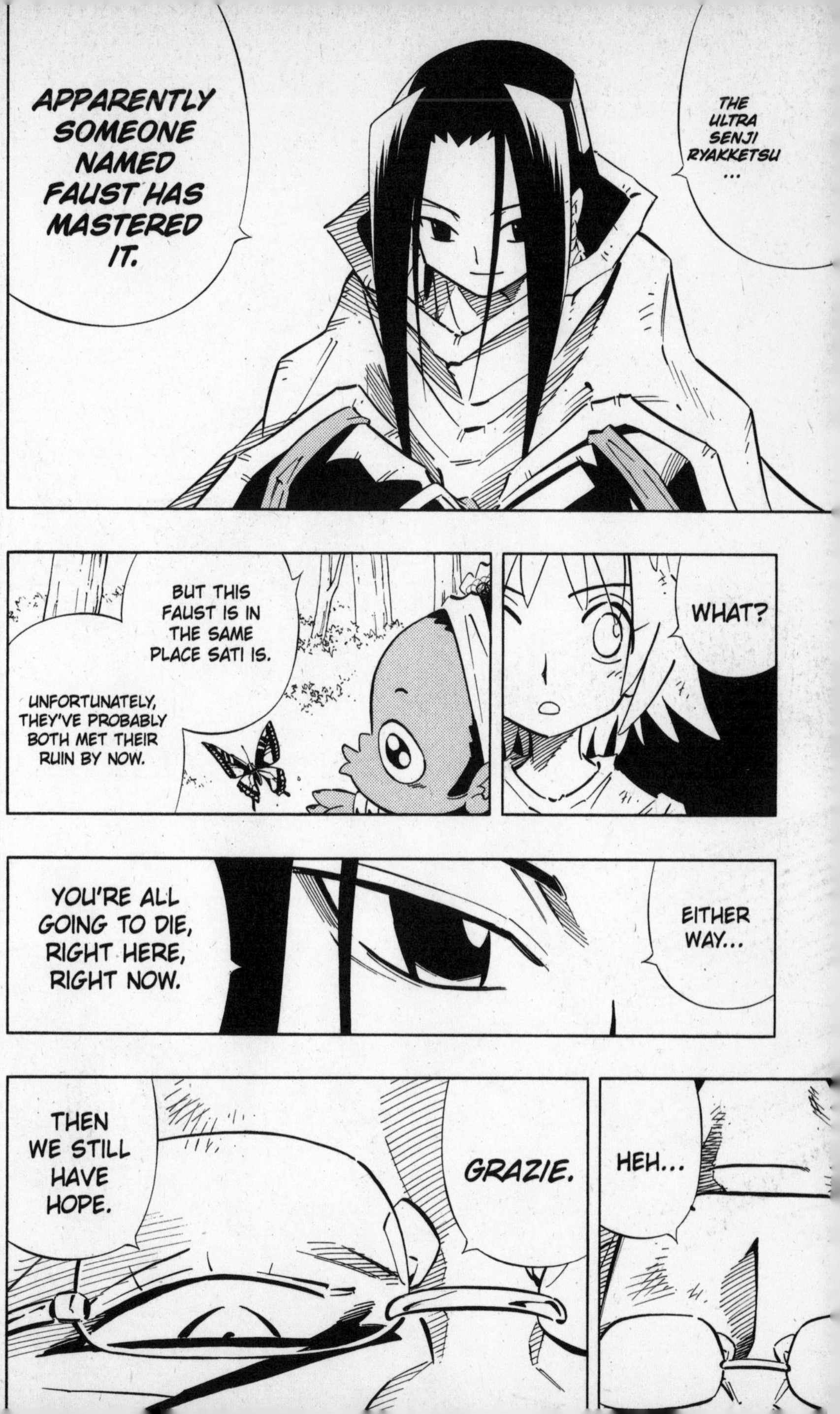
THE ULTRA SENJI RYAKKETSU...
APPARENTLY SOMEONE NAMED FAUST HAS MASTERED IT.
WHAT?
BUT THIS FAUST IS IN THE SAME PLACE SATI IS.
UNFORTUNATELY, THEY'VE PROBABLY BOTH MET THEIR RUIN BY NOW.
EITHER WAY...
YOU'RE ALL GOING TO DIE, RIGHT HERE, RIGHT NOW.
HEH...
GRAZIE.
THEN WE STILL HAVE HOPE.

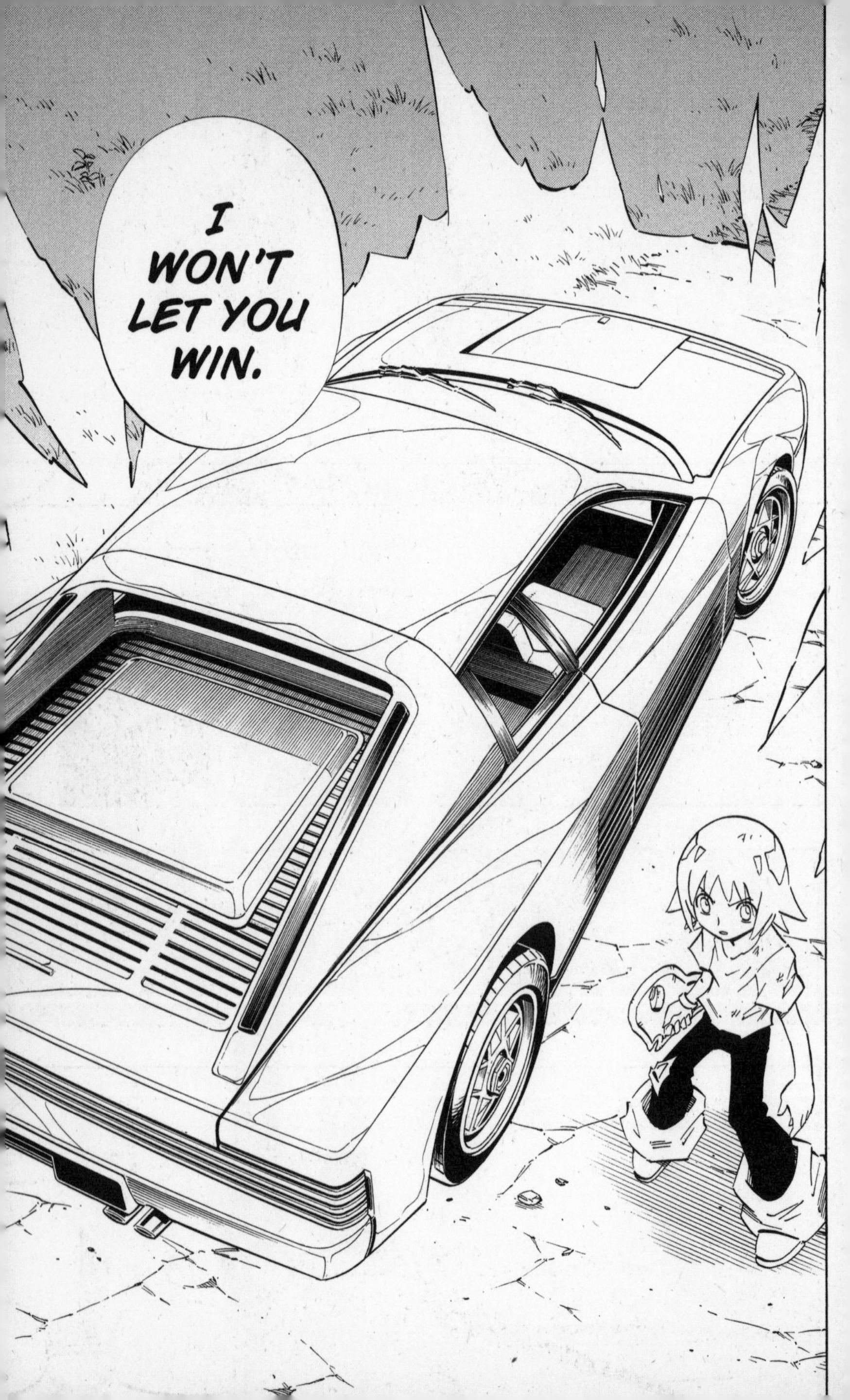
I WON'T LET YOU WIN.

SHAMAN KING CHARACTER FILE No.144

田村崎 緑

MIDORI TAMURAZAKI

2001
(JAN)

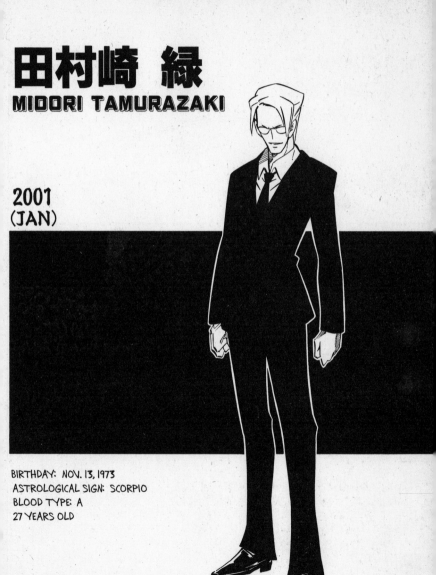

BIRTHDAY: NOV. 13, 1973
ASTROLOGICAL SIGN: SCORPIO
BLOOD TYPE: A
27 YEARS OLD

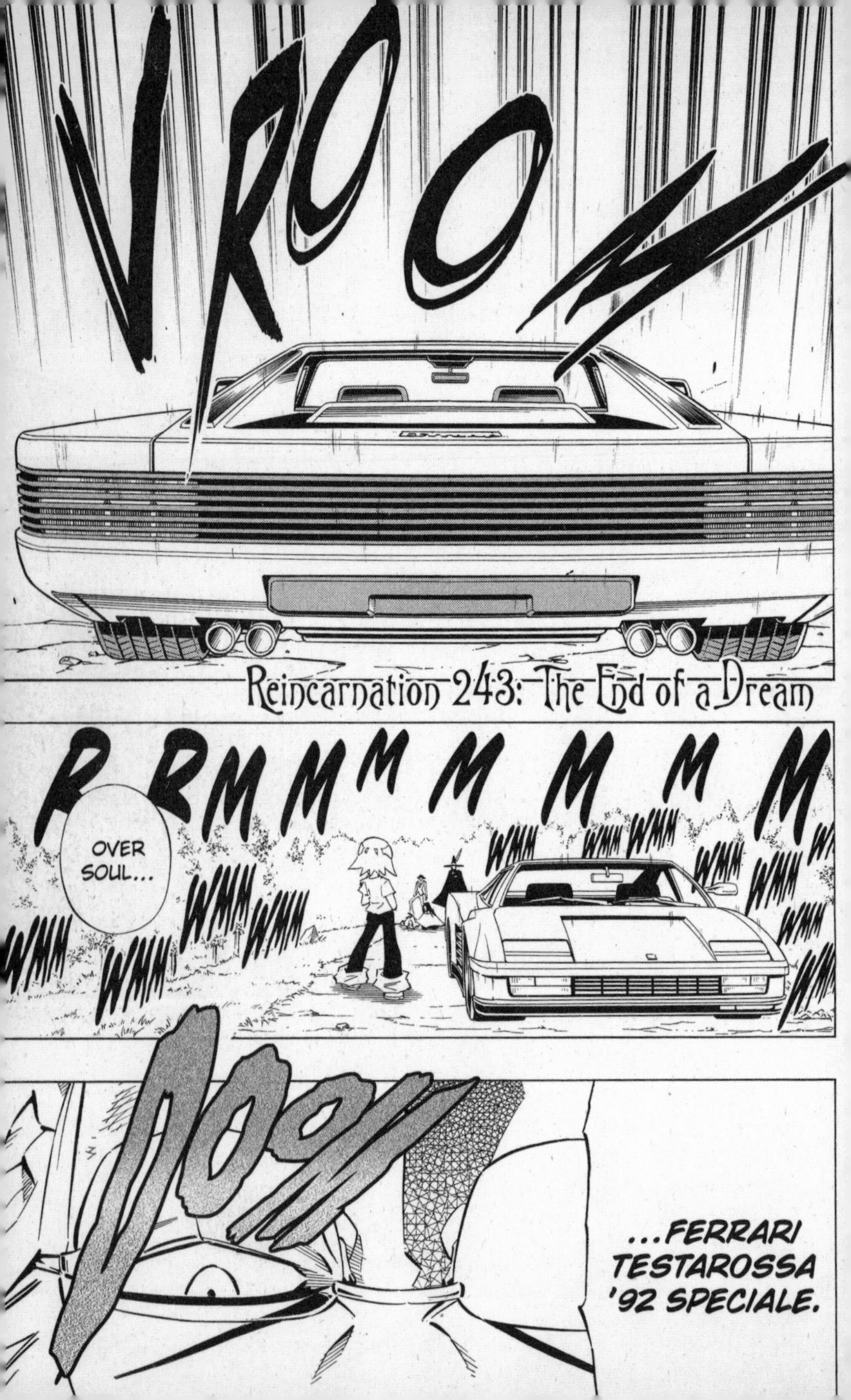
VROOOM
Reincarnation 243: The End of a Dream
RRMMMMMMM
OVER SOUL...
WHM
VOOM
...FERRARI TESTAROSSA '92 SPECIALE.

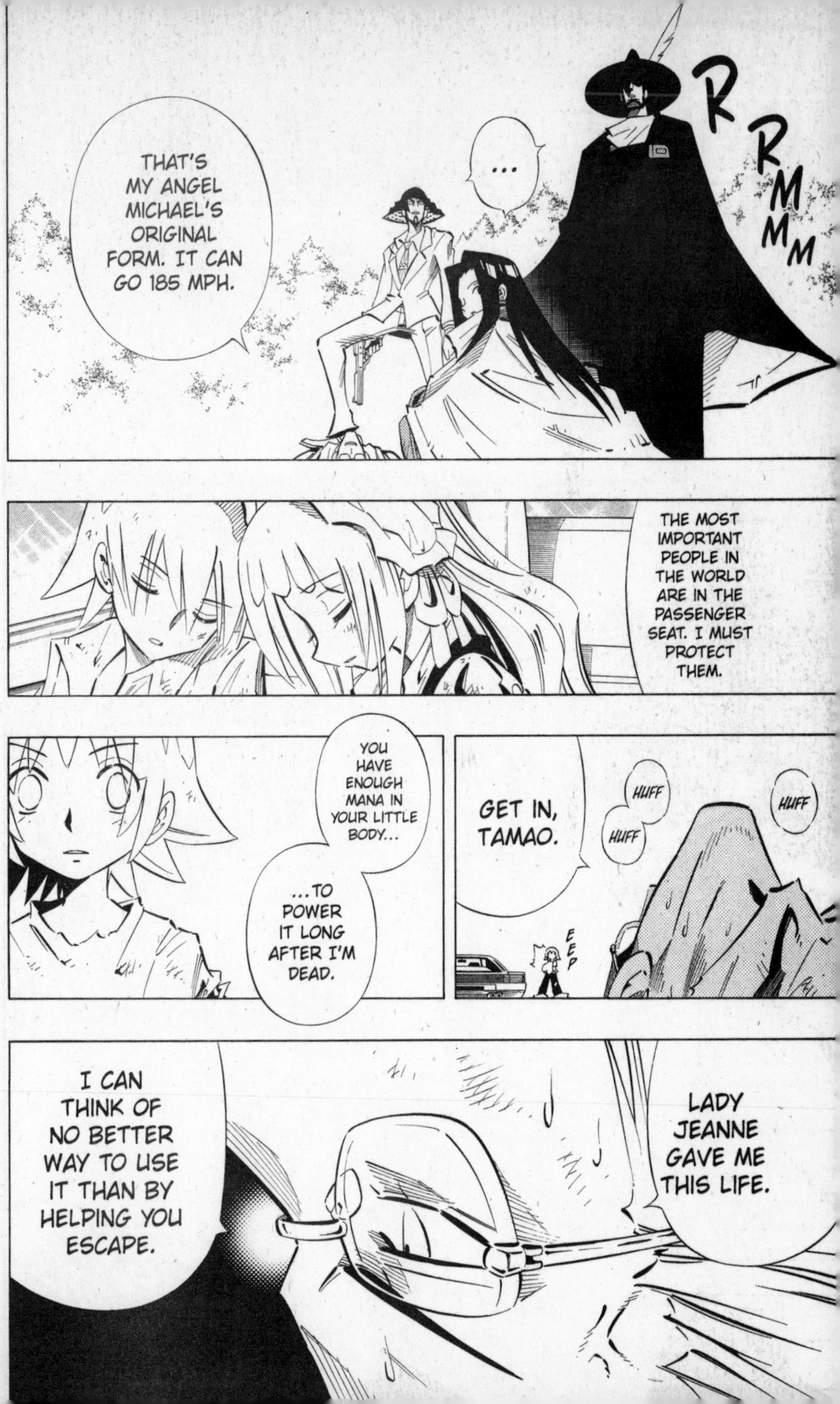
RRMMM
...
THAT'S MY ANGEL MICHAEL'S ORIGINAL FORM. IT CAN GO 185 MPH.
THE MOST IMPORTANT PEOPLE IN THE WORLD ARE IN THE PASSENGER SEAT. I MUST PROTECT THEM.
HUFF
HUFF
HUFF
GET IN, TAMAO.
EEP
YOU HAVE ENOUGH MANA IN YOUR LITTLE BODY...
...TO POWER IT LONG AFTER I'M DEAD.
LADY JEANNE GAVE ME THIS LIFE.
I CAN THINK OF NO BETTER WAY TO USE IT THAN BY HELPING YOU ESCAPE.

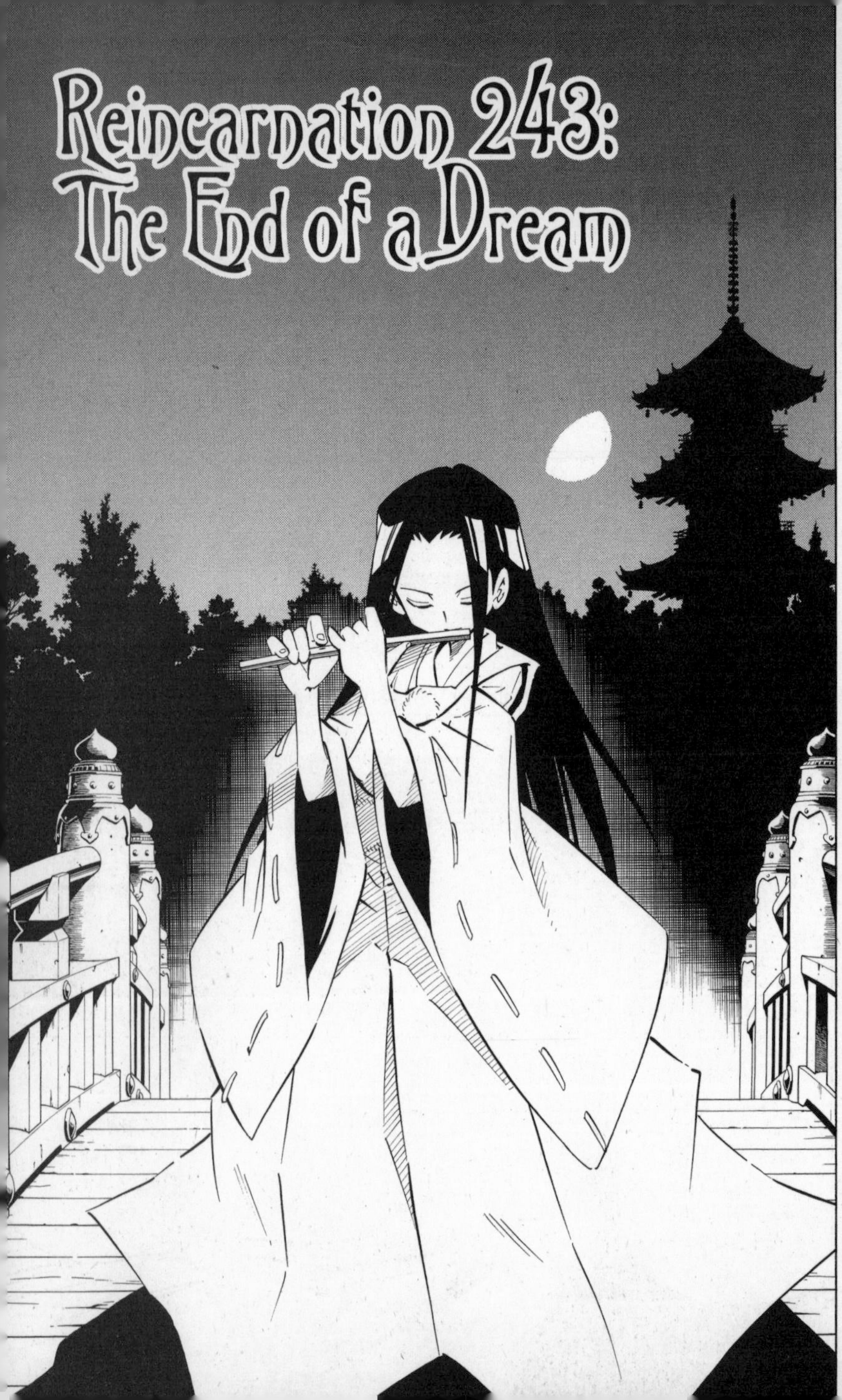
Reincarnation 243:
The End of a Dream

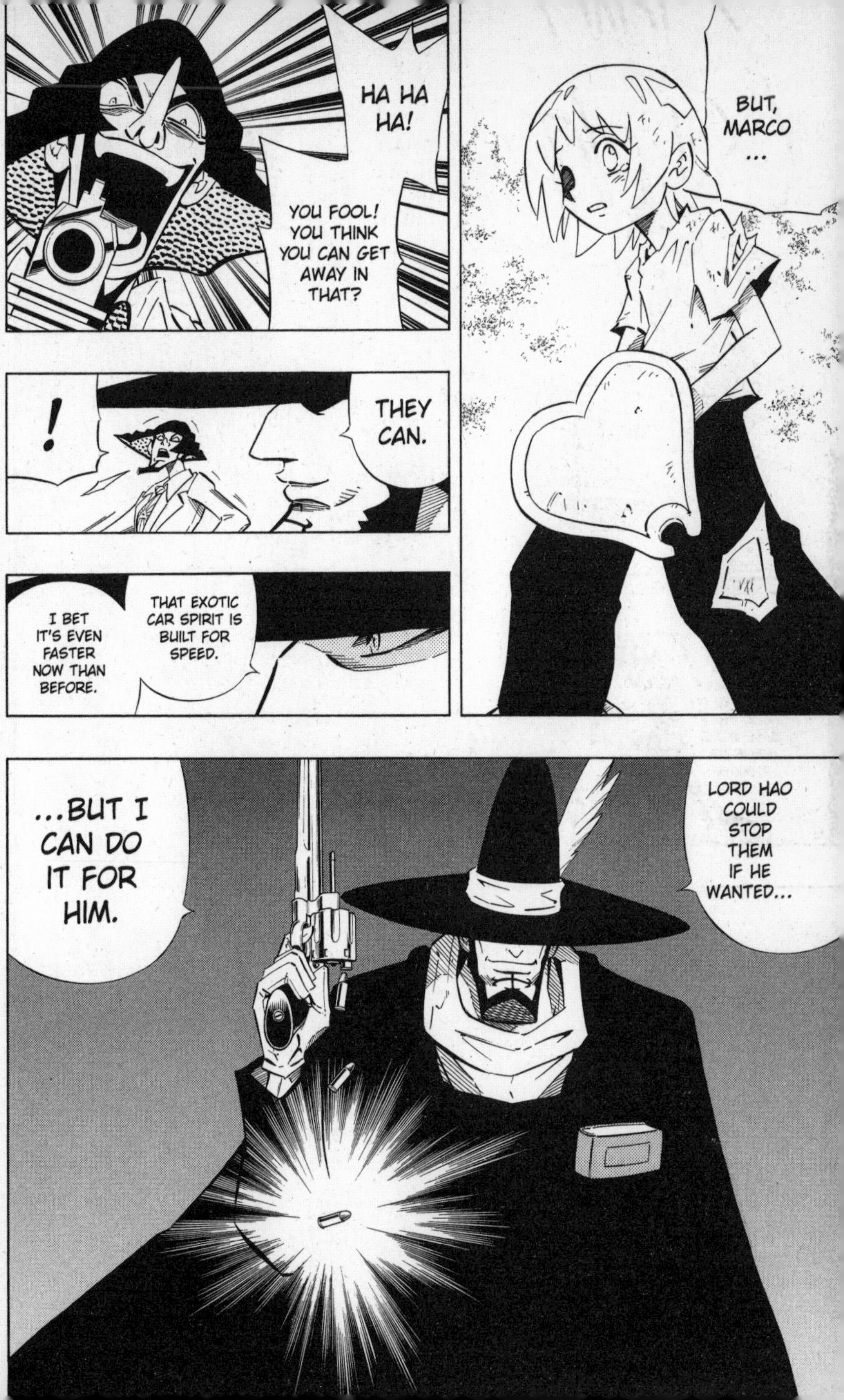
BUT, MARCO ...
HA HA HA!
YOU FOOL! YOU THINK YOU CAN GET AWAY IN THAT?
!
THEY CAN.
THAT EXOTIC CAR SPIRIT IS BUILT FOR SPEED.
I BET IT'S EVEN FASTER NOW THAN BEFORE.
LORD HAO COULD STOP THEM IF HE WANTED...
...BUT I CAN DO IT FOR HIM.

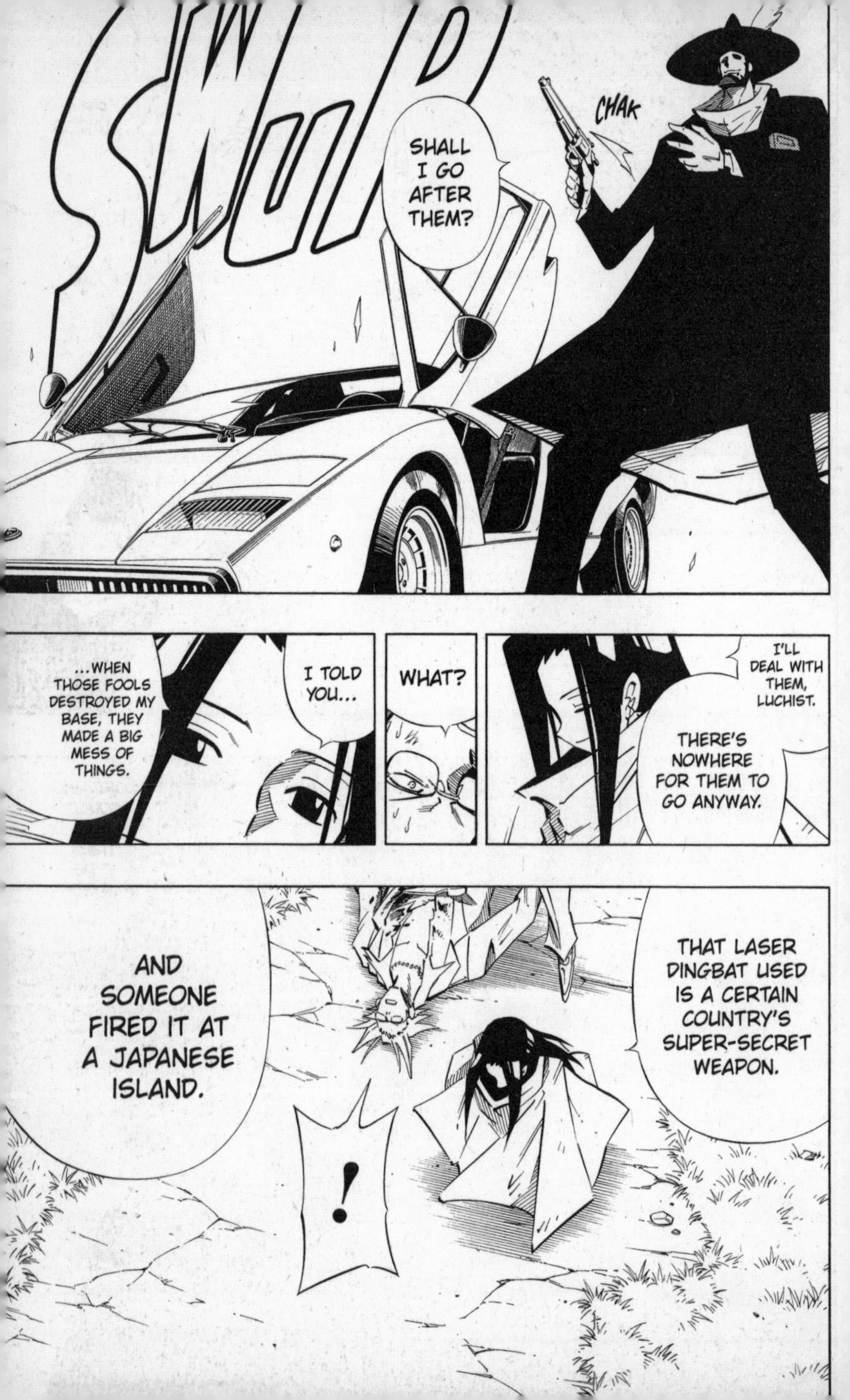
CHAK
SHALL I GO AFTER THEM?
I'LL DEAL WITH THEM, LUCHIST.
THERE'S NOWHERE FOR THEM TO GO ANYWAY.
WHAT?
I TOLD YOU...
...WHEN THOSE FOOLS DESTROYED MY BASE, THEY MADE A BIG MESS OF THINGS.
THAT LASER DINGBAT USED IS A CERTAIN COUNTRY'S SUPER-SECRET WEAPON.
!
AND SOMEONE FIRED IT AT A JAPANESE ISLAND.

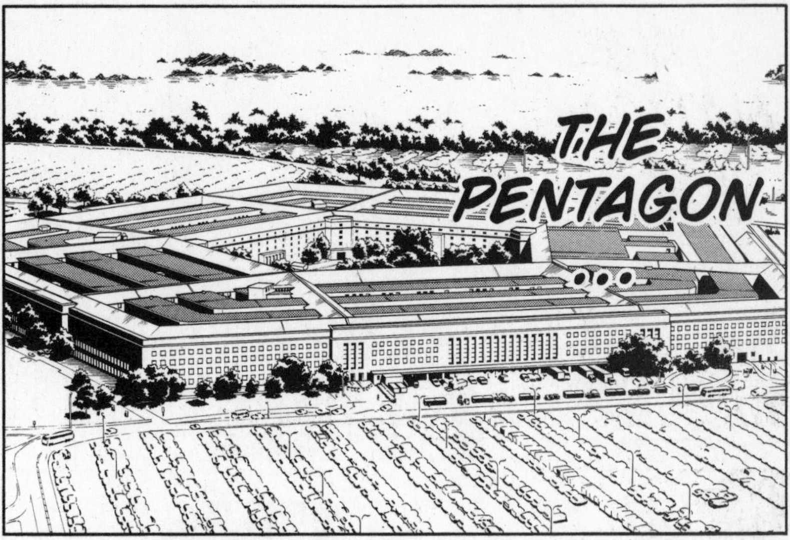
THE PENTAGON...
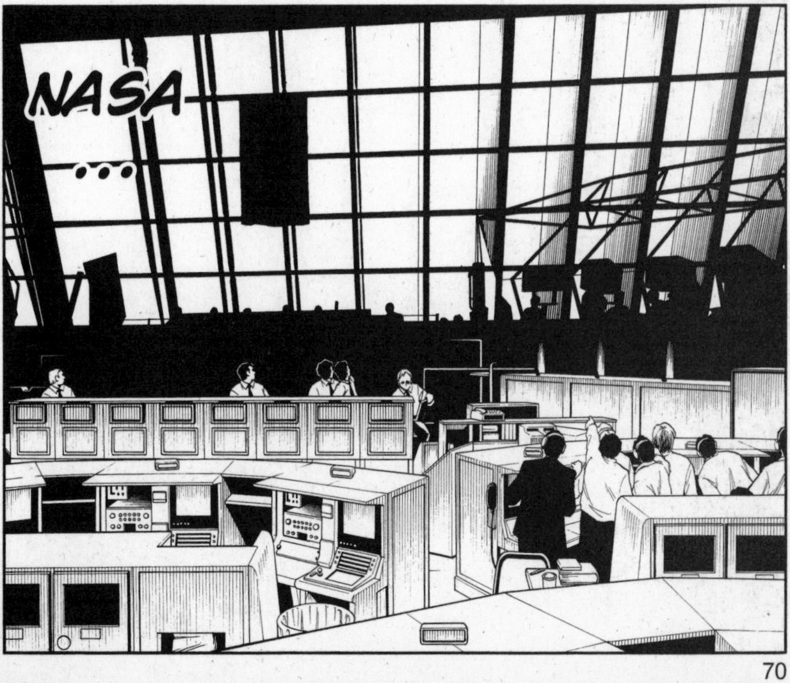
NASA...

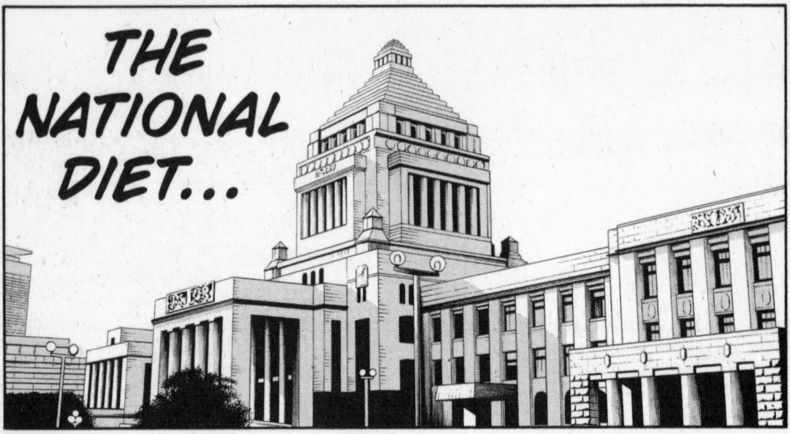
THE NATIONAL DIET...

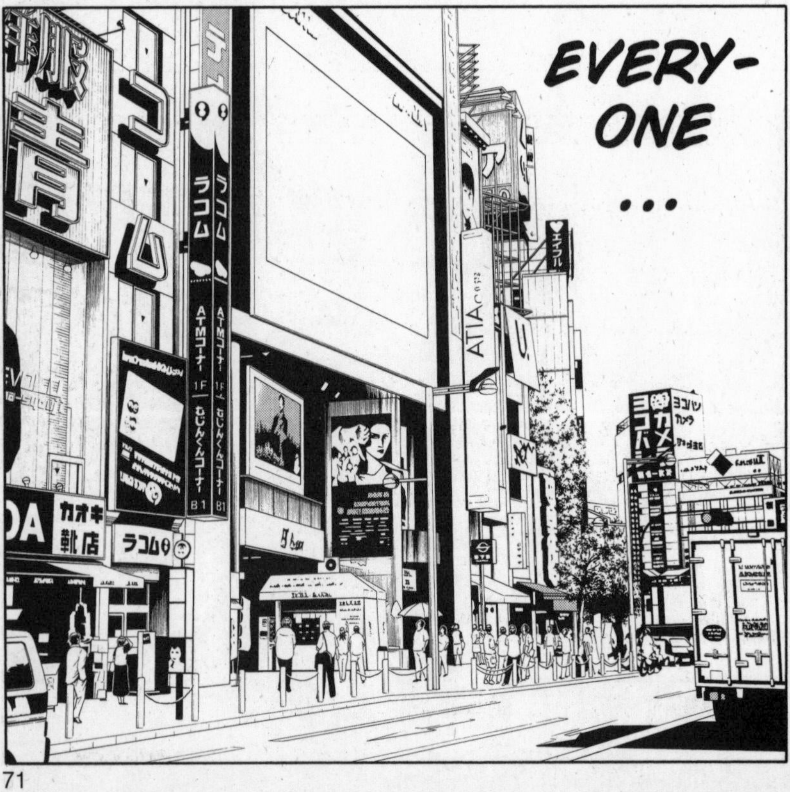
EVERY-ONE ...
ラコム
ATMコーナー 1F
むじんくんコーナー B1
ATIA

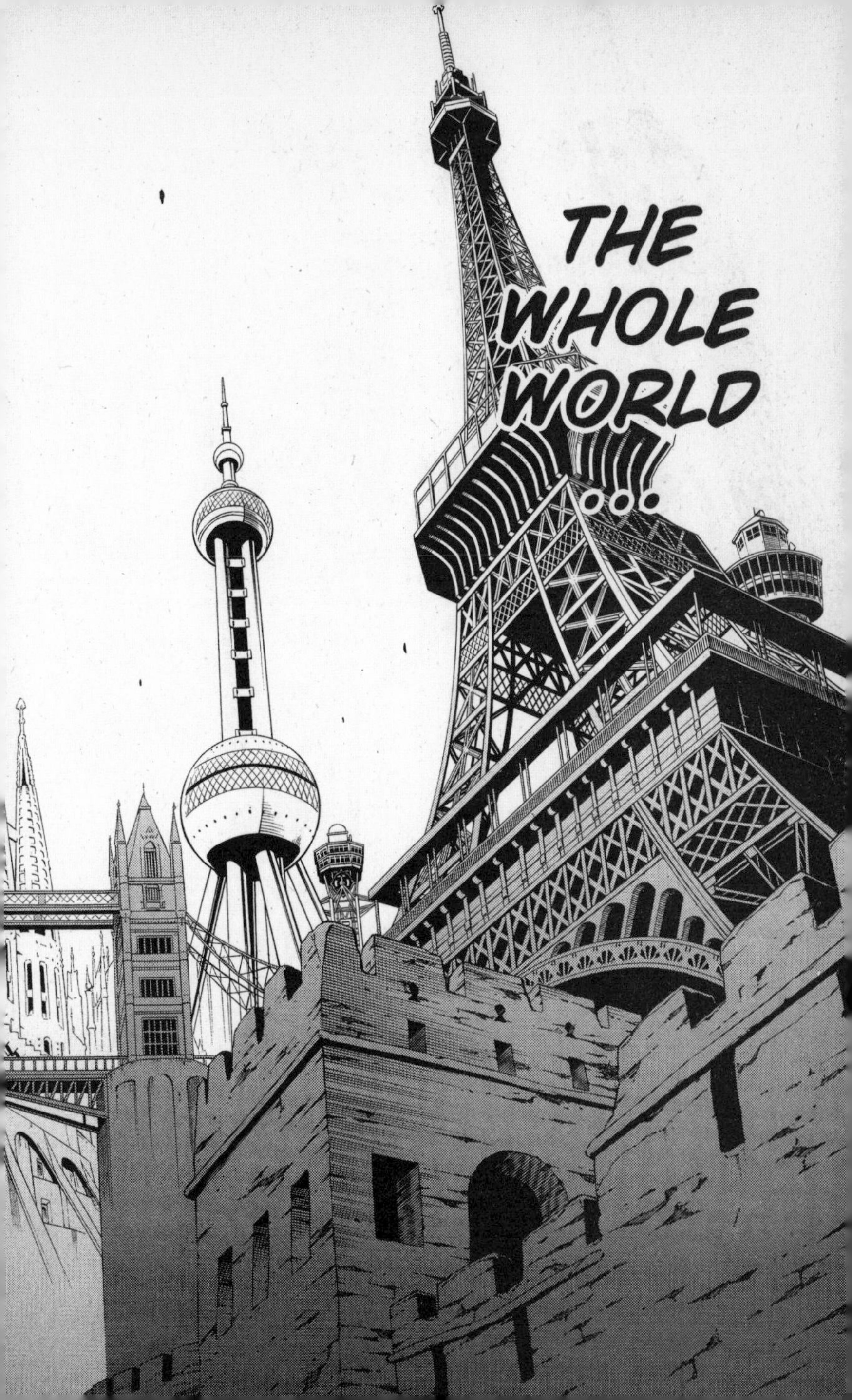
THE WHOLE WORLD!!!...!

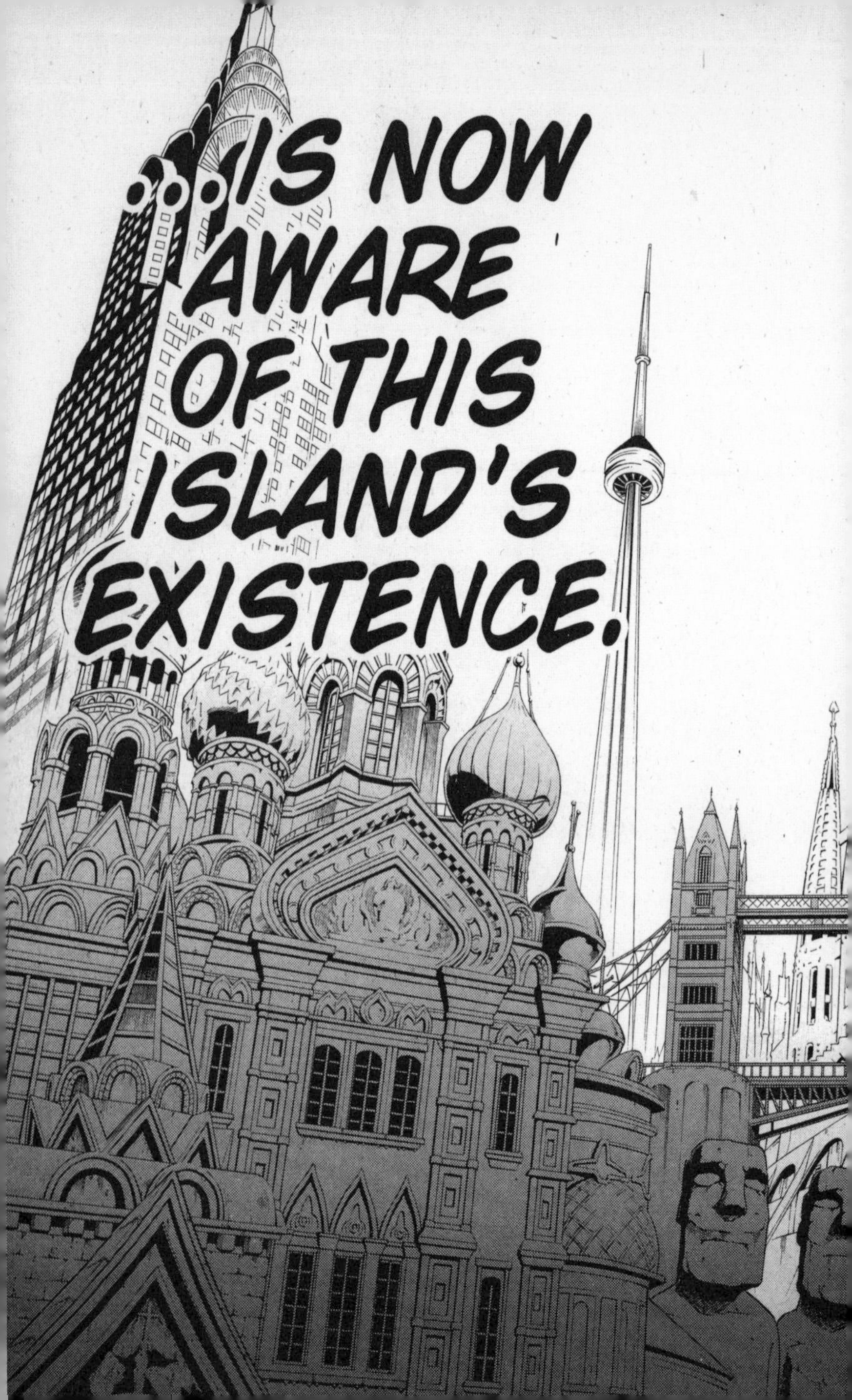
...IS NOW AWARE OF THIS ISLAND'S EXISTENCE.

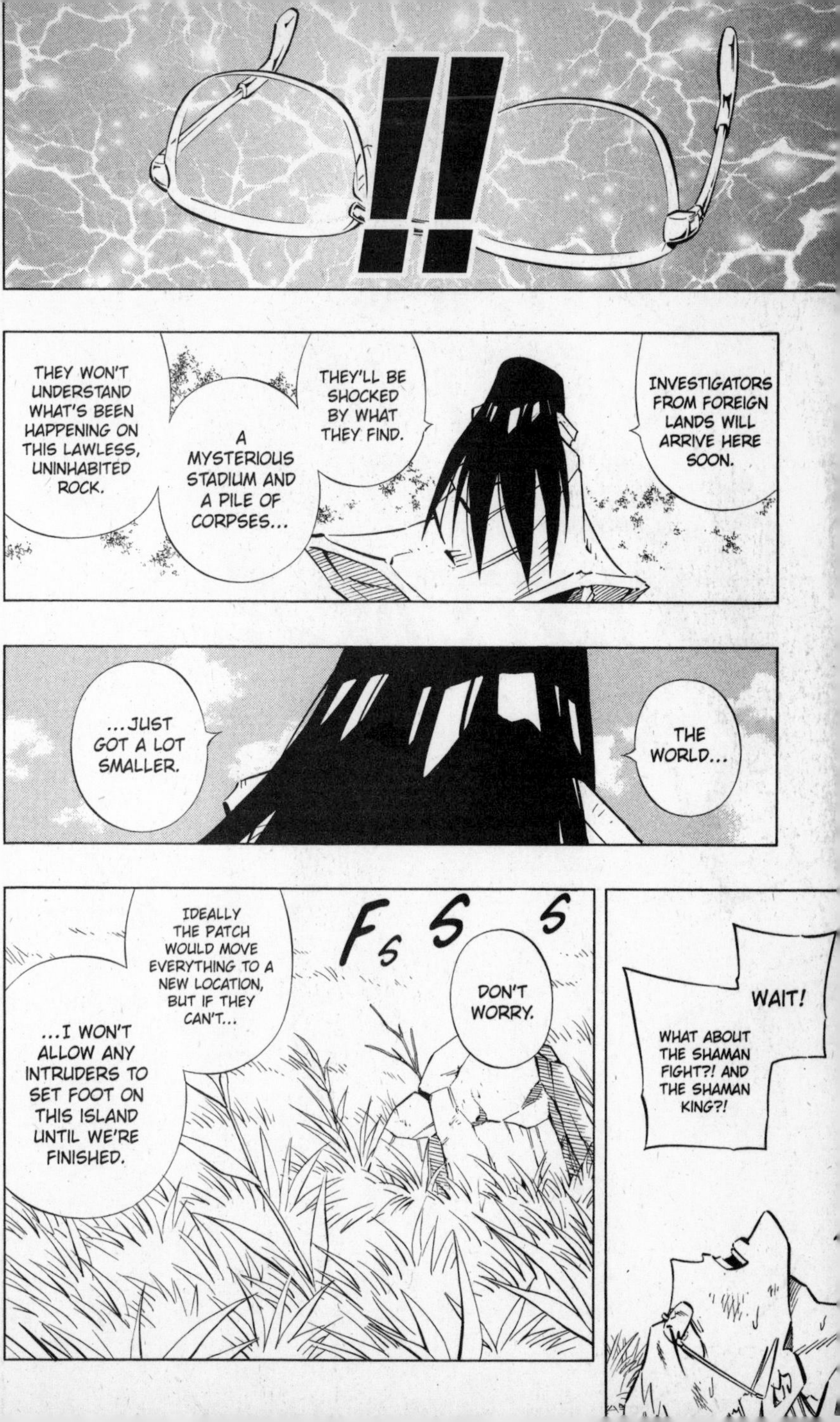
!!
INVESTIGATORS FROM FOREIGN LANDS WILL ARRIVE HERE SOON.
THEY'LL BE SHOCKED BY WHAT THEY FIND.
A MYSTERIOUS STADIUM AND A PILE OF CORPSES...
THEY WON'T UNDERSTAND WHAT'S BEEN HAPPENING ON THIS LAWLESS, UNINHABITED ROCK.
THE WORLD...
...JUST GOT A LOT SMALLER.
WAIT!
WHAT ABOUT THE SHAMAN FIGHT?! AND THE SHAMAN KING?!
FsSS
DON'T WORRY.
IDEALLY THE PATCH WOULD MOVE EVERYTHING TO A NEW LOCATION, BUT IF THEY CAN'T...
...I WON'T ALLOW ANY INTRUDERS TO SET FOOT ON THIS ISLAND UNTIL WE'RE FINISHED.

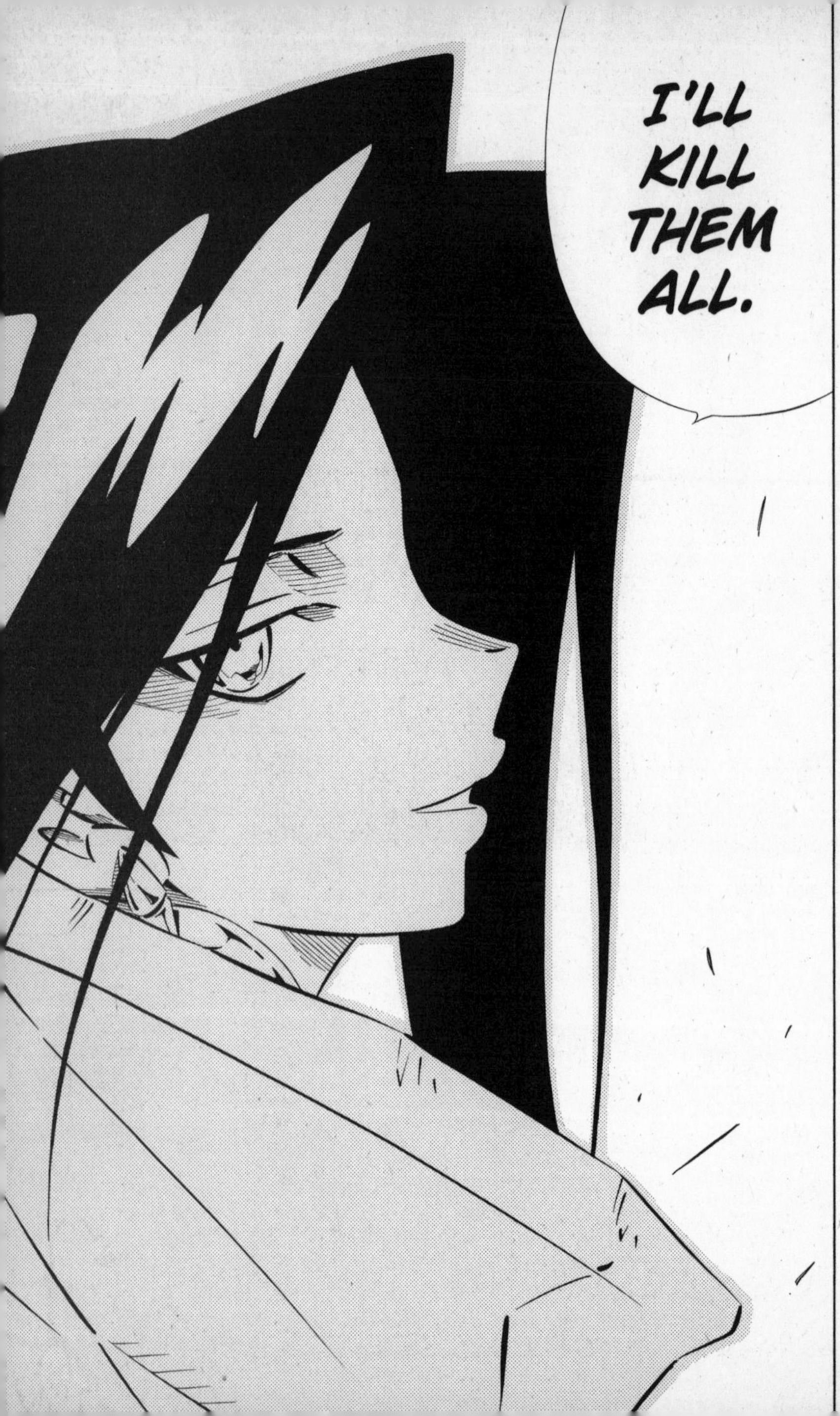
I'LL KILL THEM ALL.

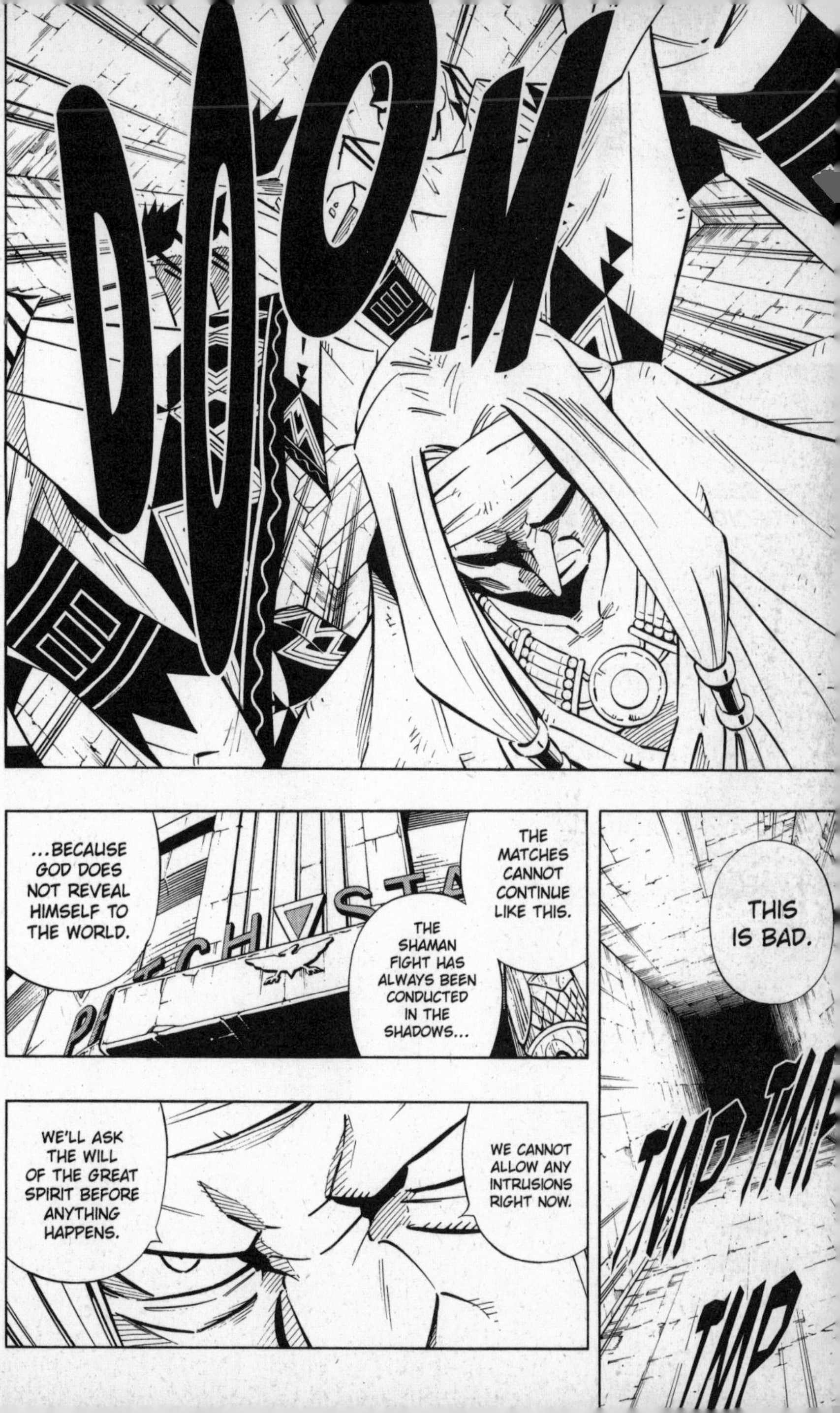
DOOM
THIS IS BAD.
TMP TMP
TMP
THE MATCHES CANNOT CONTINUE LIKE THIS.
THE SHAMAN FIGHT HAS ALWAYS BEEN CONDUCTED IN THE SHADOWS...
...BECAUSE GOD DOES NOT REVEAL HIMSELF TO THE WORLD.
WE CANNOT ALLOW ANY INTRUSIONS RIGHT NOW.
WE'LL ASK THE WILL OF THE GREAT SPIRIT BEFORE ANYTHING HAPPENS.

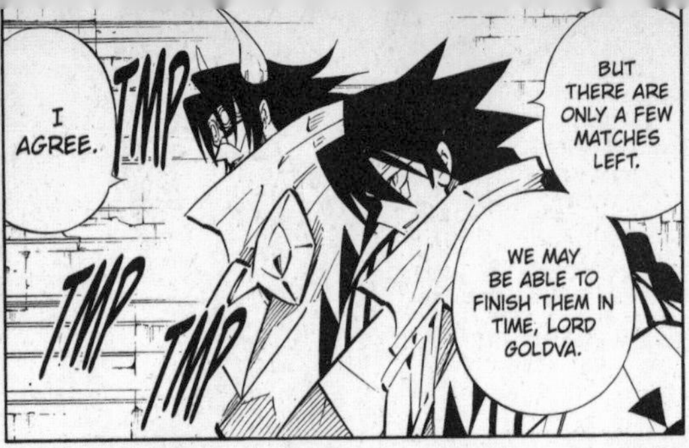
BUT THERE ARE ONLY A FEW MATCHES LEFT.
WE MAY BE ABLE TO FINISH THEM IN TIME, LORD GOLDVA.
I AGREE.
TMP
TMP
TMP
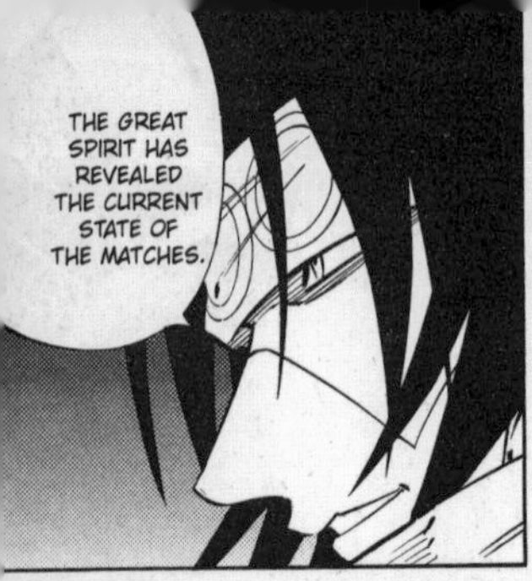
THE GREAT SPIRIT HAS REVEALED THE CURRENT STATE OF THE MATCHES.
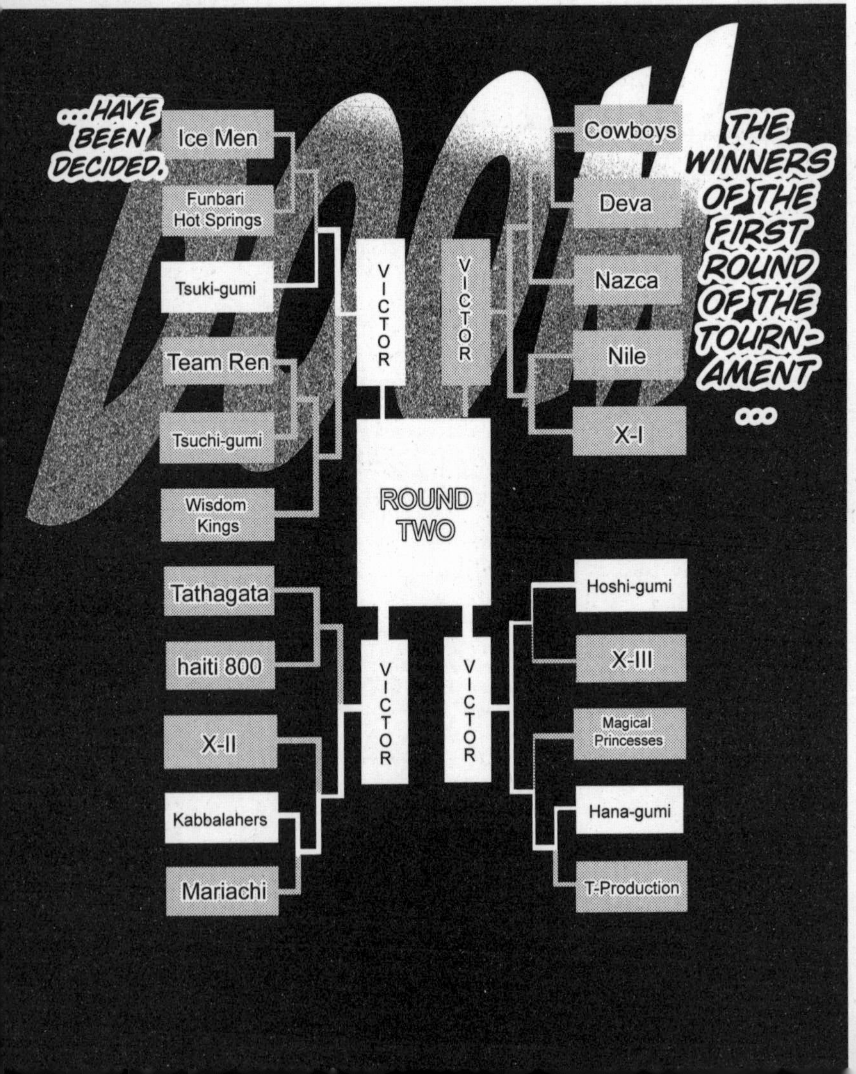
THE WINNERS OF THE FIRST ROUND OF THE TOURN-AMENT...
...HAVE BEEN DECIDED.
Ice Men
Funbari Hot Springs
Tsuki-gumi
Team Ren
Tsuchi-gumi
Wisdom Kings
Tathagata
haiti 800
X-II
Kabbalahers
Mariachi
VICTOR
VICTOR
ROUND TWO
VICTOR
VICTOR
Cowboys
Deva
Nazca
Nile
X-I
Hoshi-gumi
X-III
Magical Princesses
Hana-gumi
T-Production

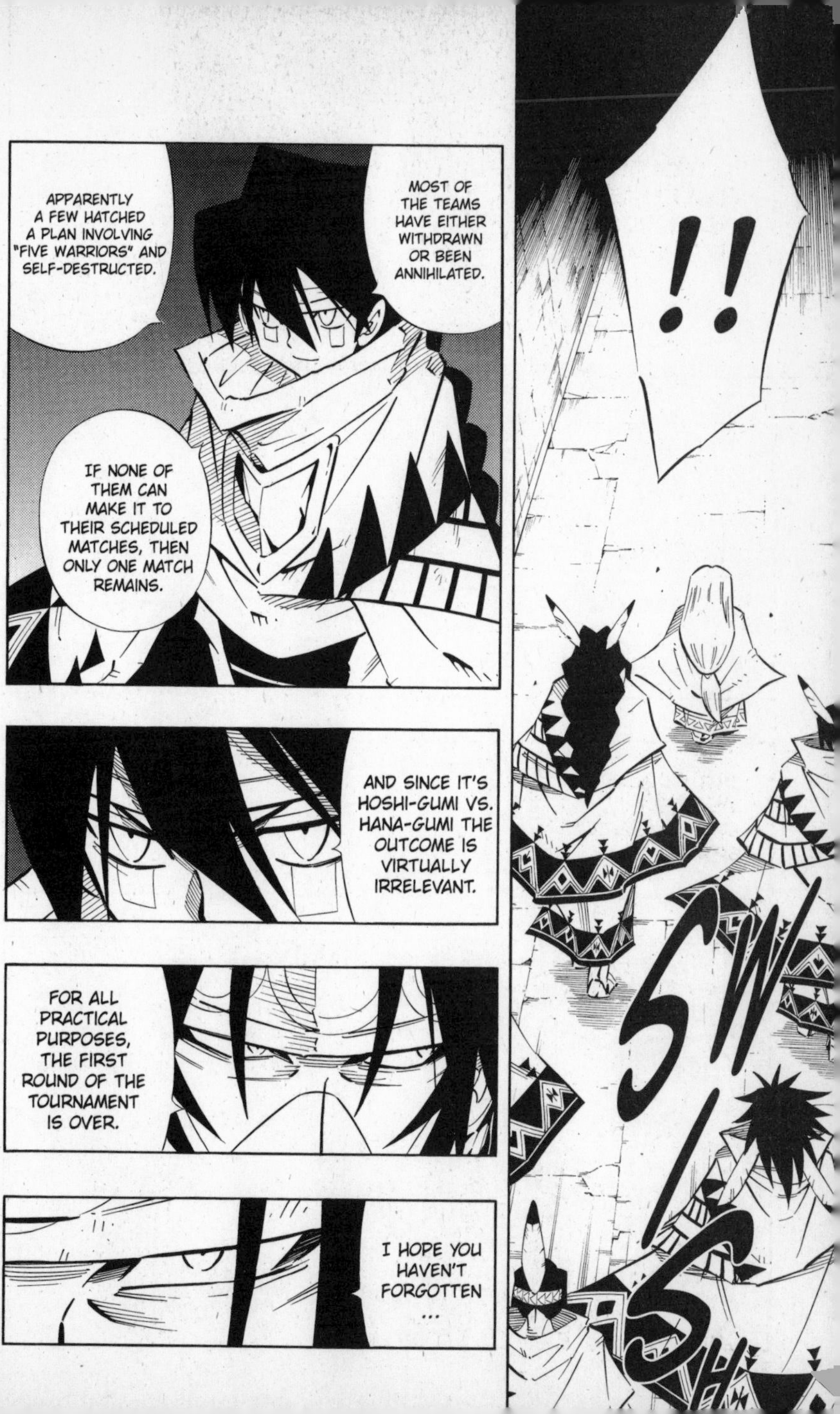
!!
MOST OF THE TEAMS HAVE EITHER WITHDRAWN OR BEEN ANNIHILATED.
APPARENTLY A FEW HATCHED A PLAN INVOLVING "FIVE WARRIORS" AND SELF-DESTRUCTED.
IF NONE OF THEM CAN MAKE IT TO THEIR SCHEDULED MATCHES, THEN ONLY ONE MATCH REMAINS.
AND SINCE IT'S HOSHI-GUMI VS. HANA-GUMI THE OUTCOME IS VIRTUALLY IRRELEVANT.
FOR ALL PRACTICAL PURPOSES, THE FIRST ROUND OF THE TOURNAMENT IS OVER.
I HOPE YOU HAVEN'T FORGOTTEN ...

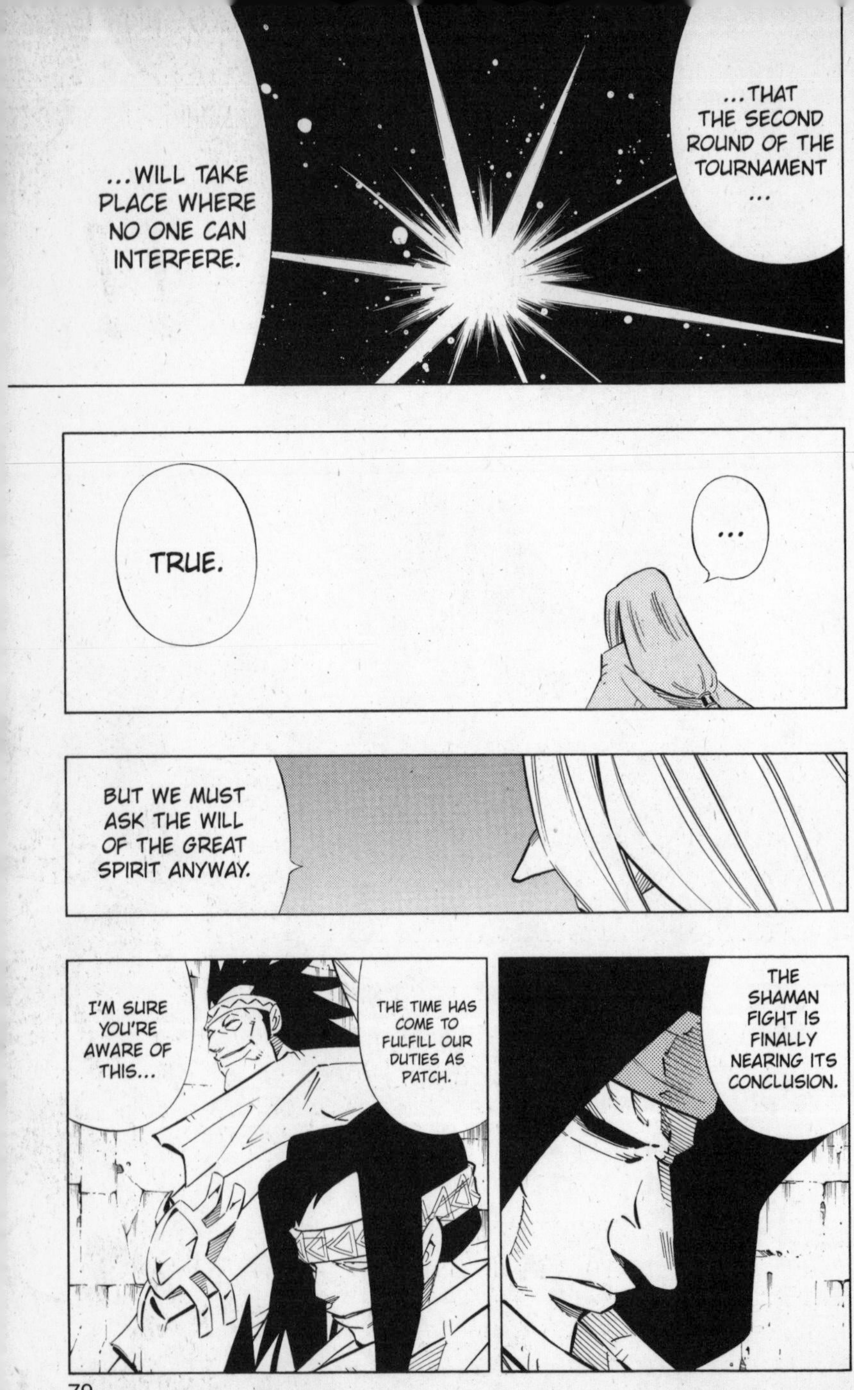
...THAT THE SECOND ROUND OF THE TOURNAMENT ...
...WILL TAKE PLACE WHERE NO ONE CAN INTERFERE.
...
TRUE.
BUT WE MUST ASK THE WILL OF THE GREAT SPIRIT ANYWAY.
THE SHAMAN FIGHT IS FINALLY NEARING ITS CONCLUSION.
THE TIME HAS COME TO FULFILL OUR DUTIES AS PATCH.
I'M SURE YOU'RE AWARE OF THIS...

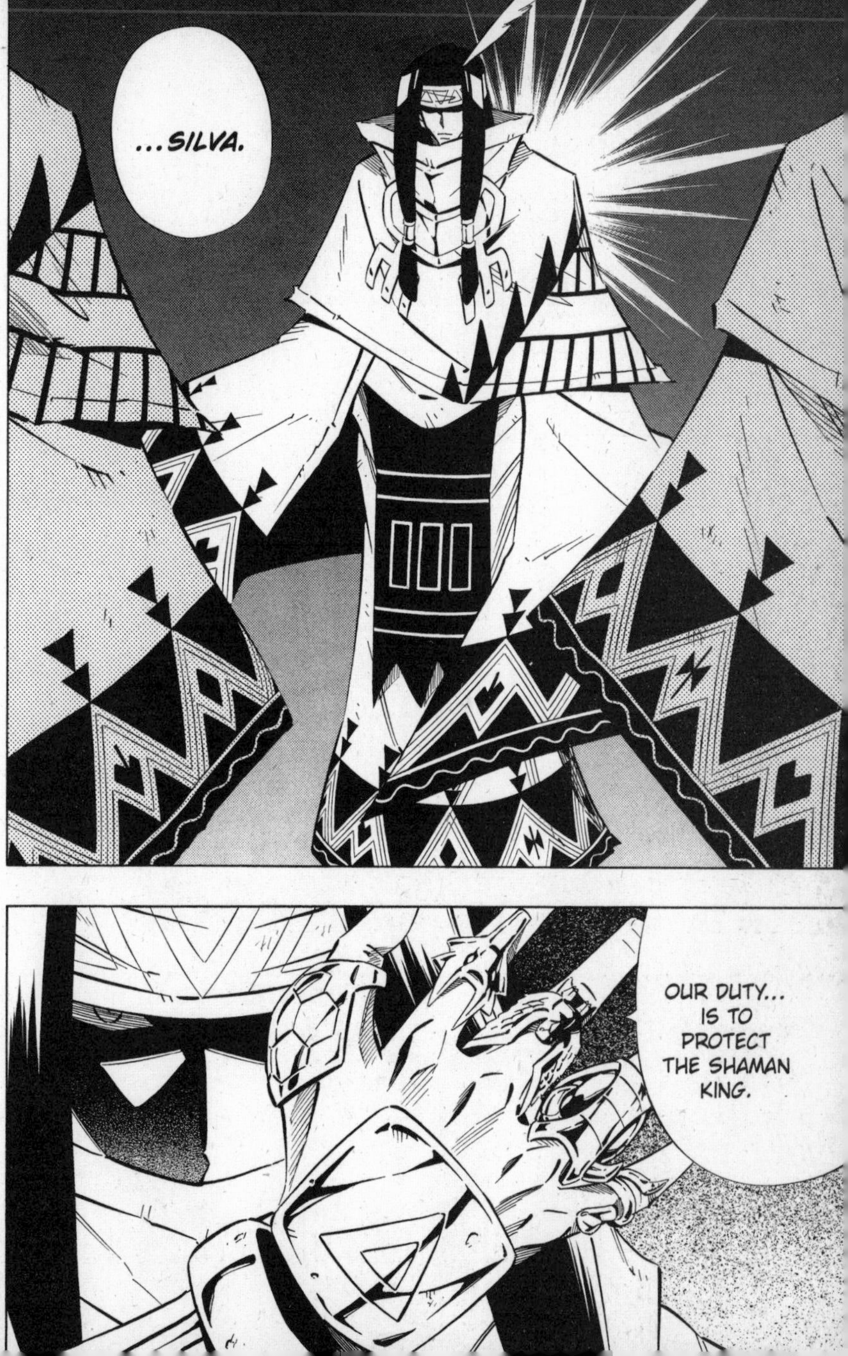
...SILVA.
OUR DUTY... IS TO PROTECT THE SHAMAN KING.

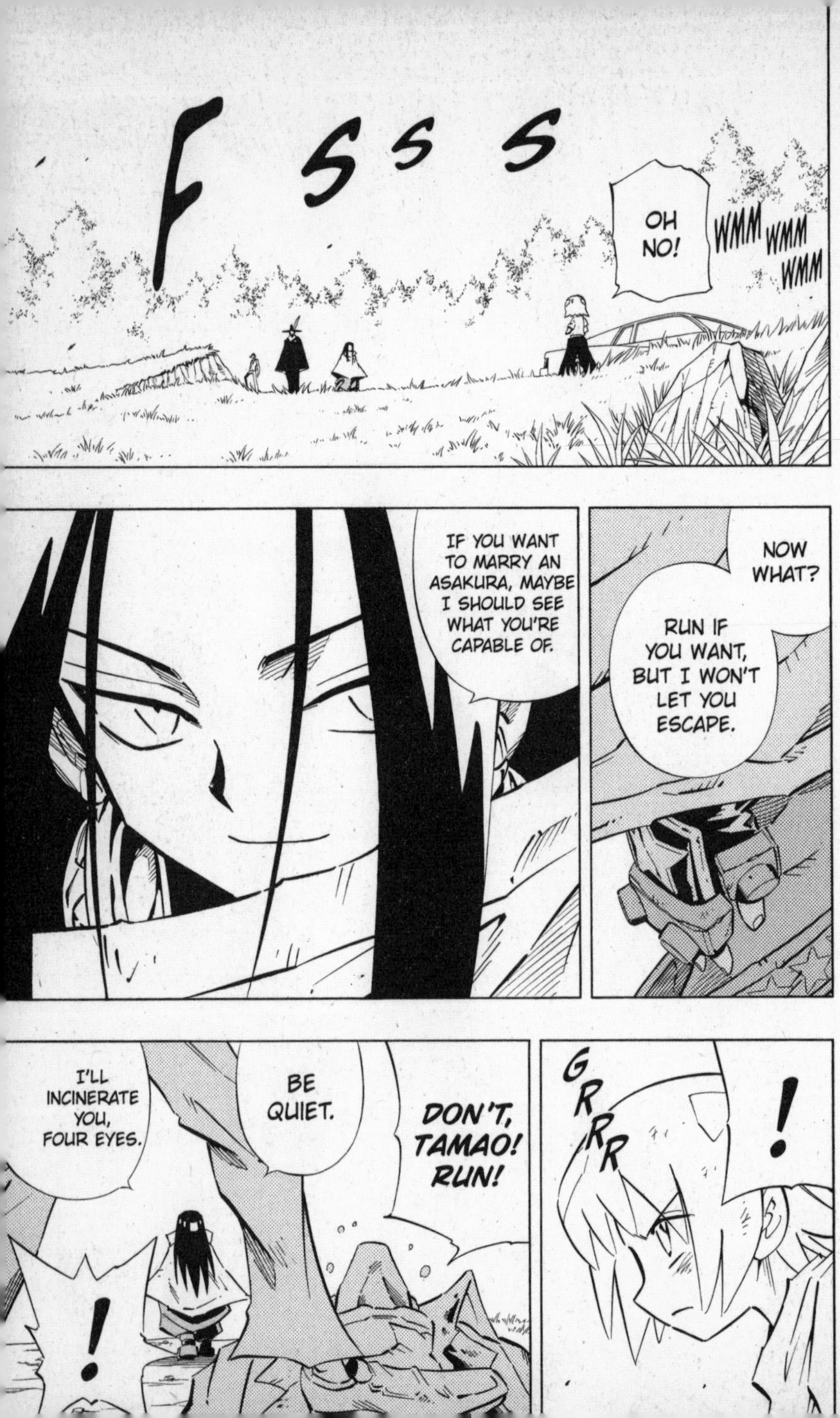
OH NO!
WMM WMM WMM
FSSS
NOW WHAT?
RUN IF YOU WANT, BUT I WON'T LET YOU ESCAPE.
IF YOU WANT TO MARRY AN ASAKURA, MAYBE I SHOULD SEE WHAT YOU'RE CAPABLE OF.
!
GRRR
DON'T, TAMAO! RUN!
BE QUIET.
I'LL INCINERATE YOU, FOUR EYES.
!

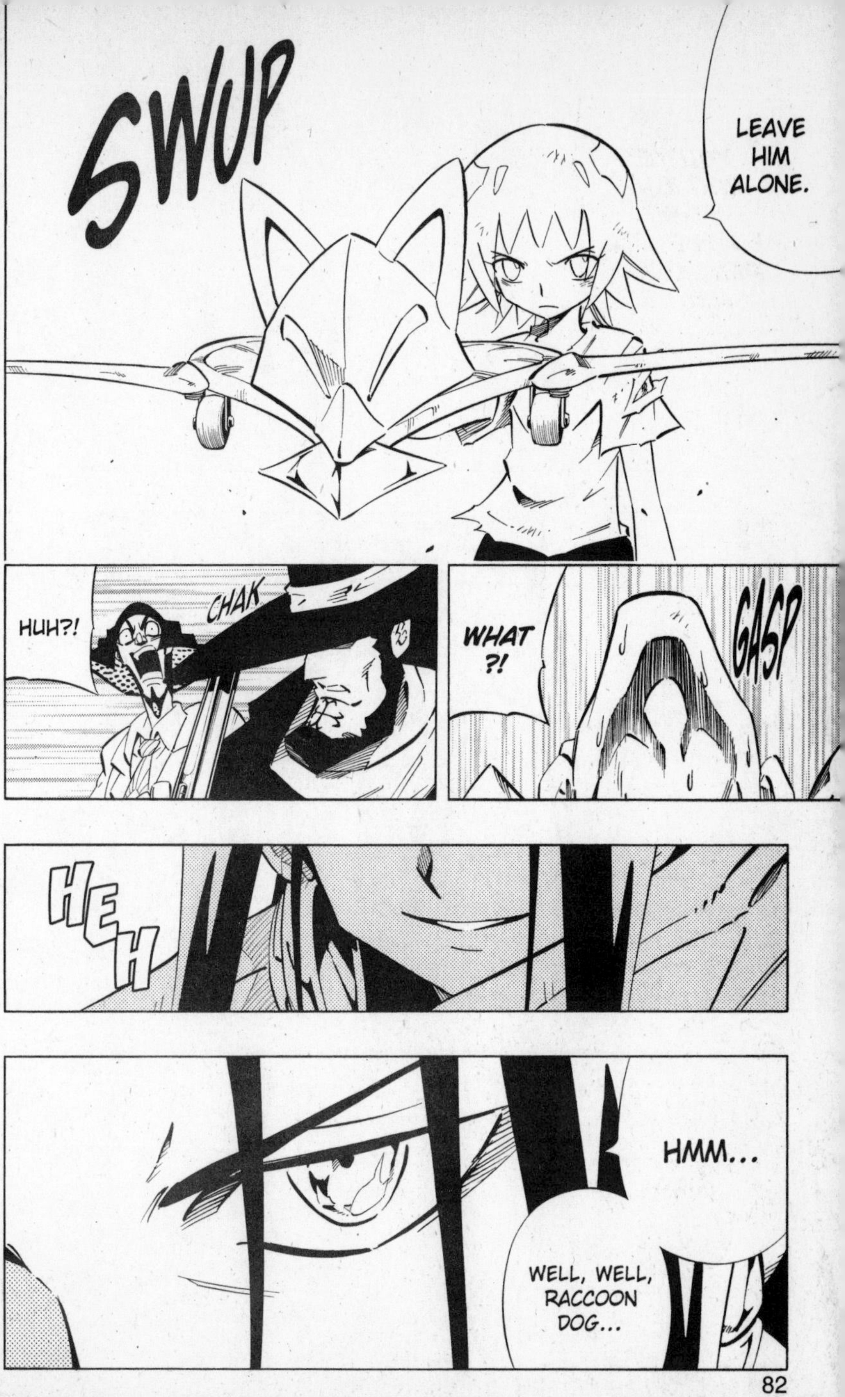
LEAVE HIM ALONE.
SWUP
GASP
WHAT?!
CHAK
HUH?!
HEH
HMM...
WELL, WELL, RACCOON DOG...

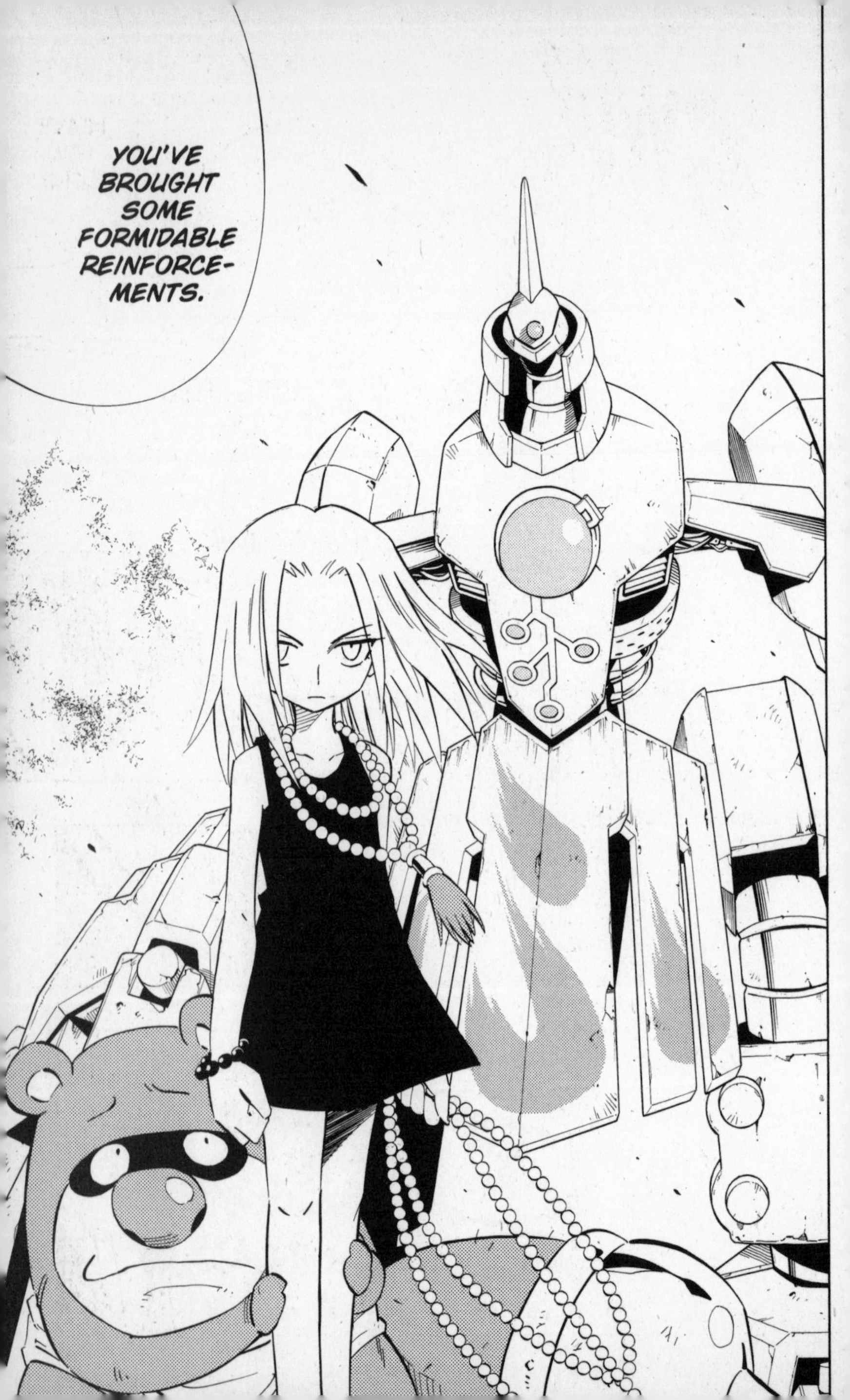
YOU'VE BROUGHT SOME FORMIDABLE REINFORCE-MENTS.

Shaman King

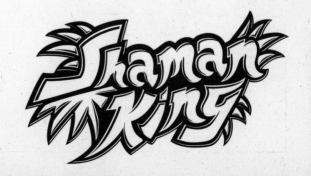

Reincarnation 244: Seriously

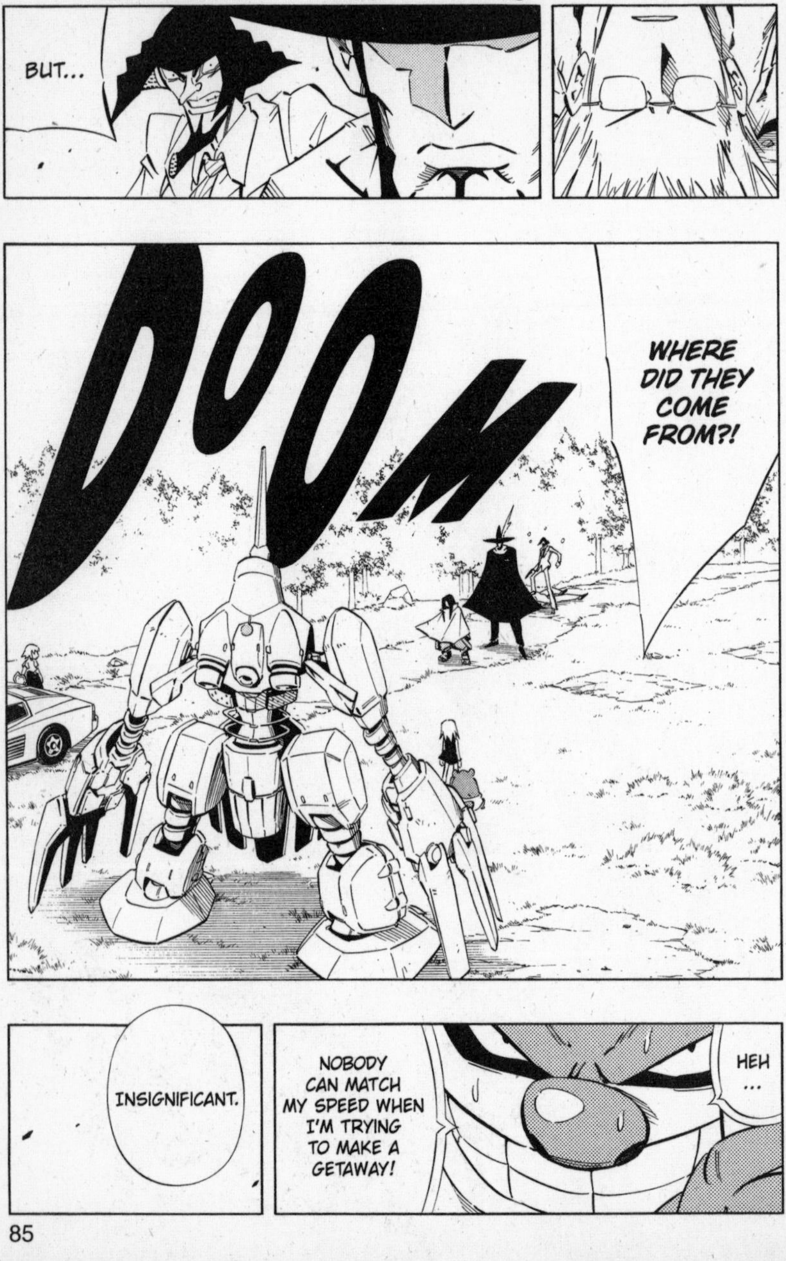
BUT...
WHERE DID THEY COME FROM?!
DOOM
HEH ...
NOBODY CAN MATCH MY SPEED WHEN I'M TRYING TO MAKE A GETAWAY!
INSIGNIFICANT.

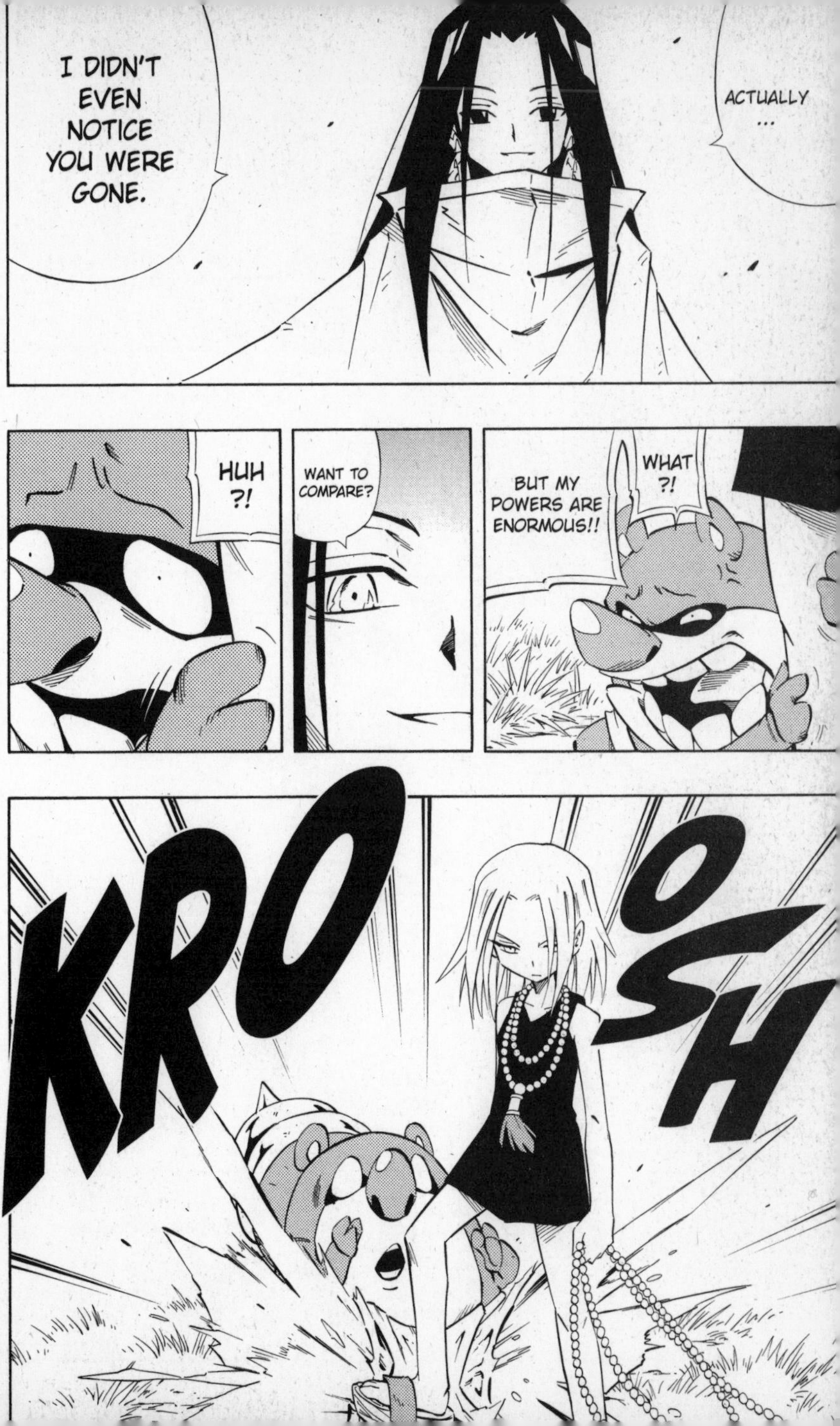
ACTUALLY ...
I DIDN'T EVEN NOTICE YOU WERE GONE.
WHAT ?!
BUT MY POWERS ARE ENORMOUS!!
WANT TO COMPARE?
HUH ?!
KROOSH

Reincarnation 244: Seriously

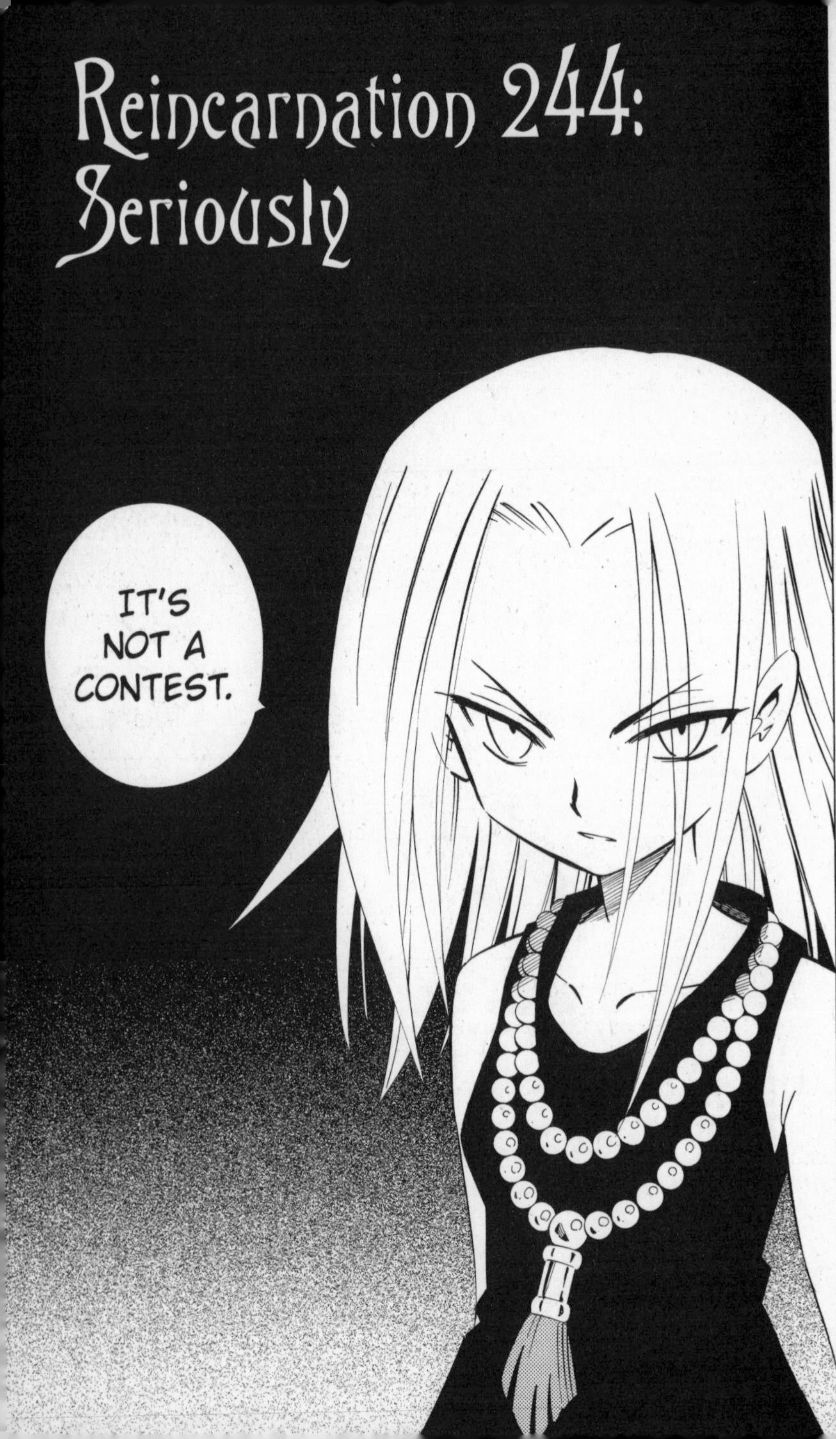
IT'S NOT A CONTEST.

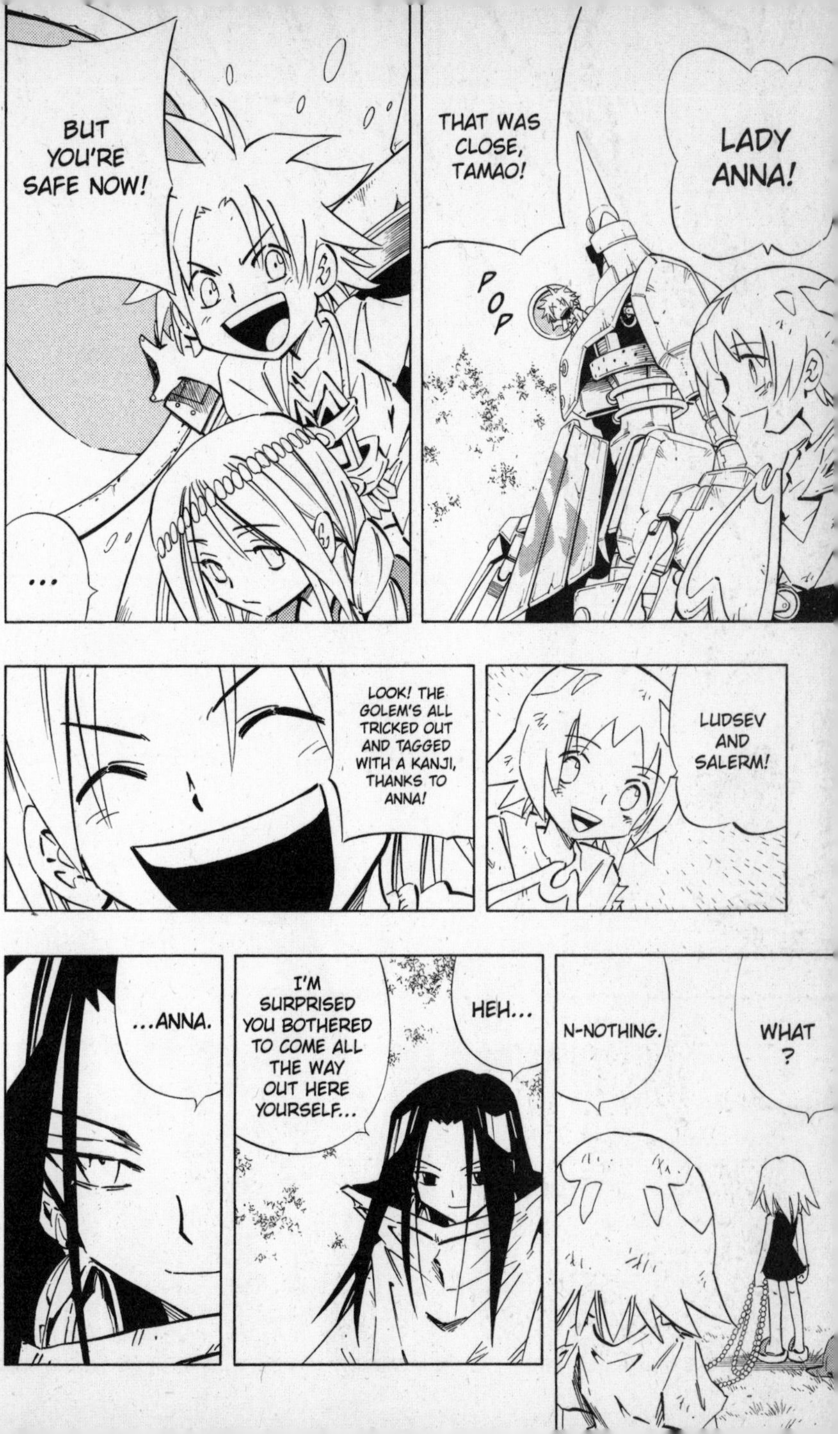

LADY ANNA!
THAT WAS CLOSE, TAMAO!
POP
BUT YOU'RE SAFE NOW!
...
LUDSEV AND SALERM!
LOOK! THE GOLEM'S ALL TRICKED OUT AND TAGGED WITH A KANJI, THANKS TO ANNA!
WHAT?
N-NOTHING.
HEH...
I'M SURPRISED YOU BOTHERED TO COME ALL THE WAY OUT HERE YOURSELF...
...ANNA.

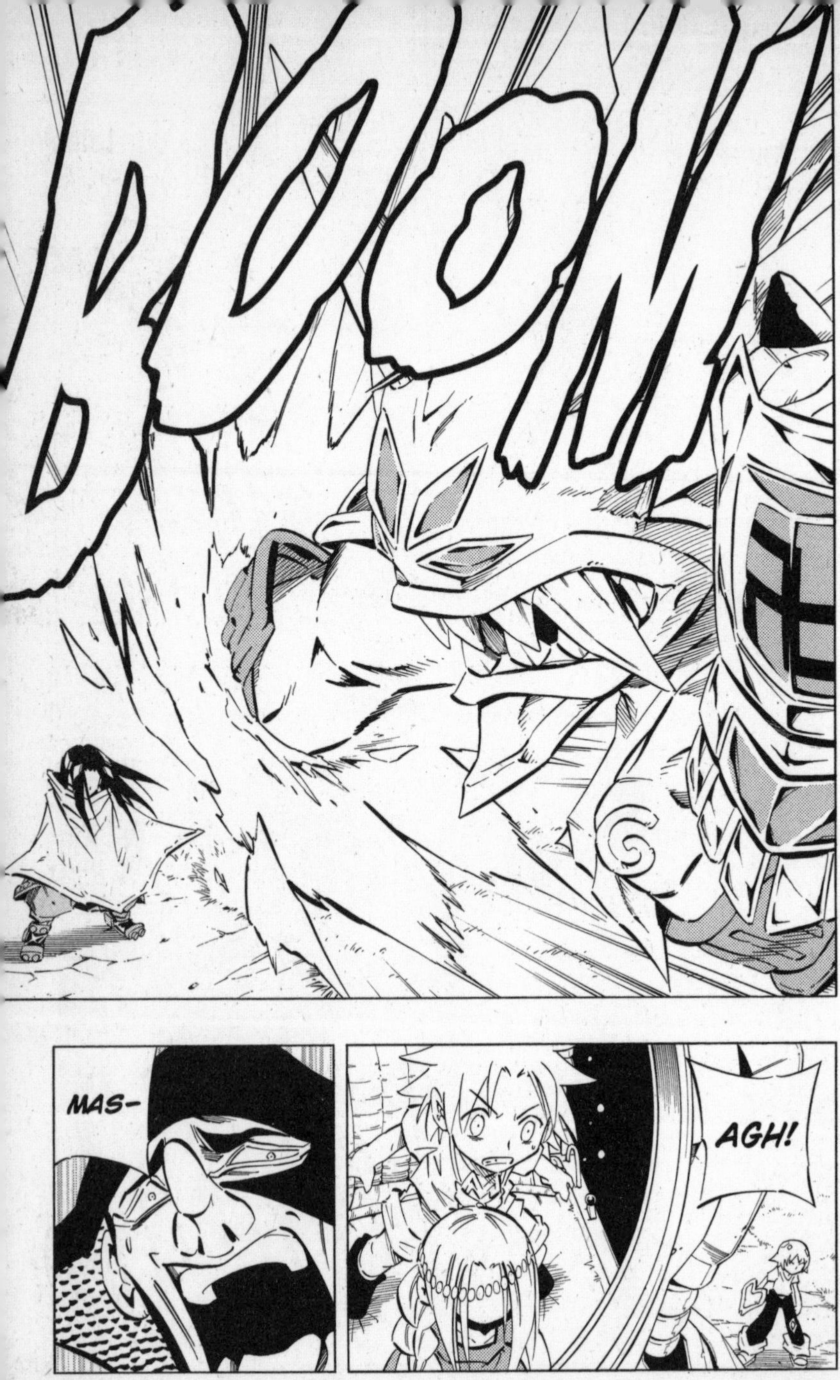
BOOM!
AGH!
MAS-

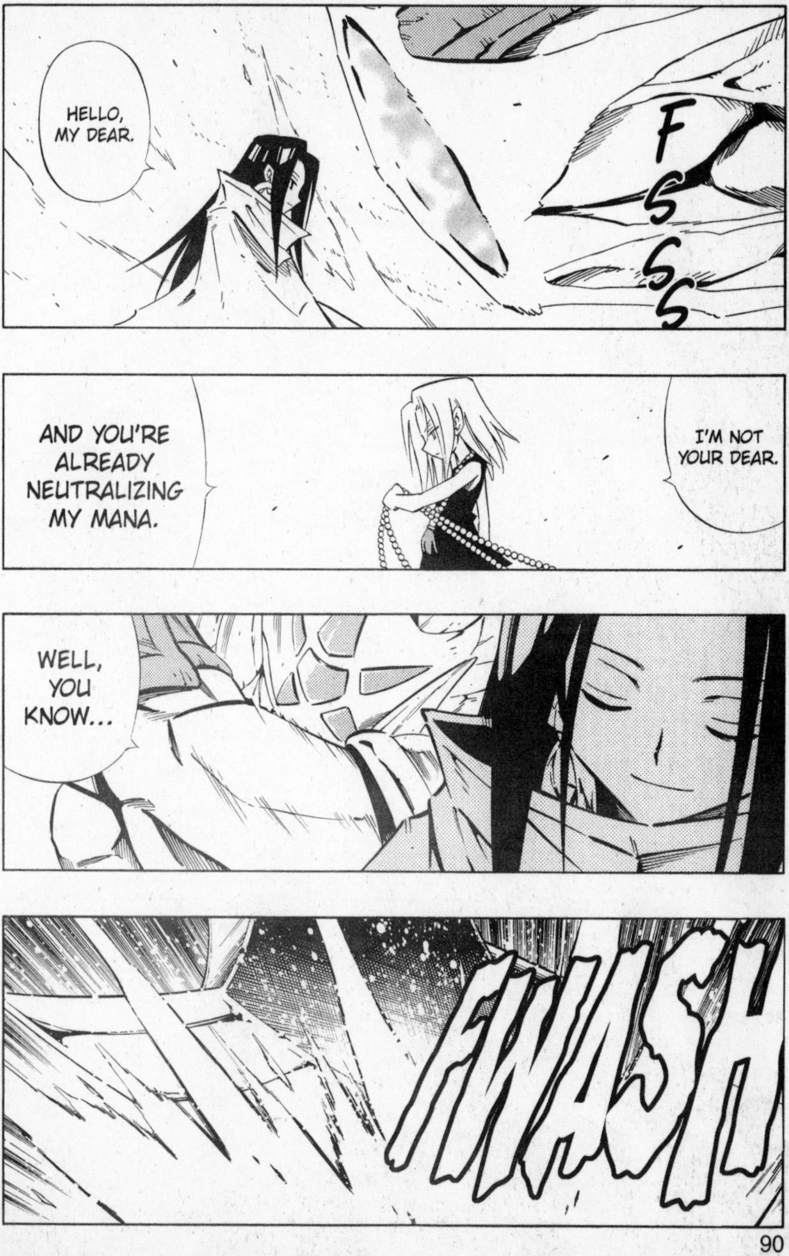
FSSSS
HELLO, MY DEAR.
I'M NOT YOUR DEAR.
AND YOU'RE ALREADY NEUTRALIZING MY MANA.
WELL, YOU KNOW...
FWASH

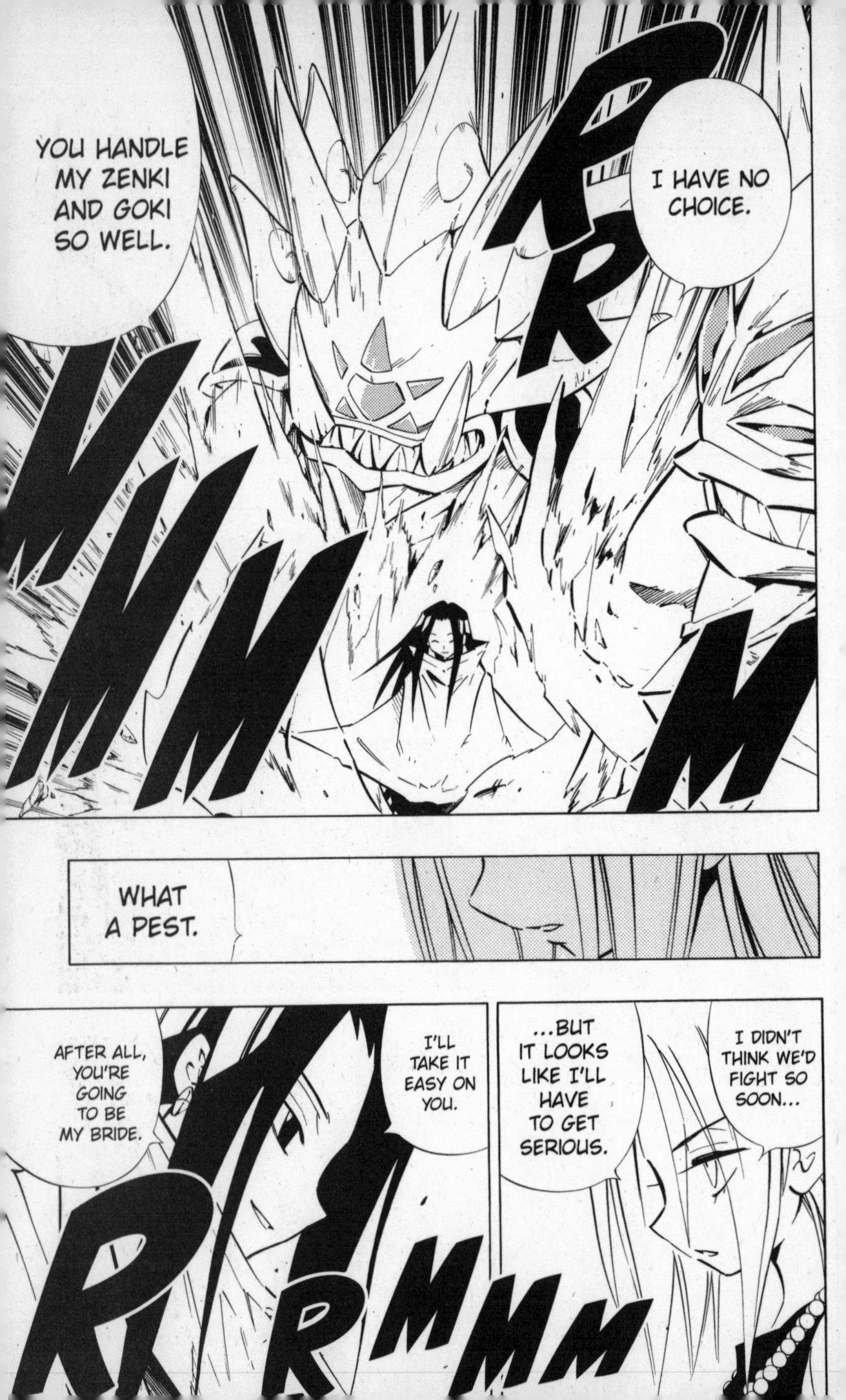
I HAVE NO CHOICE.
YOU HANDLE MY ZENKI AND GOKI SO WELL.
WHAT A PEST.
I DIDN'T THINK WE'D FIGHT SO SOON...
...BUT IT LOOKS LIKE I'LL HAVE TO GET SERIOUS.
I'LL TAKE IT EASY ON YOU.
AFTER ALL, YOU'RE GOING TO BE MY BRIDE.
RRMMMM

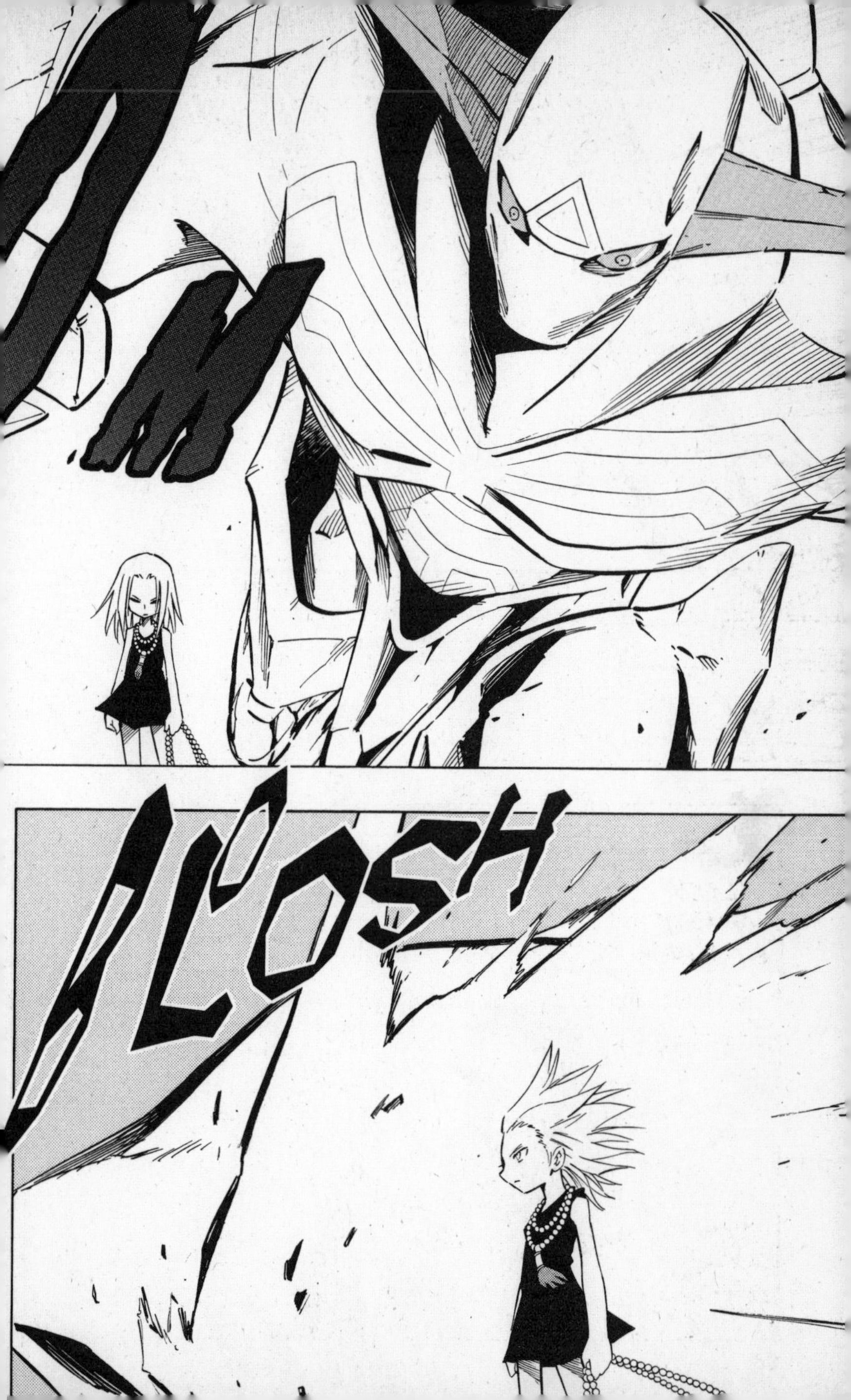

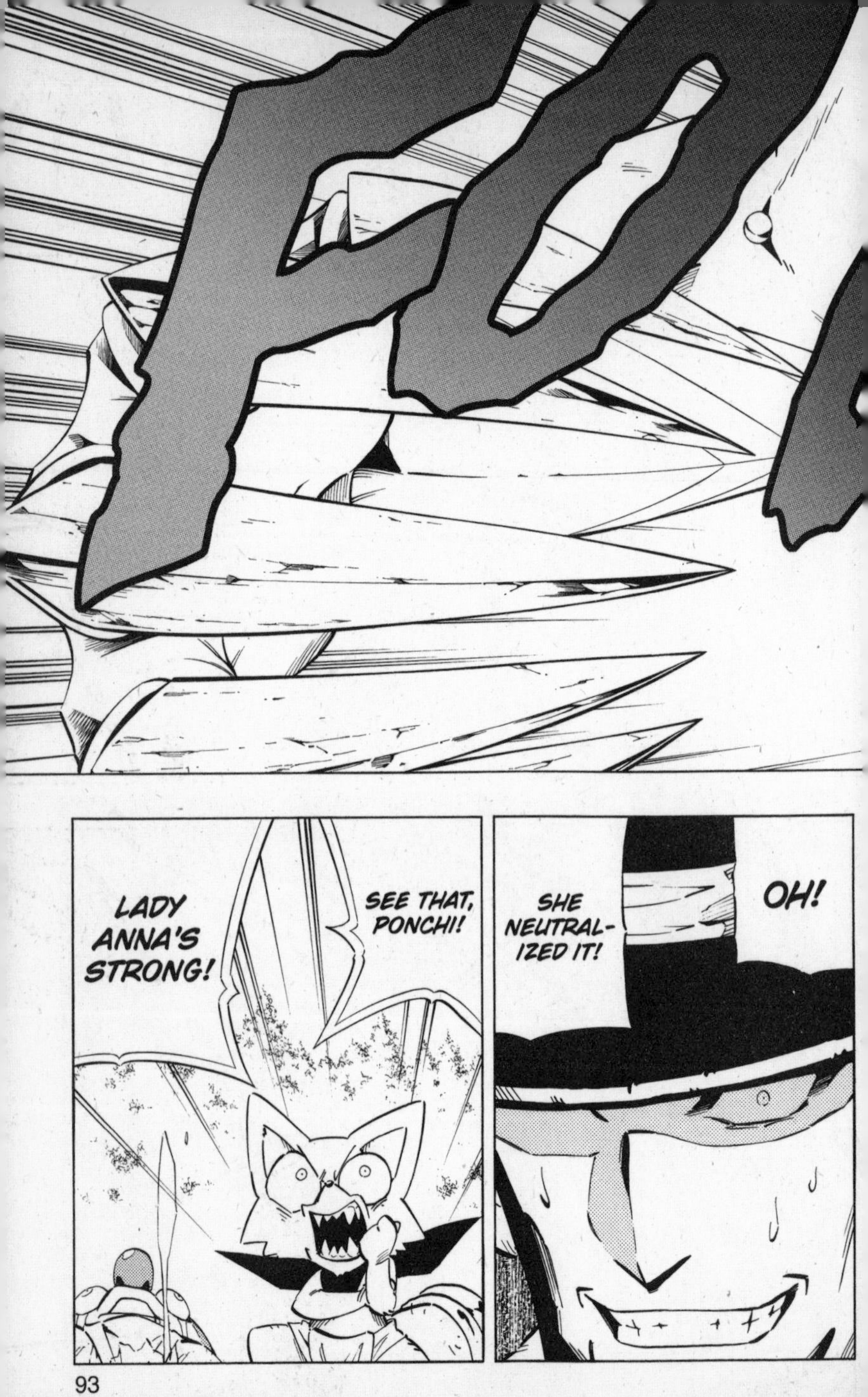
OH!
SHE NEUTRAL-IZED IT!
SEE THAT, PONCHI!
LADY ANNA'S STRONG!

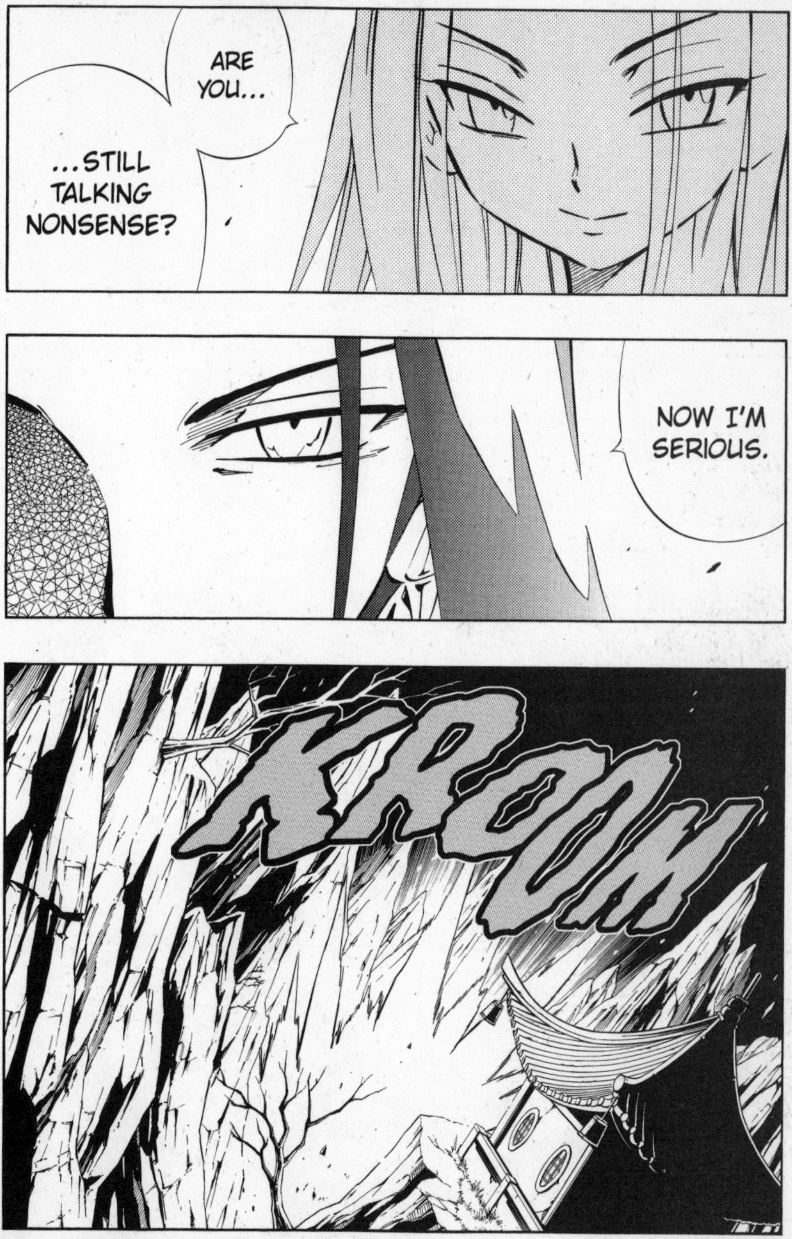
ARE YOU...
...STILL TALKING NONSENSE?
NOW I'M SERIOUS.
KROM

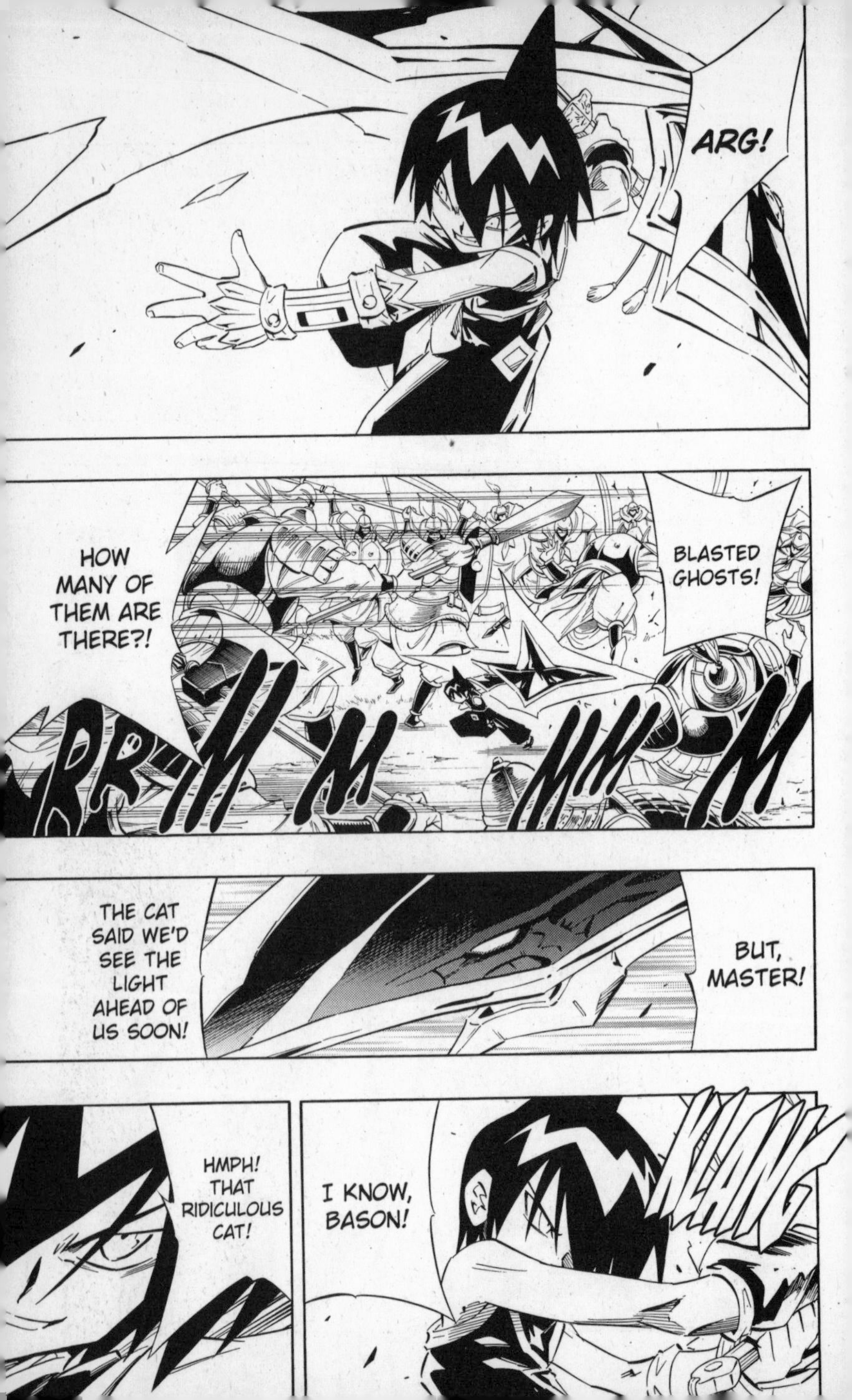
ARG!
BLASTED GHOSTS!
HOW MANY OF THEM ARE THERE?!
BUT, MASTER!
THE CAT SAID WE'D SEE THE LIGHT AHEAD OF US SOON!
I KNOW, BASON!
HMPH! THAT RIDICULOUS CAT!

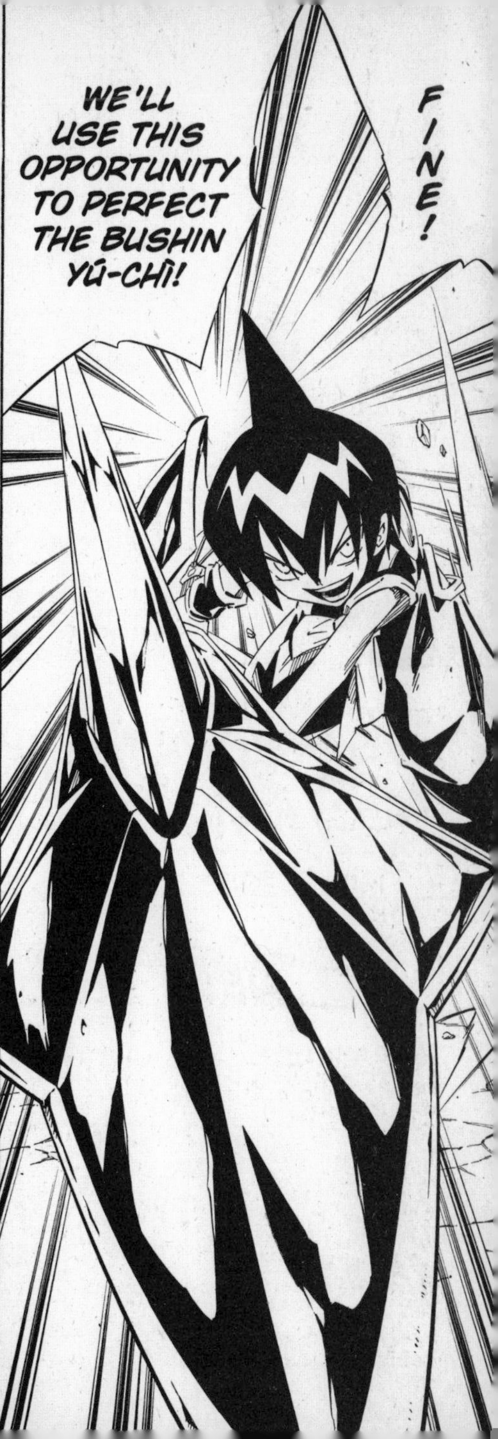
FINE!
WE'LL USE THIS OPPORTUNITY TO PERFECT THE BUSHIN YŪ-CHĪ!
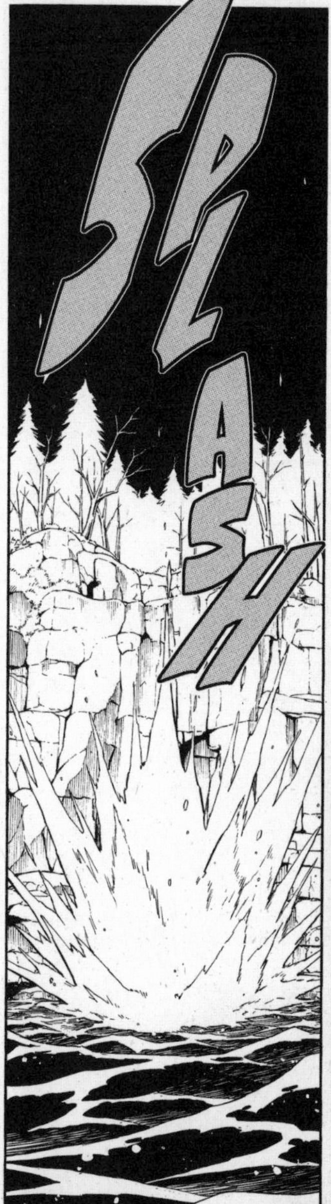
SPLASH

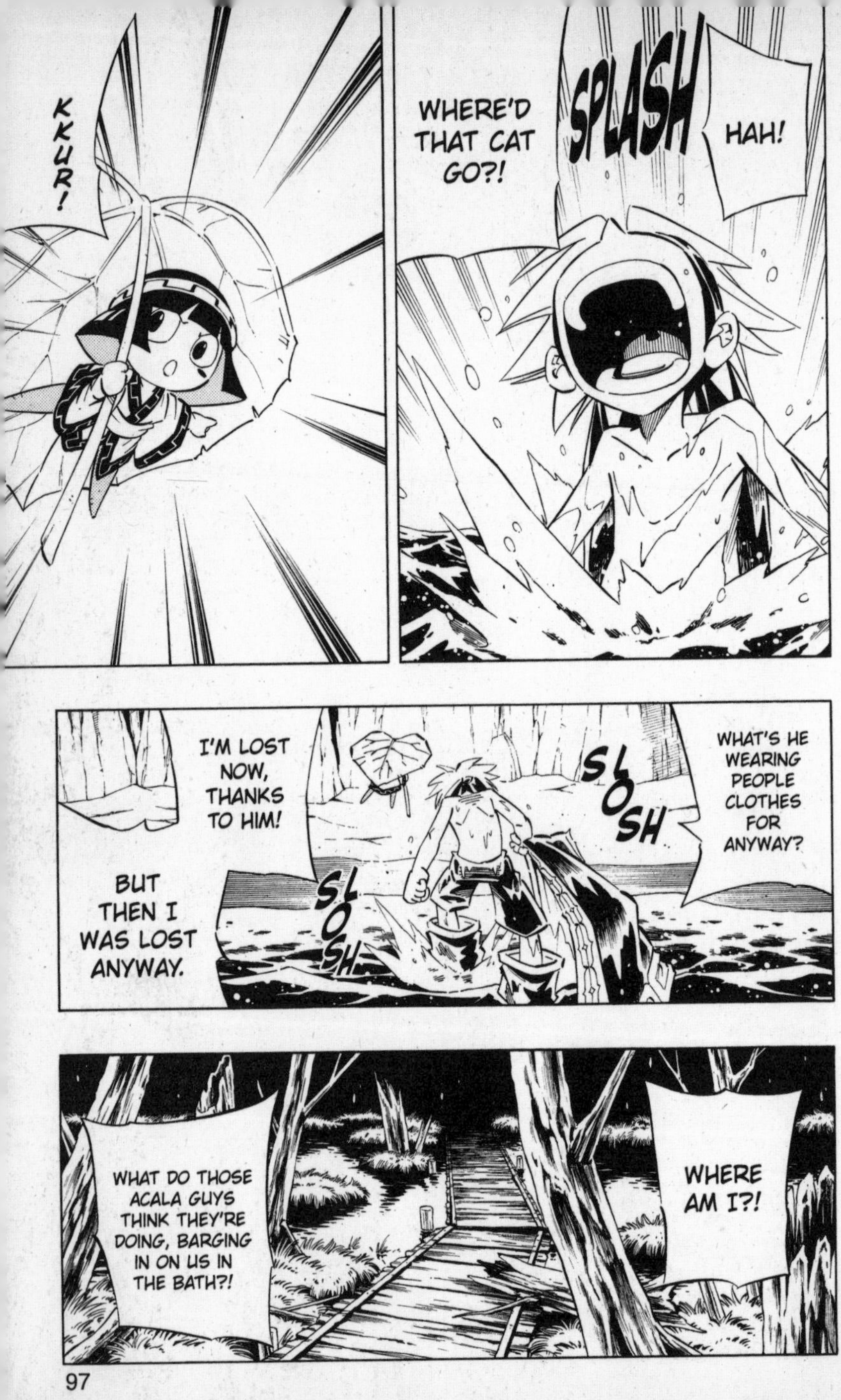
SPLASH
HAH!
WHERE'D THAT CAT GO?!
KKUR!
WHAT'S HE WEARING PEOPLE CLOTHES FOR ANYWAY?
SLOSH
SLOSH
I'M LOST NOW, THANKS TO HIM!
BUT THEN I WAS LOST ANYWAY.
WHERE AM I?!
WHAT DO THOSE ACALA GUYS THINK THEY'RE DOING, BARGING IN ON US IN THE BATH?!

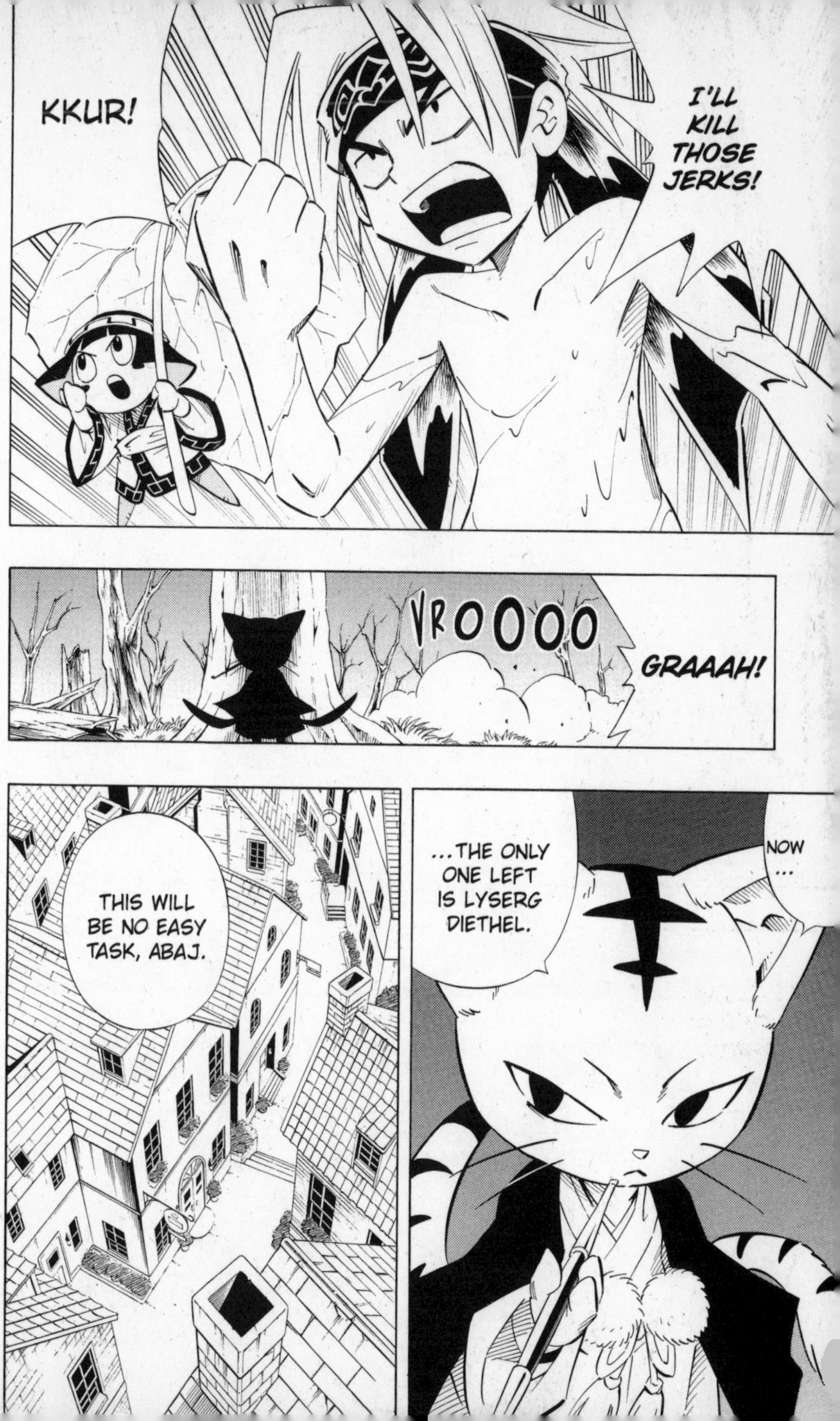
I'LL KILL THOSE JERKS!
KKUR!
GRAAAH!
VROOOO
NOW ...
...THE ONLY ONE LEFT IS LYSERG DIETHEL.
THIS WILL BE NO EASY TASK, ABAJ.

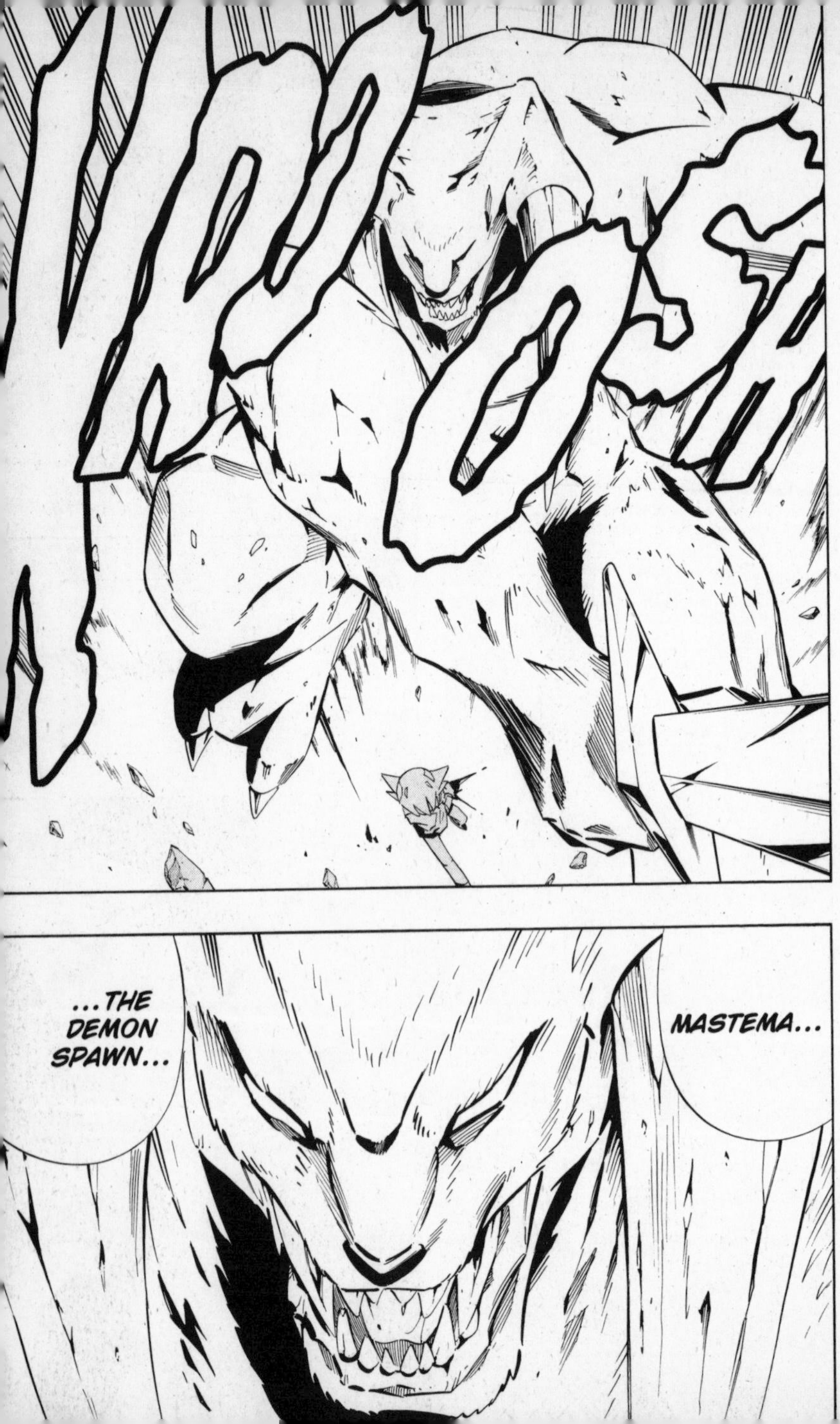
MASTEMA...
...THE DEMON SPAWN...

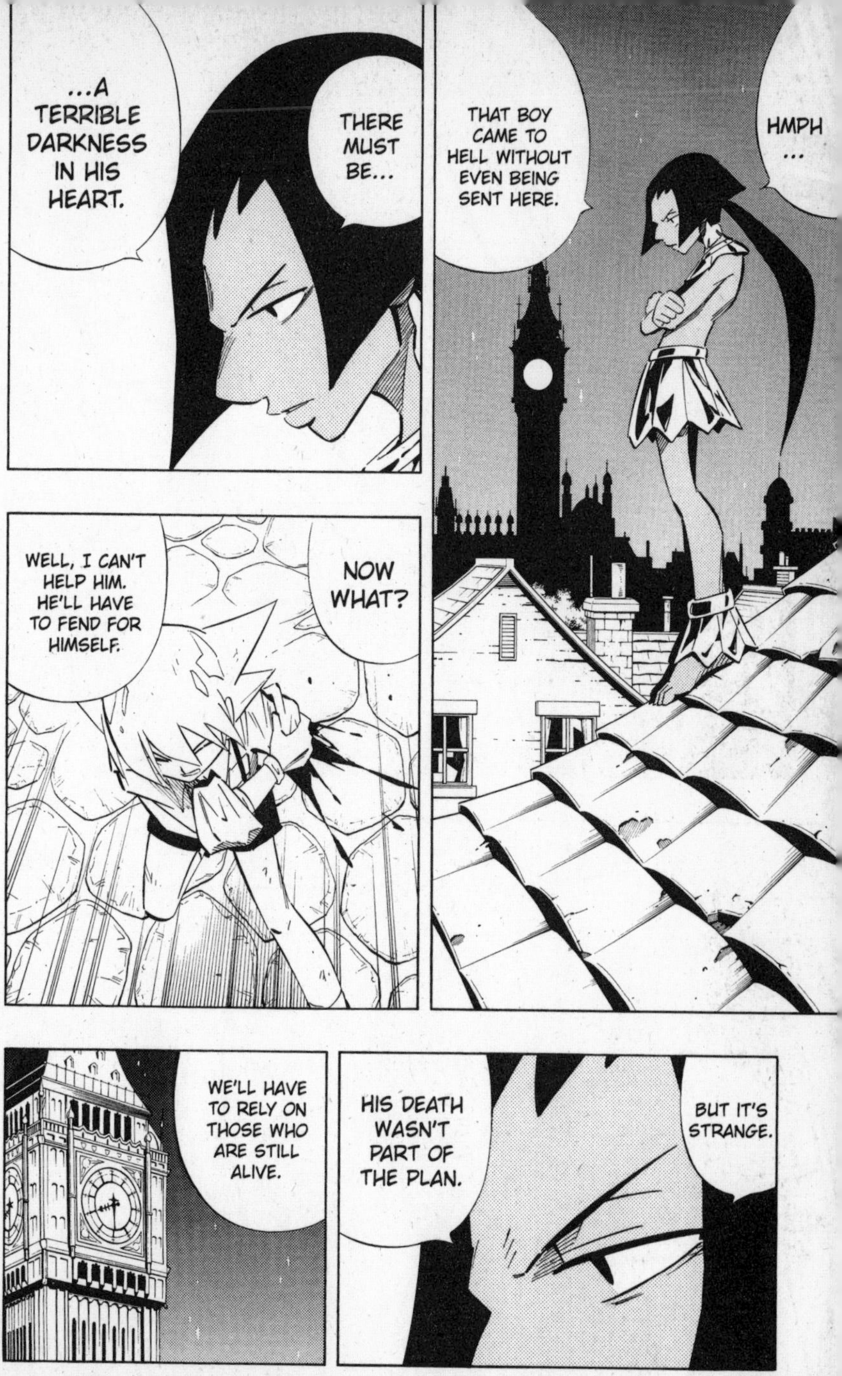
HMPH ...
THAT BOY CAME TO HELL WITHOUT EVEN BEING SENT HERE.
THERE MUST BE...
...A TERRIBLE DARKNESS IN HIS HEART.
NOW WHAT?
WELL, I CAN'T HELP HIM. HE'LL HAVE TO FEND FOR HIMSELF.
BUT IT'S STRANGE.
HIS DEATH WASN'T PART OF THE PLAN.
WE'LL HAVE TO RELY ON THOSE WHO ARE STILL ALIVE.

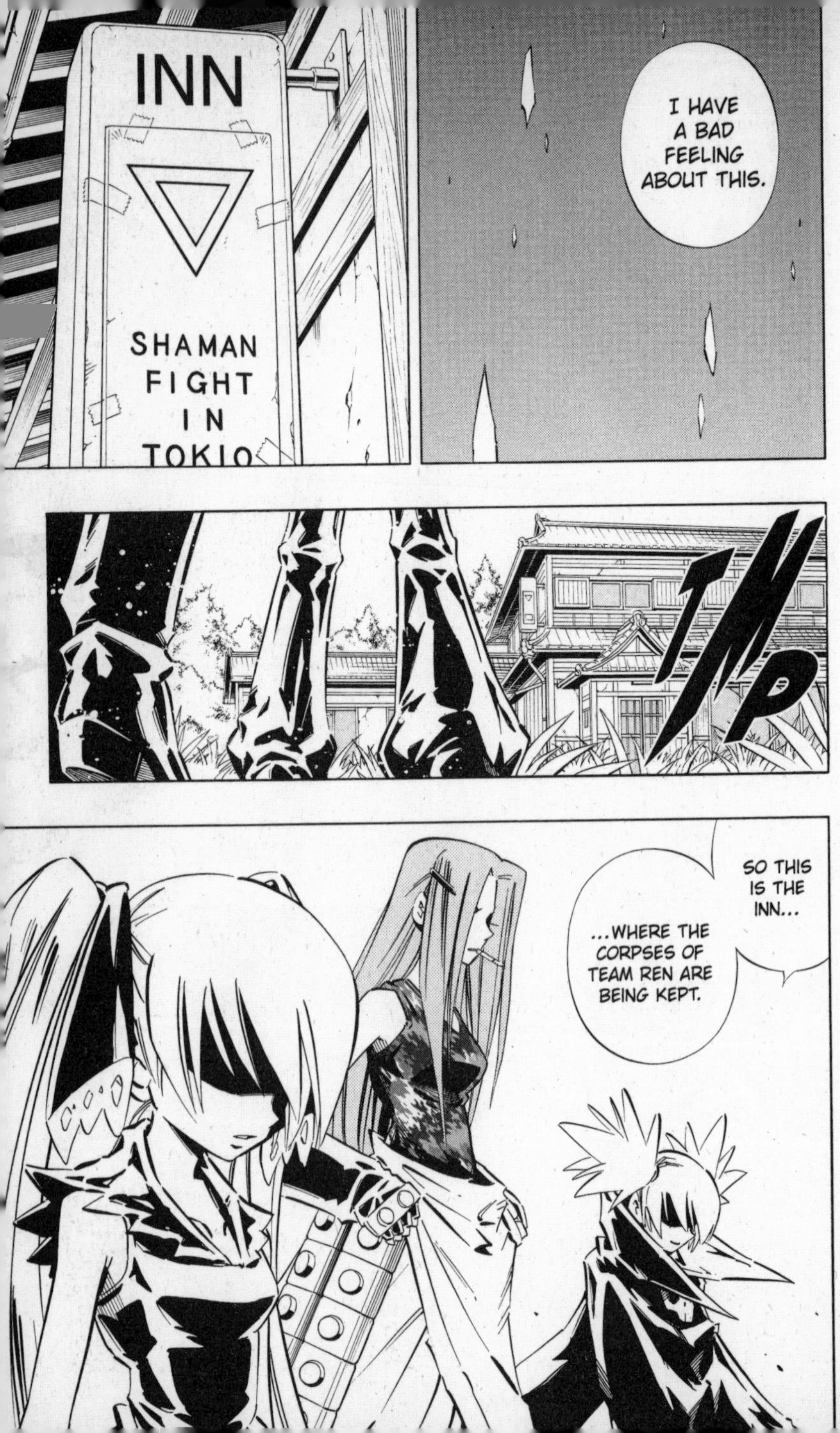
I HAVE A BAD FEELING ABOUT THIS.
INN
SHAMAN FIGHT IN TOKIO
TMP
SO THIS IS THE INN...
...WHERE THE CORPSES OF TEAM REN ARE BEING KEPT.

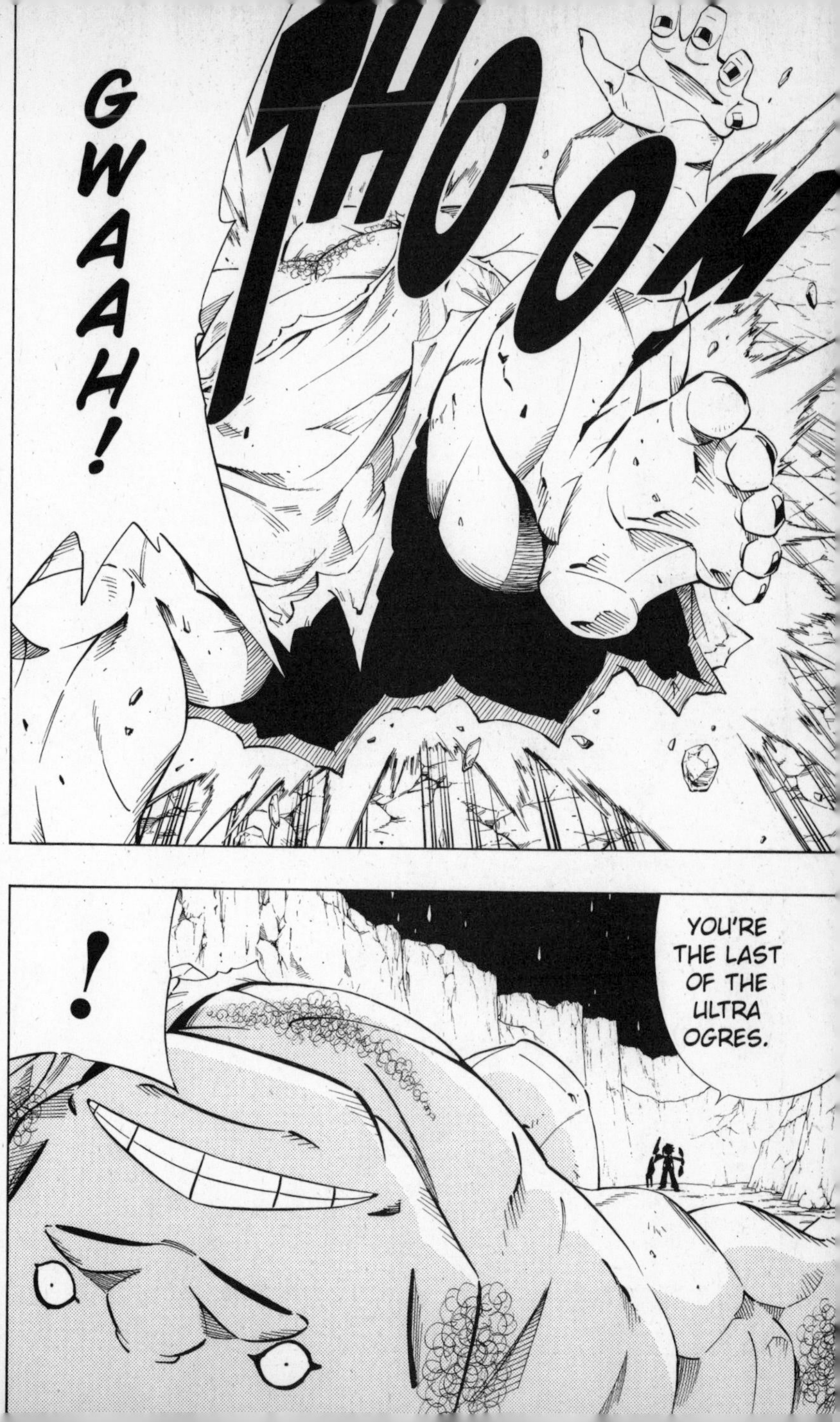
THOOM
GWAAH!
YOU'RE THE LAST OF THE ULTRA OGRES.
!

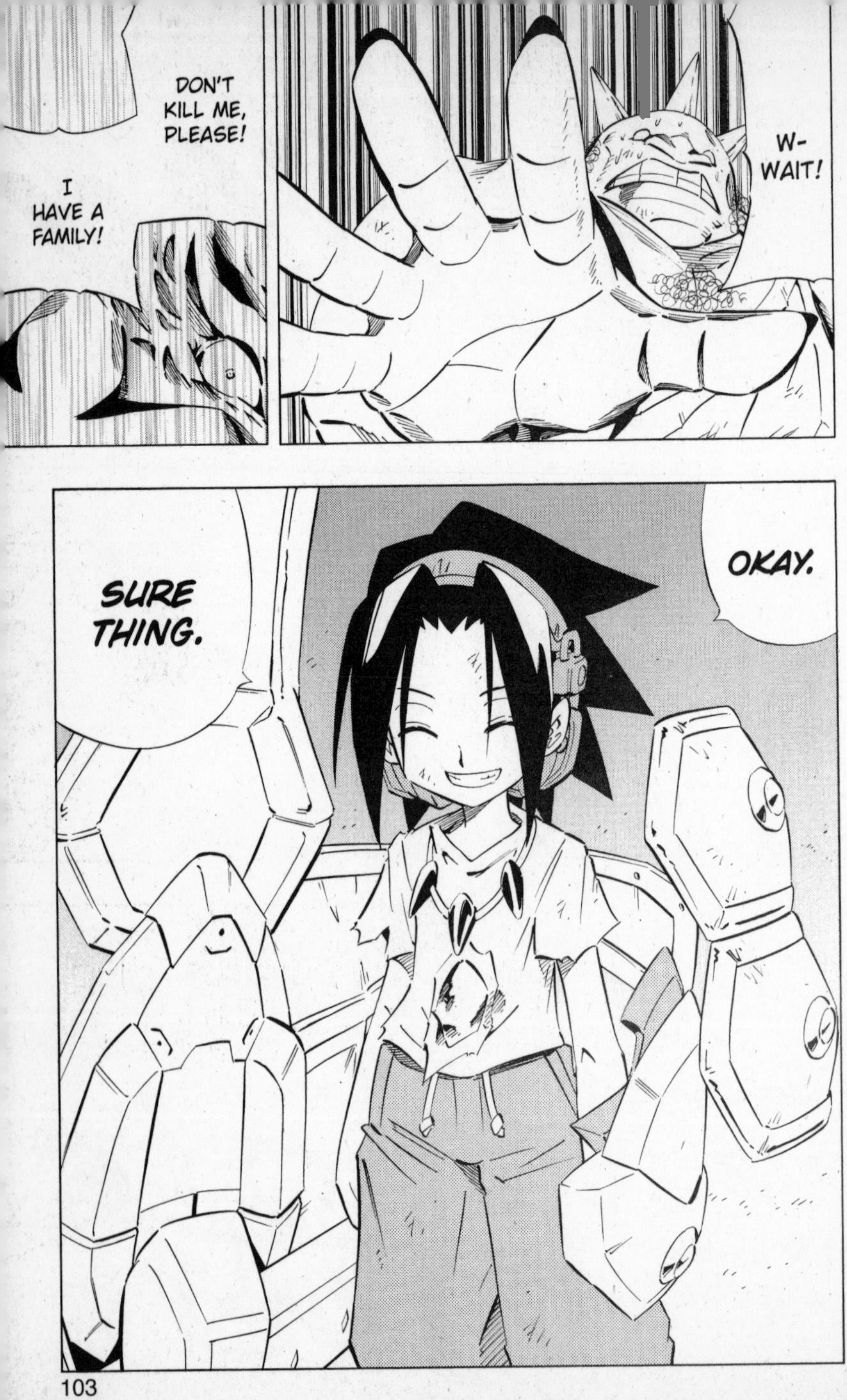
W- WAIT!
DON'T KILL ME, PLEASE!
I HAVE A FAMILY!
OKAY.
SURE THING.

Shaman King

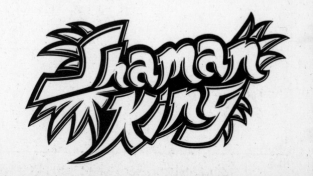

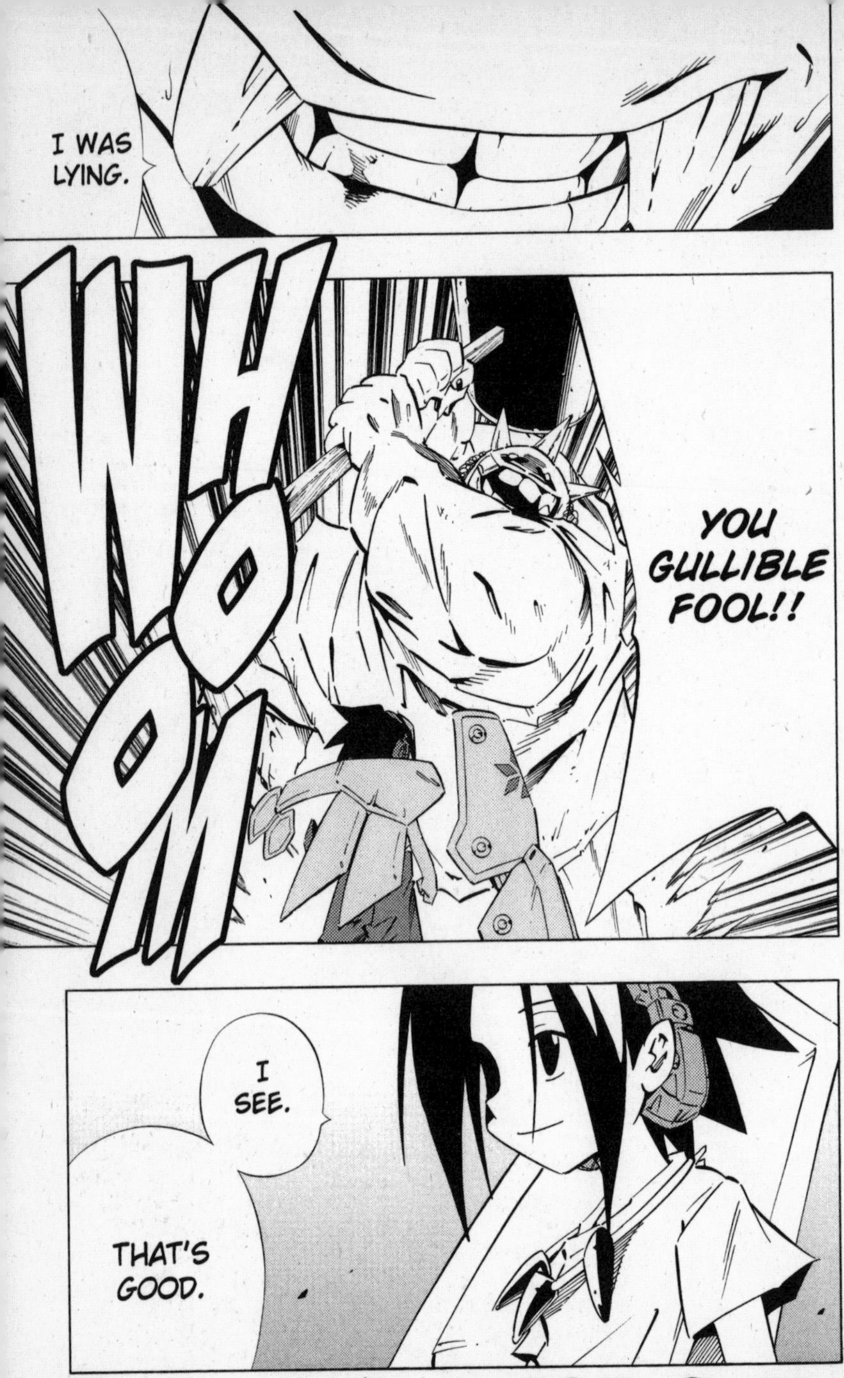
I WAS LYING.
WHOOM
YOU GULLIBLE FOOL!!
I SEE.
THAT'S GOOD.

Reincarnation 245: One Person I Can't Lose To

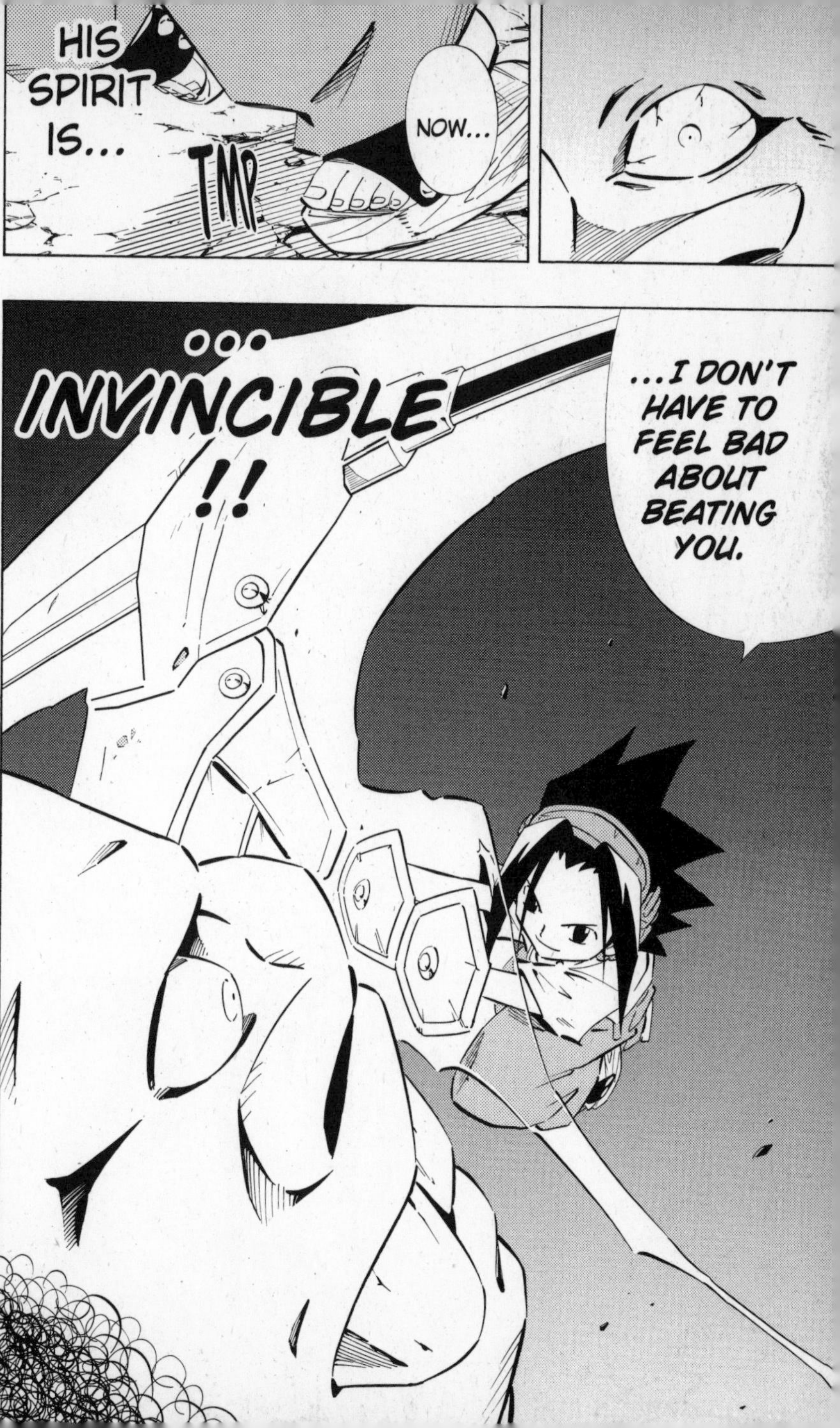

HIS SPIRIT IS...
NOW...
TMP
...I DON'T HAVE TO FEEL BAD ABOUT BEATING YOU.
...INVINCIBLE!!

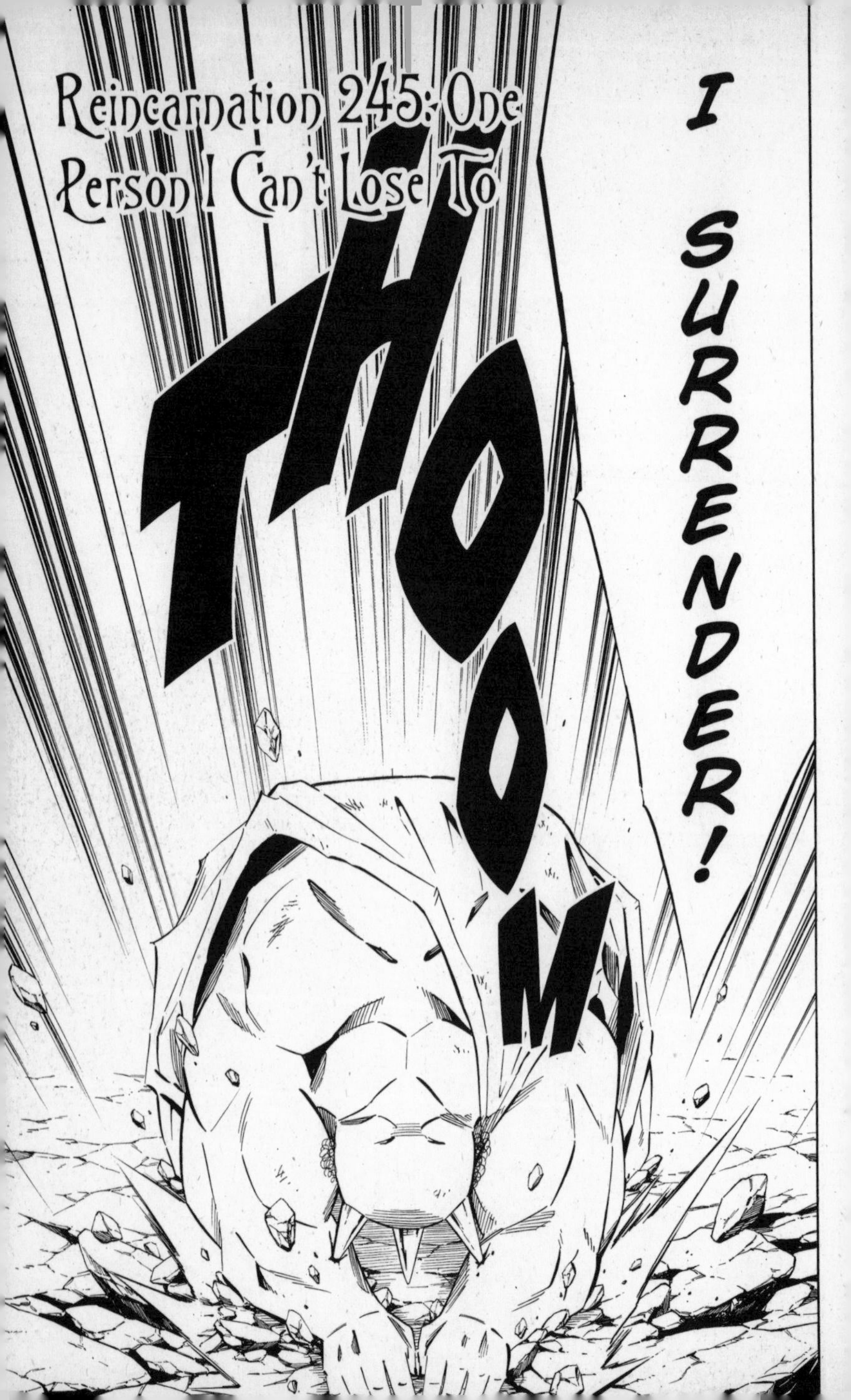
Reincarnation 245: One Person I Can't Lose To
I SURRENDER!
THOOM

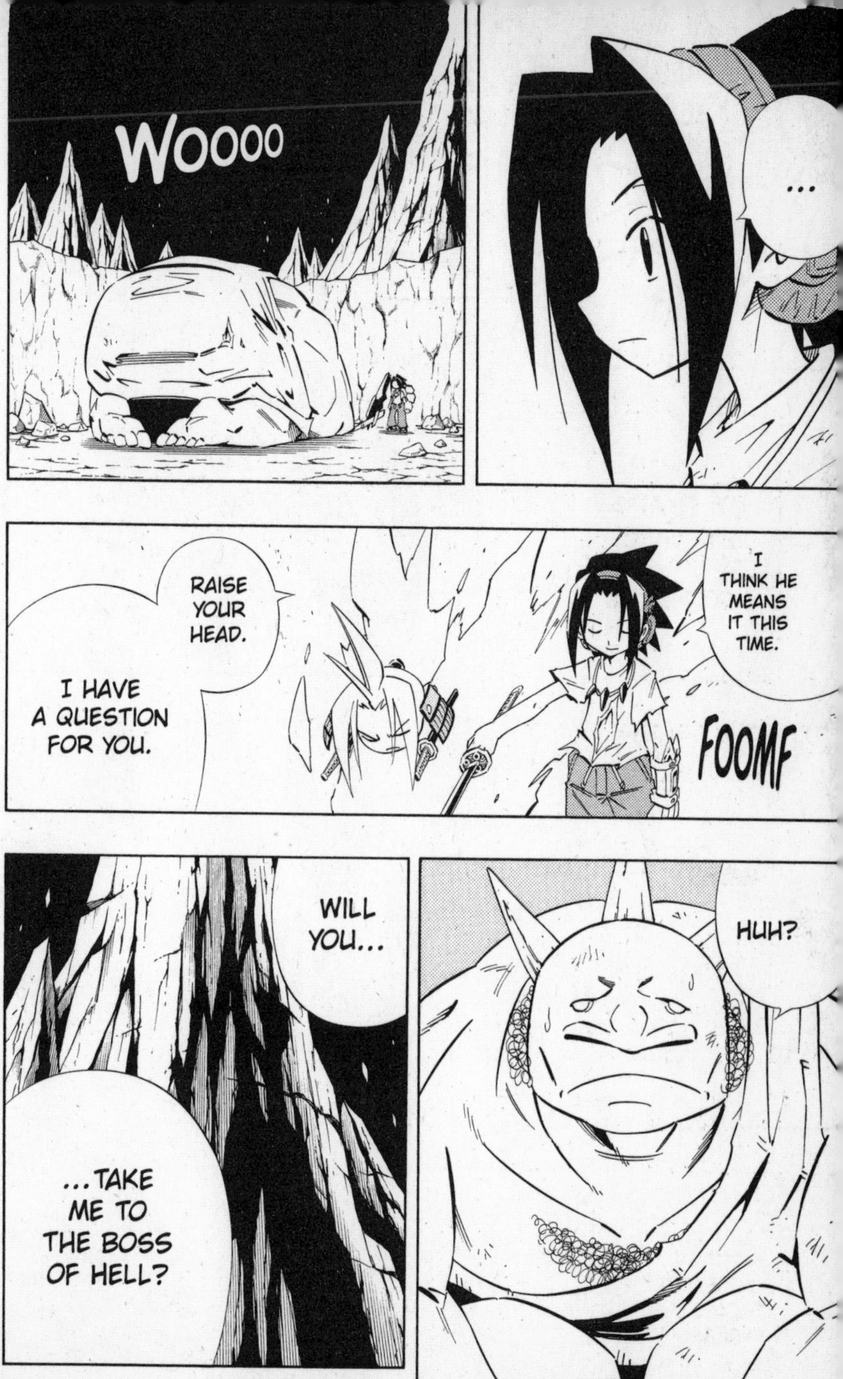
...
WOOOO
I THINK HE MEANS IT THIS TIME.
FOOMF
RAISE YOUR HEAD.
I HAVE A QUESTION FOR YOU.
HUH?
WILL YOU...
...TAKE ME TO THE BOSS OF HELL?

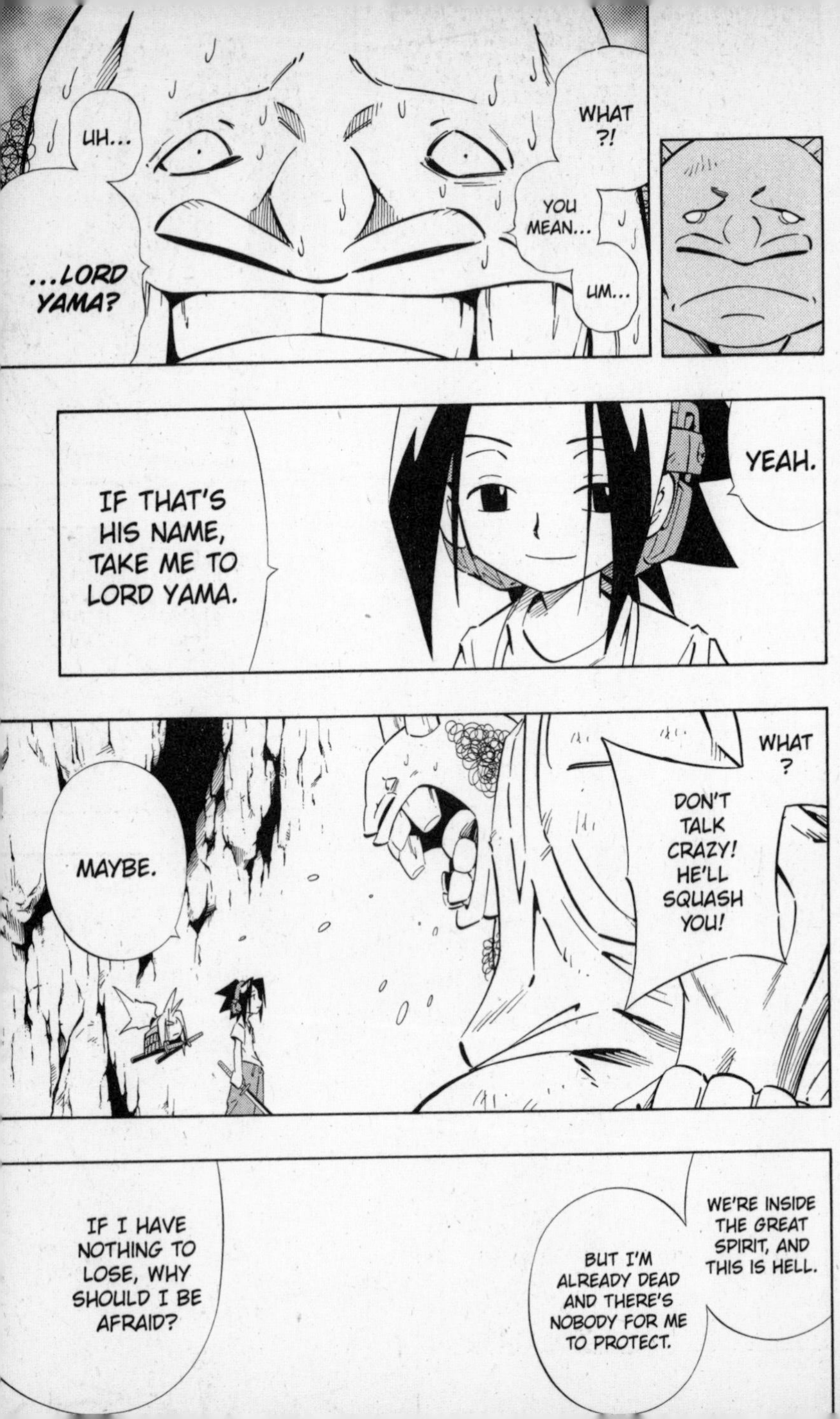
WHAT ?!
YOU MEAN...
UM...
UH...
...LORD YAMA?
YEAH.
IF THAT'S HIS NAME, TAKE ME TO LORD YAMA.
WHAT ?
DON'T TALK CRAZY! HE'LL SQUASH YOU!
MAYBE.
WE'RE INSIDE THE GREAT SPIRIT, AND THIS IS HELL.
BUT I'M ALREADY DEAD AND THERE'S NOBODY FOR ME TO PROTECT.
IF I HAVE NOTHING TO LOSE, WHY SHOULD I BE AFRAID?

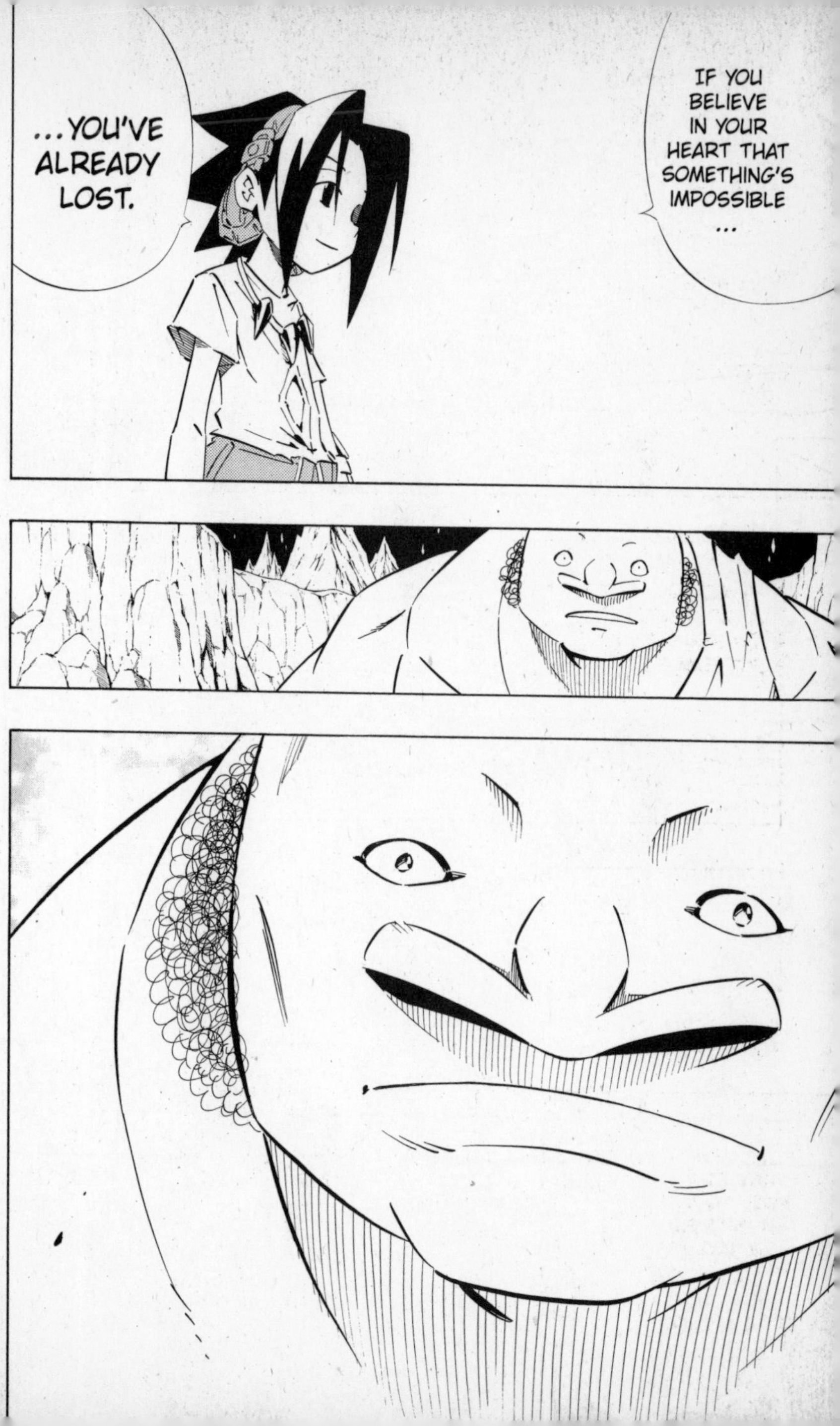
IF YOU BELIEVE IN YOUR HEART THAT SOMETHING'S IMPOSSIBLE ...
...YOU'VE ALREADY LOST.

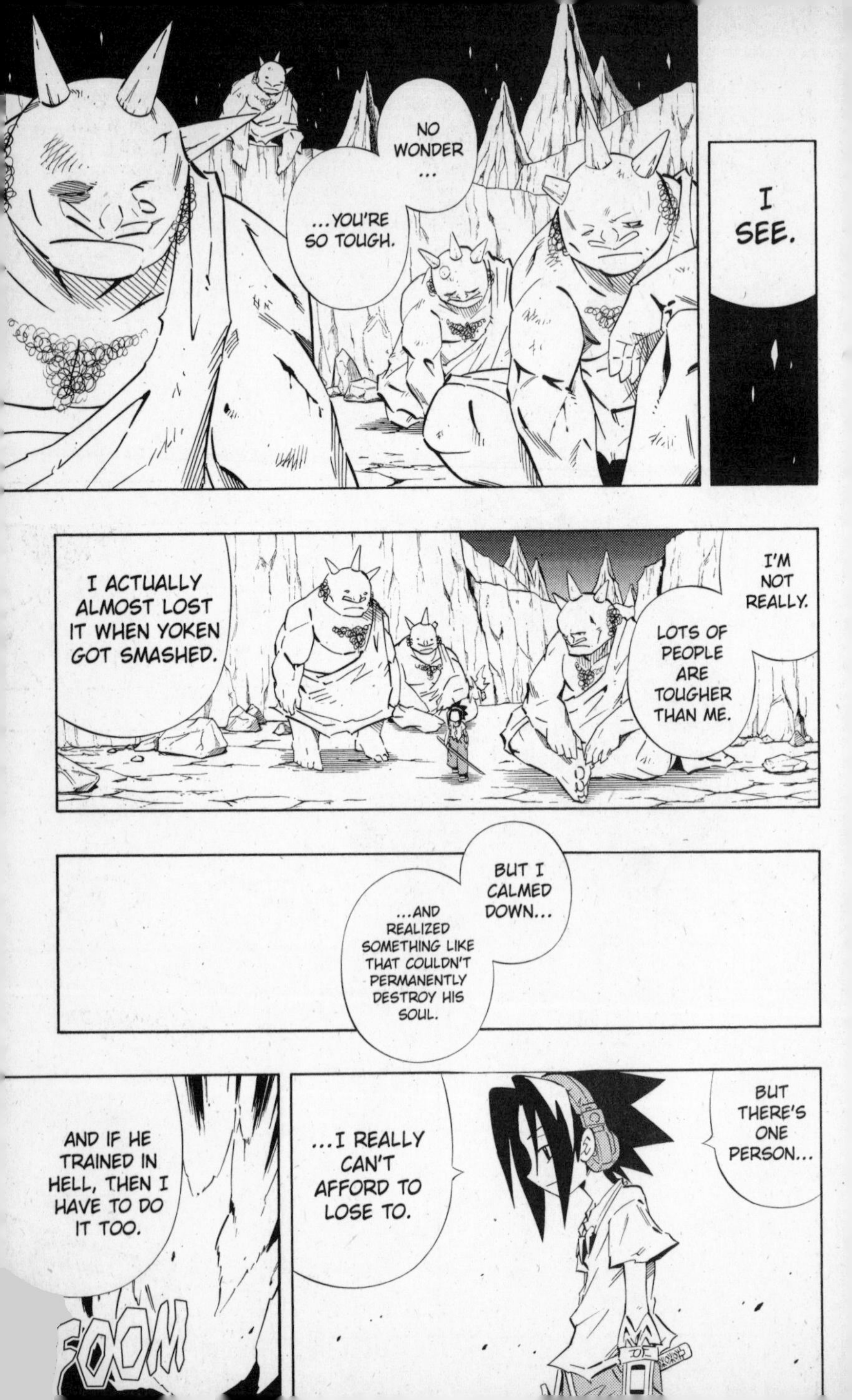
I SEE.
NO WONDER...
...YOU'RE SO TOUGH.
I'M NOT REALLY.
LOTS OF PEOPLE ARE TOUGHER THAN ME.
I ACTUALLY ALMOST LOST IT WHEN YOKEN GOT SMASHED.
BUT I CALMED DOWN...
...AND REALIZED SOMETHING LIKE THAT COULDN'T PERMANENTLY DESTROY HIS SOUL.
BUT THERE'S ONE PERSON...
...I REALLY CAN'T AFFORD TO LOSE TO.
AND IF HE TRAINED IN HELL, THEN I HAVE TO DO IT TOO.
FOOM

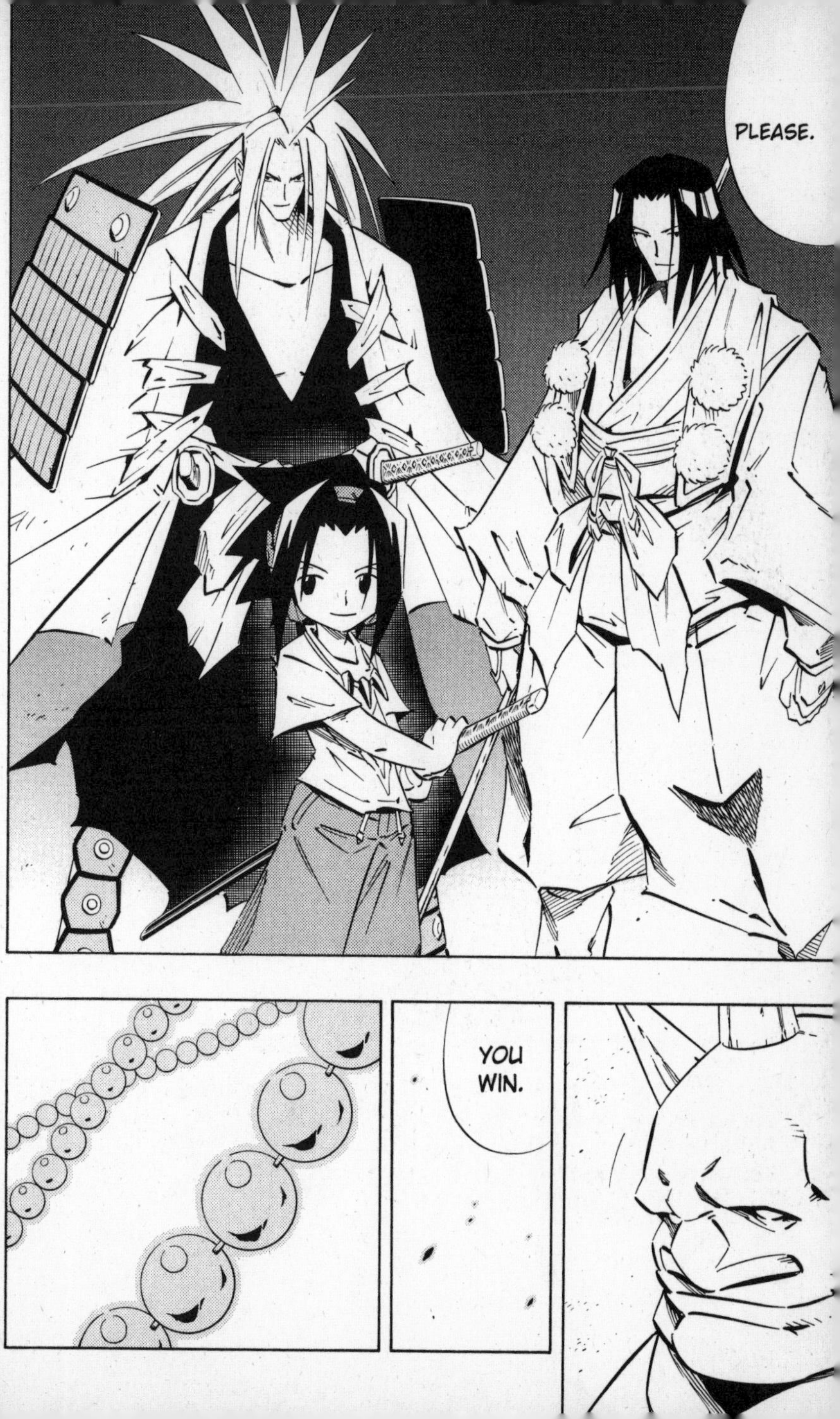
PLEASE.
YOU WIN.

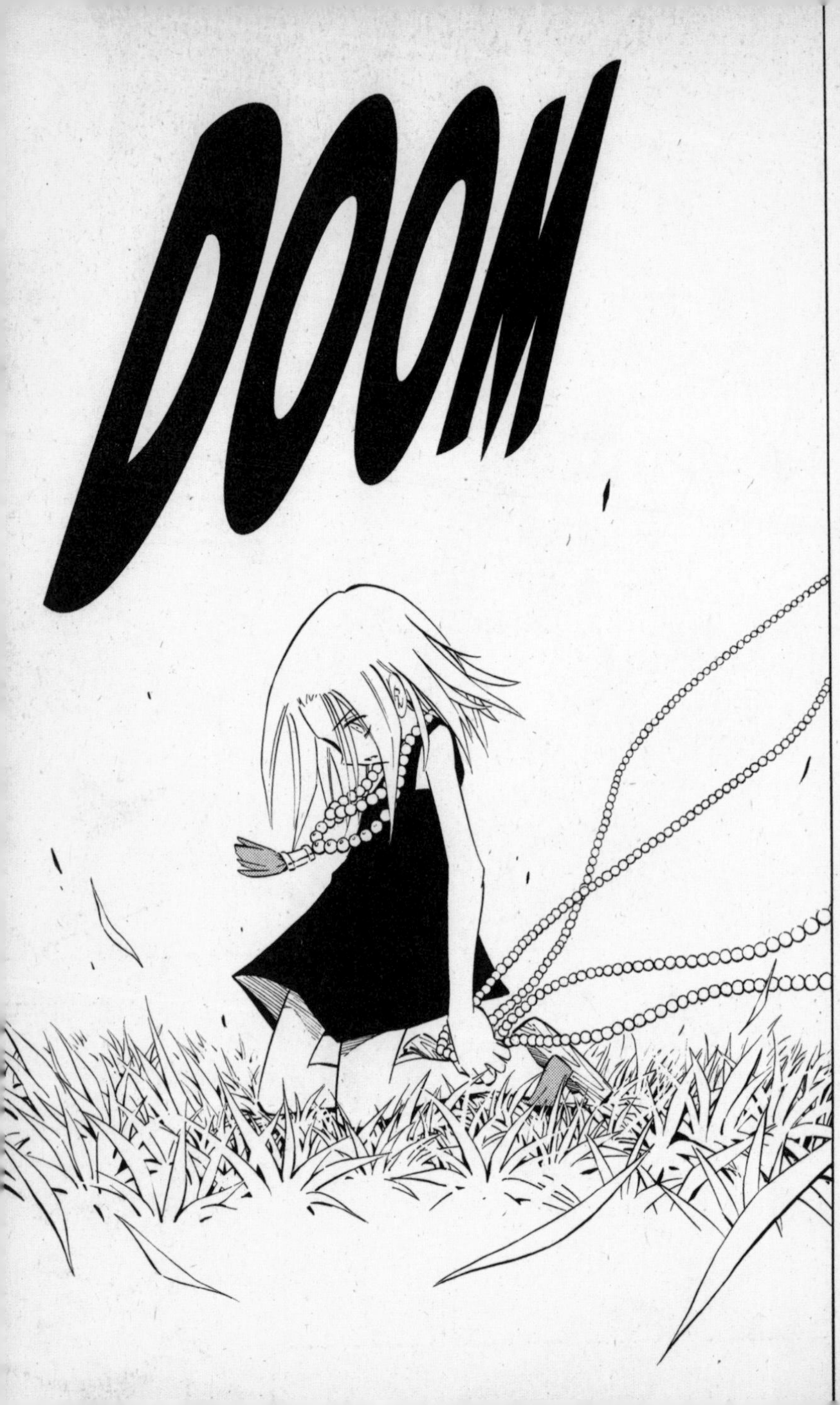
DOOM

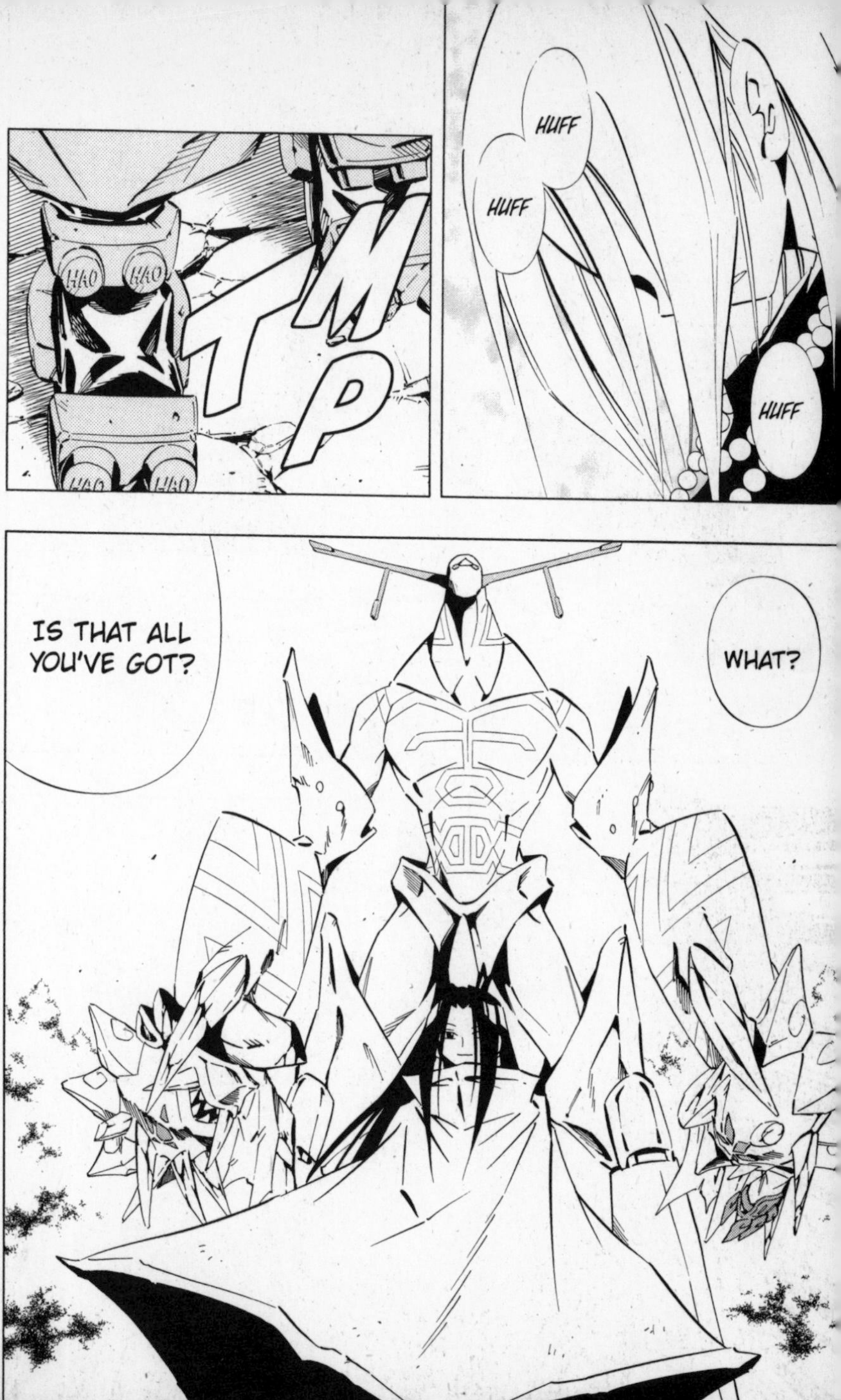
HUFF
HUFF
HUFF
HAO
HAO
HAO
HAO
TMP
WHAT?
IS THAT ALL YOU'VE GOT?

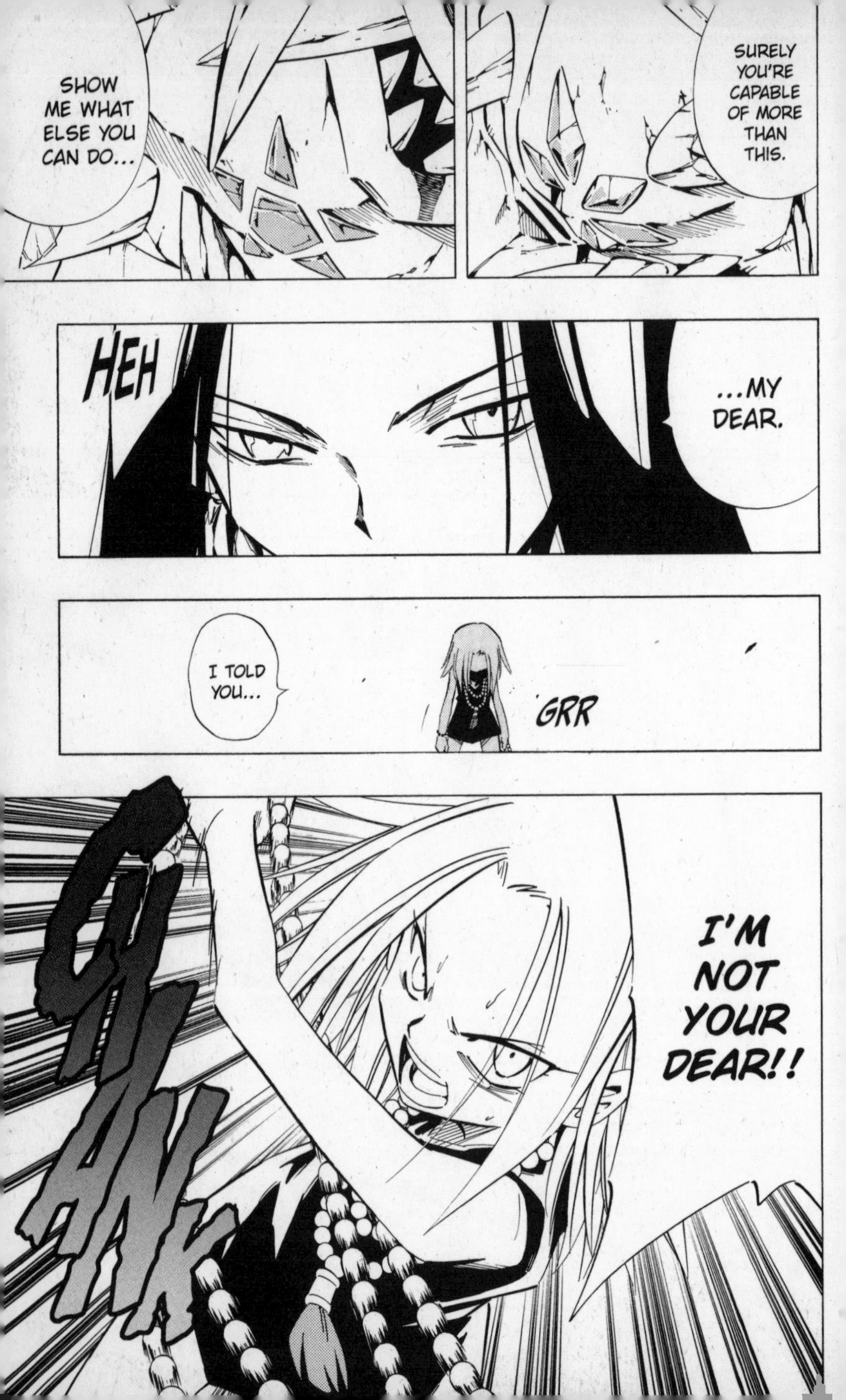
SURELY YOU'RE CAPABLE OF MORE THAN THIS.
SHOW ME WHAT ELSE YOU CAN DO...
...MY DEAR.
HEH
GRR
I TOLD YOU...
I'M NOT YOUR DEAR!!

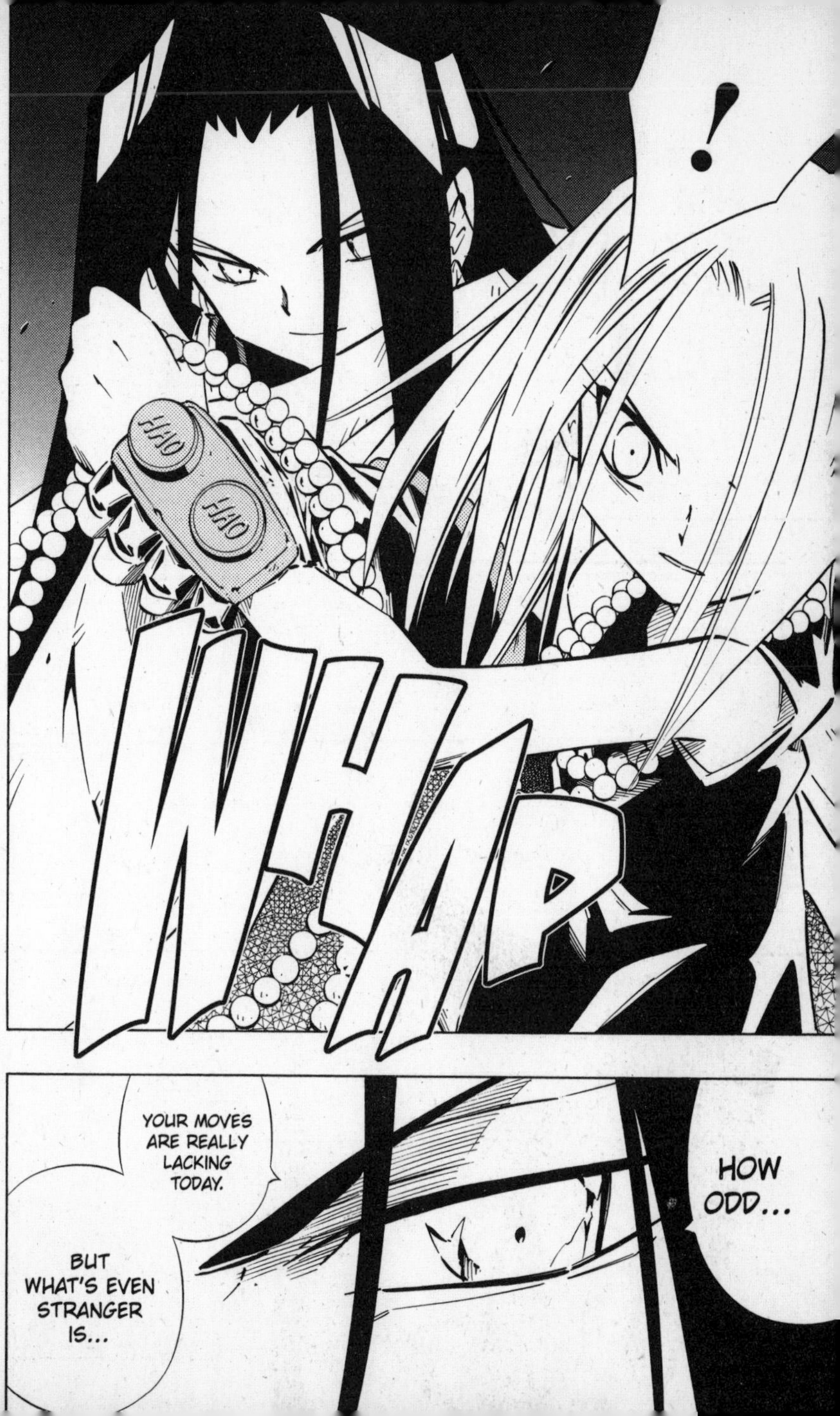
!
WHAP
HOW ODD...
YOUR MOVES ARE REALLY LACKING TODAY.
BUT WHAT'S EVEN STRANGER IS...

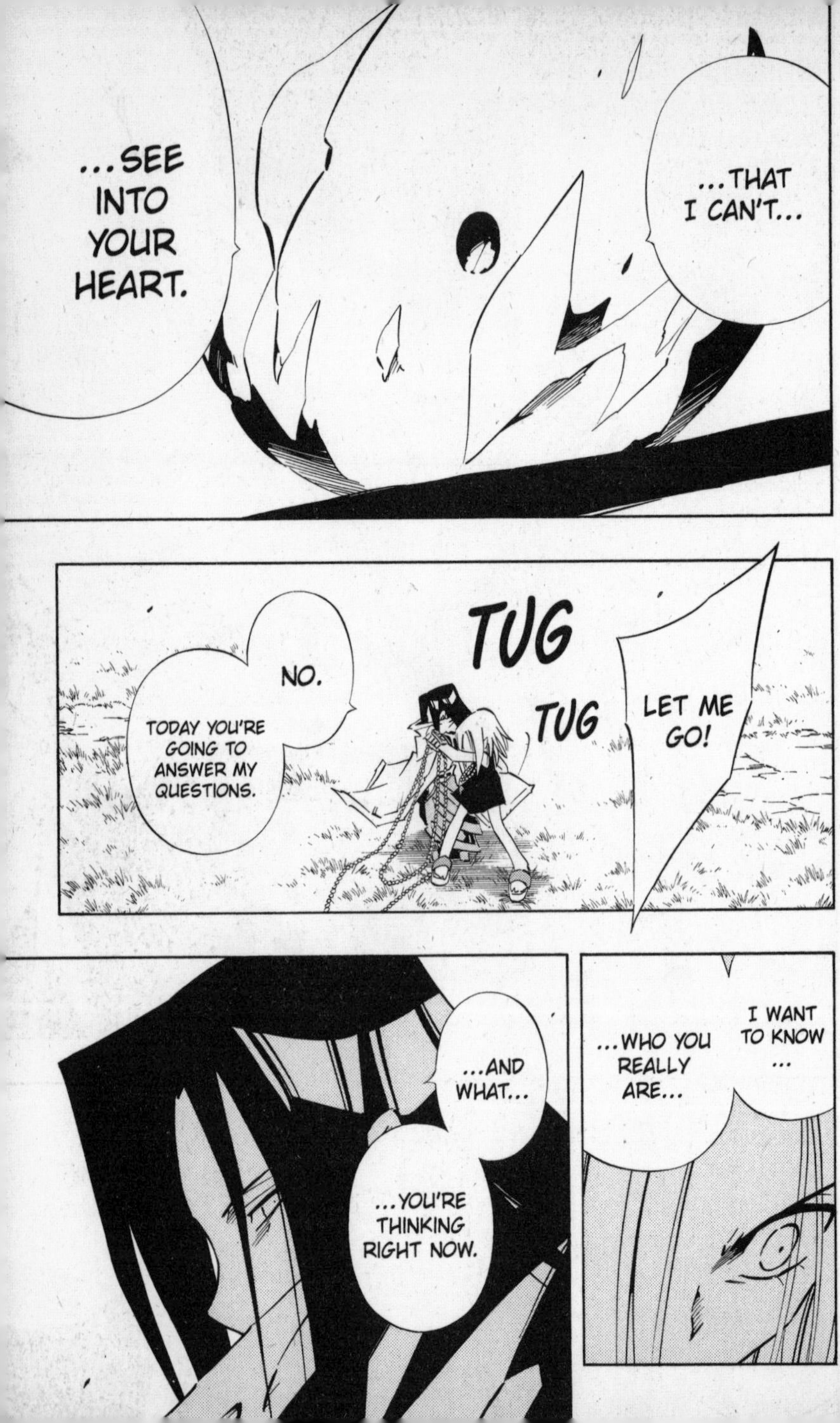
...THAT I CAN'T...
...SEE INTO YOUR HEART.
LET ME GO!
TUG
TUG
NO.
TODAY YOU'RE GOING TO ANSWER MY QUESTIONS.
I WANT TO KNOW ...
...WHO YOU REALLY ARE...
...AND WHAT...
...YOU'RE THINKING RIGHT NOW.

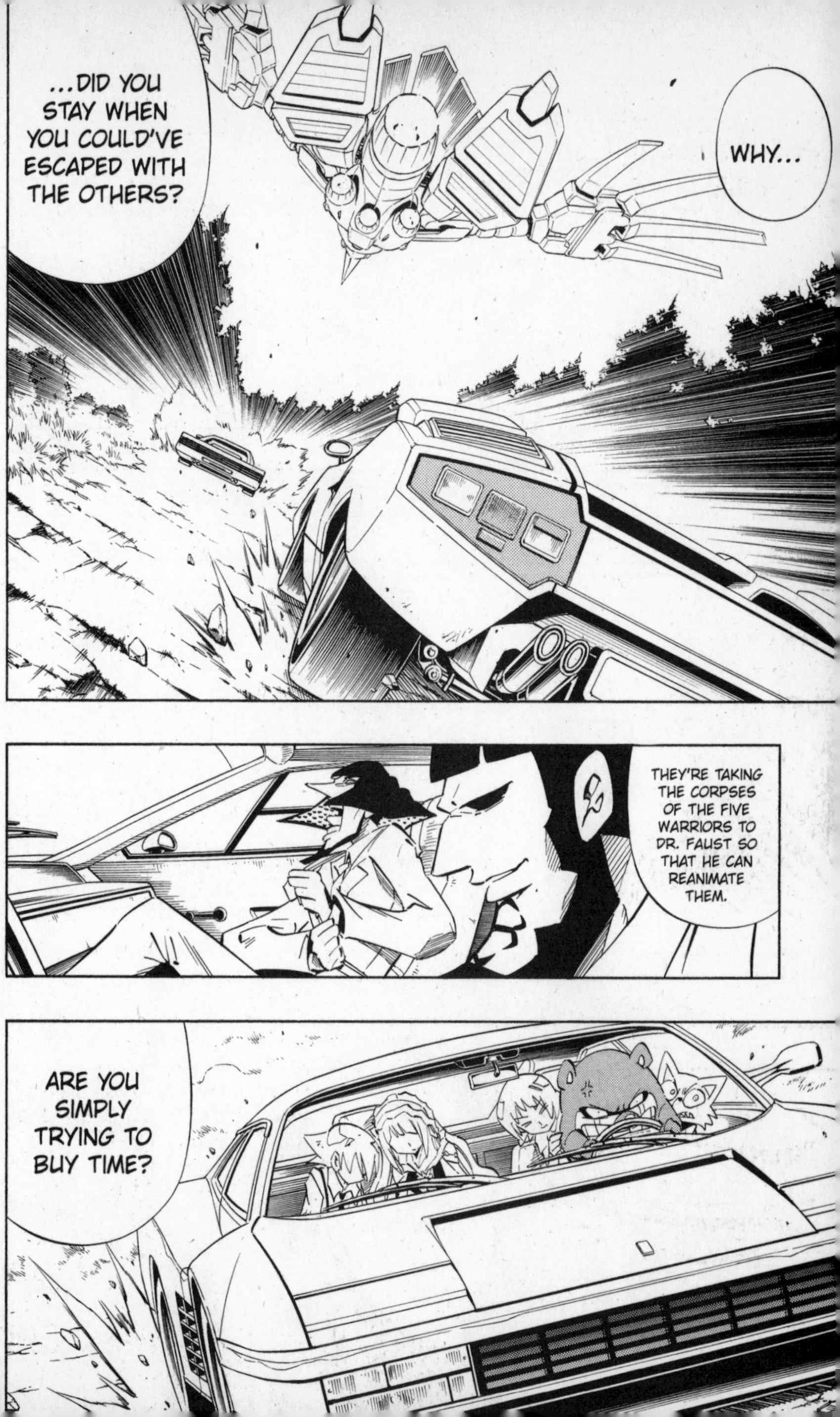
WHY...
...DID YOU STAY WHEN YOU COULD'VE ESCAPED WITH THE OTHERS?
THEY'RE TAKING THE CORPSES OF THE FIVE WARRIORS TO DR. FAUST SO THAT HE CAN REANIMATE THEM.
ARE YOU SIMPLY TRYING TO BUY TIME?

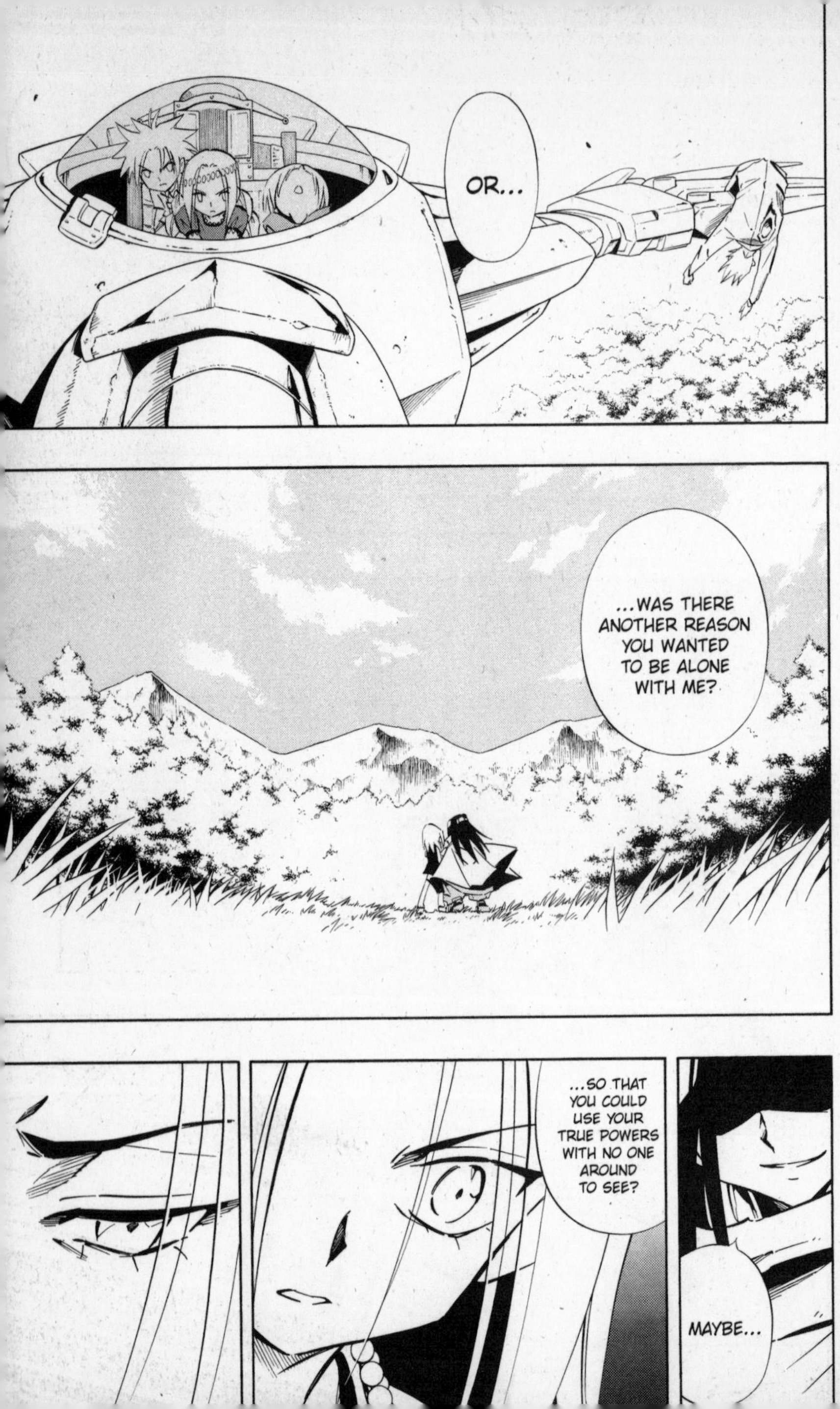
OR...
...WAS THERE ANOTHER REASON YOU WANTED TO BE ALONE WITH ME?
...SO THAT YOU COULD USE YOUR TRUE POWERS WITH NO ONE AROUND TO SEE?
MAYBE...

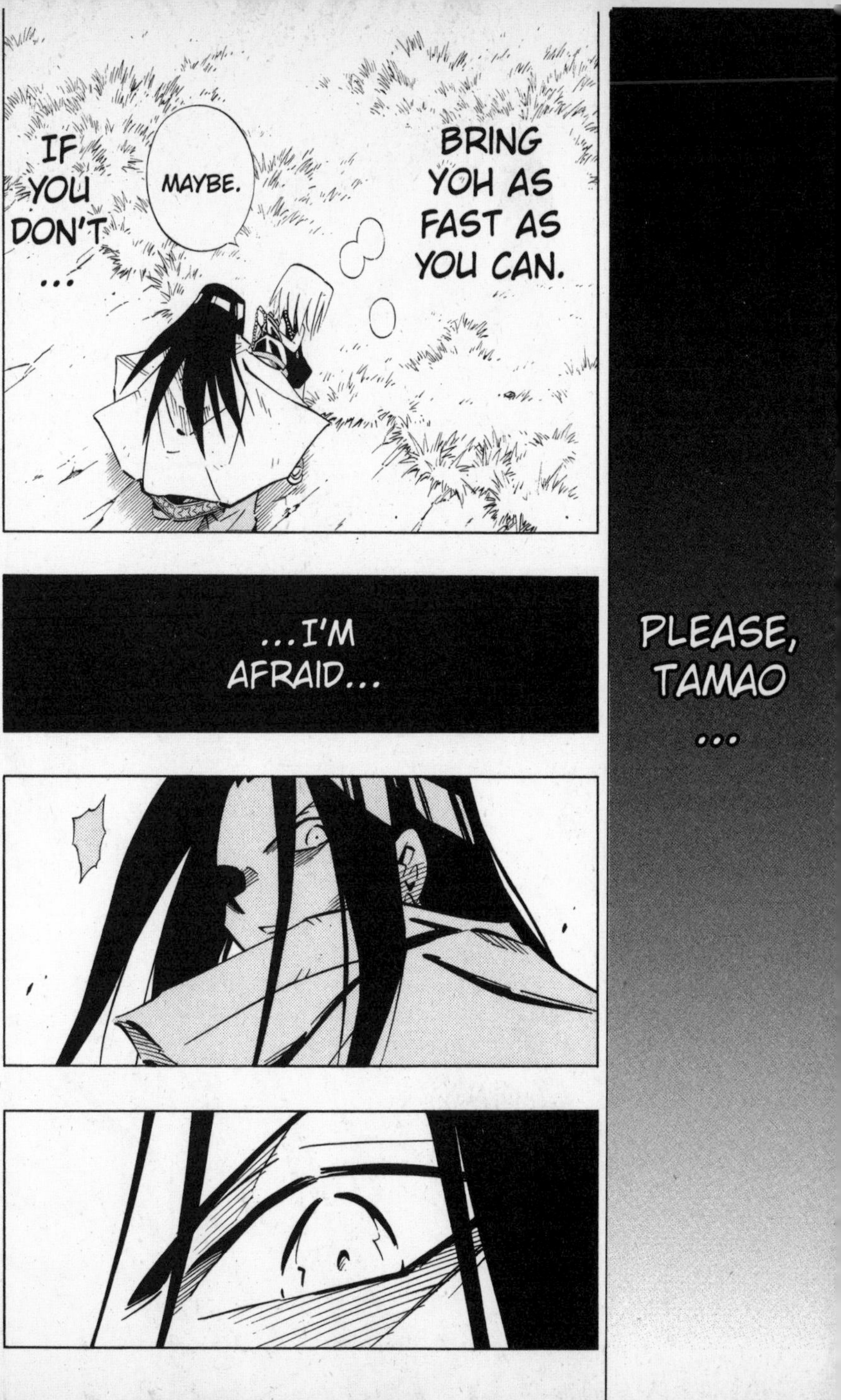
PLEASE, TAMAO ...
BRING YOH AS FAST AS YOU CAN.
MAYBE.
IF YOU DON'T ...
...I'M AFRAID...

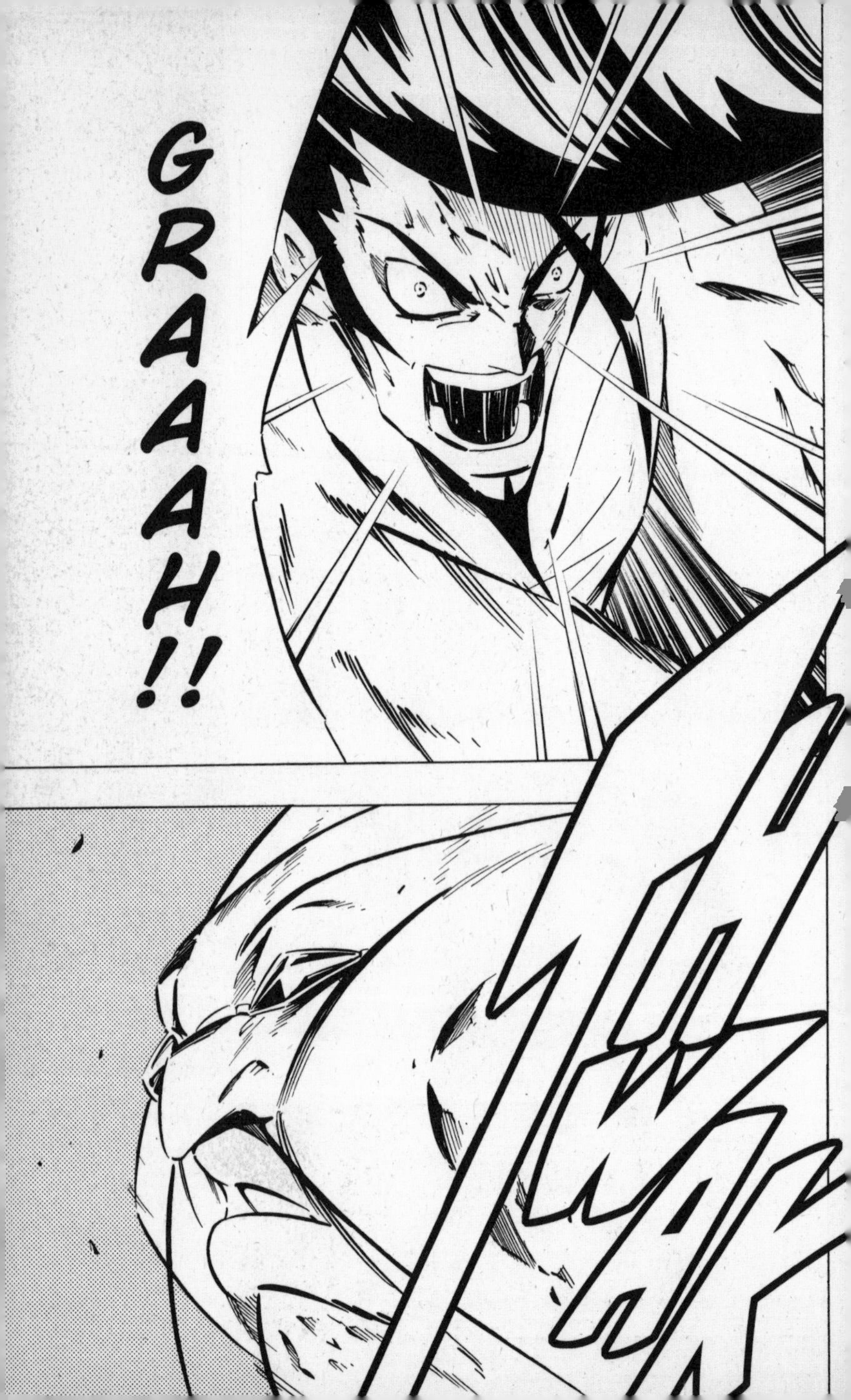
GRAAAH!!

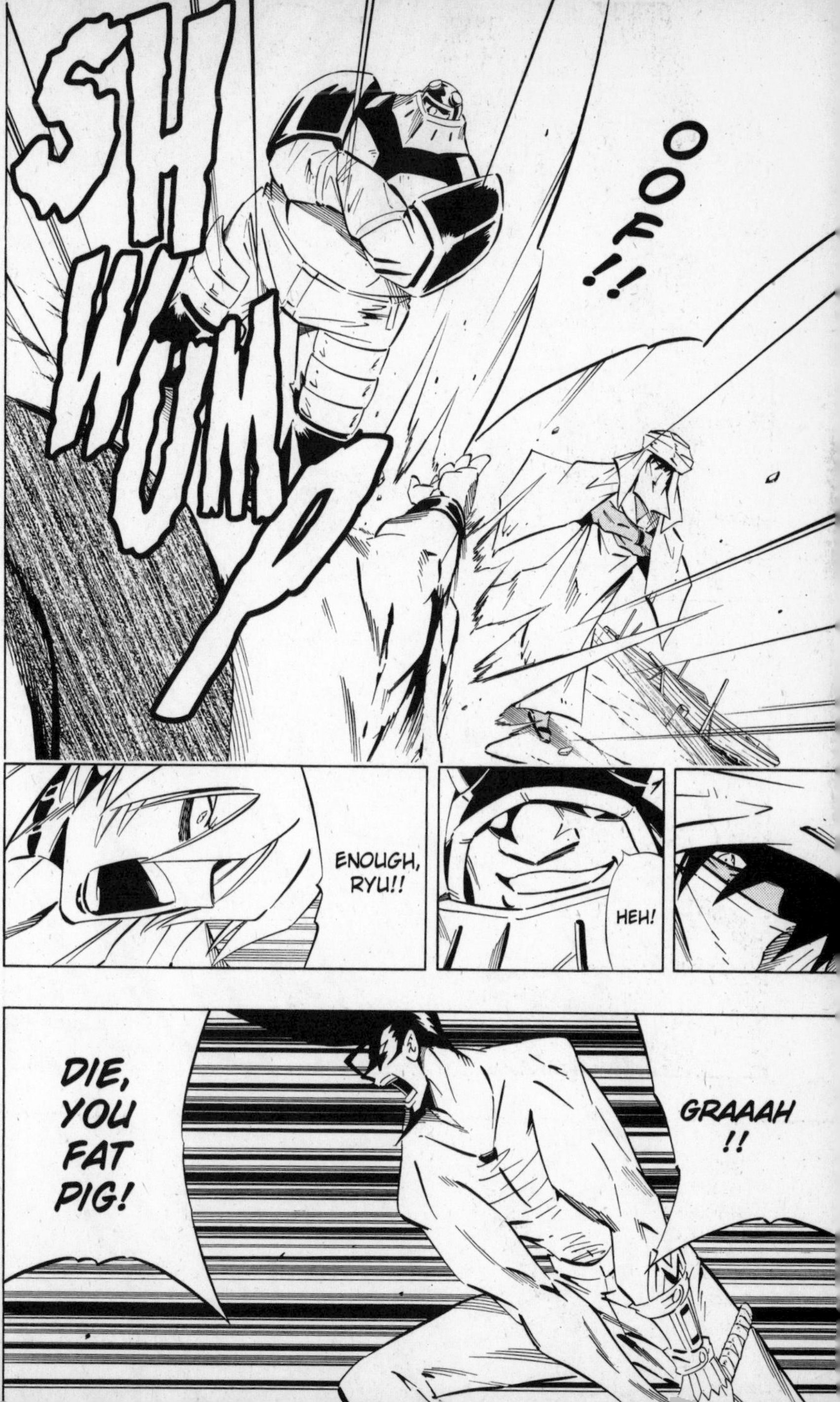
OOF!!
SHWOMP
HEH!
ENOUGH, RYU!!
GRAAAH!!
DIE, YOU FAT PIG!

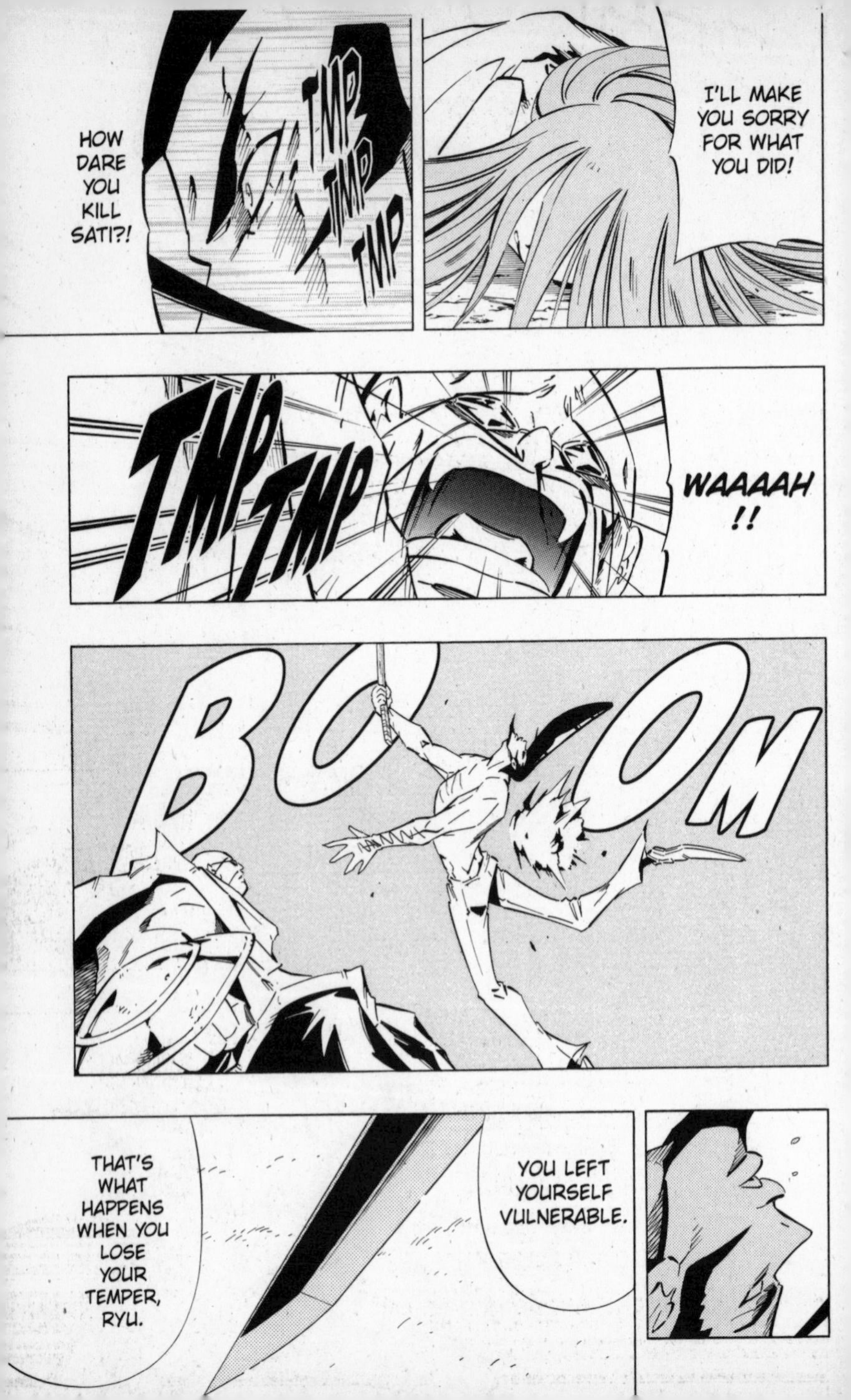
I'LL MAKE YOU SORRY FOR WHAT YOU DID!
TMP TMP TMP
HOW DARE YOU KILL SATI?!
WAAAAH !!
TMP TMP
BOOM
YOU LEFT YOURSELF VULNERABLE.
THAT'S WHAT HAPPENS WHEN YOU LOSE YOUR TEMPER, RYU.

Shaman King

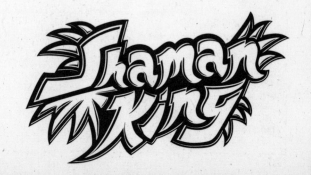

Reincarnation 246: Come Back to Life

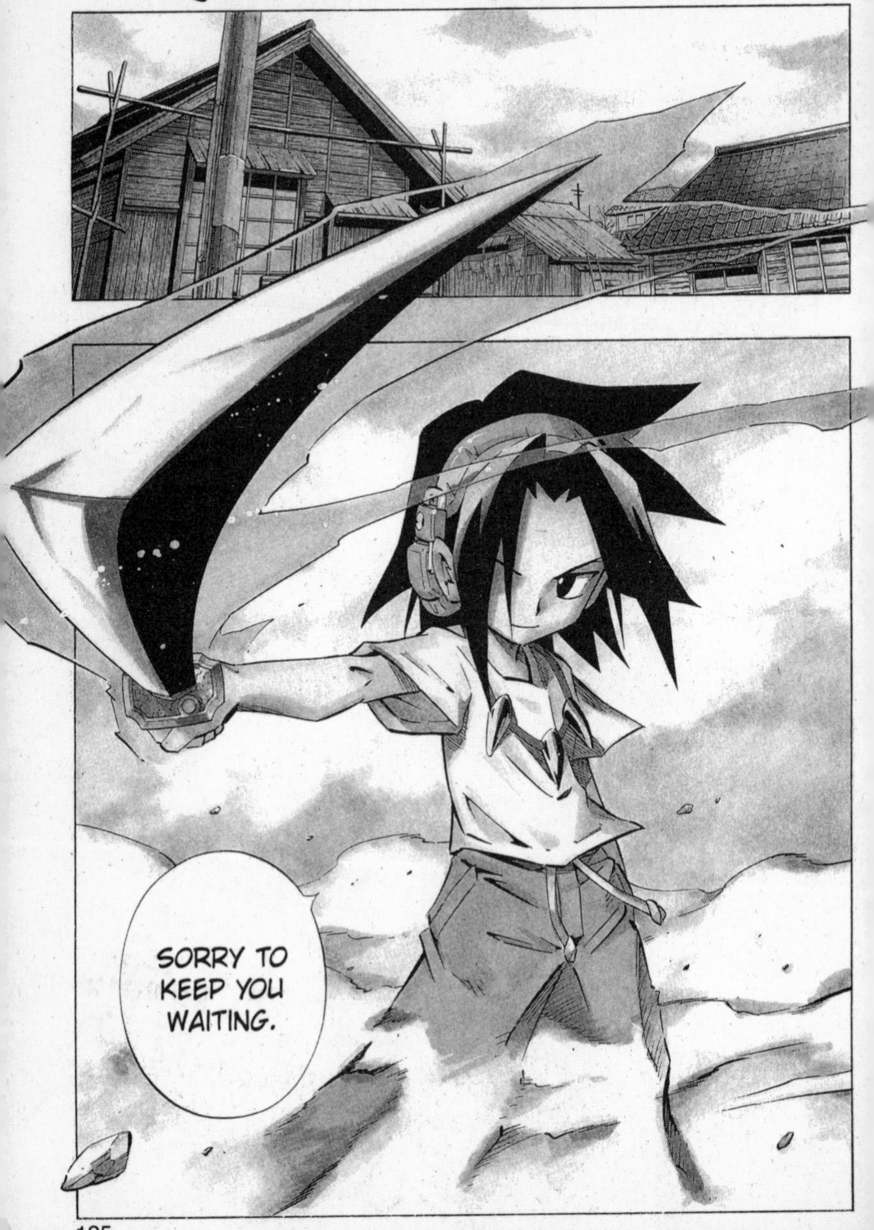
SORRY TO KEEP YOU WAITING.

Reincarnation 246: Come Back to Life

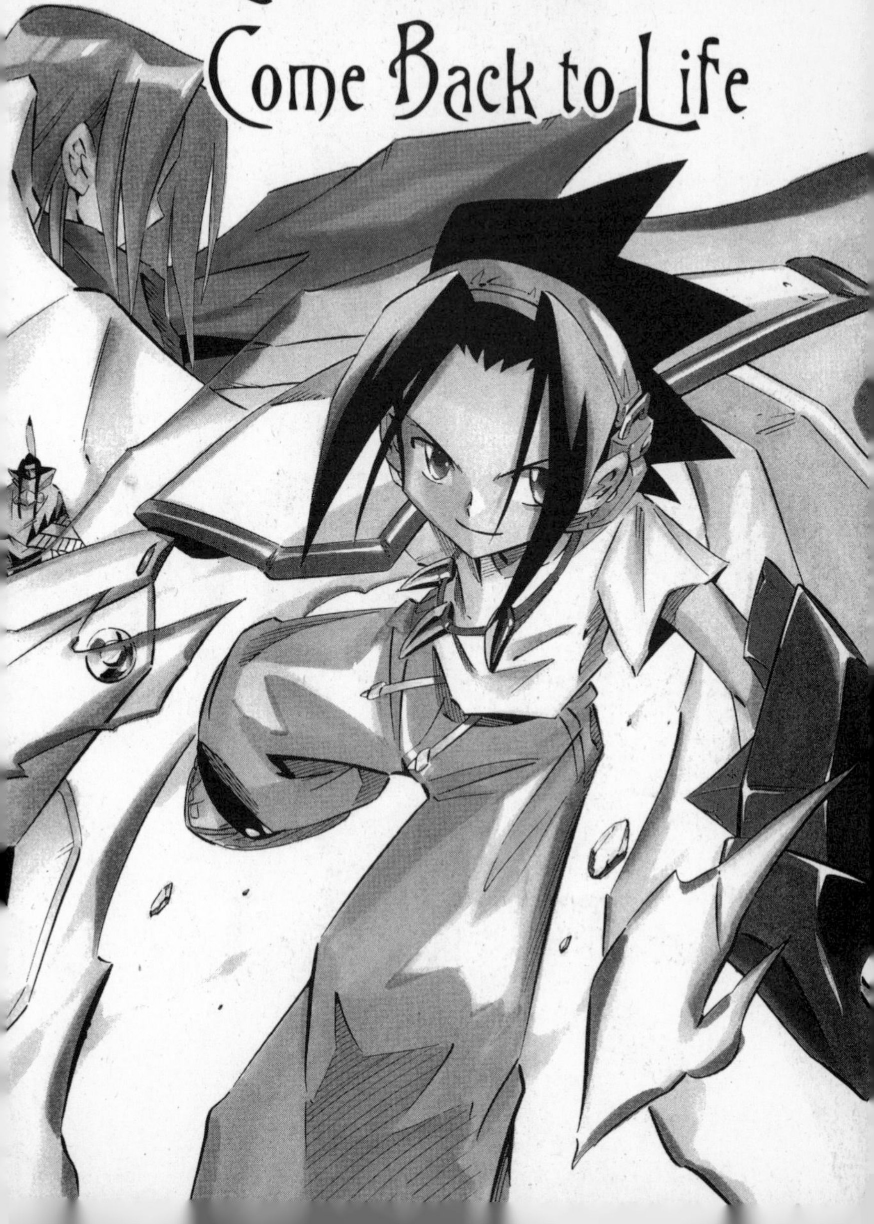

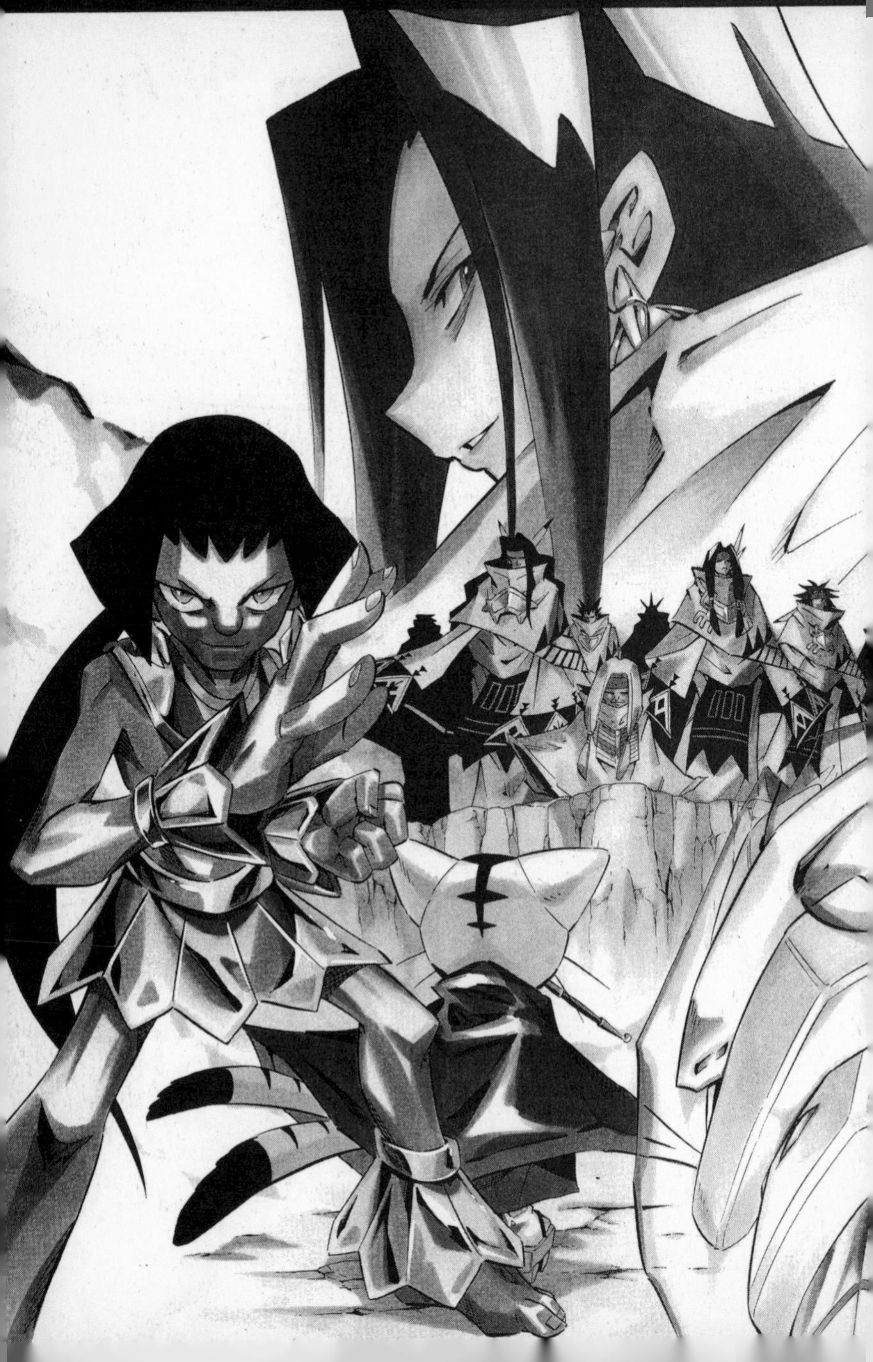

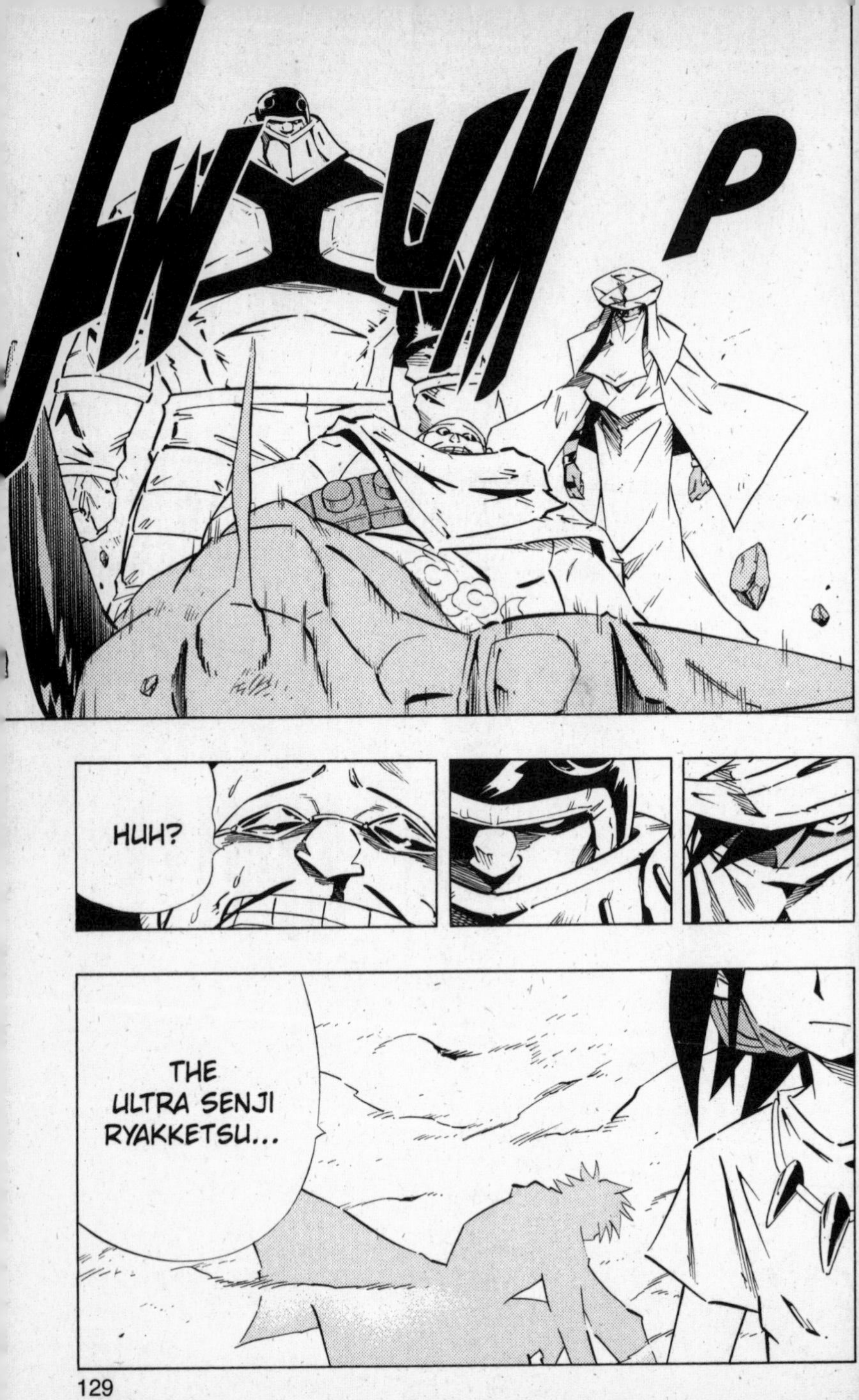
FWUMP
HUH?
THE ULTRA SENJI RYAKKETSU...

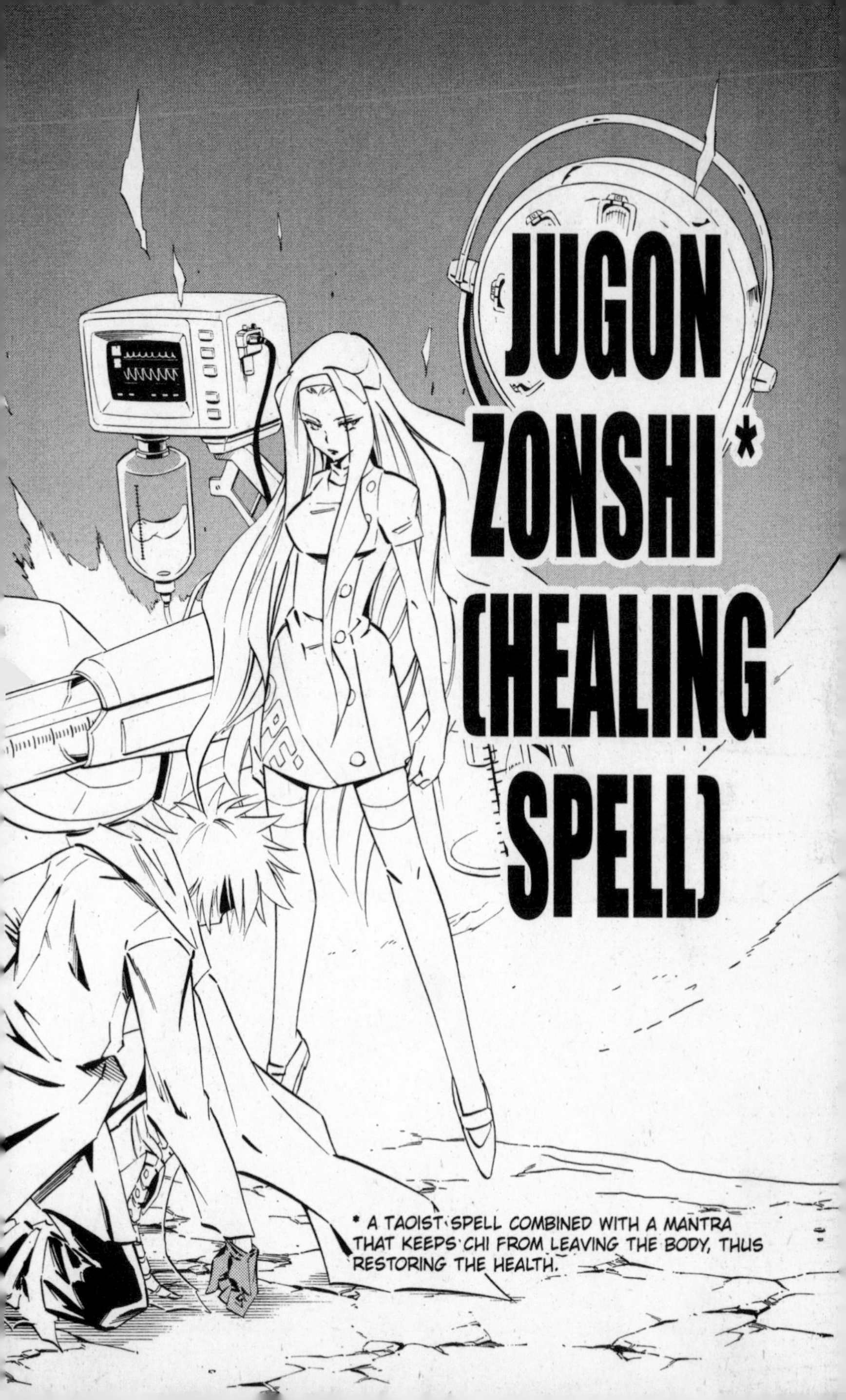
JUGON ZONSHI* (HEALING SPELL)
* A TAOIST SPELL COMBINED WITH A MANTRA THAT KEEPS CHI FROM LEAVING THE BODY, THUS RESTORING THE HEALTH.

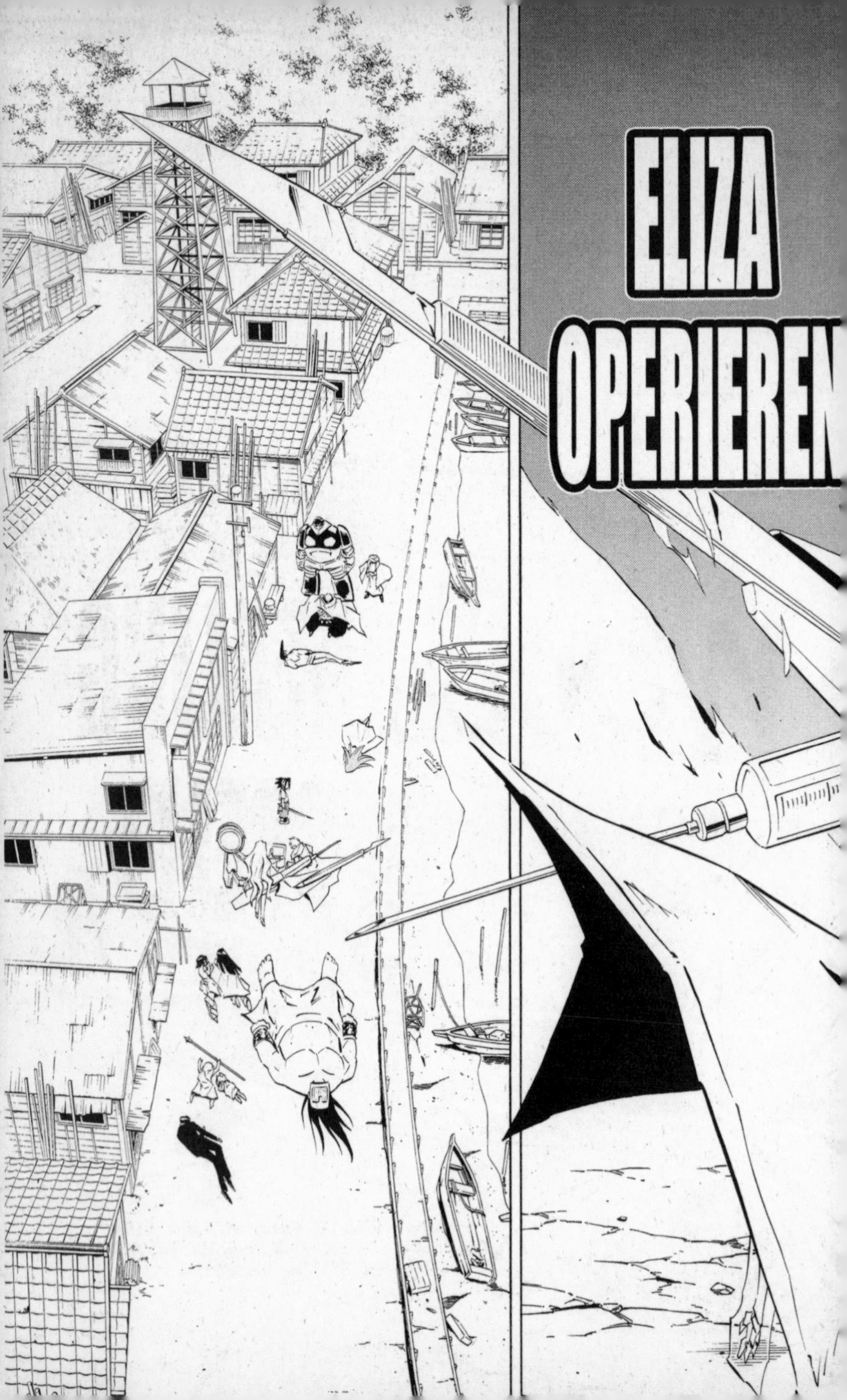
ELIZA
OPERIEREN

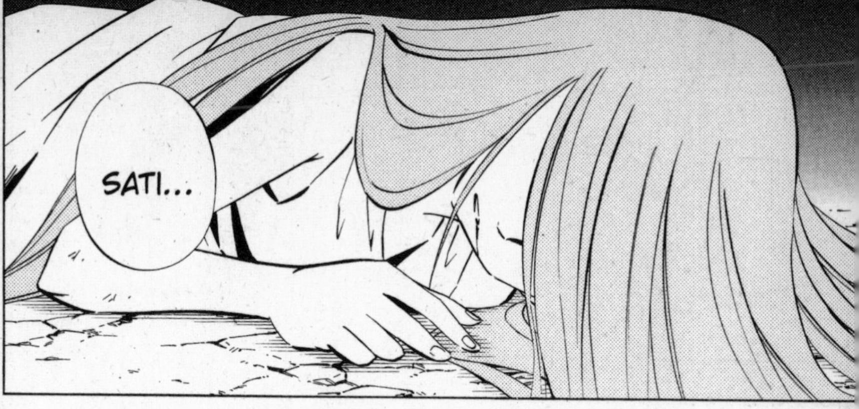
SATI...

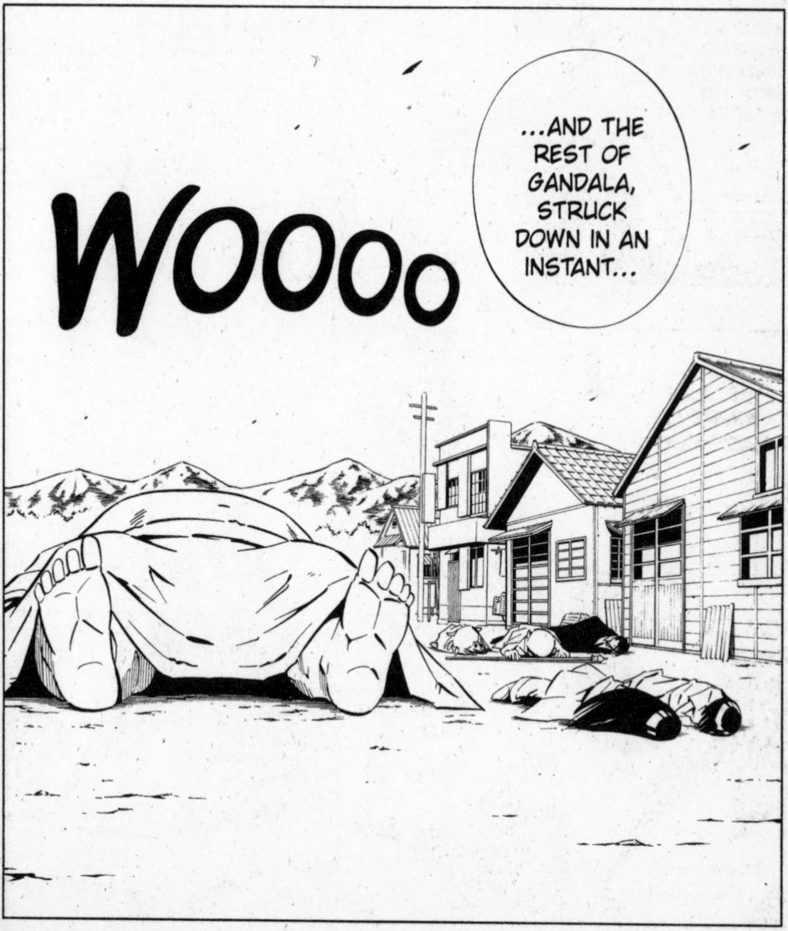
...AND THE REST OF GANDALA, STRUCK DOWN IN AN INSTANT...
WOOOO

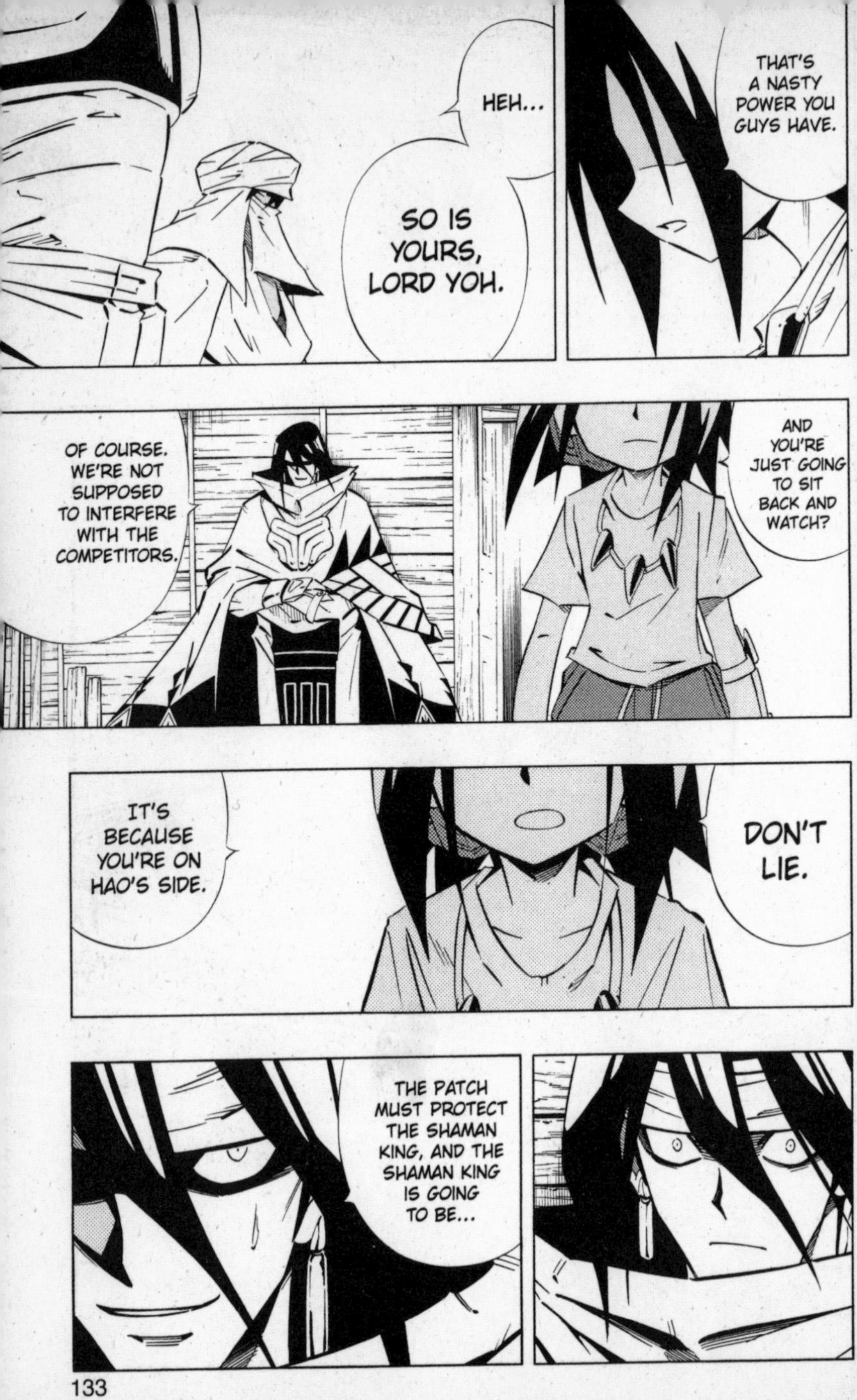
THAT'S A NASTY POWER YOU GUYS HAVE.
HEH...
SO IS YOURS, LORD YOH.
AND YOU'RE JUST GOING TO SIT BACK AND WATCH?
OF COURSE. WE'RE NOT SUPPOSED TO INTERFERE WITH THE COMPETITORS.
DON'T LIE.
IT'S BECAUSE YOU'RE ON HAO'S SIDE.
THE PATCH MUST PROTECT THE SHAMAN KING, AND THE SHAMAN KING IS GOING TO BE...

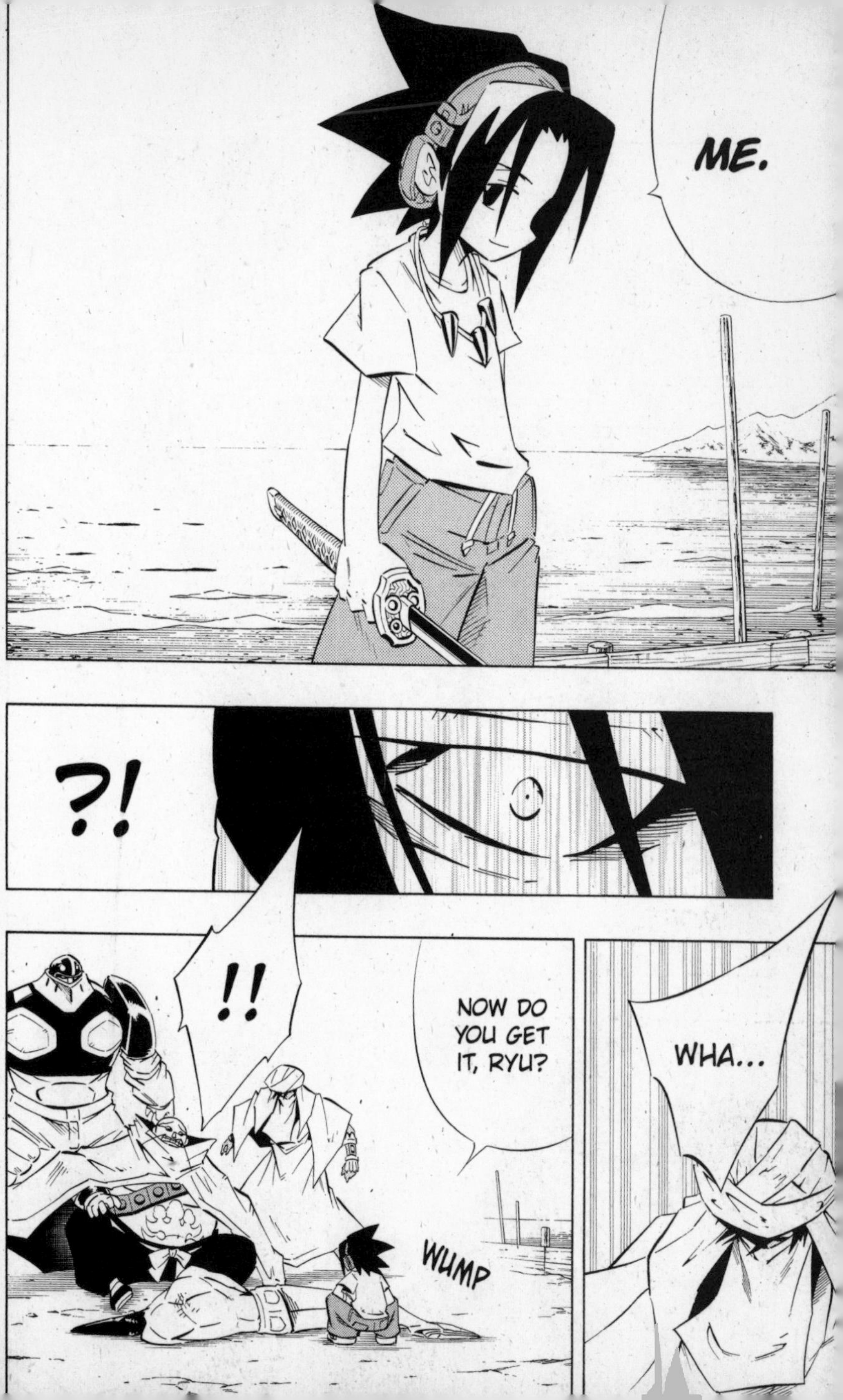
ME.
?!
WHA...
NOW DO YOU GET IT, RYU?
!!
WUMP

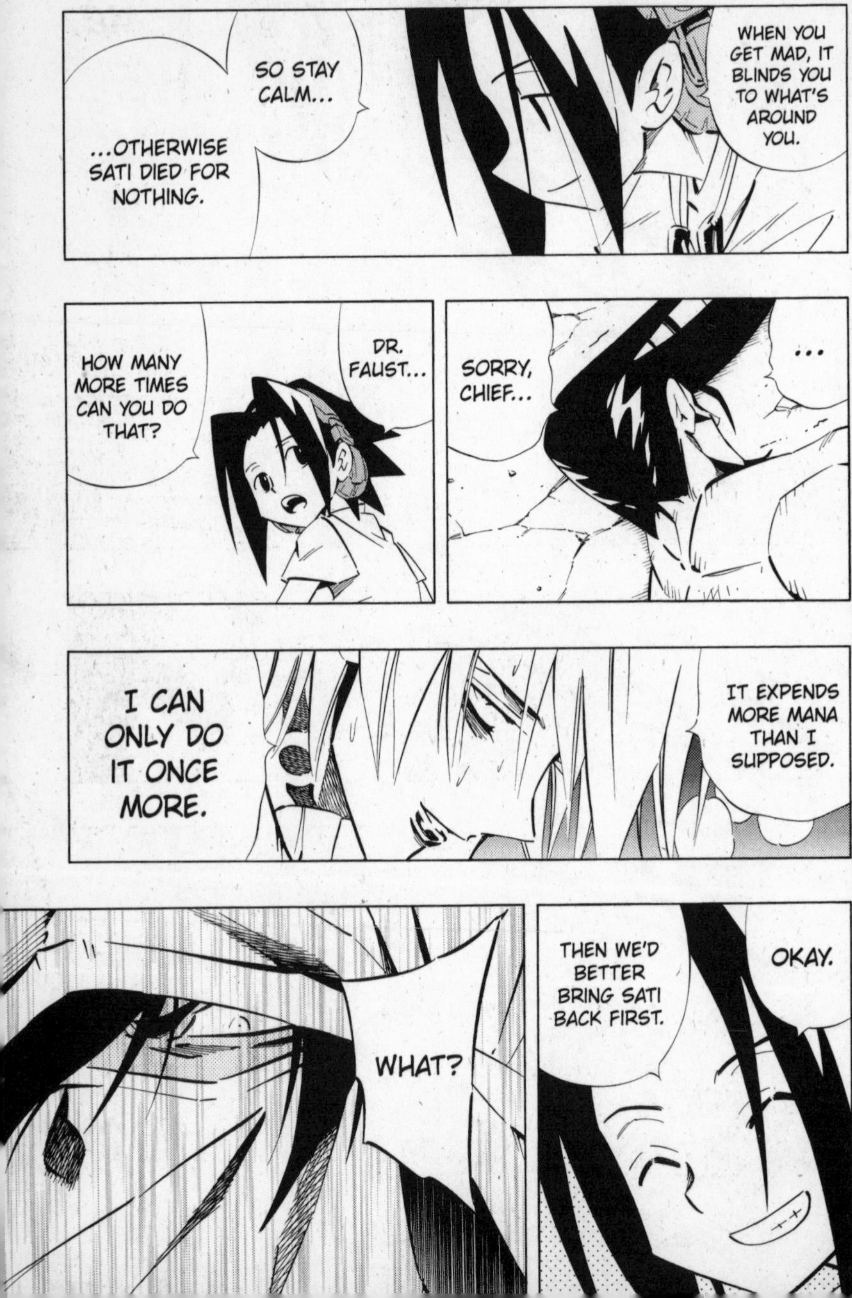
WHEN YOU GET MAD, IT BLINDS YOU TO WHAT'S AROUND YOU.
SO STAY CALM...
...OTHERWISE SATI DIED FOR NOTHING.
...
SORRY, CHIEF...
DR. FAUST...
HOW MANY MORE TIMES CAN YOU DO THAT?
IT EXPENDS MORE MANA THAN I SUPPOSED.
I CAN ONLY DO IT ONCE MORE.
OKAY.
THEN WE'D BETTER BRING SATI BACK FIRST.
WHAT?

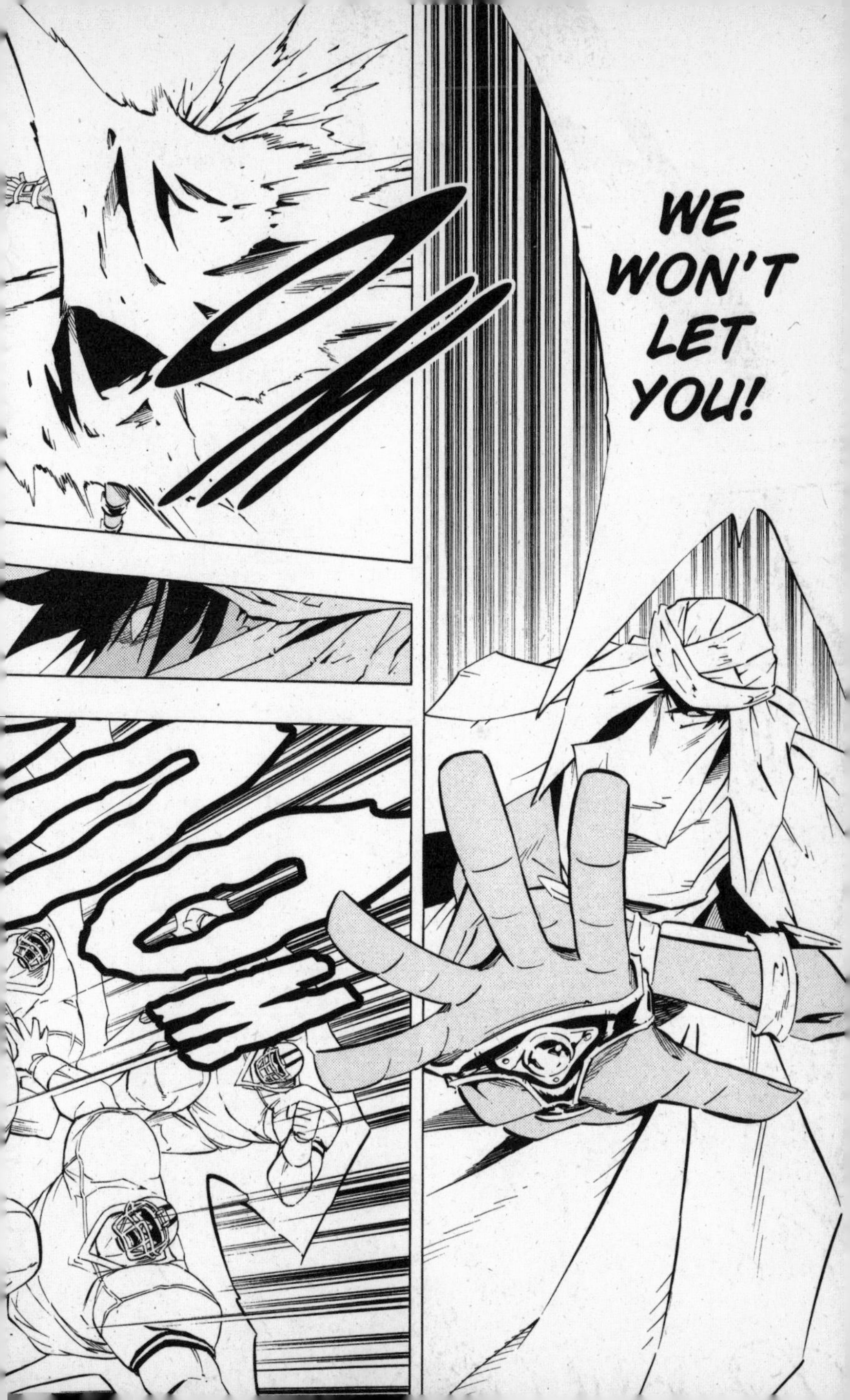
WE WON'T LET YOU!

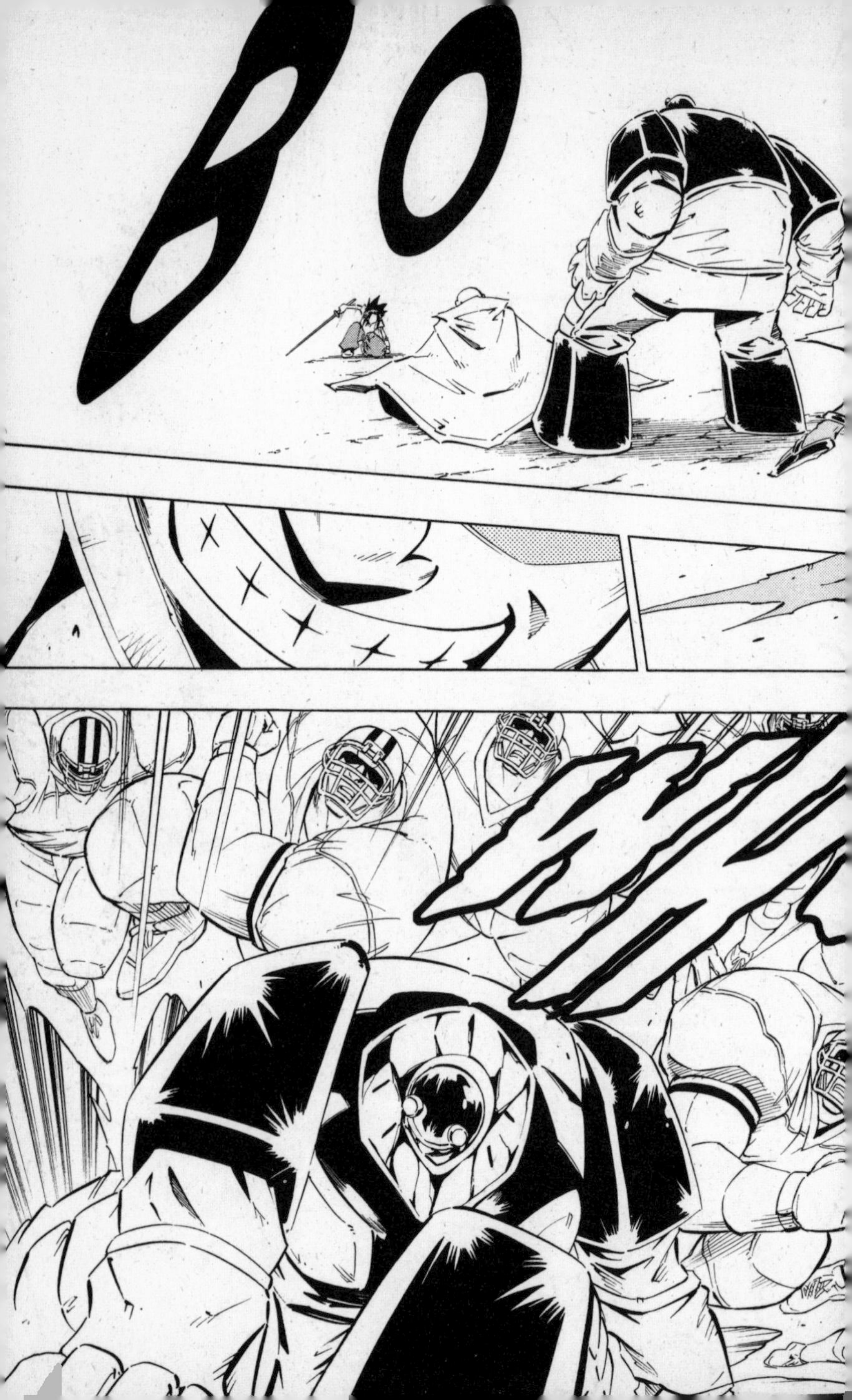
BO

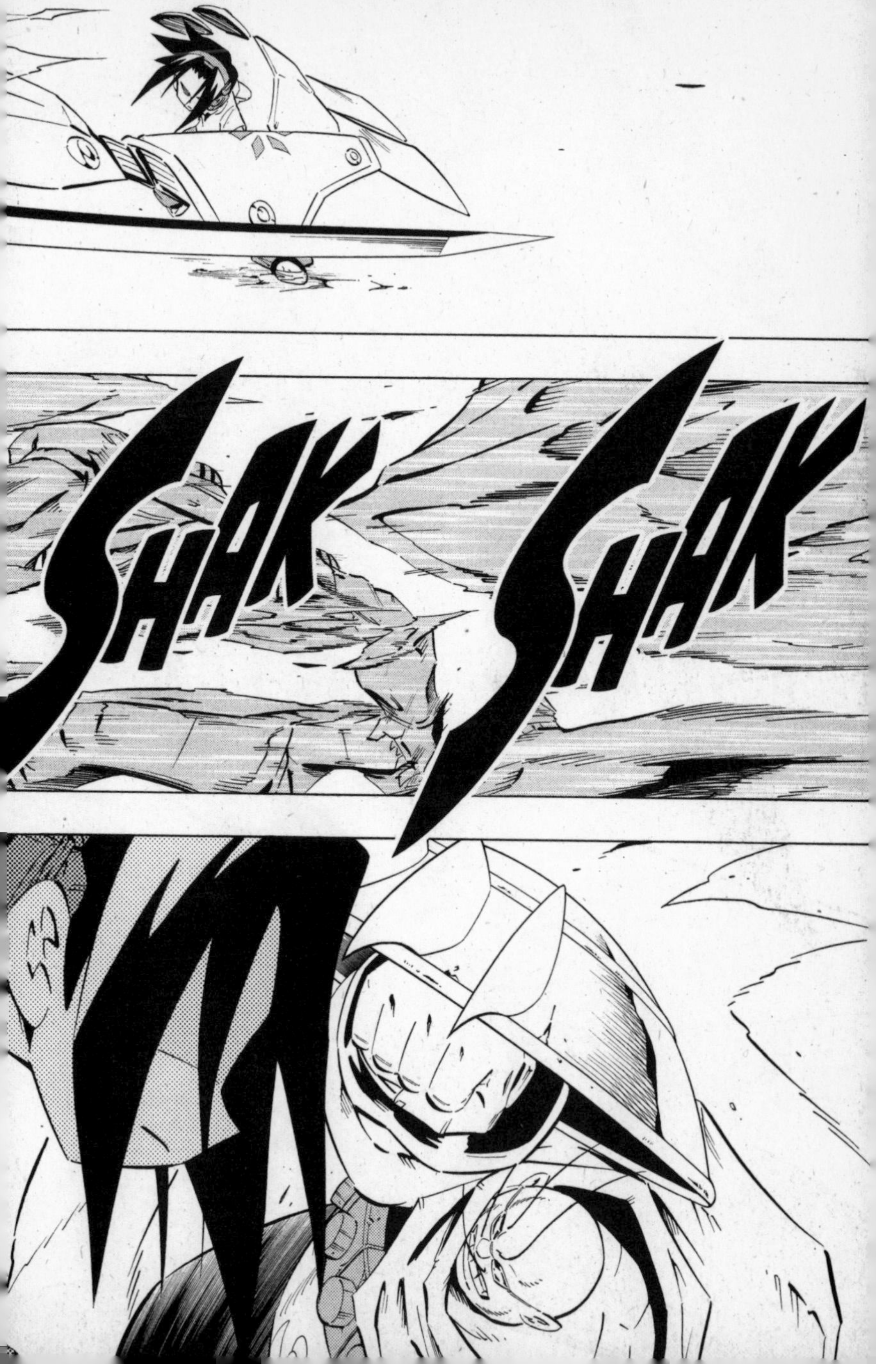
SHAK SHAK

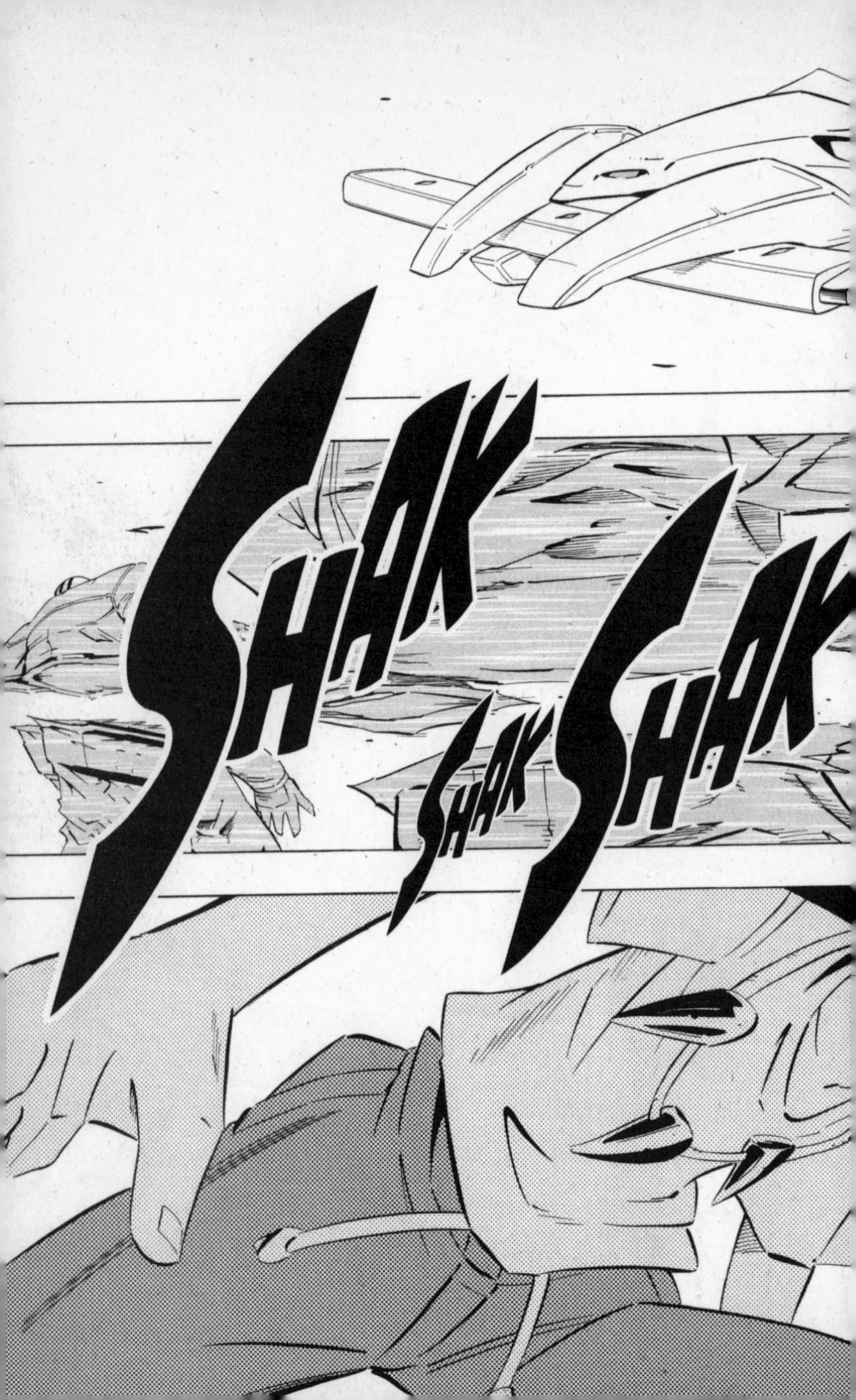
SHAK
SHAK
SHAK

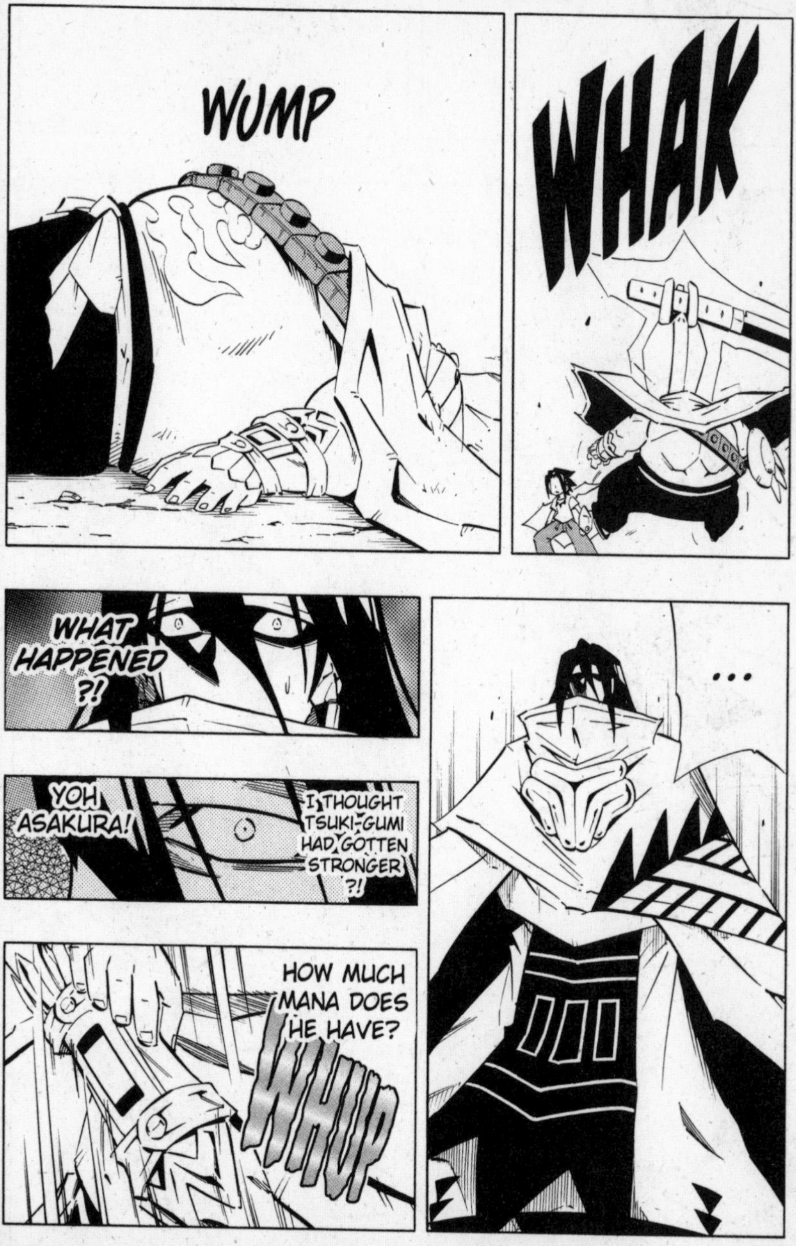

WHAK
WUMP
...
WHAT HAPPENED ?!
I THOUGHT TSUKI-GUMI HAD GOTTEN STRONGER ?!
YOH ASAKURA!
HOW MUCH MANA DOES HE HAVE?
WHIP

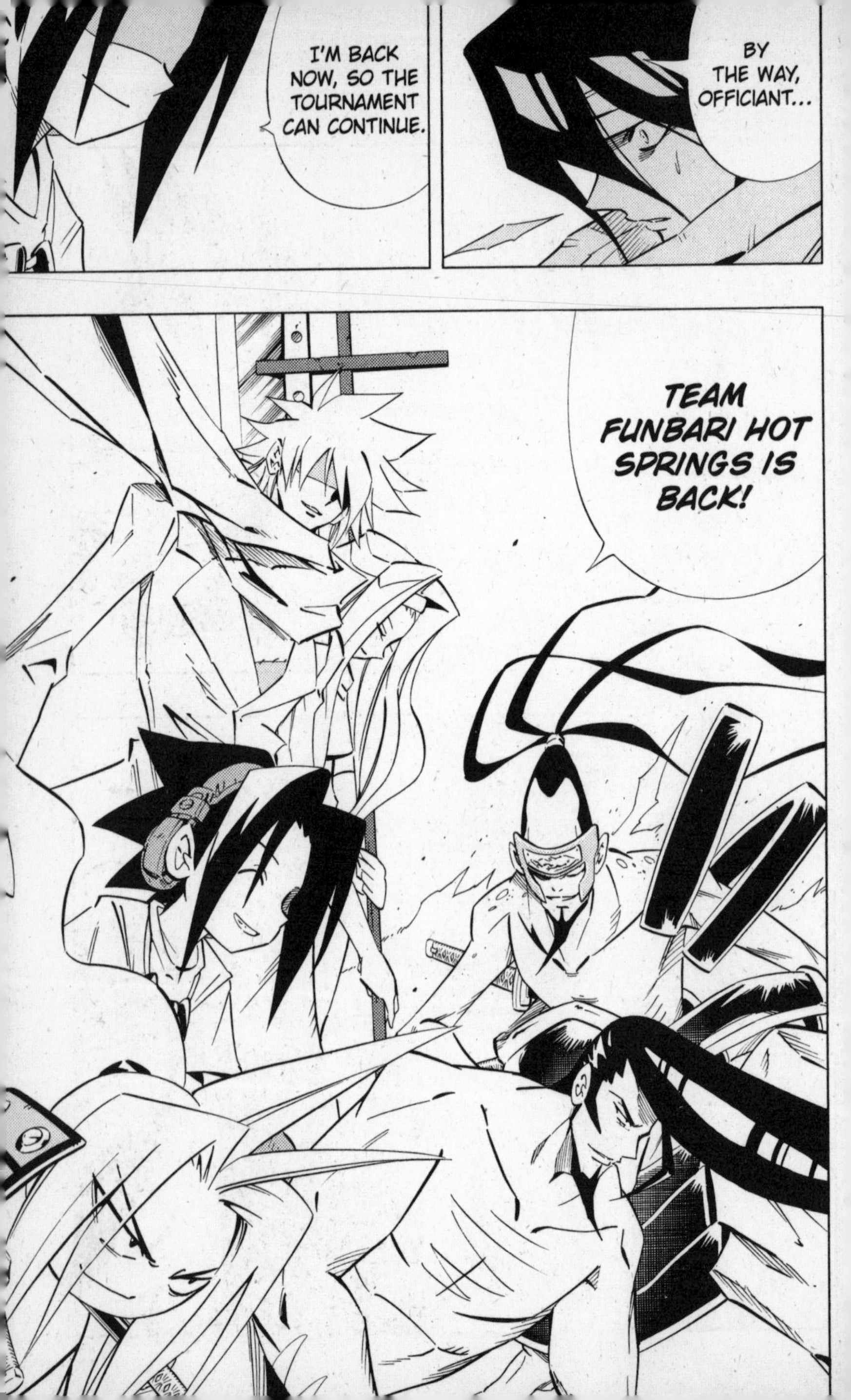
BY THE WAY, OFFICIANT...
I'M BACK NOW, SO THE TOURNAMENT CAN CONTINUE.
TEAM FUNBARI HOT SPRINGS IS BACK!

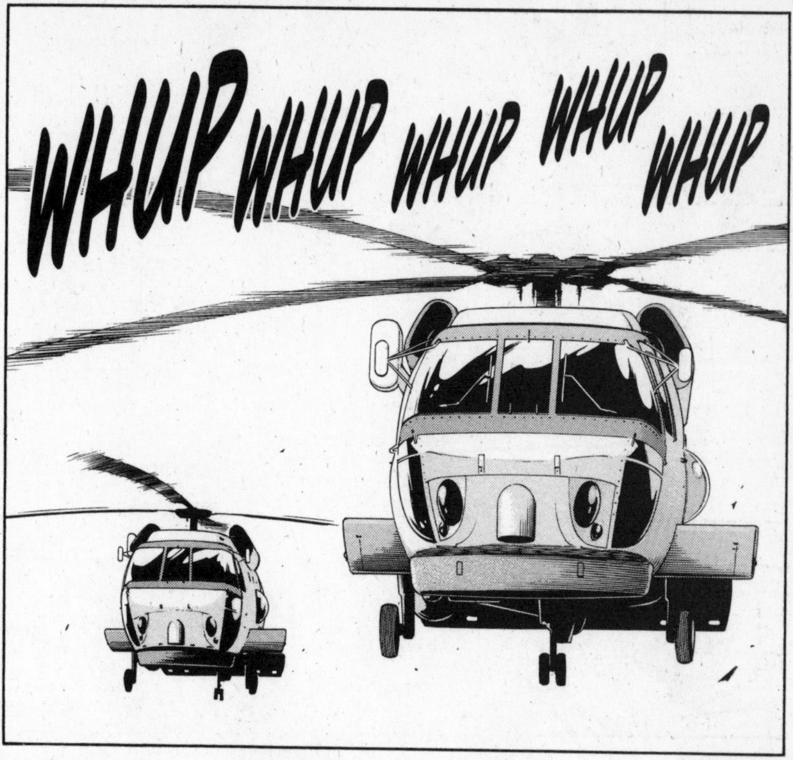
WHUP WHUP WHUP WHUP WHUP
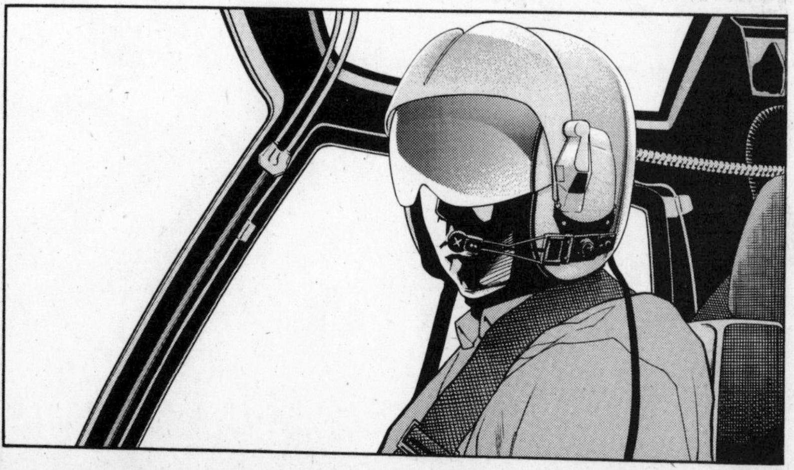

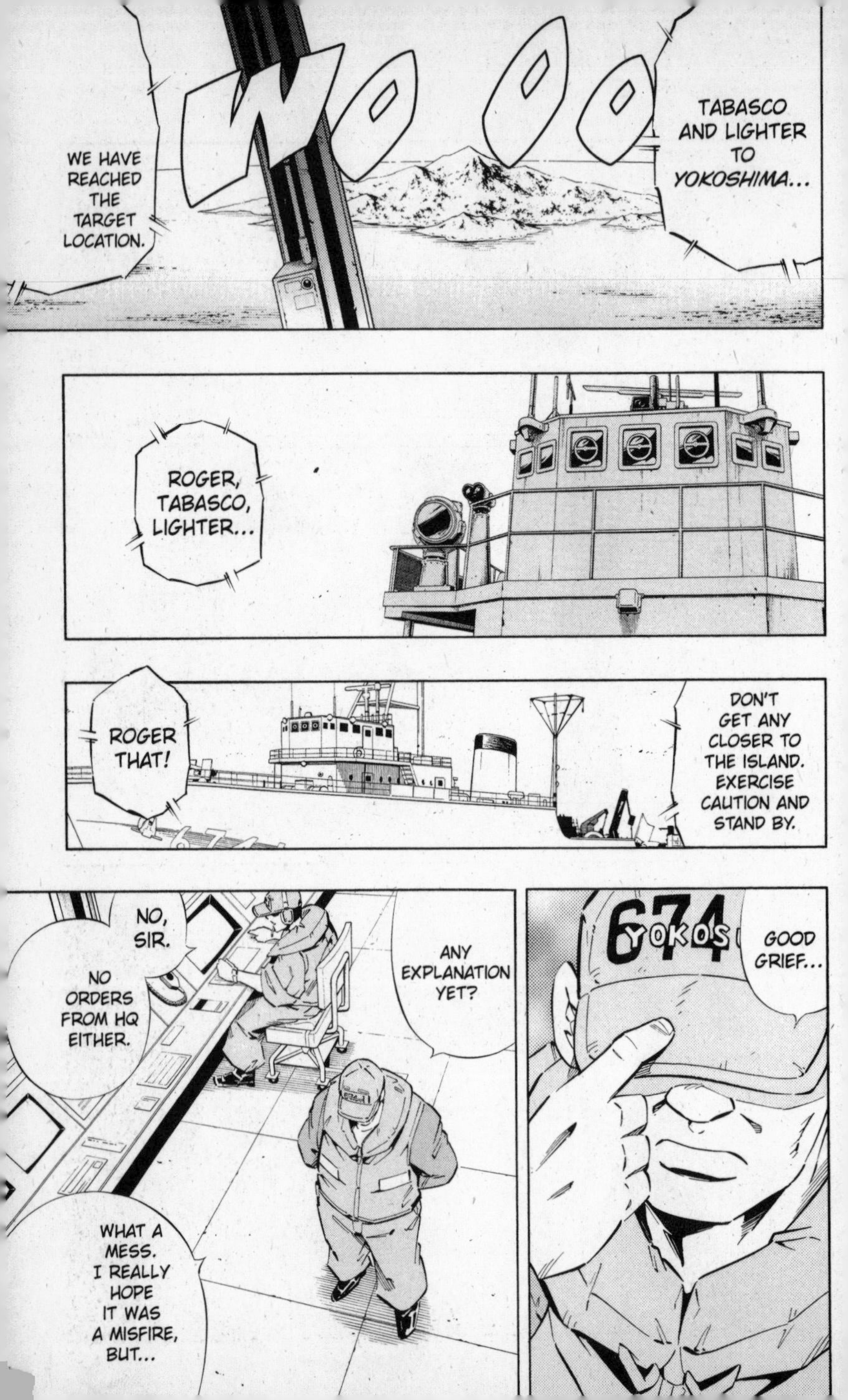
TABASCO AND LIGHTER TO YOKOSHIMA...
WOOO
WE HAVE REACHED THE TARGET LOCATION.
ROGER, TABASCO, LIGHTER...
DON'T GET ANY CLOSER TO THE ISLAND. EXERCISE CAUTION AND STAND BY.
ROGER THAT!
674 YOKOS
GOOD GRIEF...
ANY EXPLANATION YET?
NO, SIR.
NO ORDERS FROM HQ EITHER.
WHAT A MESS. I REALLY HOPE IT WAS A MISFIRE, BUT...

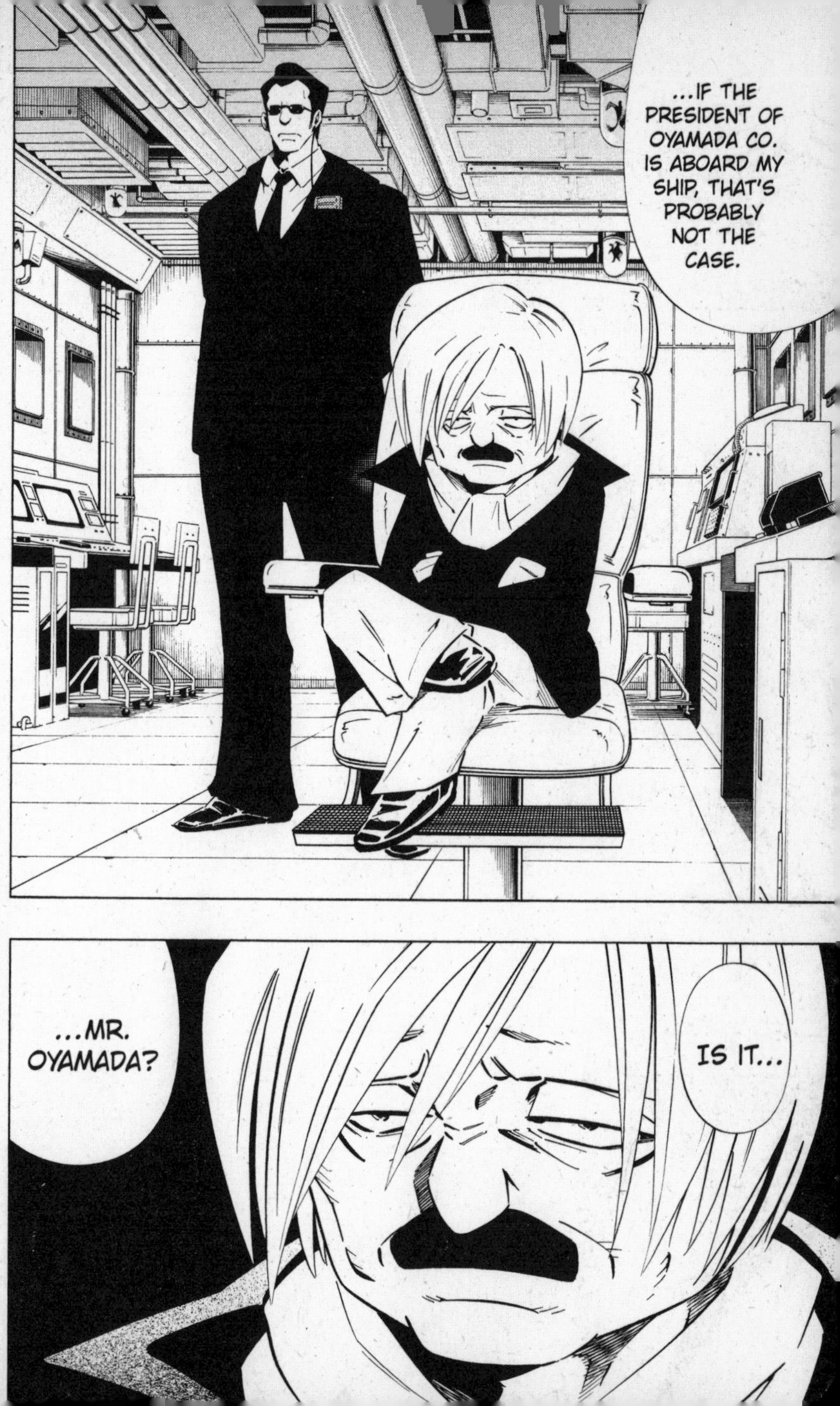
...IF THE PRESIDENT OF OYAMADA CO. IS ABOARD MY SHIP, THAT'S PROBABLY NOT THE CASE.
IS IT...
...MR. OYAMADA?

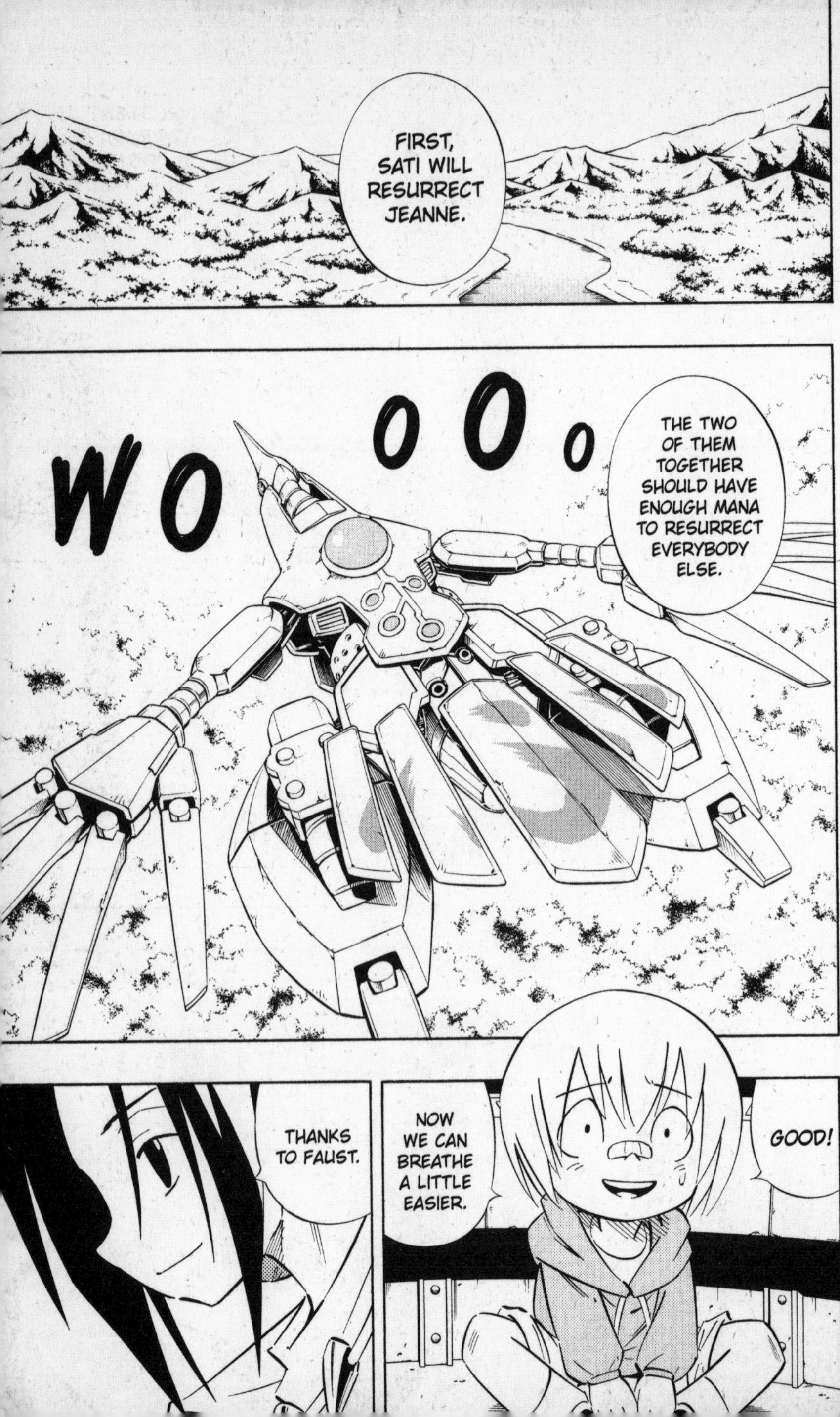
FIRST, SATI WILL RESURRECT JEANNE.
THE TWO OF THEM TOGETHER SHOULD HAVE ENOUGH MANA TO RESURRECT EVERYBODY ELSE.
WOOOO
GOOD!
NOW WE CAN BREATHE A LITTLE EASIER.
THANKS TO FAUST.

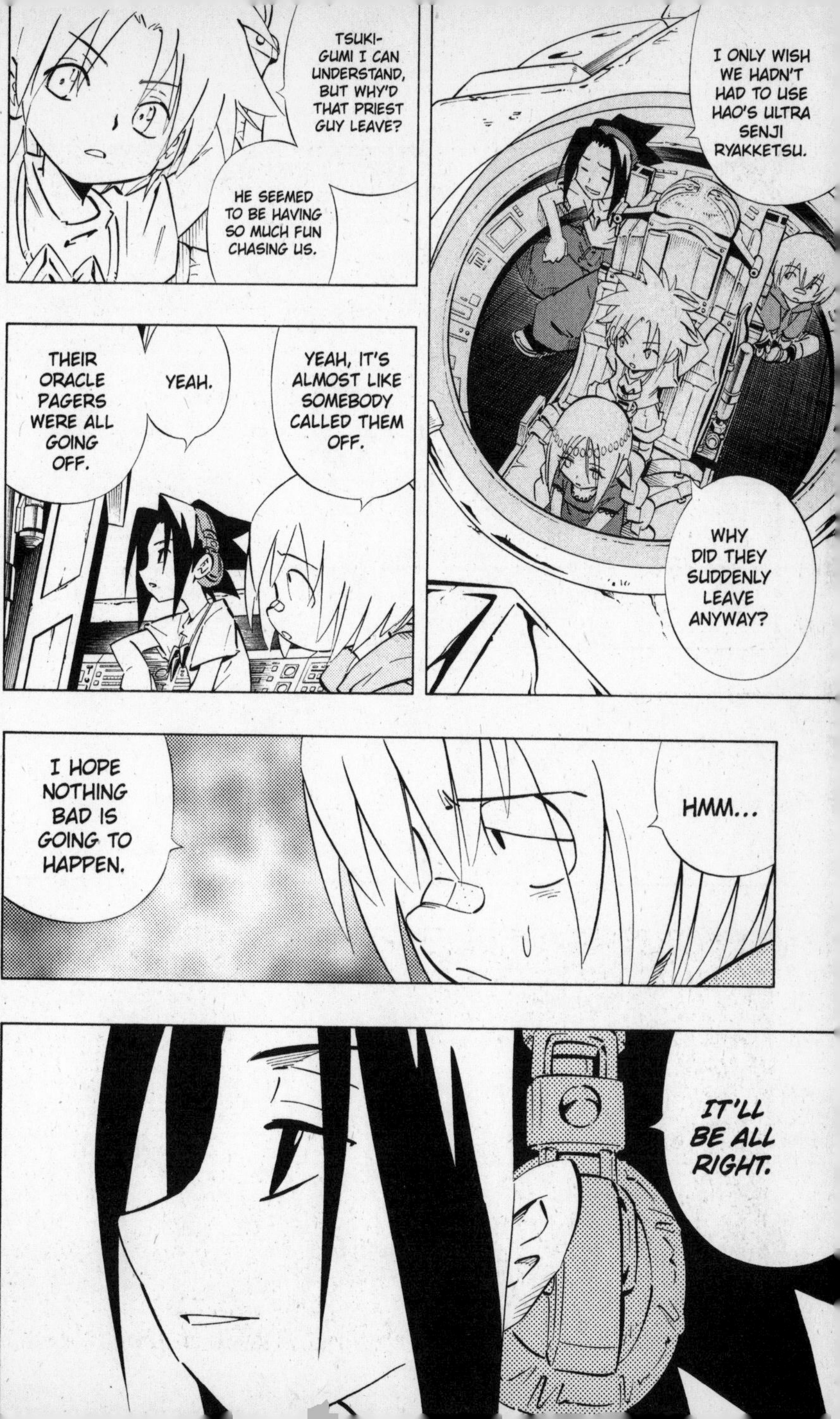
I ONLY WISH WE HADN'T HAD TO USE HAO'S ULTRA SENJI RYAKKETSU.
WHY DID THEY SUDDENLY LEAVE ANYWAY?
TSUKI-GUMI I CAN UNDERSTAND, BUT WHY'D THAT PRIEST GUY LEAVE?
HE SEEMED TO BE HAVING SO MUCH FUN CHASING US.
YEAH, IT'S ALMOST LIKE SOMEBODY CALLED THEM OFF.
YEAH.
THEIR ORACLE PAGERS WERE ALL GOING OFF.
HMM...
I HOPE NOTHING BAD IS GOING TO HAPPEN.
IT'LL BE ALL RIGHT.

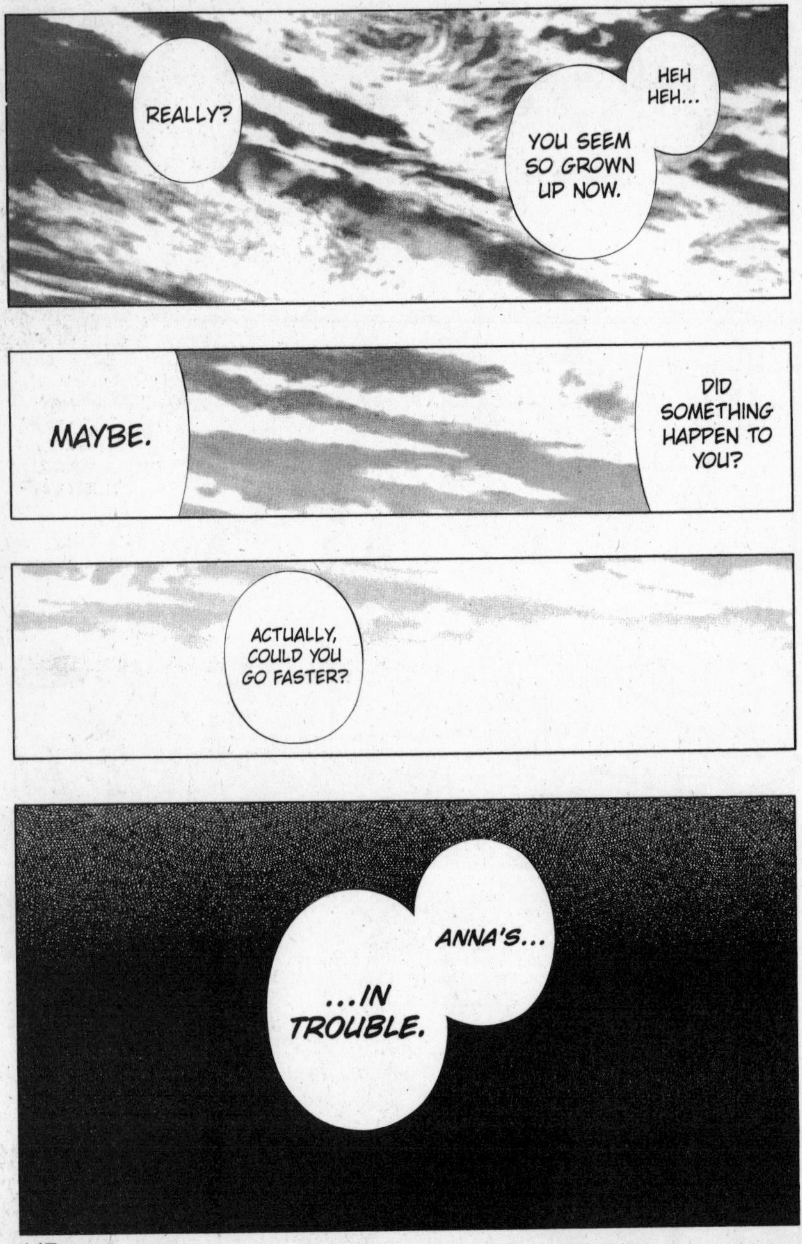
HEH HEH...
YOU SEEM SO GROWN UP NOW.
REALLY?
DID SOMETHING HAPPEN TO YOU?
MAYBE.
ACTUALLY, COULD YOU GO FASTER?
ANNA'S...
...IN TROUBLE.

SHAMAN KING CHARACTER FILE No.145

エリザ オペリーレン
ELIZA OPERIEREN

2001
(JAN)

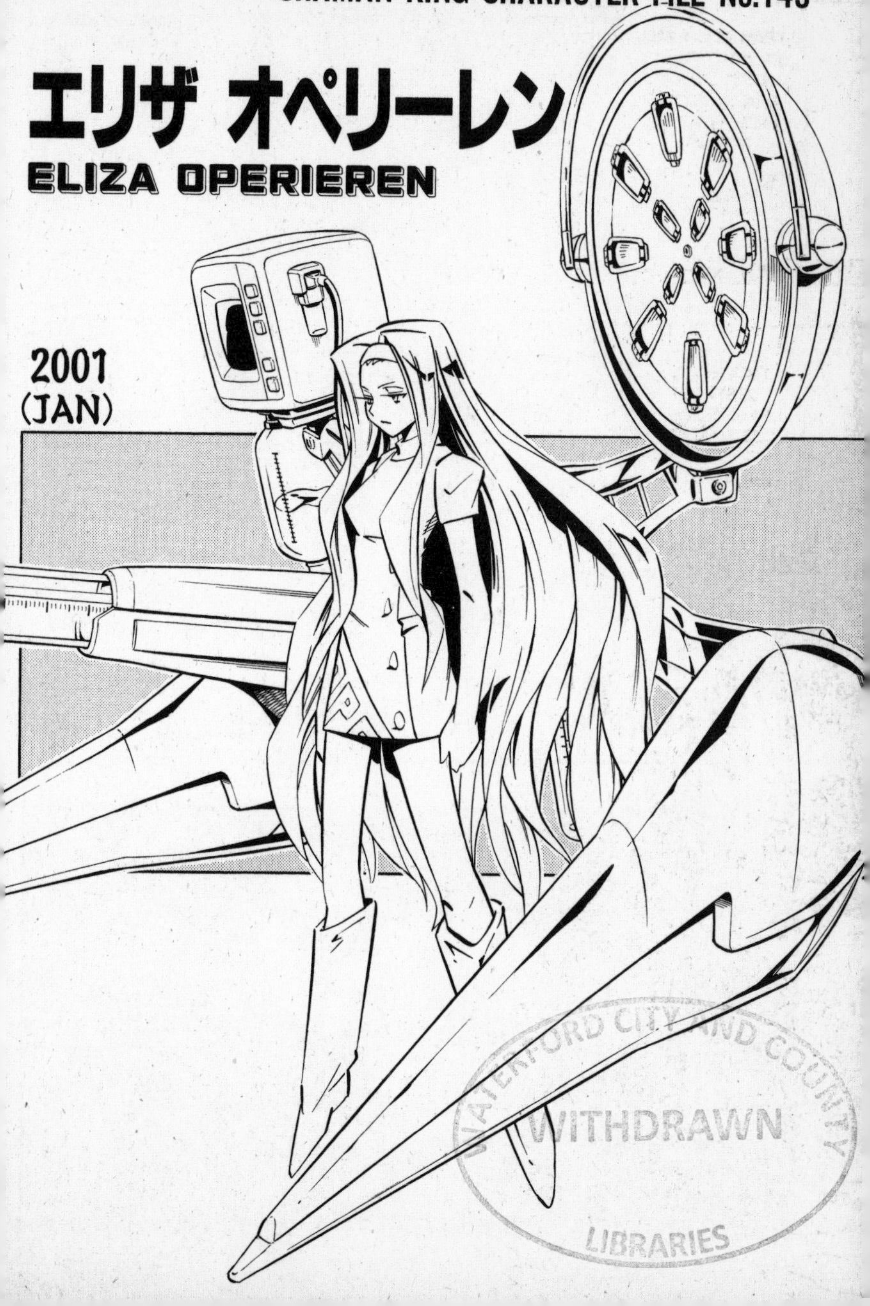

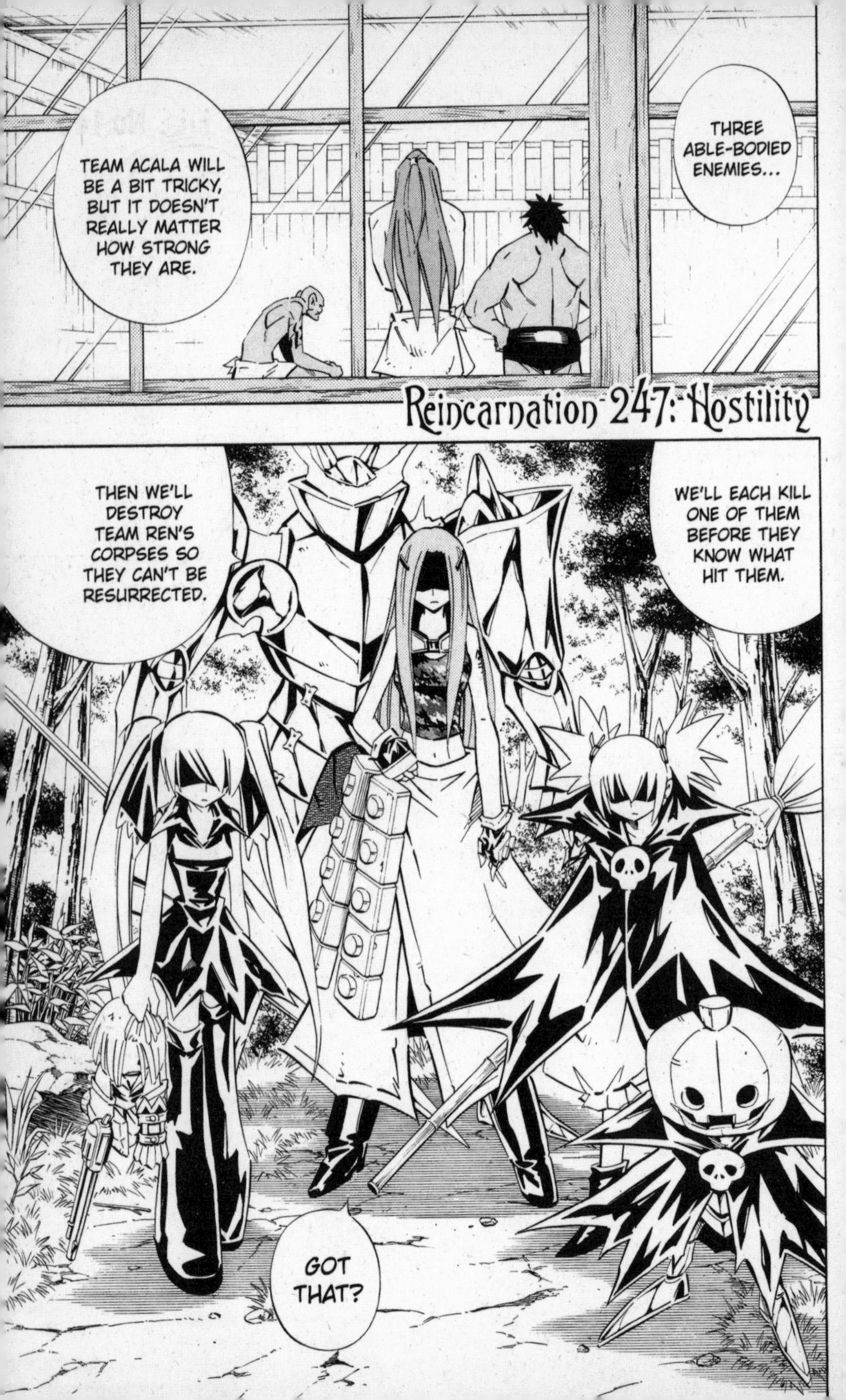
THREE ABLE-BODIED ENEMIES...
TEAM ACALA WILL BE A BIT TRICKY, BUT IT DOESN'T REALLY MATTER HOW STRONG THEY ARE.
Reincarnation 247: Hostility
WE'LL EACH KILL ONE OF THEM BEFORE THEY KNOW WHAT HIT THEM.
THEN WE'LL DESTROY TEAM REN'S CORPSES SO THEY CAN'T BE RESURRECTED.
GOT THAT?

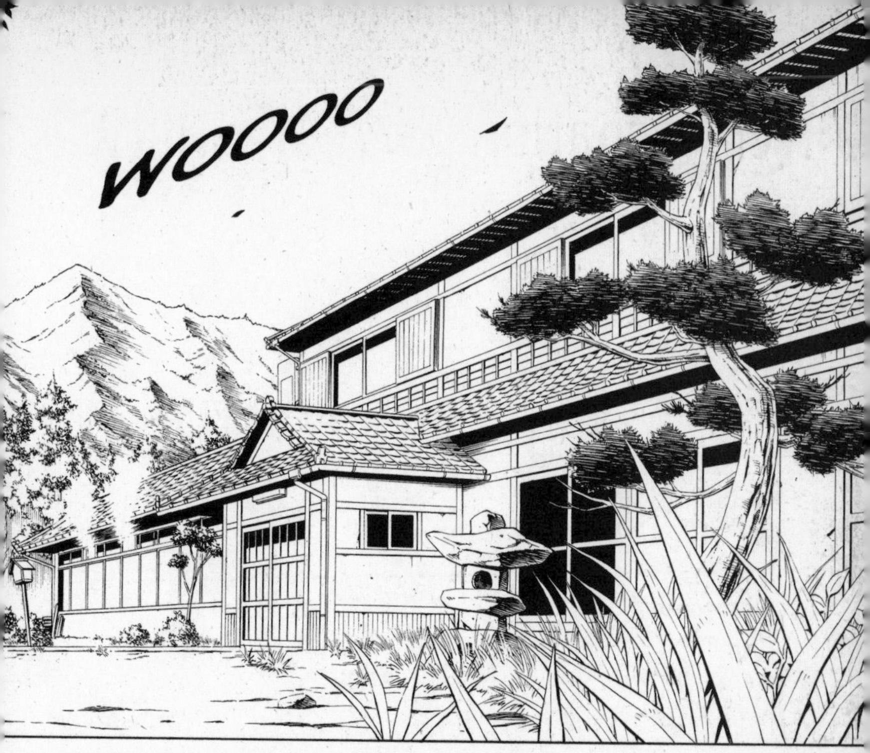
WOOOO
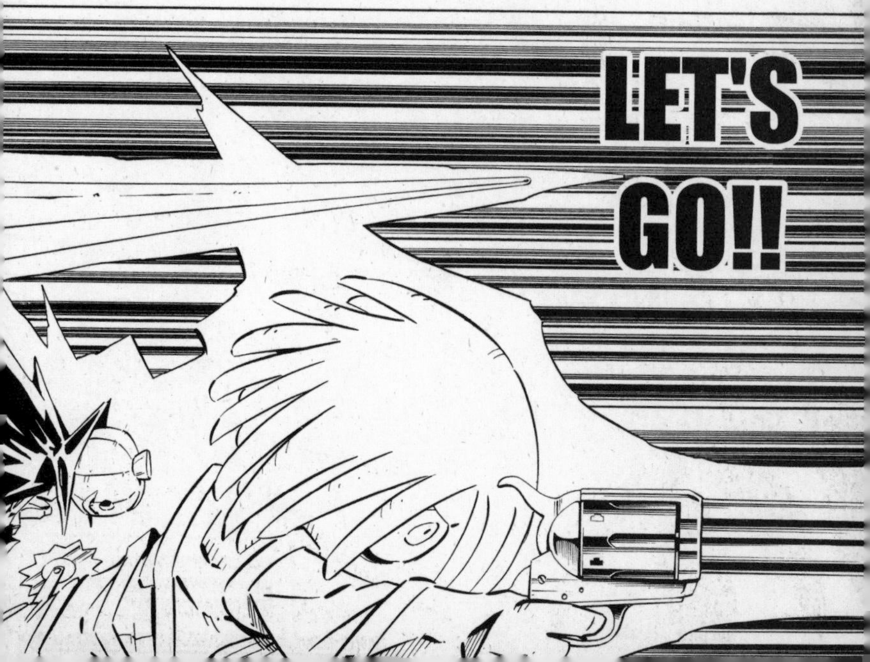
LET'S GO!!

Reincarnation 247: Hostility

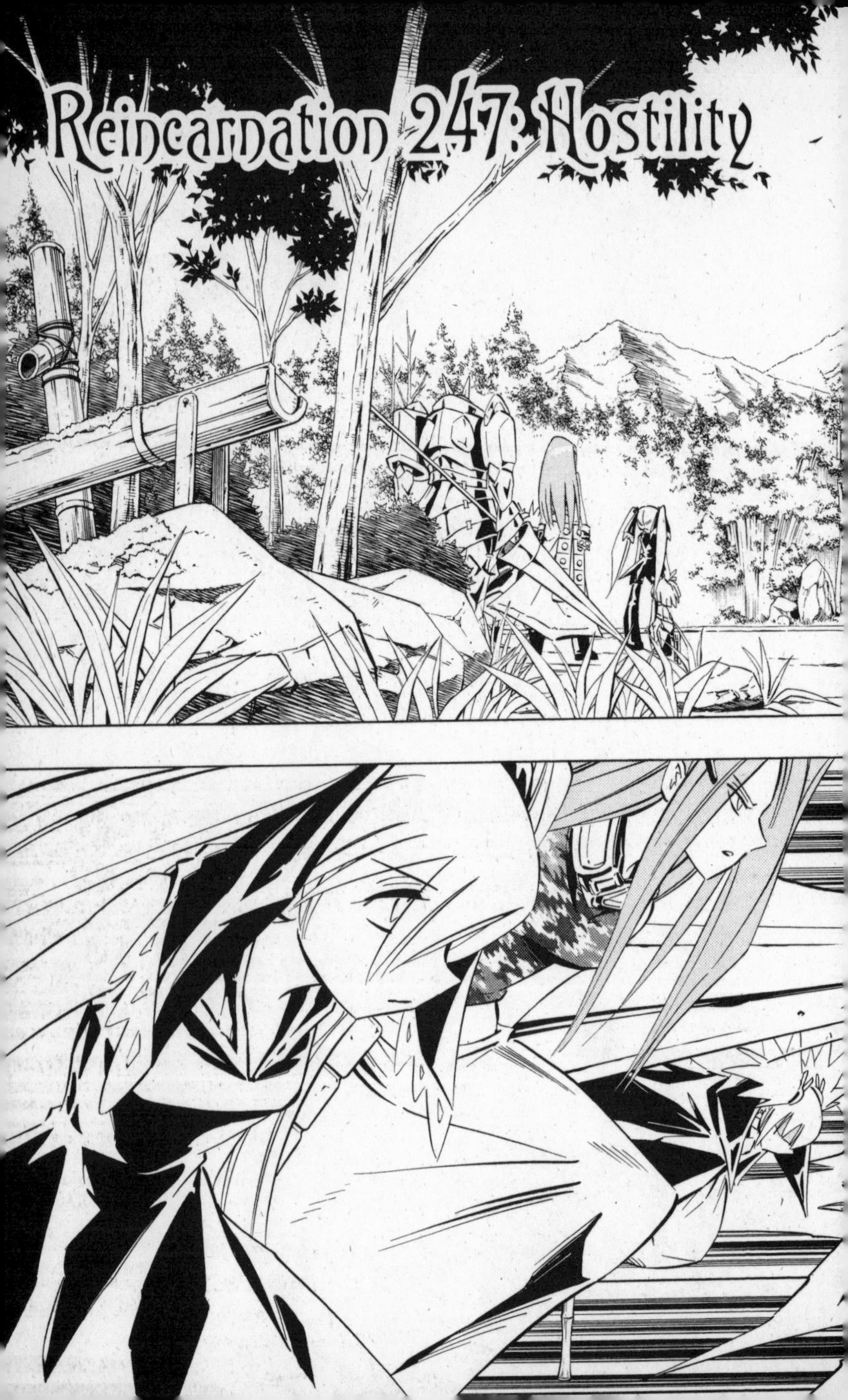

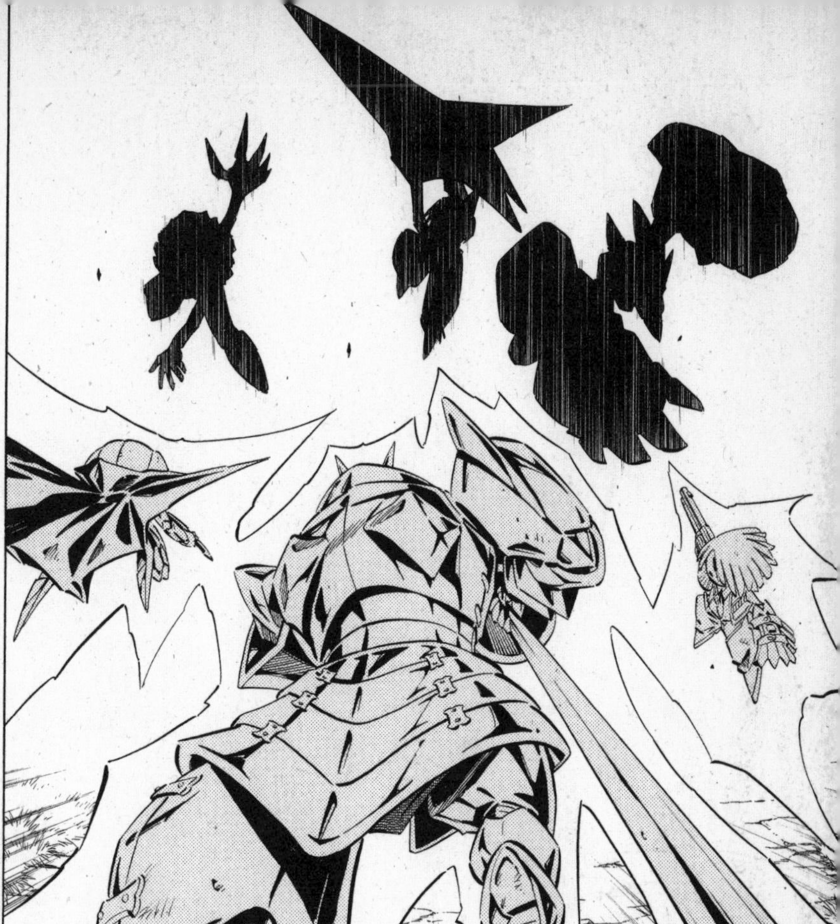

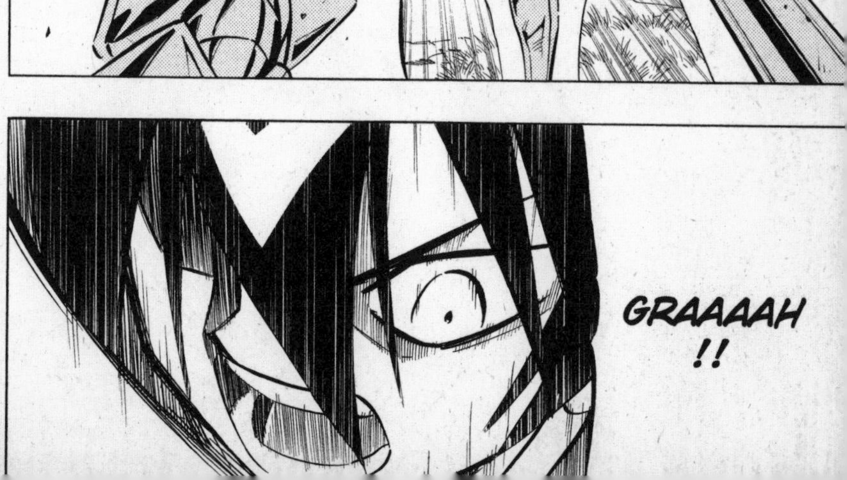
GRAAAAH
!!

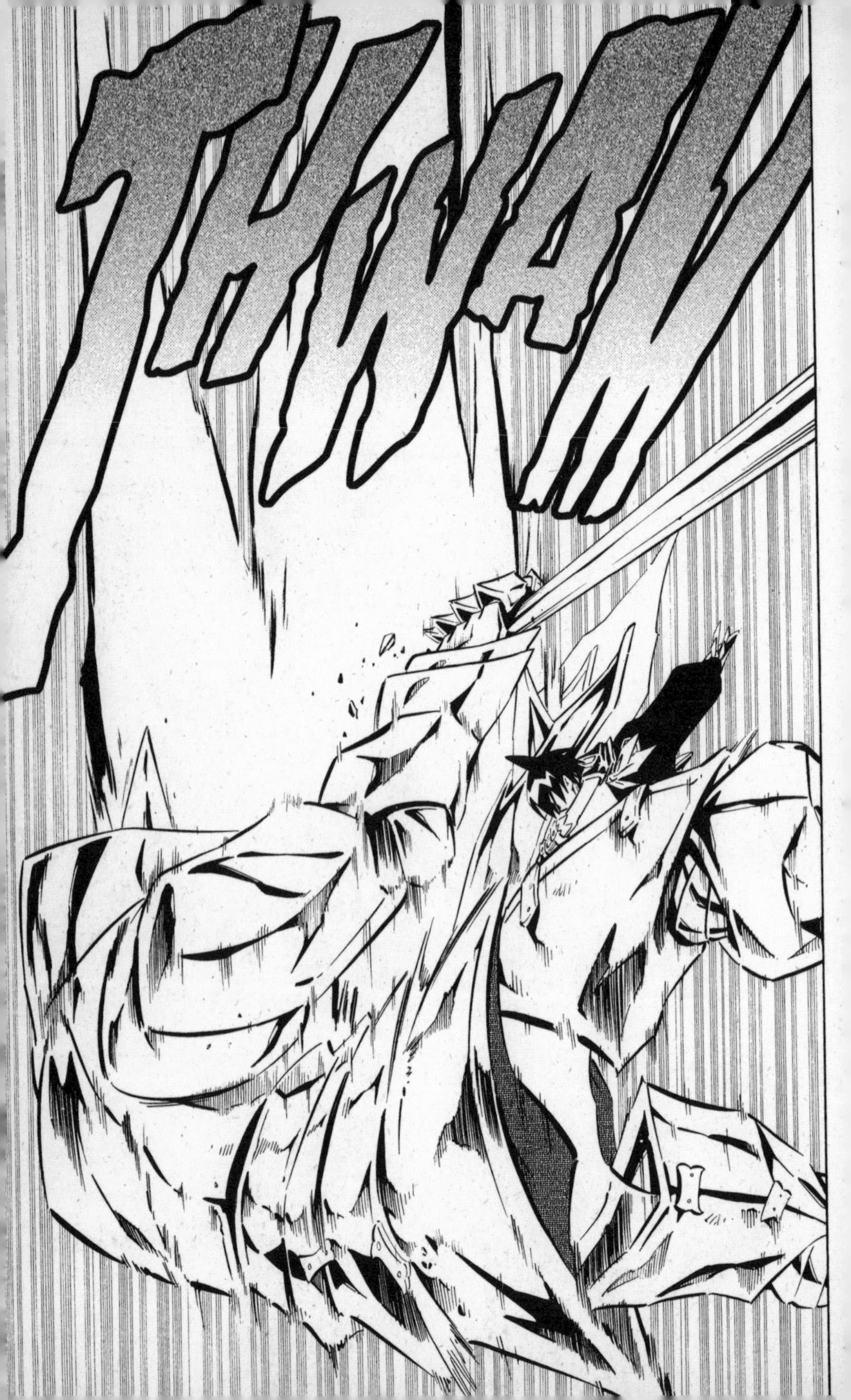
THWAM

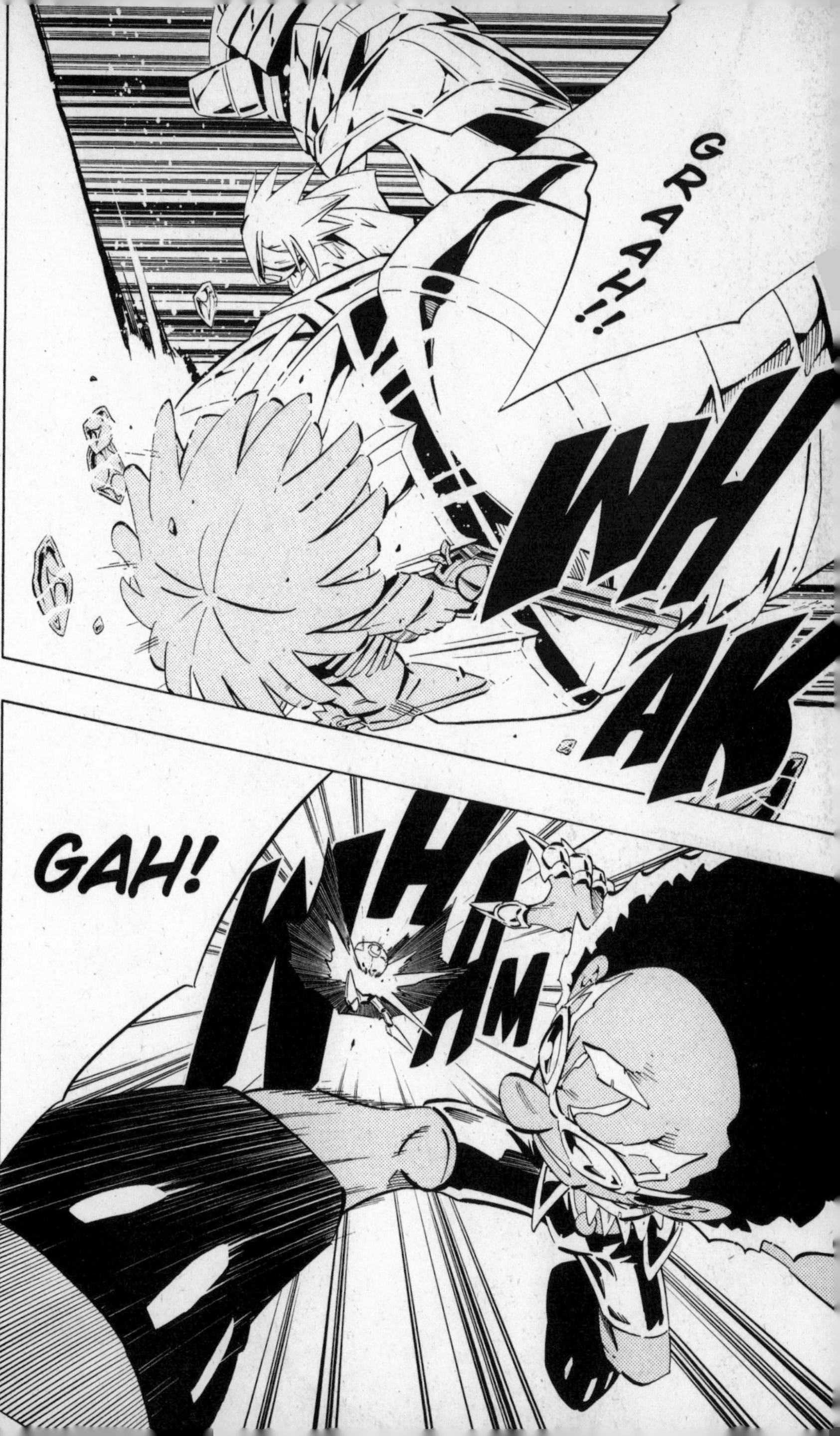
GRAAH!!
WHAK
GAH!
WHAM

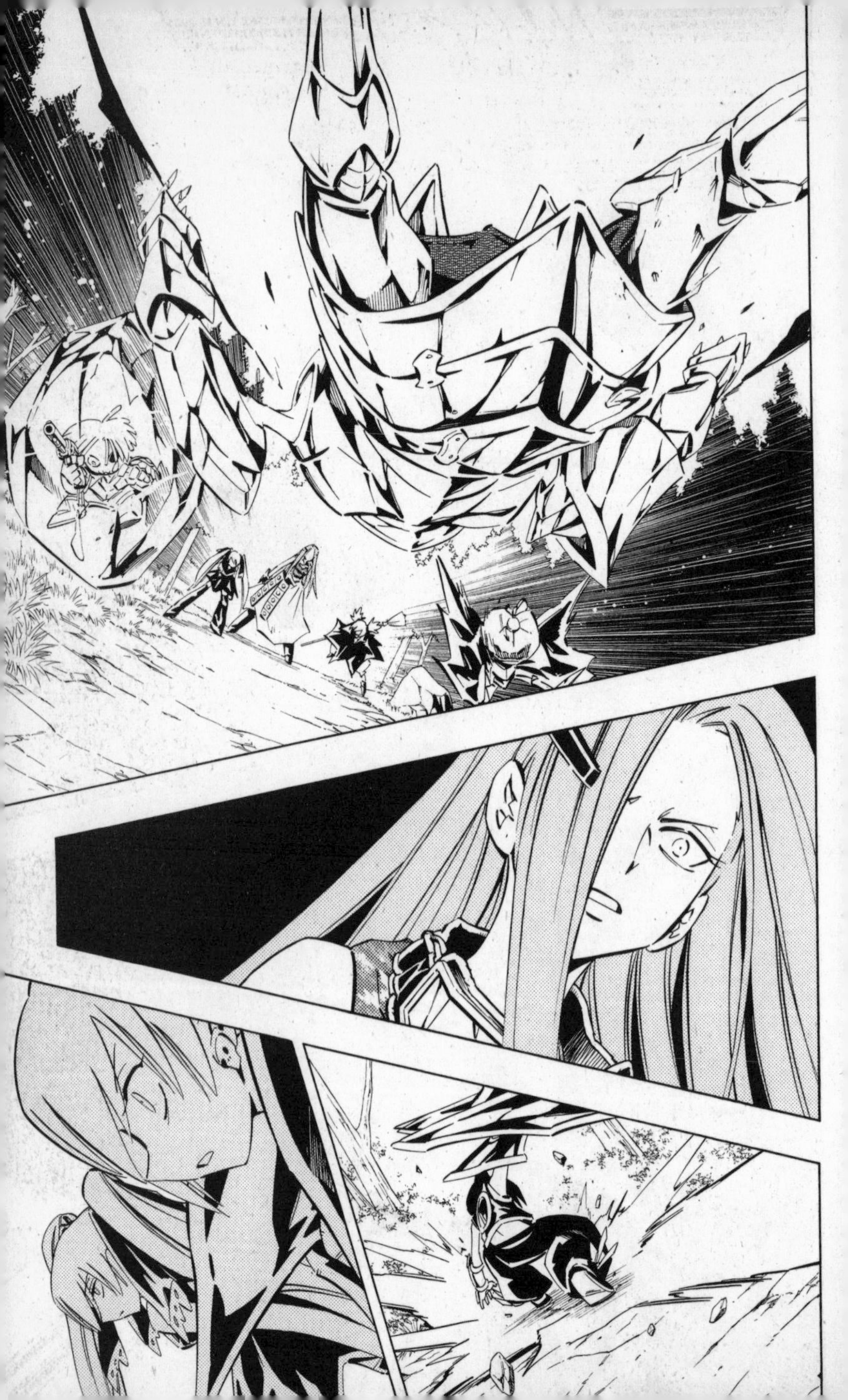

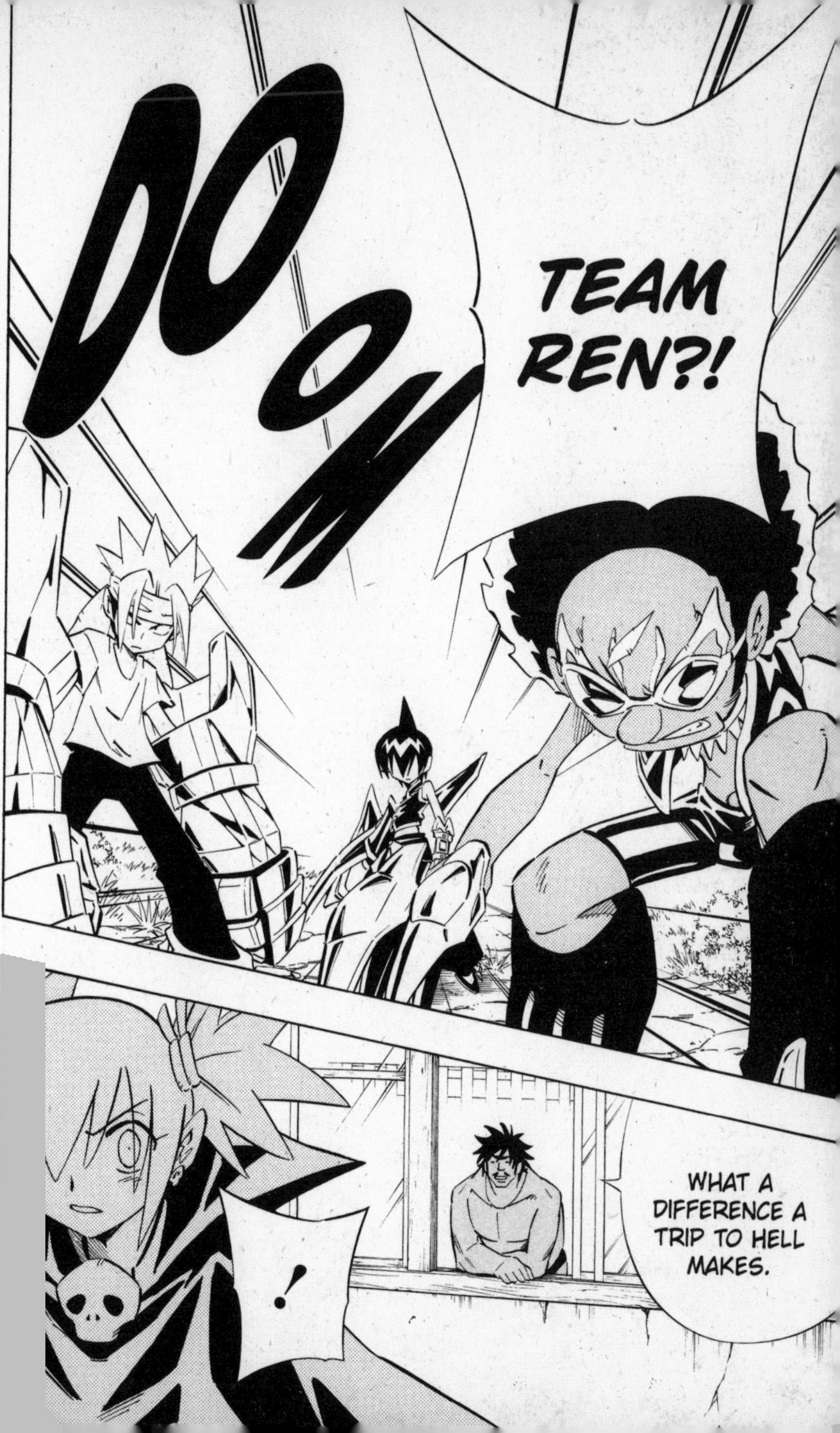
TEAM REN?!
DOOOM
WHAT A DIFFERENCE A TRIP TO HELL MAKES.
!

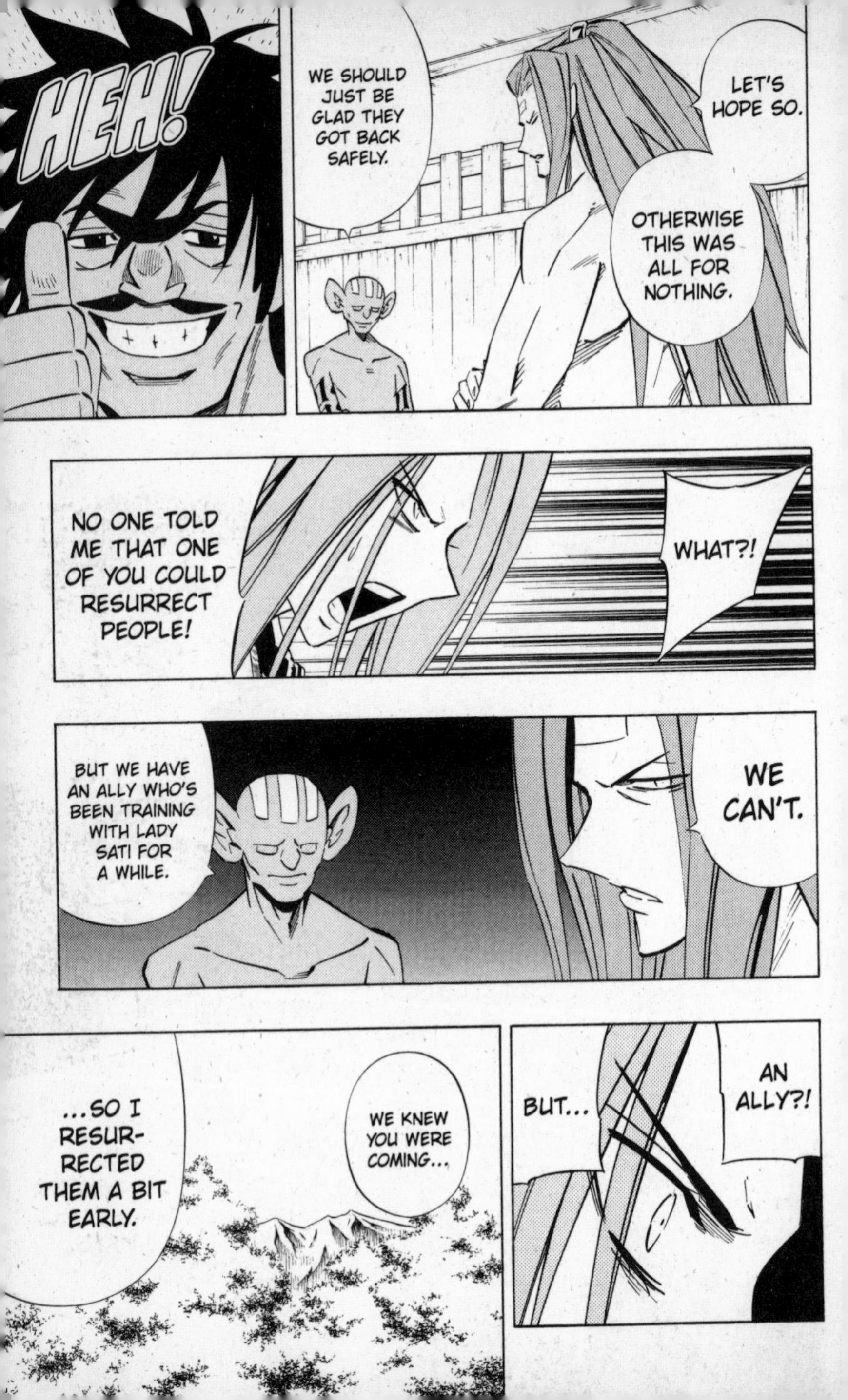
WE SHOULD JUST BE GLAD THEY GOT BACK SAFELY.
LET'S HOPE SO.
OTHERWISE THIS WAS ALL FOR NOTHING.
HEH!
WHAT?!
NO ONE TOLD ME THAT ONE OF YOU COULD RESURRECT PEOPLE!
WE CAN'T.
BUT WE HAVE AN ALLY WHO'S BEEN TRAINING WITH LADY SATI FOR A WHILE.
AN ALLY?!
BUT...
WE KNEW YOU WERE COMING...
...SO I RESURRECTED THEM A BIT EARLY.

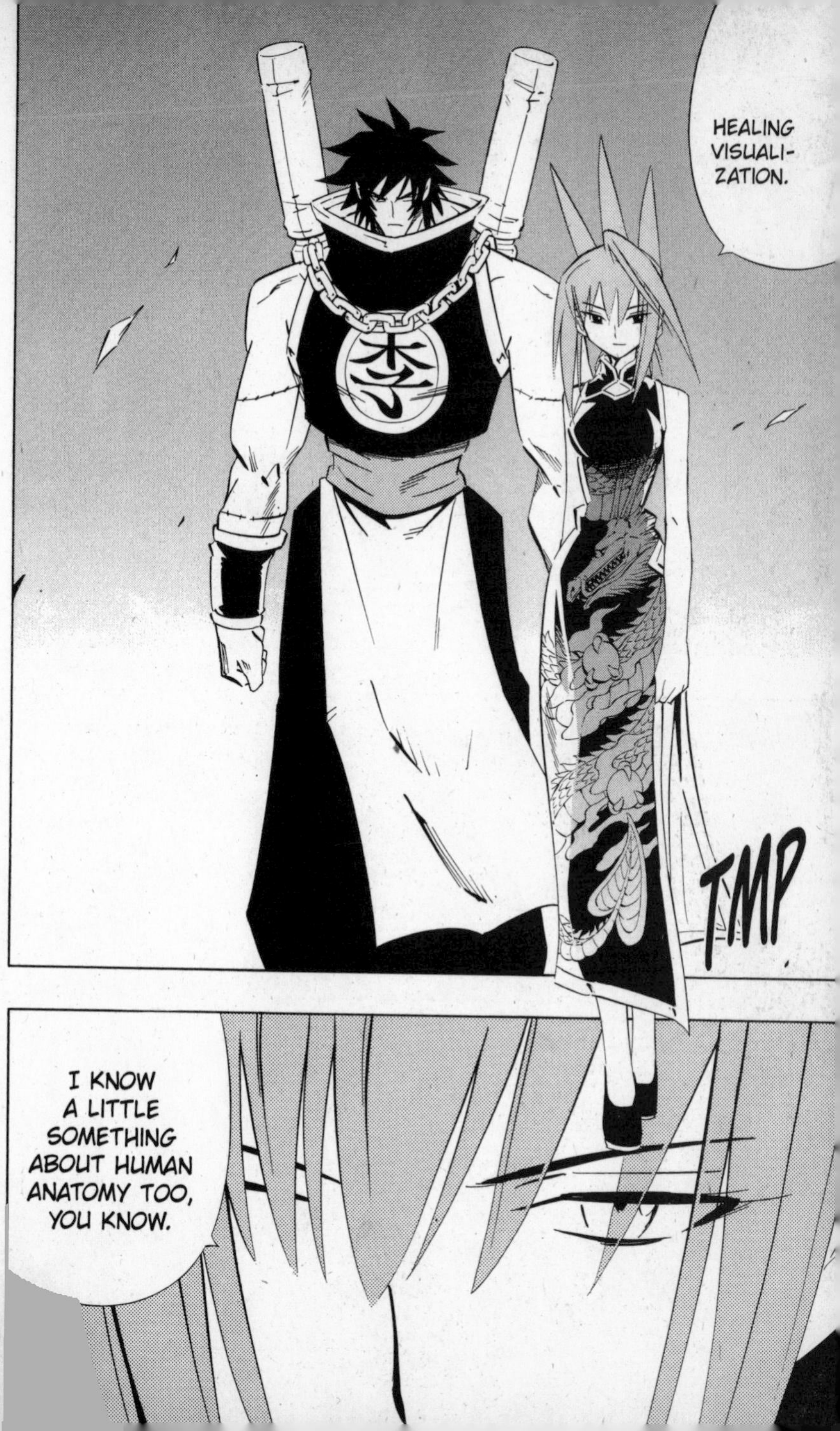
HEALING VISUALI-ZATION.
TMP
I KNOW A LITTLE SOMETHING ABOUT HUMAN ANATOMY TOO, YOU KNOW.

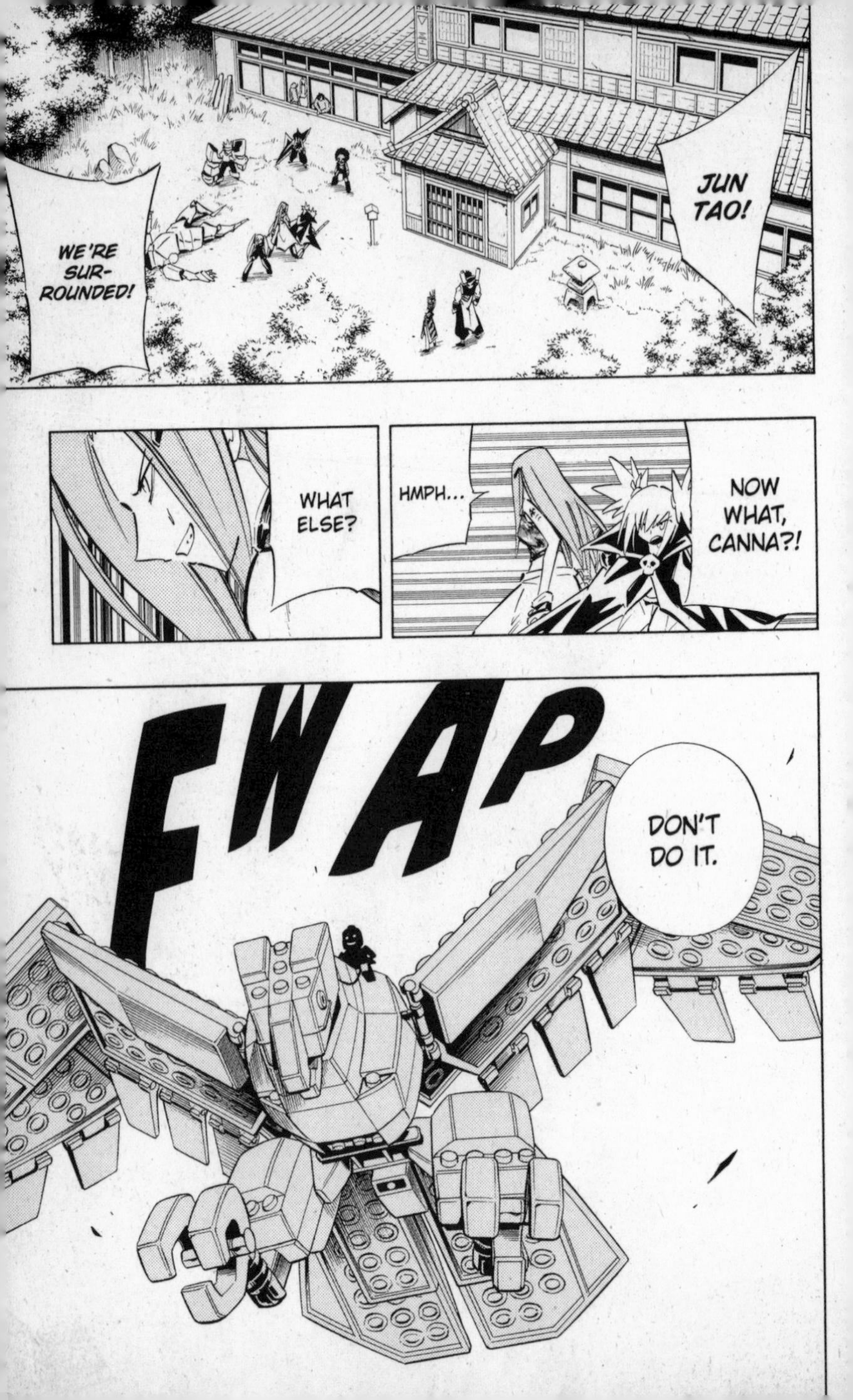
JUN TAO!
WE'RE SUR-ROUNDED!
NOW WHAT, CANNA?!
HMPH...
WHAT ELSE?
FWAP
DON'T DO IT.

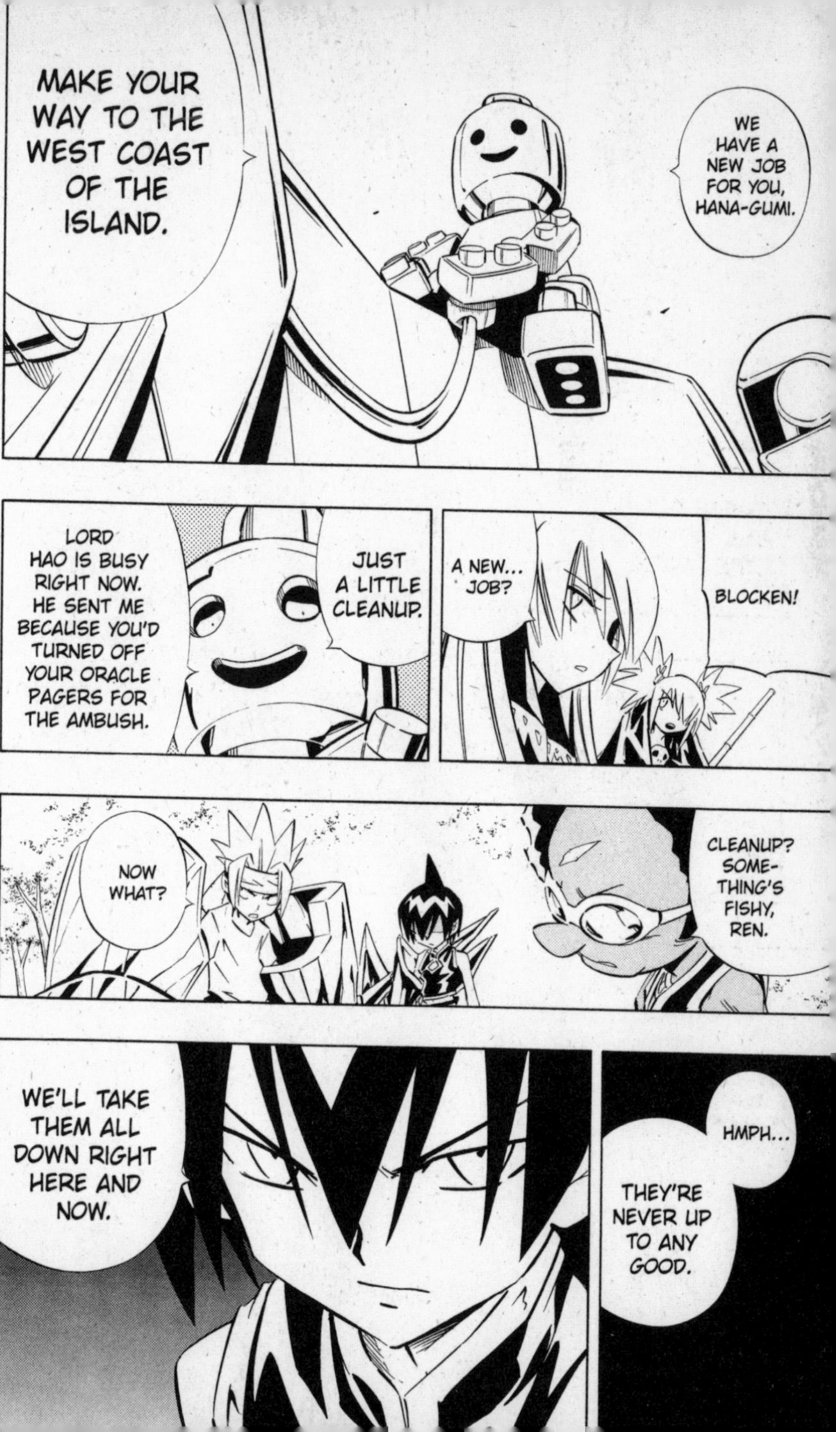
WE HAVE A NEW JOB FOR YOU, HANA-GUMI.
MAKE YOUR WAY TO THE WEST COAST OF THE ISLAND.
BLOCKEN!
A NEW... JOB?
JUST A LITTLE CLEANUP.
LORD HAO IS BUSY RIGHT NOW. HE SENT ME BECAUSE YOU'D TURNED OFF YOUR ORACLE PAGERS FOR THE AMBUSH.
CLEANUP? SOME-THING'S FISHY, REN.
NOW WHAT?
HMPH...
THEY'RE NEVER UP TO ANY GOOD.
WE'LL TAKE THEM ALL DOWN RIGHT HERE AND NOW.

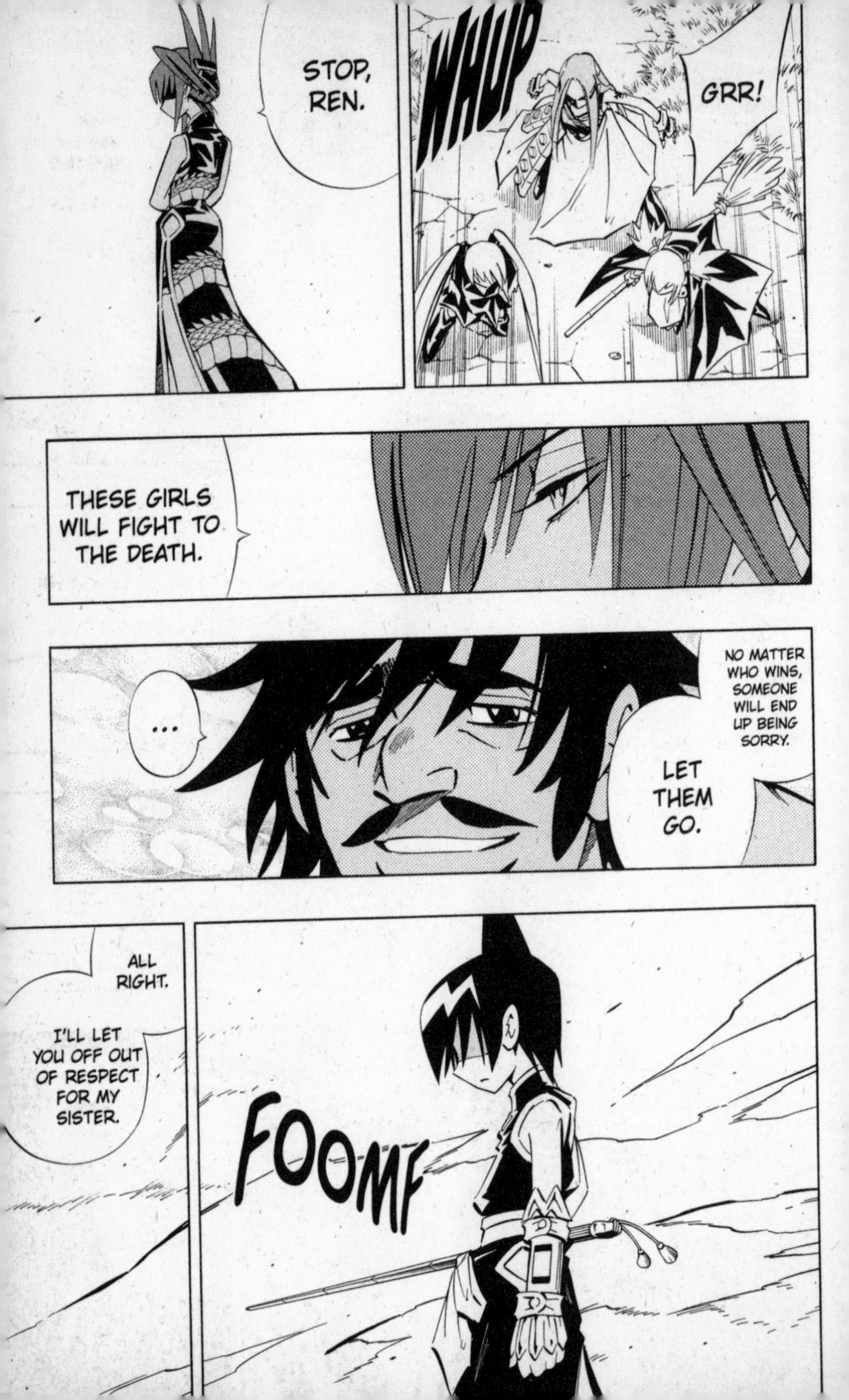
GRR!
WHUP
STOP, REN.
THESE GIRLS WILL FIGHT TO THE DEATH.
NO MATTER WHO WINS, SOMEONE WILL END UP BEING SORRY.
LET THEM GO.
...
FOOMF
ALL RIGHT.
I'LL LET YOU OFF OUT OF RESPECT FOR MY SISTER.

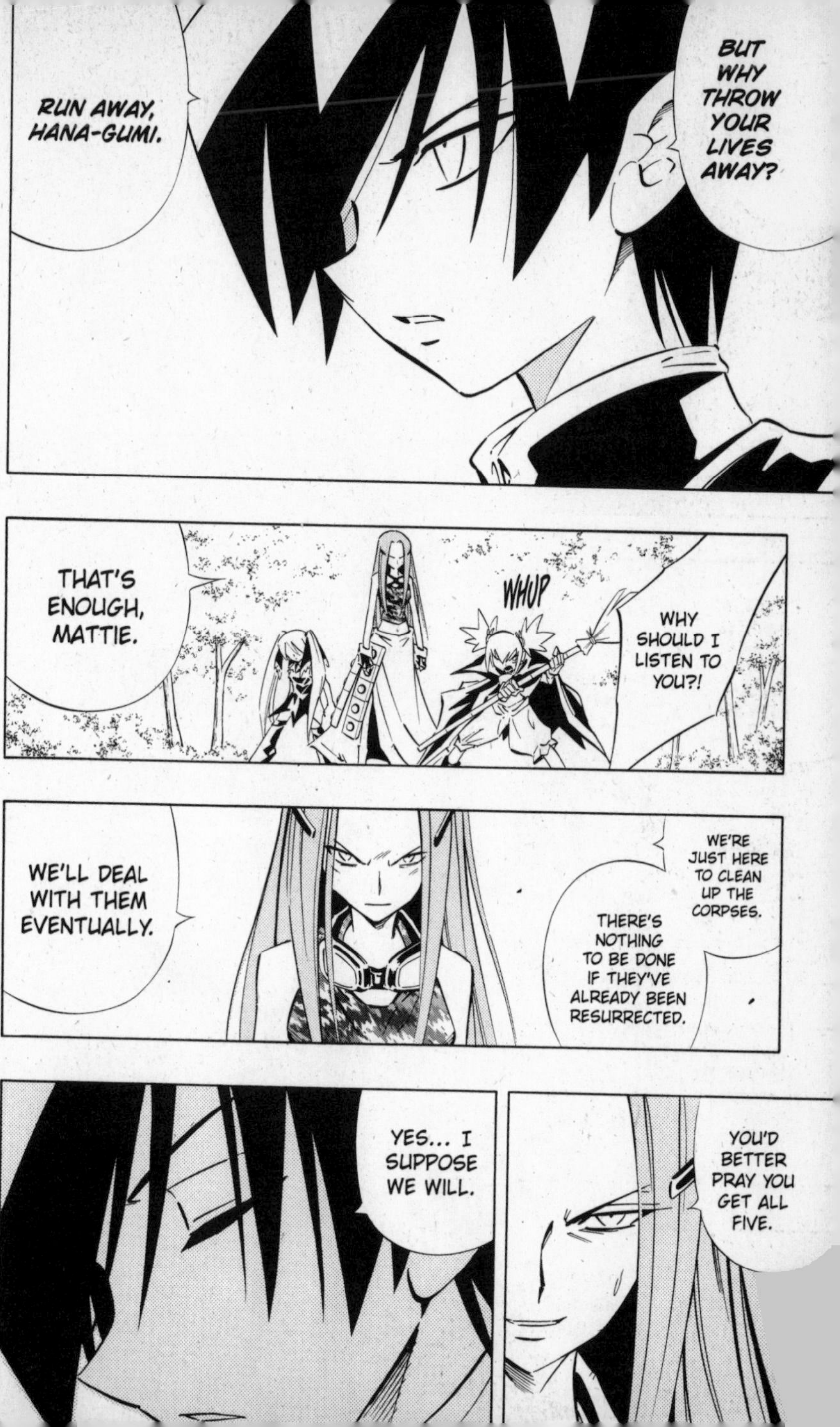
BUT WHY THROW YOUR LIVES AWAY?
RUN AWAY, HANA-GUMI.
WHUP
WHY SHOULD I LISTEN TO YOU?!
THAT'S ENOUGH, MATTIE.
WE'RE JUST HERE TO CLEAN UP THE CORPSES.
THERE'S NOTHING TO BE DONE IF THEY'VE ALREADY BEEN RESURRECTED.
WE'LL DEAL WITH THEM EVENTUALLY.
YOU'D BETTER PRAY YOU GET ALL FIVE.
YES... I SUPPOSE WE WILL.

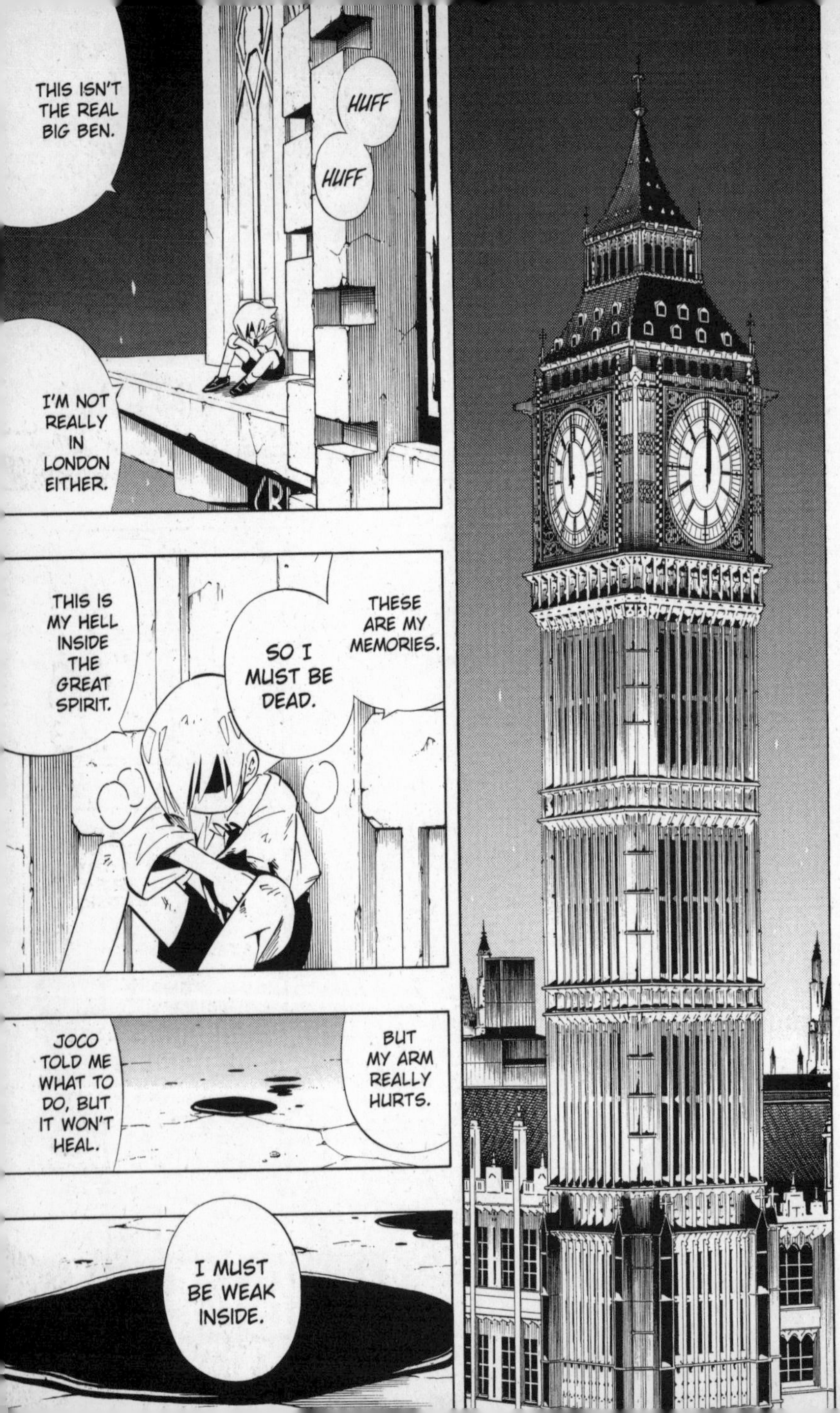
HUFF
HUFF
THIS ISN'T THE REAL BIG BEN.
I'M NOT REALLY IN LONDON EITHER.
THESE ARE MY MEMORIES.
SO I MUST BE DEAD.
THIS IS MY HELL INSIDE THE GREAT SPIRIT.
BUT MY ARM REALLY HURTS.
JOCO TOLD ME WHAT TO DO, BUT IT WON'T HEAL.
I MUST BE WEAK INSIDE.

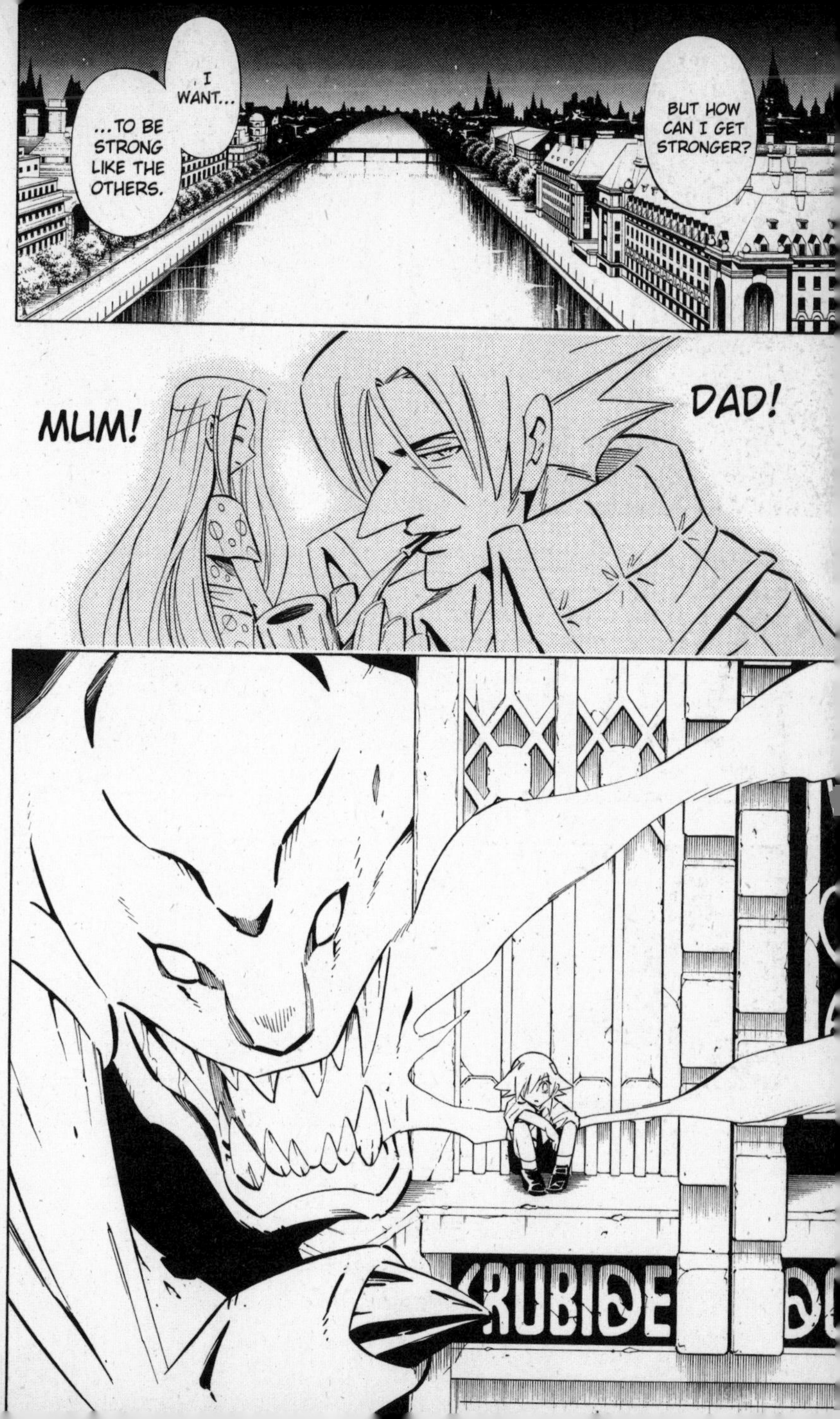
BUT HOW CAN I GET STRONGER?
I WANT...
...TO BE STRONG LIKE THE OTHERS.
DAD!
MUM!
RUBIDE

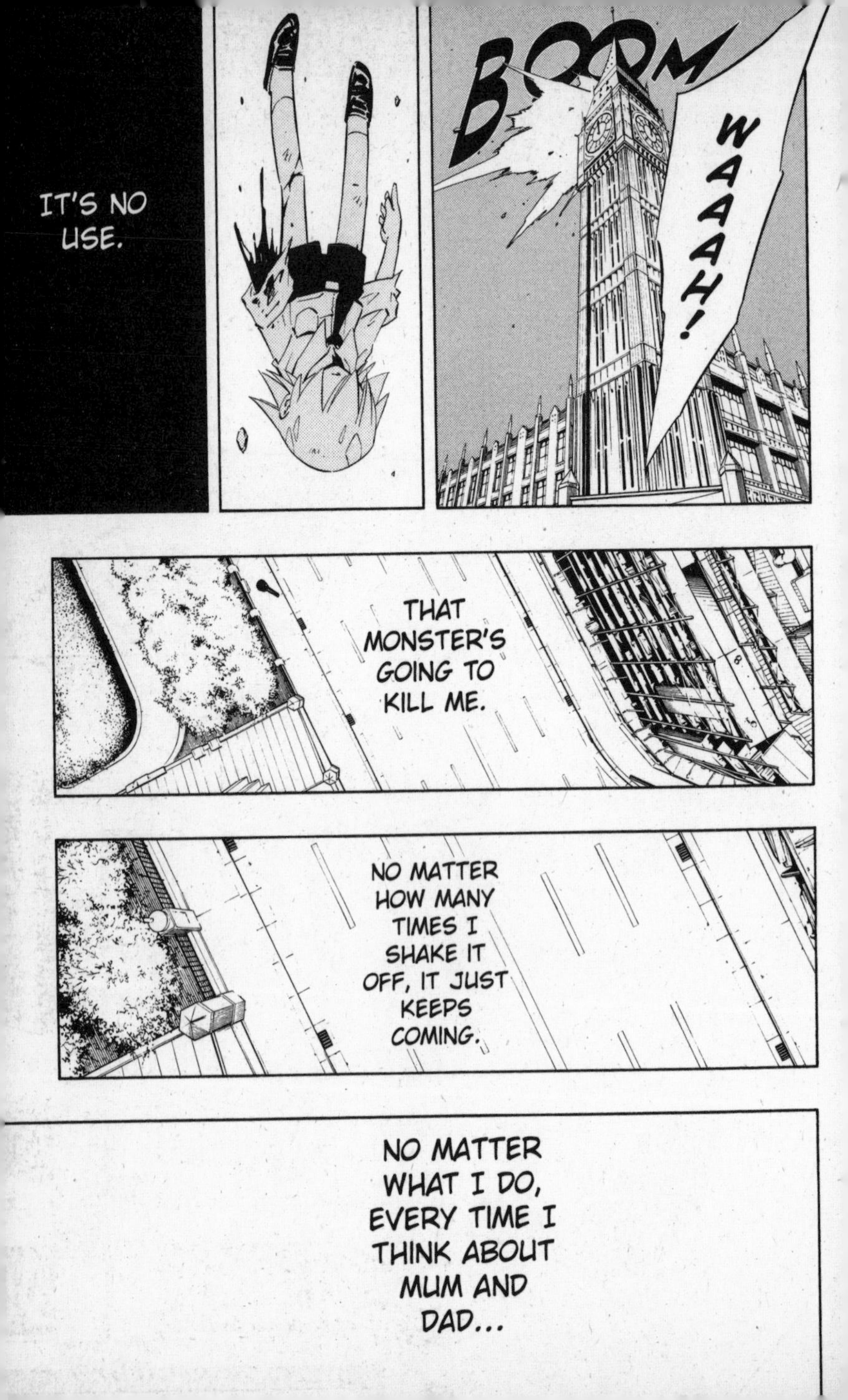
BOOM
WAAAAH!
IT'S NO USE.
THAT MONSTER'S GOING TO KILL ME.
NO MATTER HOW MANY TIMES I SHAKE IT OFF, IT JUST KEEPS COMING.
NO MATTER WHAT I DO, EVERY TIME I THINK ABOUT MUM AND DAD...

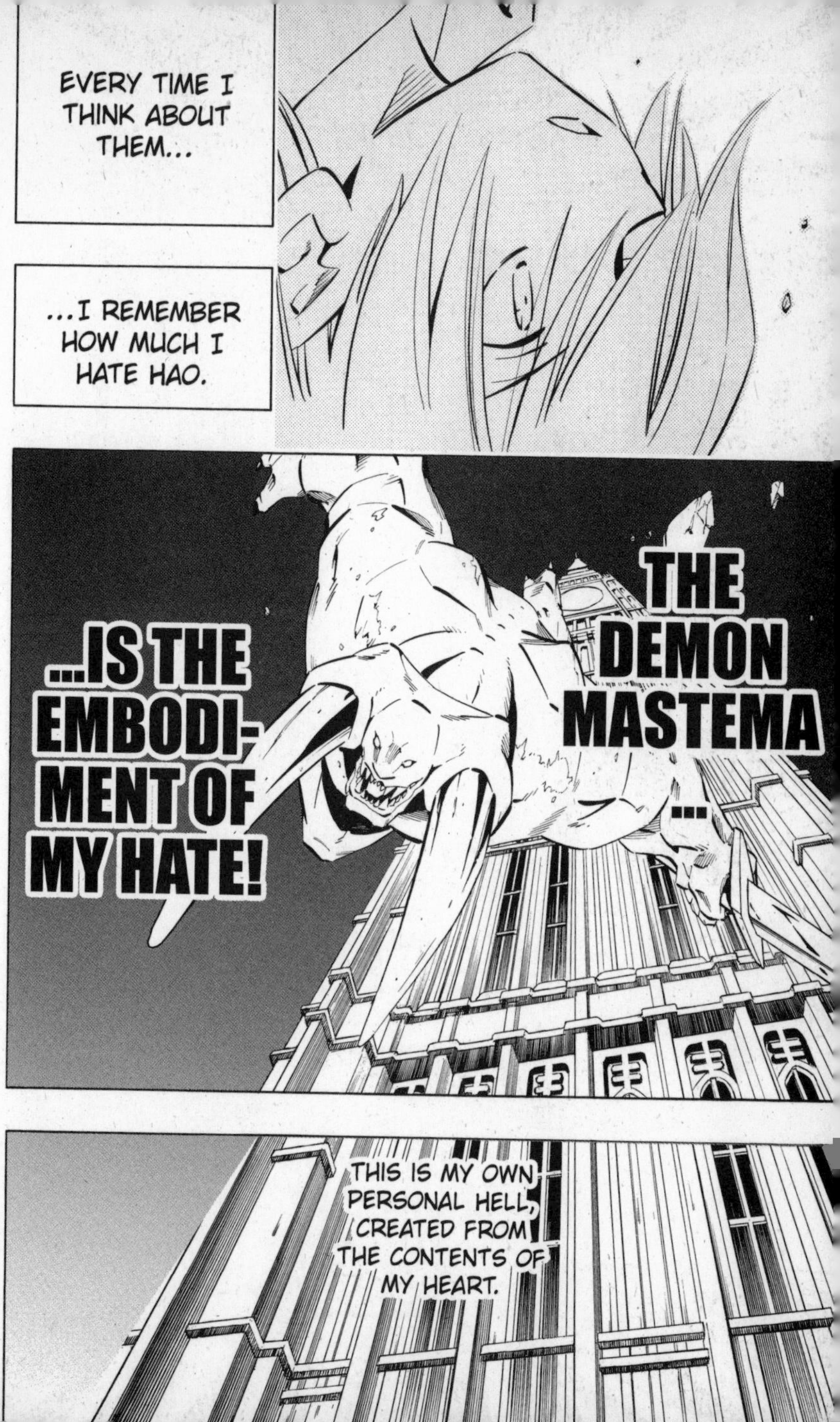
EVERY TIME I THINK ABOUT THEM...
...I REMEMBER HOW MUCH I HATE HAO.
THE DEMON MASTEMA...
...IS THE EMBODI-MENT OF MY HATE!
THIS IS MY OWN PERSONAL HELL, CREATED FROM THE CONTENTS OF MY HEART.

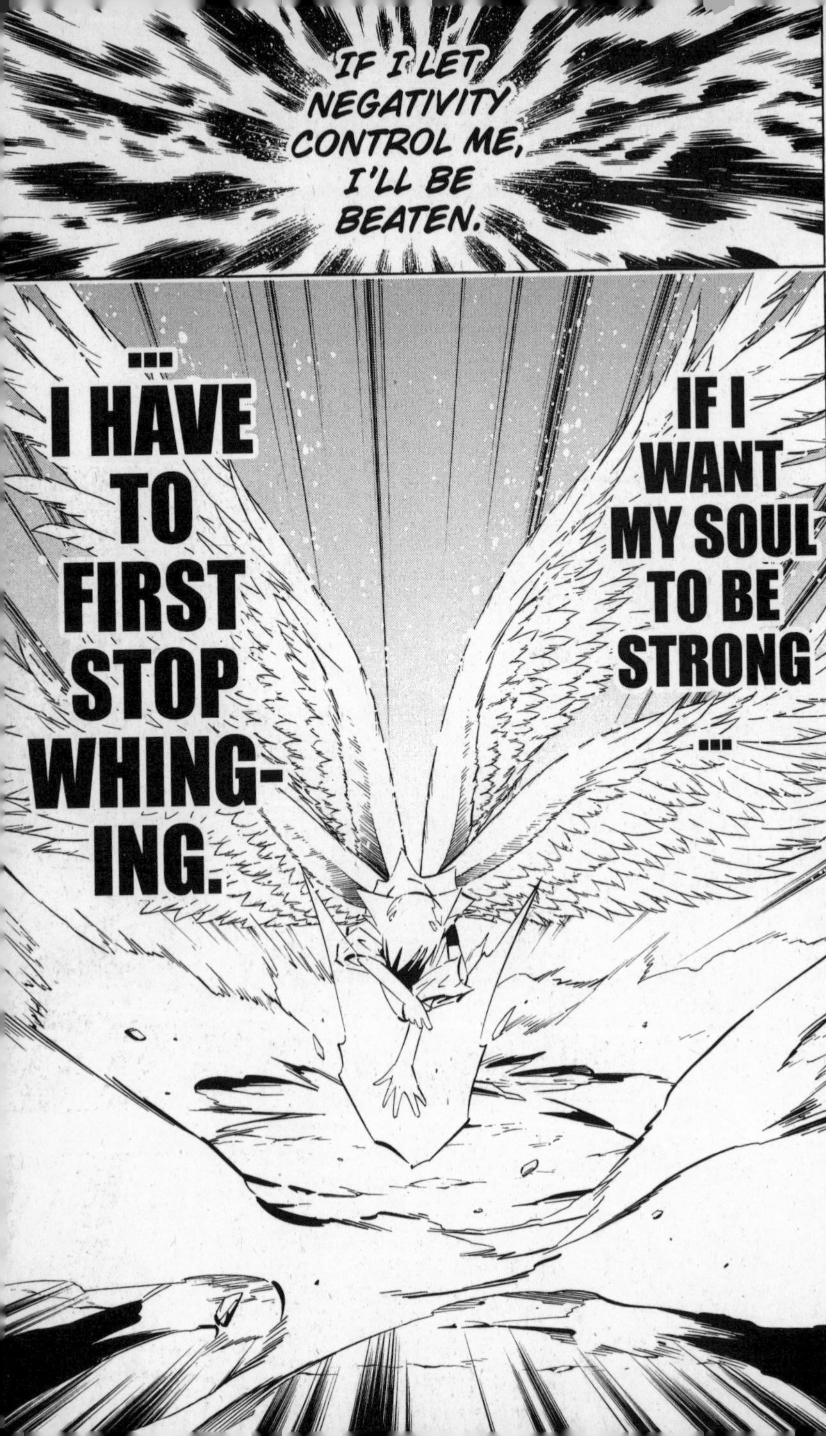
IF I LET NEGATIVITY CONTROL ME, I'LL BE BEATEN.
IF I WANT MY SOUL TO BE STRONG...
...I HAVE TO FIRST STOP WHING-ING.

SHAMAN KING CHARACTER FILE No.146

悪魔　マステマ

DEMON MASTEMA

2001
(JAN)

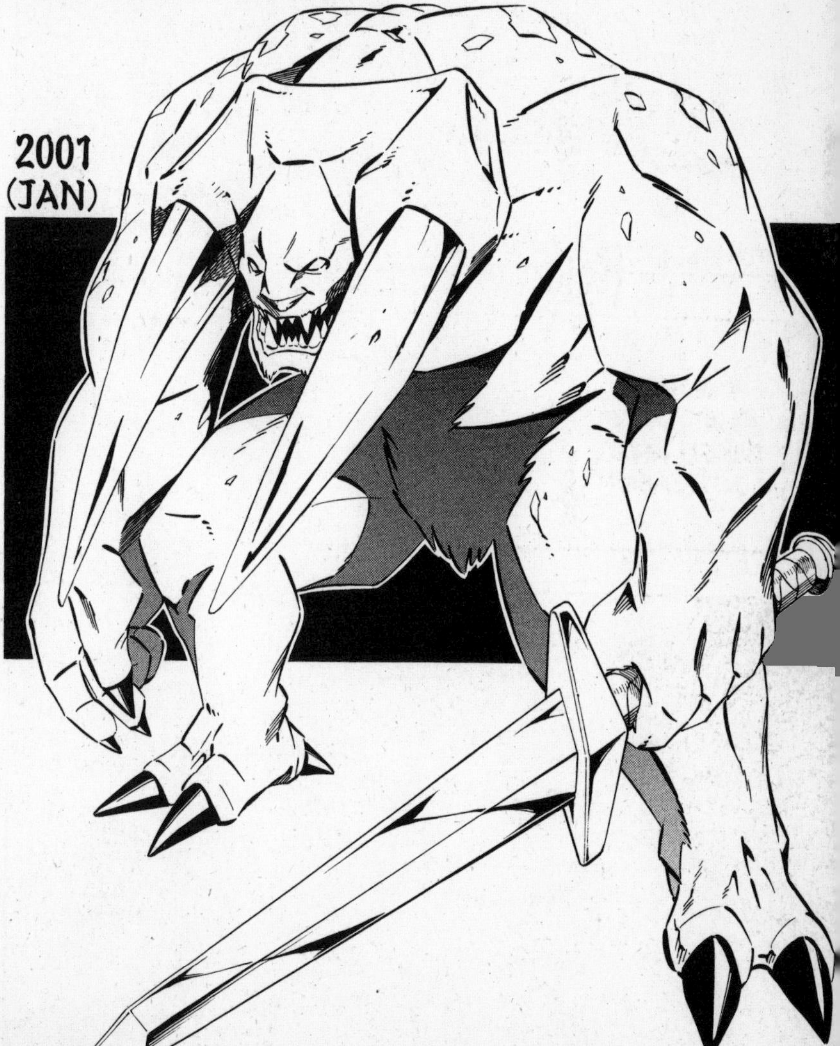

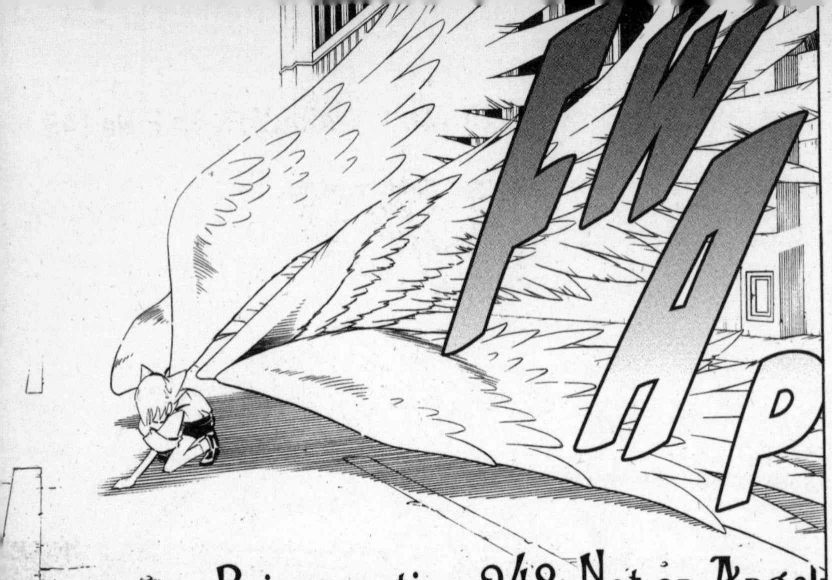
FWAP

Reincarnation 248: Not an Angel

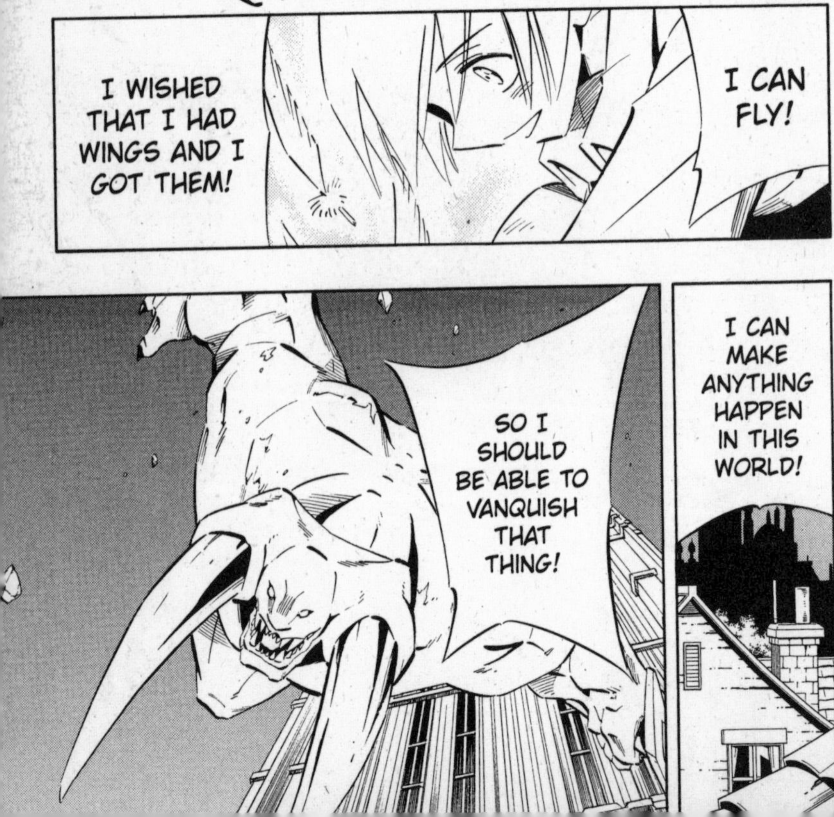
I CAN FLY!
I WISHED THAT I HAD WINGS AND I GOT THEM!
I CAN MAKE ANYTHING HAPPEN IN THIS WORLD!
SO I SHOULD BE ABLE TO VANQUISH THAT THING!

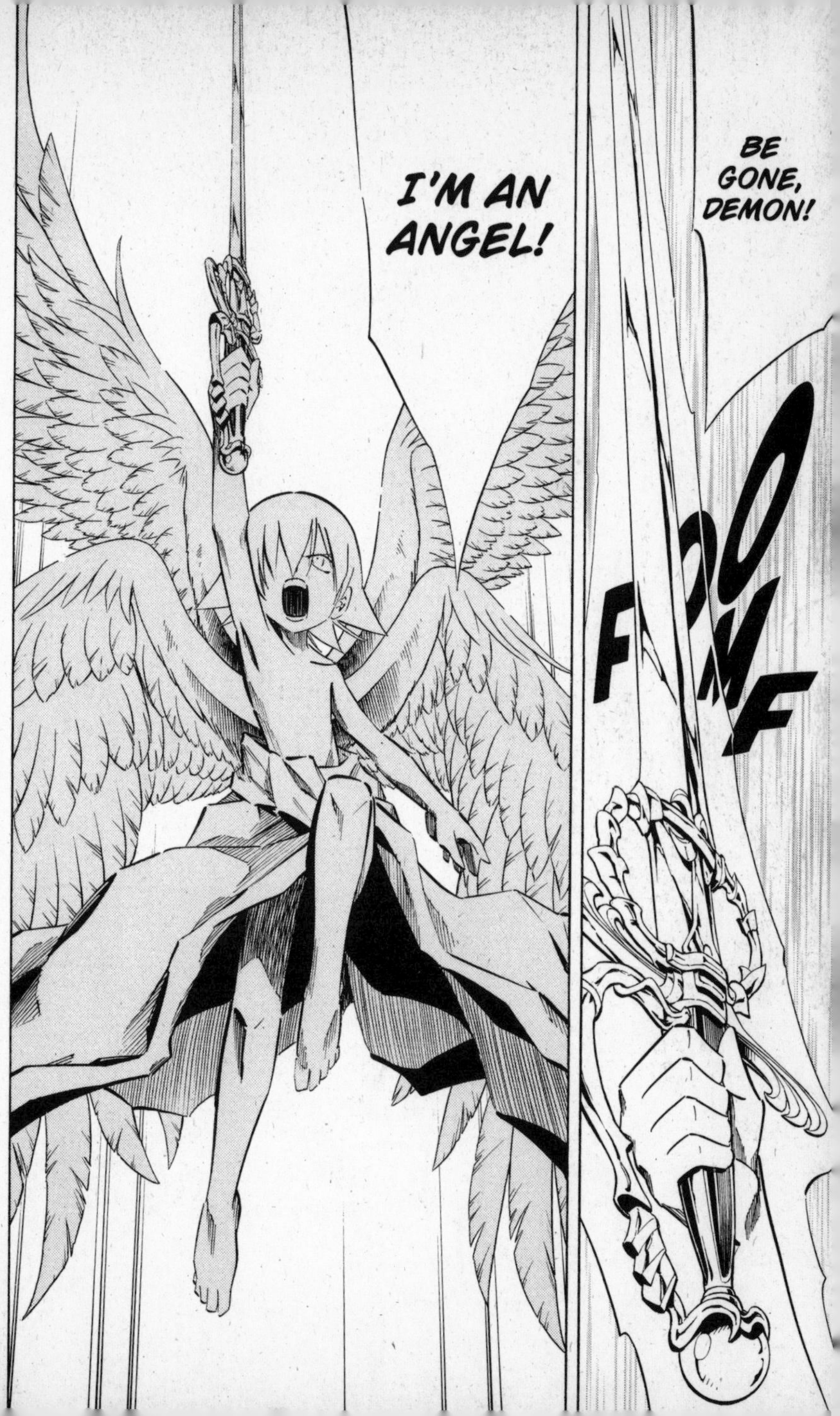
BE GONE, DEMON!
FOOMF
I'M AN ANGEL!

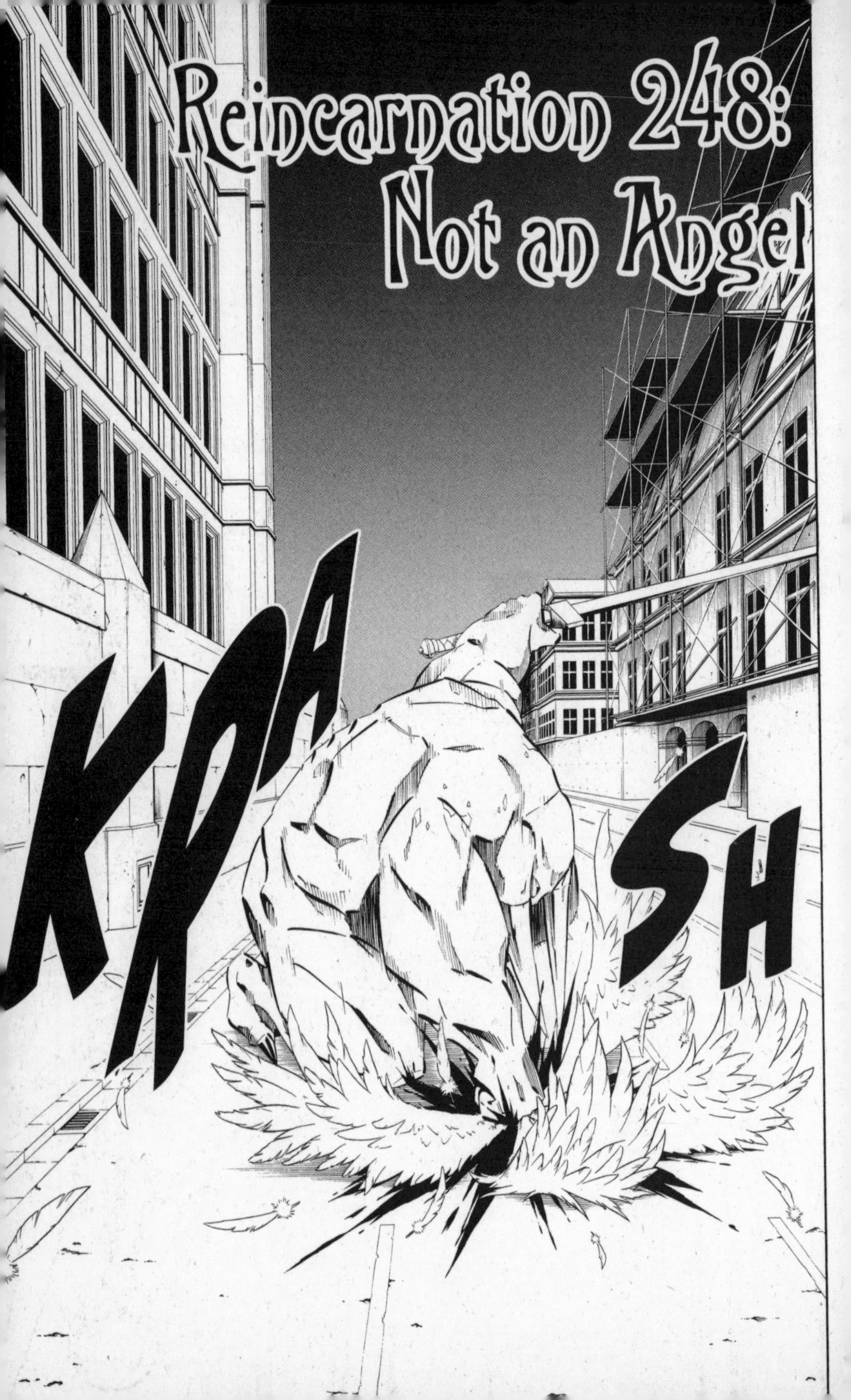
Reincarnation 248:
Not an Angel
KRRA
SH

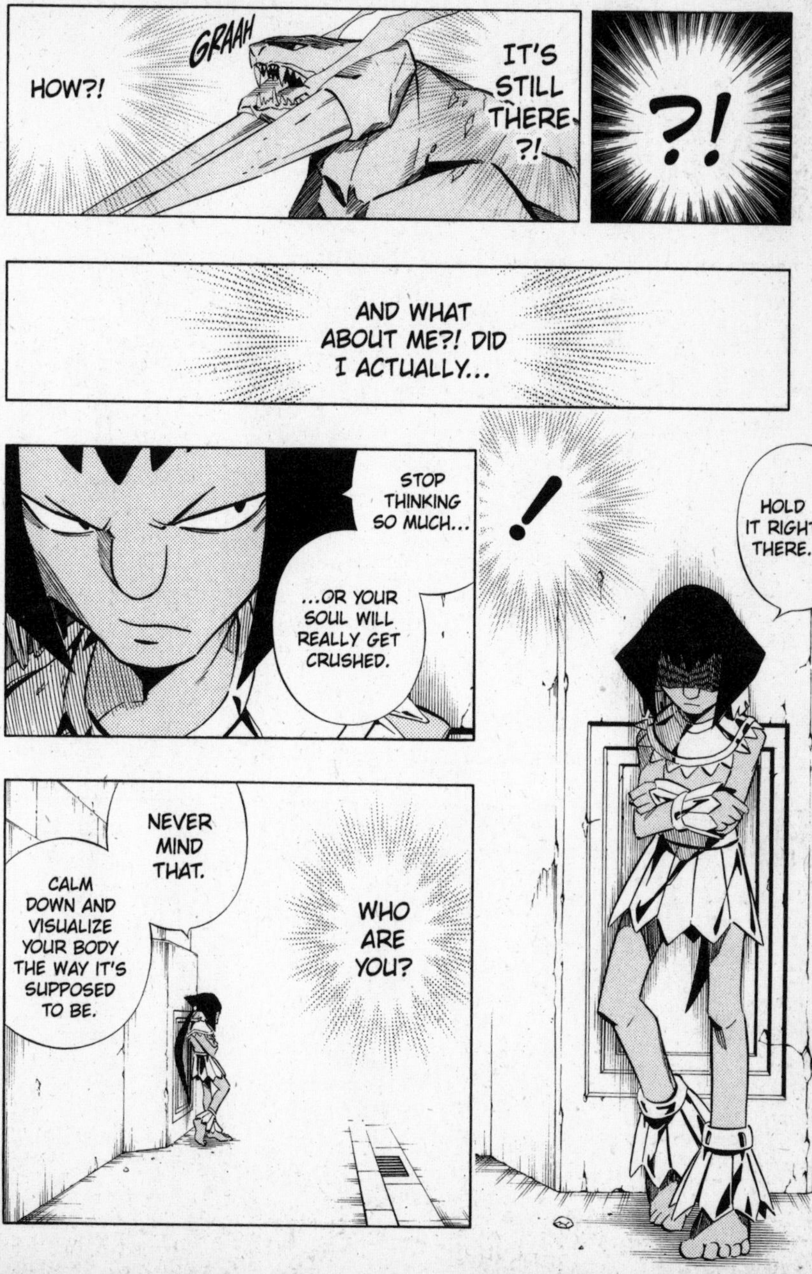
?!
IT'S STILL THERE?!
GRAAH
HOW?!
AND WHAT ABOUT ME?! DID I ACTUALLY...
HOLD IT RIGHT THERE.
!
STOP THINKING SO MUCH...
...OR YOUR SOUL WILL REALLY GET CRUSHED.
WHO ARE YOU?
NEVER MIND THAT.
CALM DOWN AND VISUALIZE YOUR BODY THE WAY IT'S SUPPOSED TO BE.

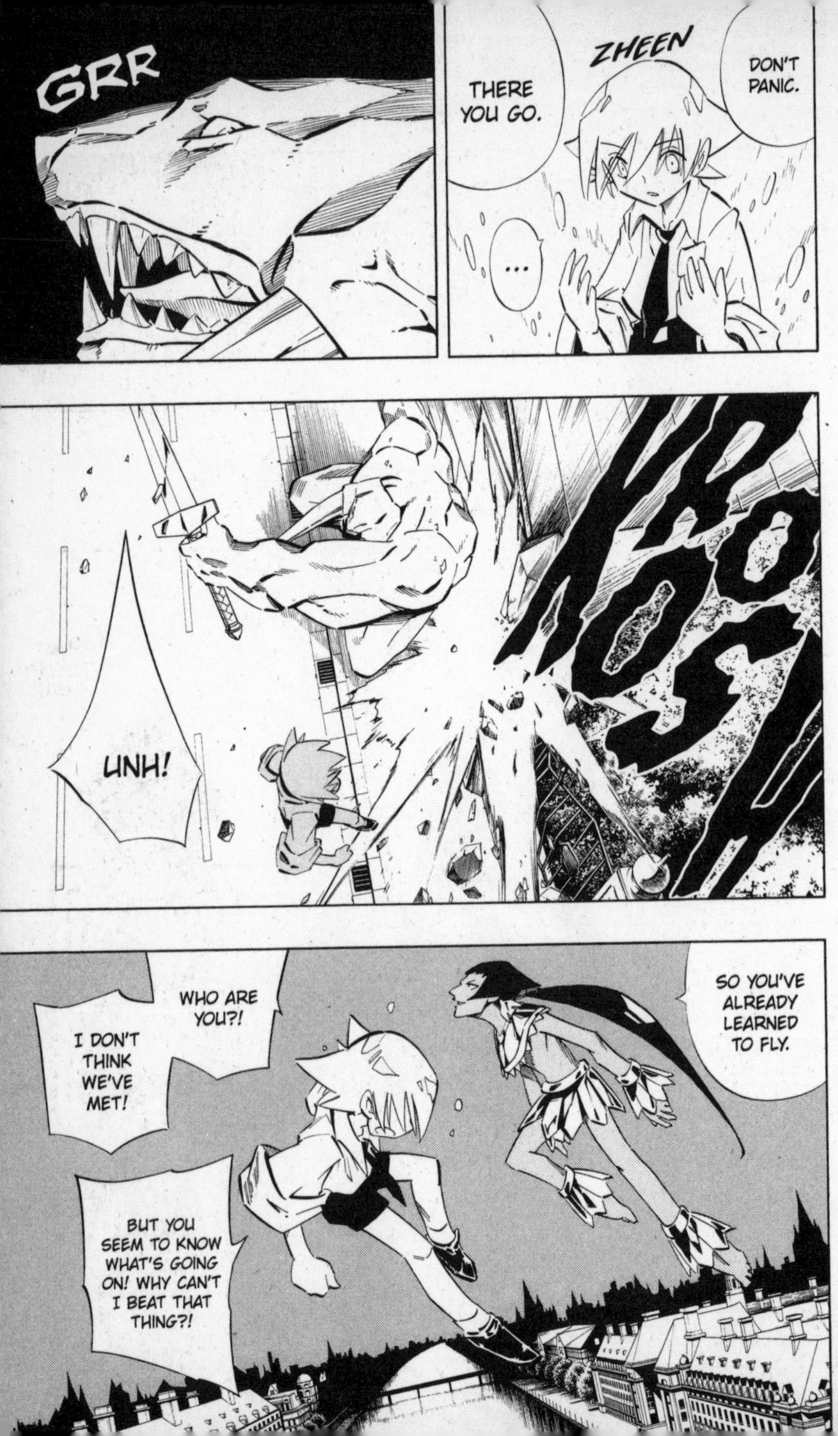
DON'T PANIC.
ZHEEN
THERE YOU GO.
...
GRR
UNH!
SO YOU'VE ALREADY LEARNED TO FLY.
WHO ARE YOU?!
I DON'T THINK WE'VE MET!
BUT YOU SEEM TO KNOW WHAT'S GOING ON! WHY CAN'T I BEAT THAT THING?!

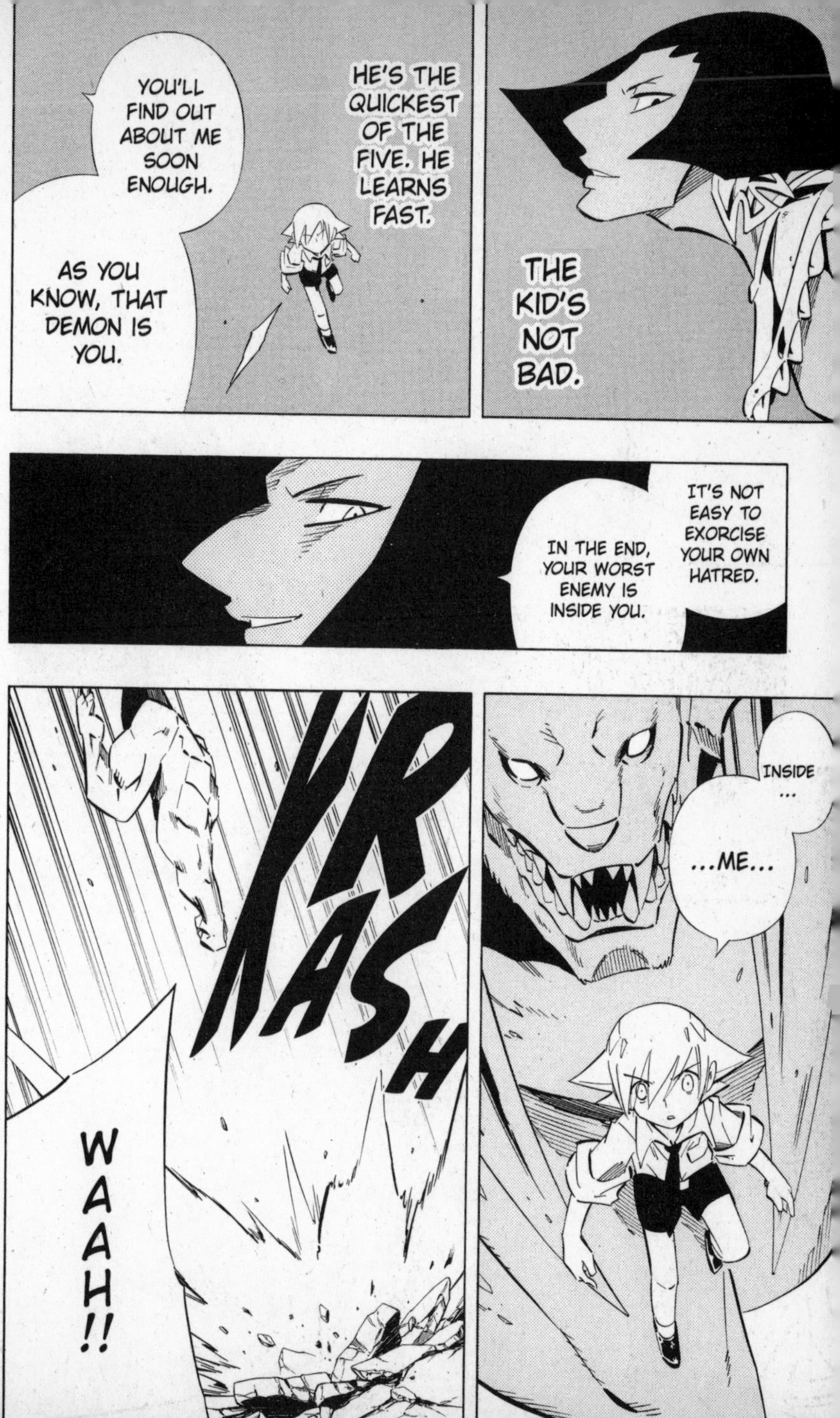
THE KID'S NOT BAD.
HE'S THE QUICKEST OF THE FIVE. HE LEARNS FAST.
YOU'LL FIND OUT ABOUT ME SOON ENOUGH.
AS YOU KNOW, THAT DEMON IS YOU.
IT'S NOT EASY TO EXORCISE YOUR OWN HATRED.
IN THE END, YOUR WORST ENEMY IS INSIDE YOU.
INSIDE ...
...ME...
KRASH
WAAAH!!

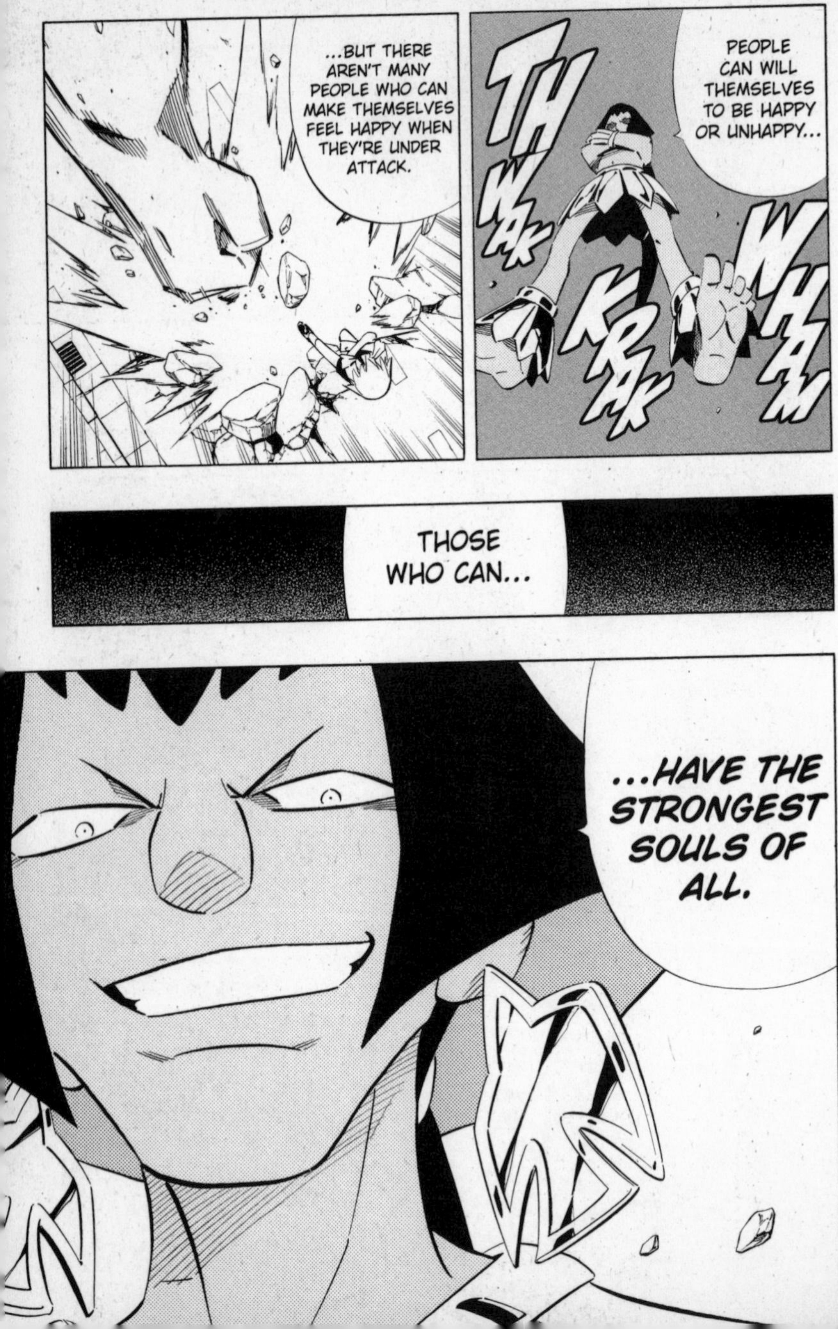
PEOPLE CAN WILL THEMSELVES TO BE HAPPY OR UNHAPPY...
THWAK
WHAM
KRAK
...BUT THERE AREN'T MANY PEOPLE WHO CAN MAKE THEMSELVES FEEL HAPPY WHEN THEY'RE UNDER ATTACK.
THOSE WHO CAN...
...HAVE THE STRONGEST SOULS OF ALL.

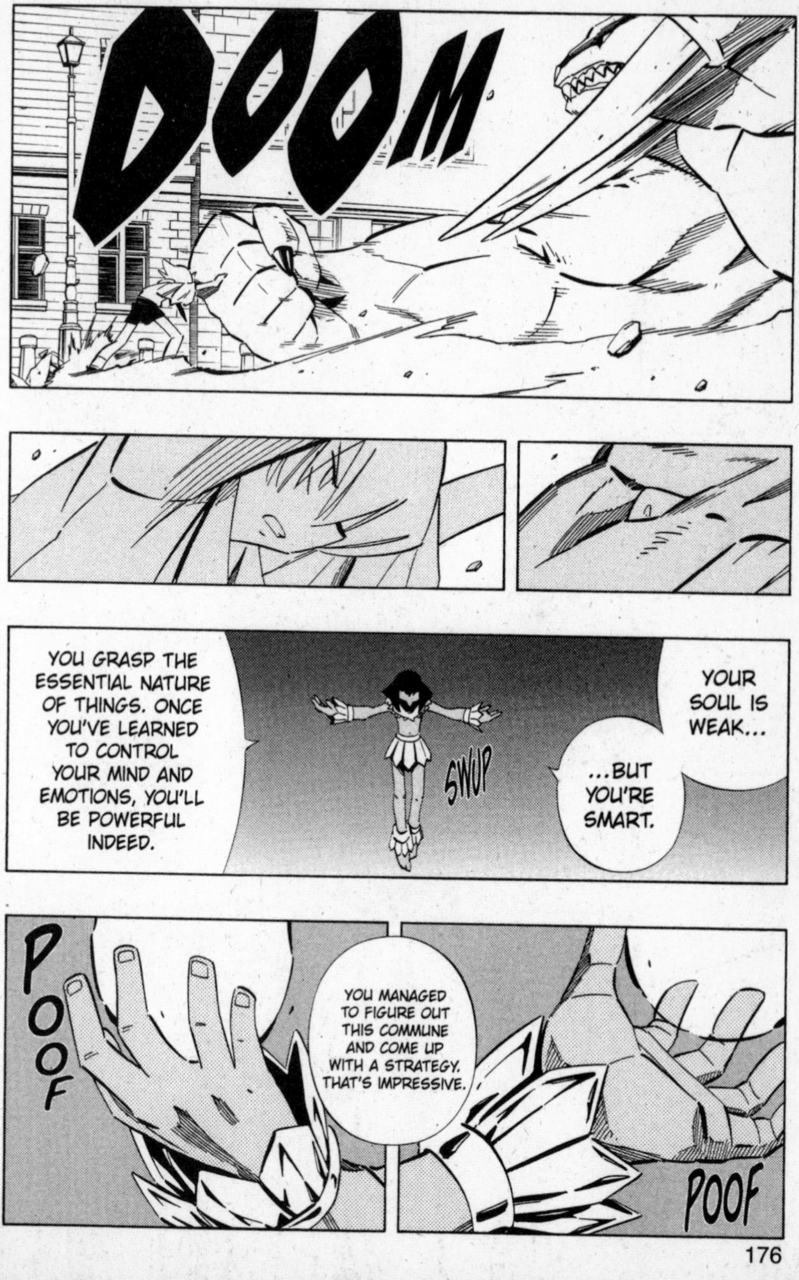
DOOM
YOUR SOUL IS WEAK...
...BUT YOU'RE SMART.
SWUP
YOU GRASP THE ESSENTIAL NATURE OF THINGS. ONCE YOU'VE LEARNED TO CONTROL YOUR MIND AND EMOTIONS, YOU'LL BE POWERFUL INDEED.
POOF
YOU MANAGED TO FIGURE OUT THIS COMMUNE AND COME UP WITH A STRATEGY. THAT'S IMPRESSIVE.
POOF

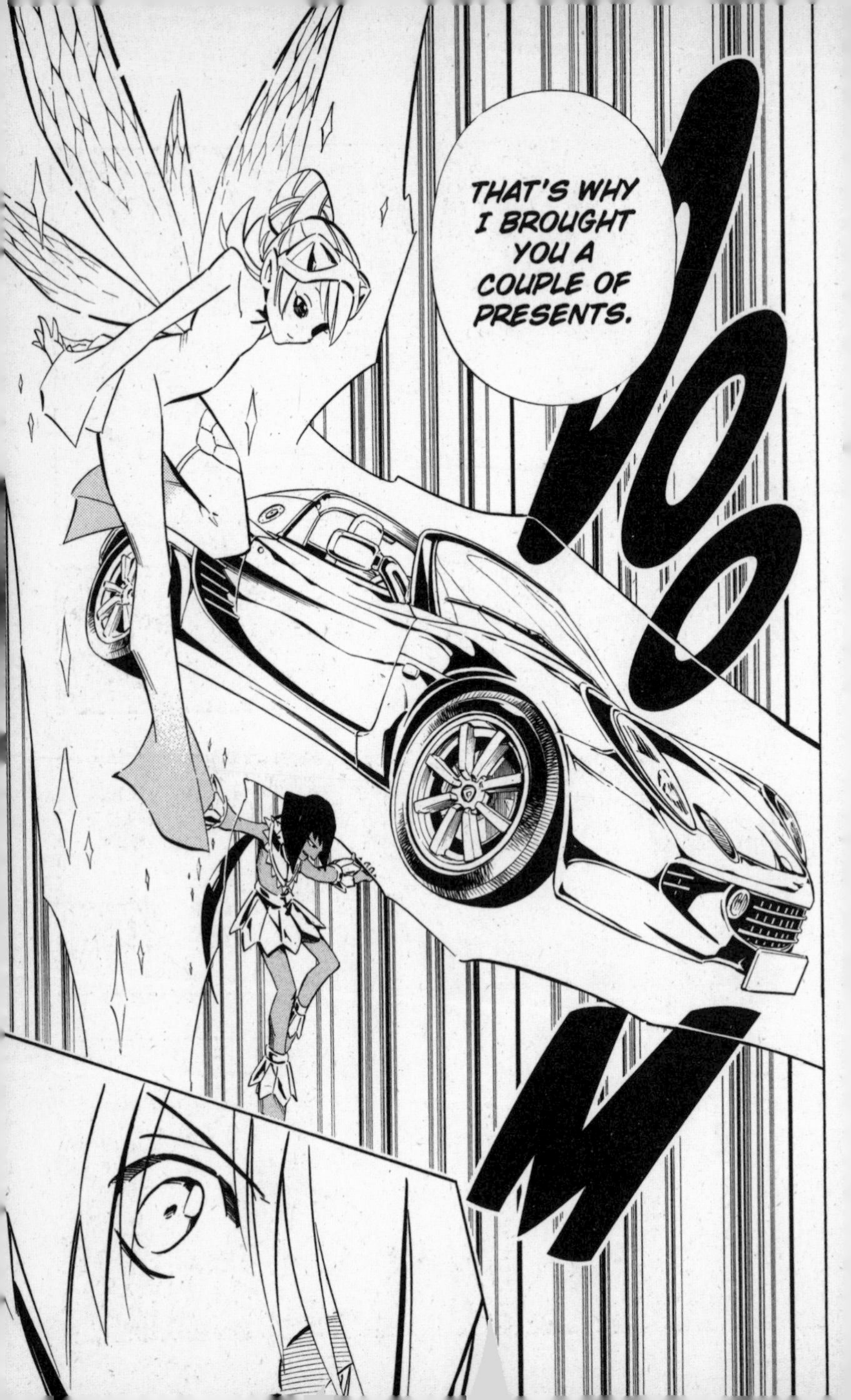
THAT'S WHY I BROUGHT YOU A COUPLE OF PRESENTS.

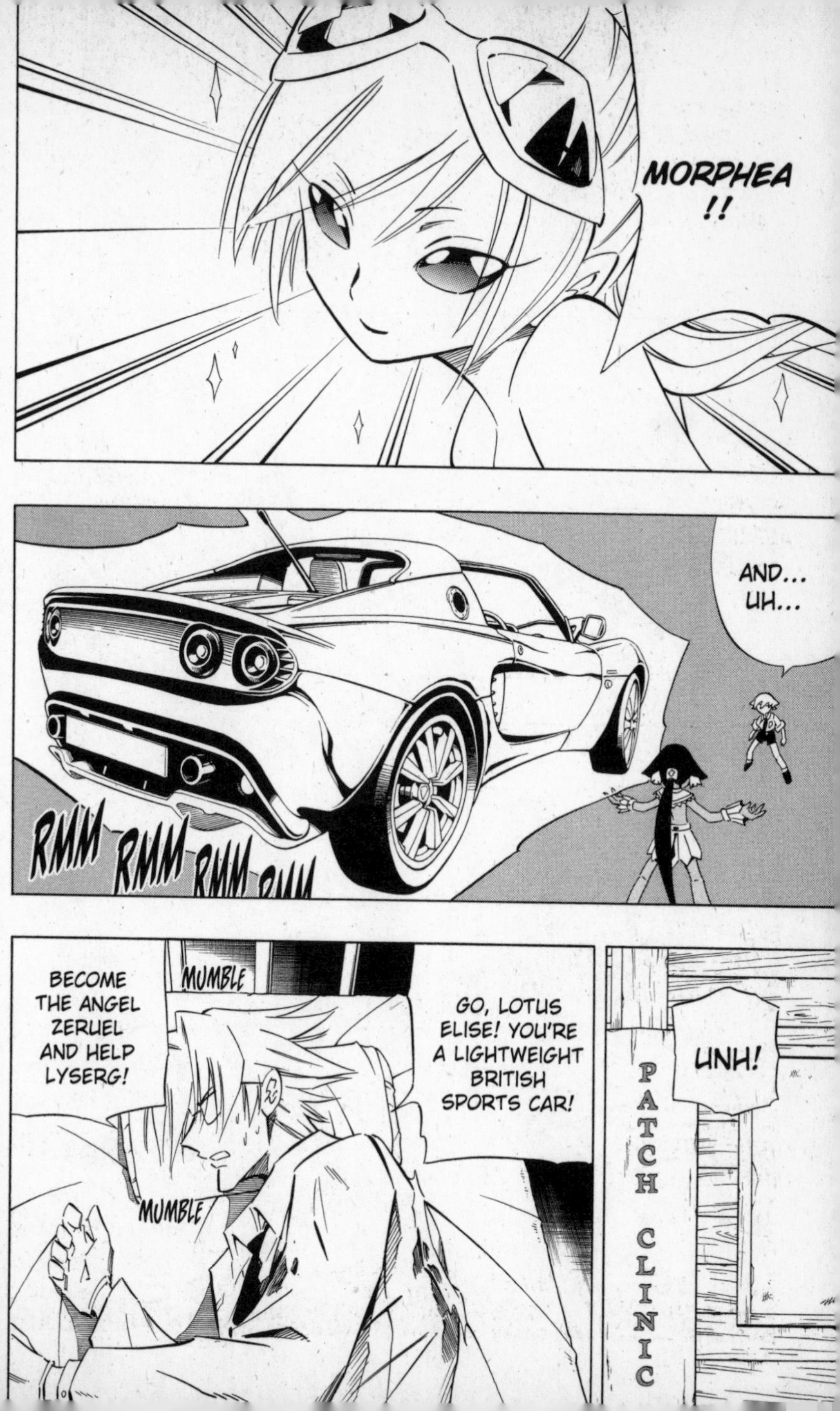

MORPHEA !!
AND... UH...
RMM RMM RMM
PATCH CLINIC
UNH!
GO, LOTUS ELISE! YOU'RE A LIGHTWEIGHT BRITISH SPORTS CAR!
MUMBLE
BECOME THE ANGEL ZERUEL AND HELP LYSERG!
MUMBLE

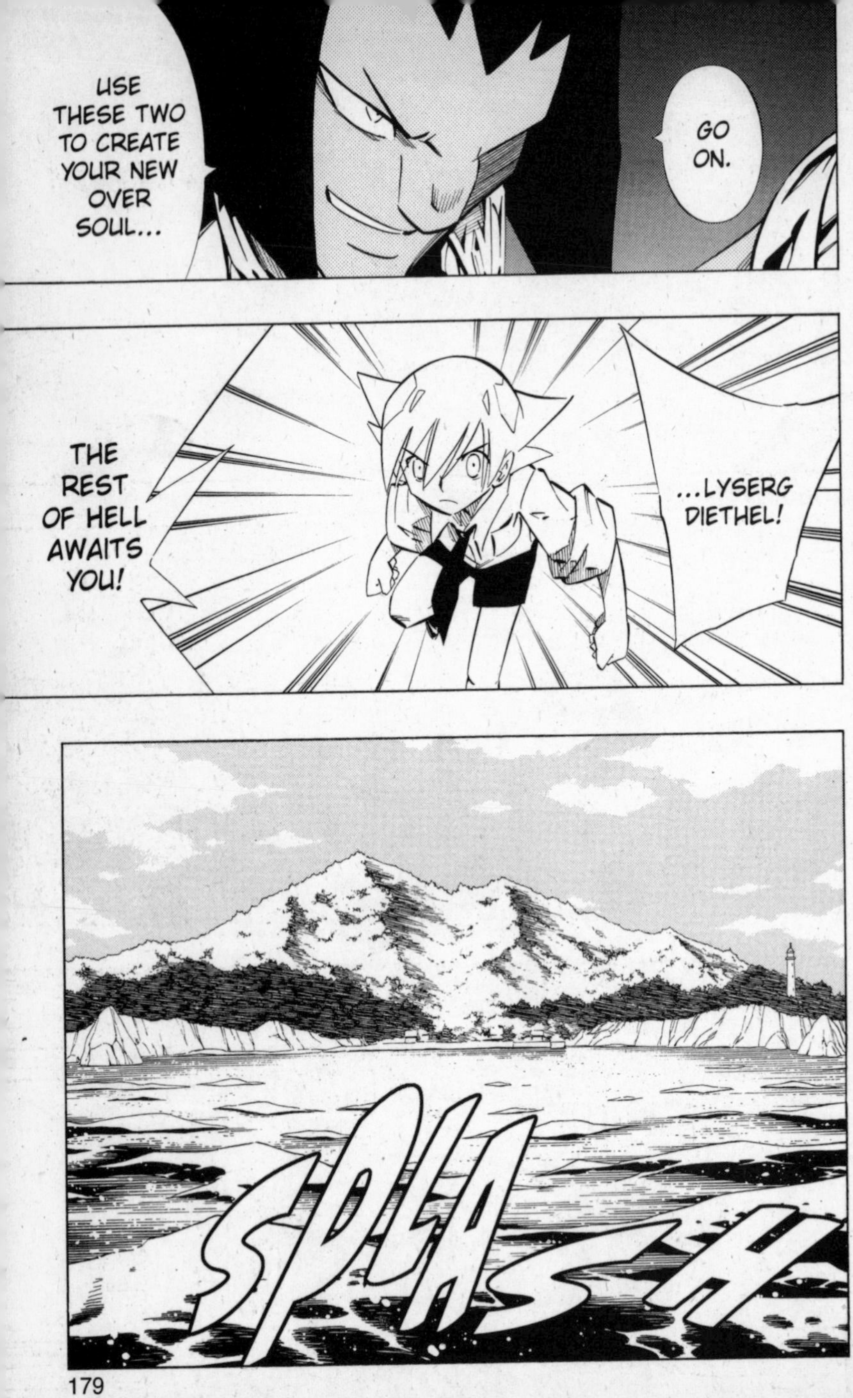
GO ON.
USE THESE TWO TO CREATE YOUR NEW OVER SOUL...
...LYSERG DIETHEL!
THE REST OF HELL AWAITS YOU!
SPLASH

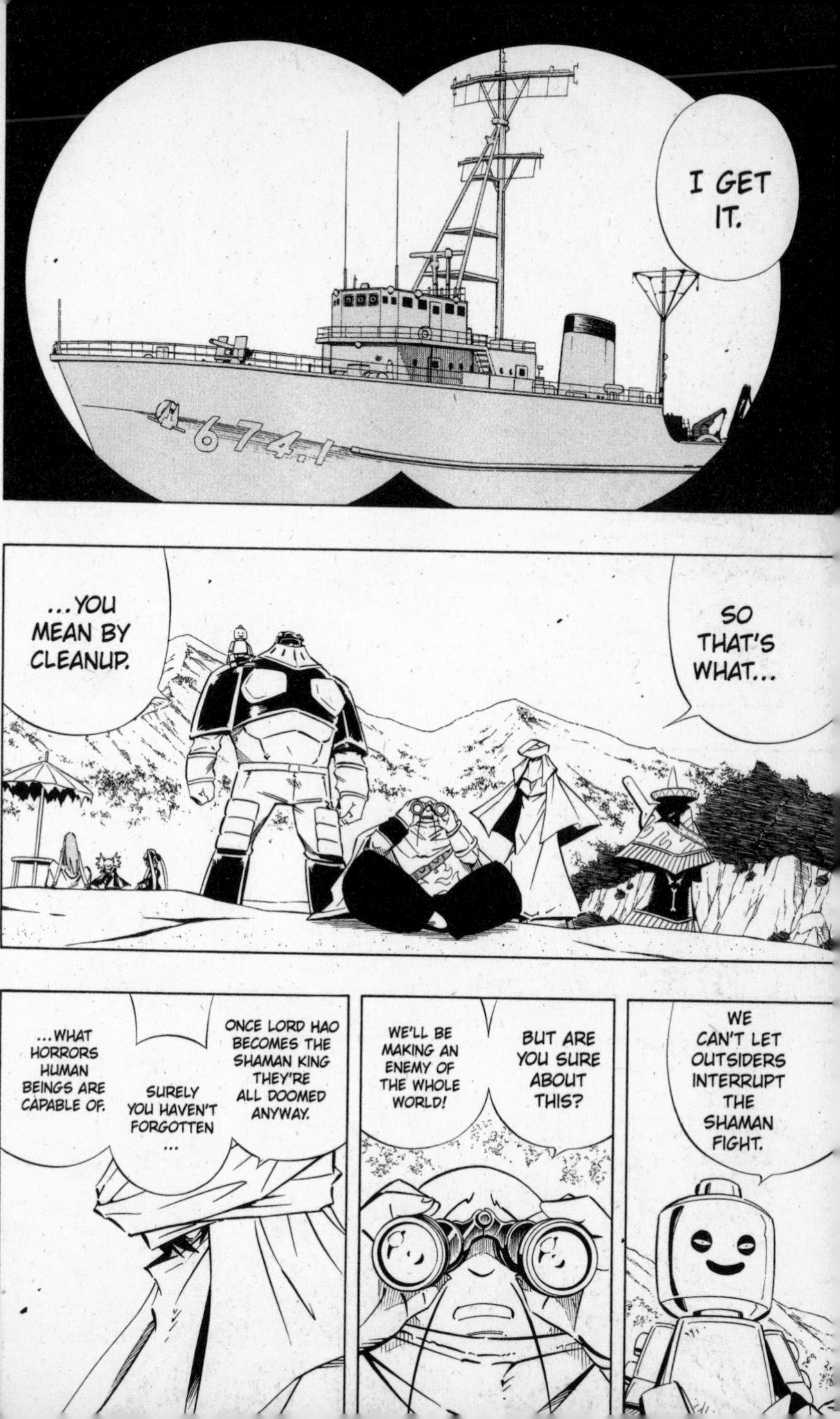
I GET IT.
SO THAT'S WHAT...
...YOU MEAN BY CLEANUP.
WE CAN'T LET OUTSIDERS INTERRUPT THE SHAMAN FIGHT.
BUT ARE YOU SURE ABOUT THIS?
WE'LL BE MAKING AN ENEMY OF THE WHOLE WORLD!
ONCE LORD HAO BECOMES THE SHAMAN KING THEY'RE ALL DOOMED ANYWAY.
SURELY YOU HAVEN'T FORGOTTEN ...
...WHAT HORRORS HUMAN BEINGS ARE CAPABLE OF.

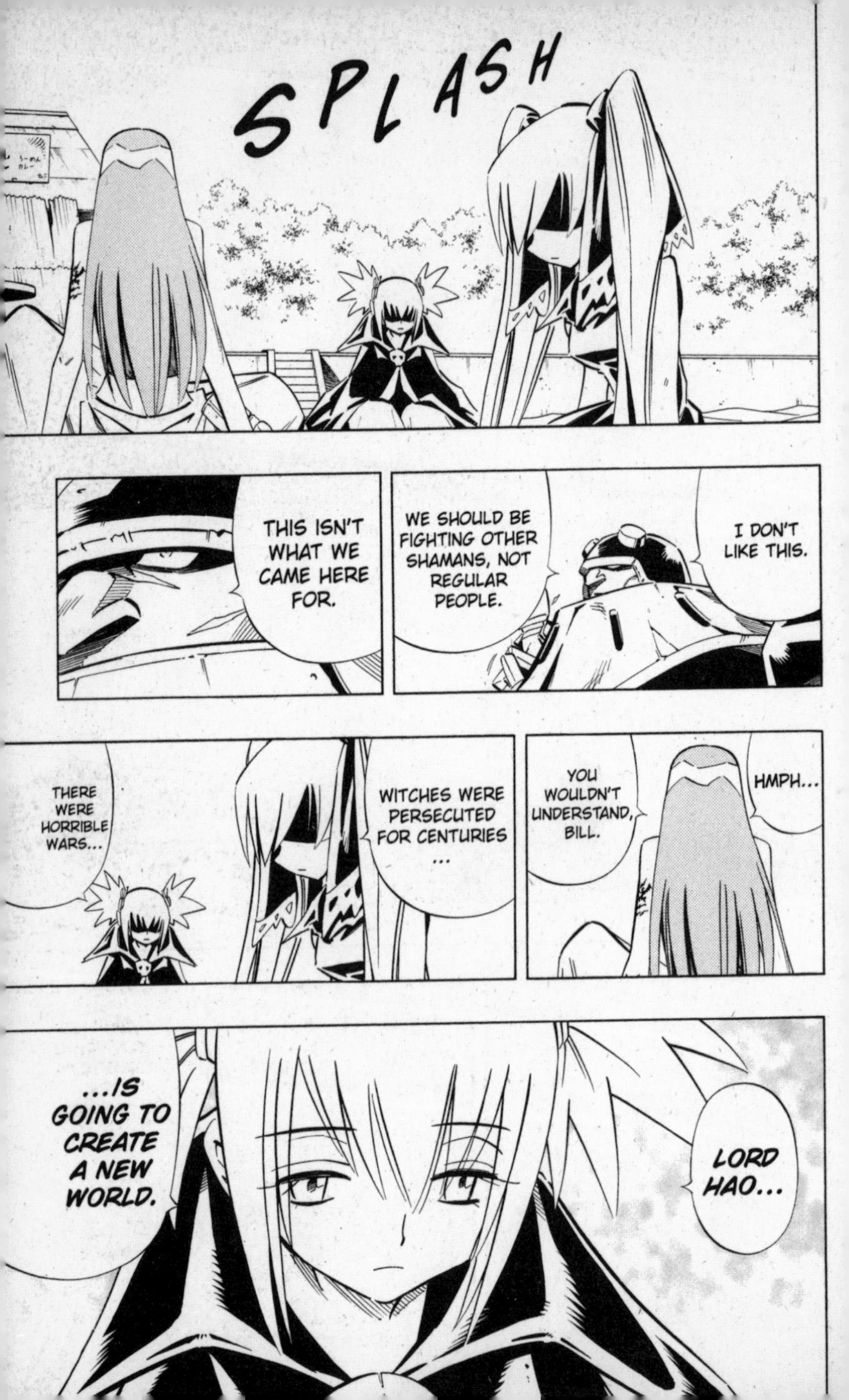
SPLASH
I DON'T LIKE THIS.
WE SHOULD BE FIGHTING OTHER SHAMANS, NOT REGULAR PEOPLE.
THIS ISN'T WHAT WE CAME HERE FOR.
HMPH...
YOU WOULDN'T UNDERSTAND, BILL.
WITCHES WERE PERSECUTED FOR CENTURIES ...
THERE WERE HORRIBLE WARS...
LORD HAO...
...IS GOING TO CREATE A NEW WORLD.

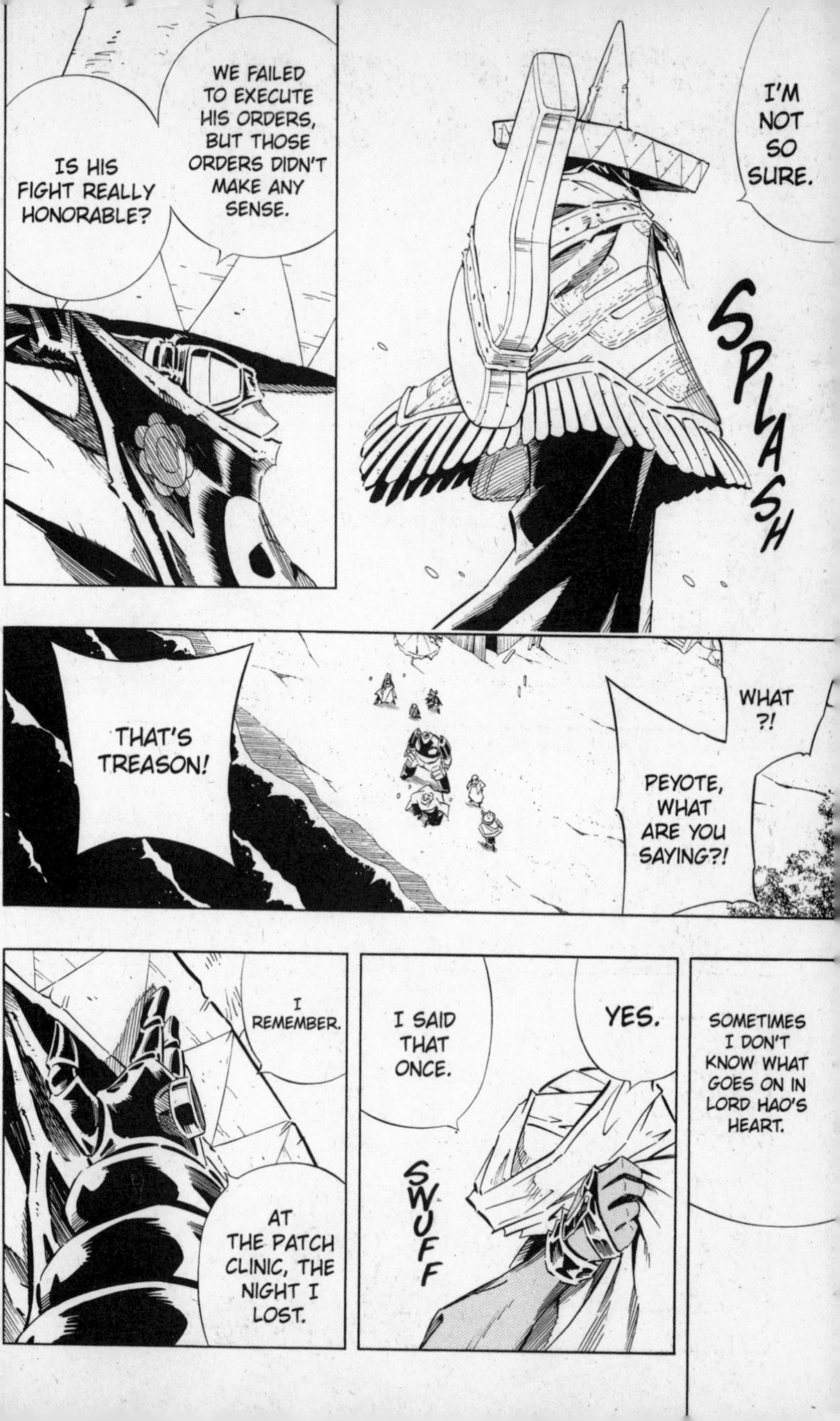
I'M NOT SO SURE.
SPLASH
WE FAILED TO EXECUTE HIS ORDERS, BUT THOSE ORDERS DIDN'T MAKE ANY SENSE.
IS HIS FIGHT REALLY HONORABLE?
WHAT ?!
PEYOTE, WHAT ARE YOU SAYING?!
THAT'S TREASON!
SOMETIMES I DON'T KNOW WHAT GOES ON IN LORD HAO'S HEART.
YES.
I SAID THAT ONCE.
SWUFF
I REMEMBER.
AT THE PATCH CLINIC, THE NIGHT I LOST.

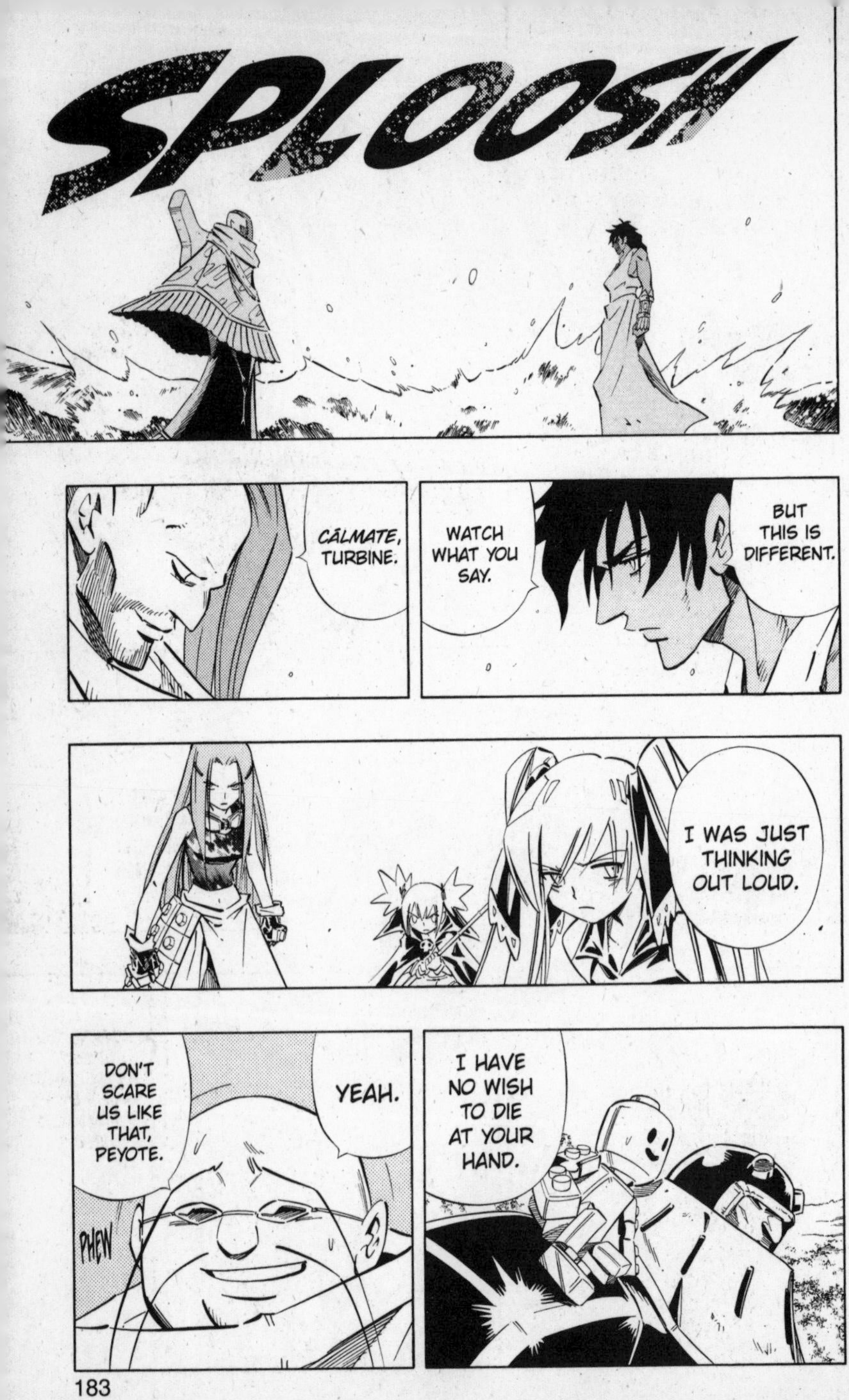
SPLOOSH
BUT THIS IS DIFFERENT.
WATCH WHAT YOU SAY.
CÁLMATE, TURBINE.
I WAS JUST THINKING OUT LOUD.
I HAVE NO WISH TO DIE AT YOUR HAND.
YEAH.
DON'T SCARE US LIKE THAT, PEYOTE.
PHEW

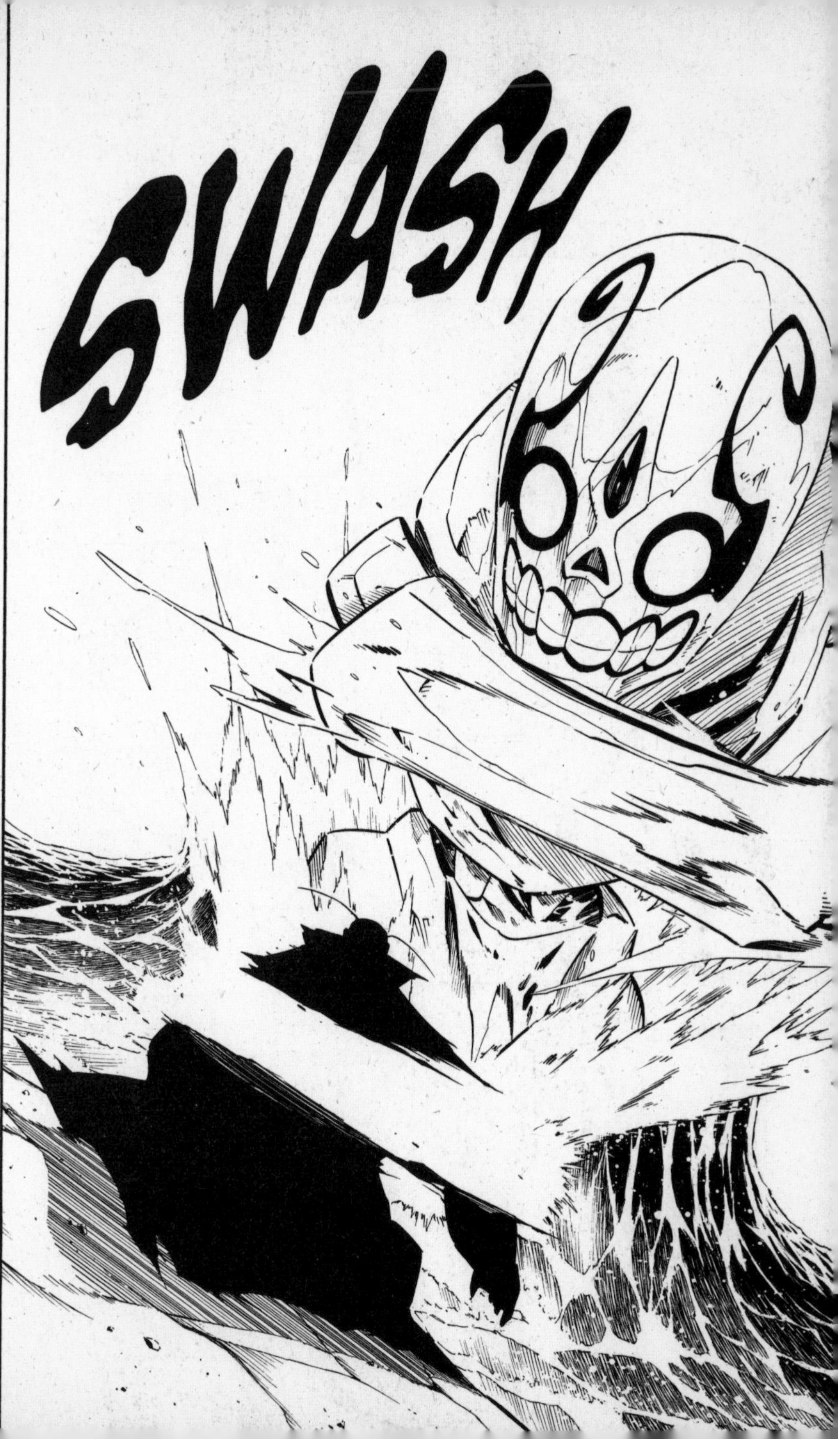
SWASH

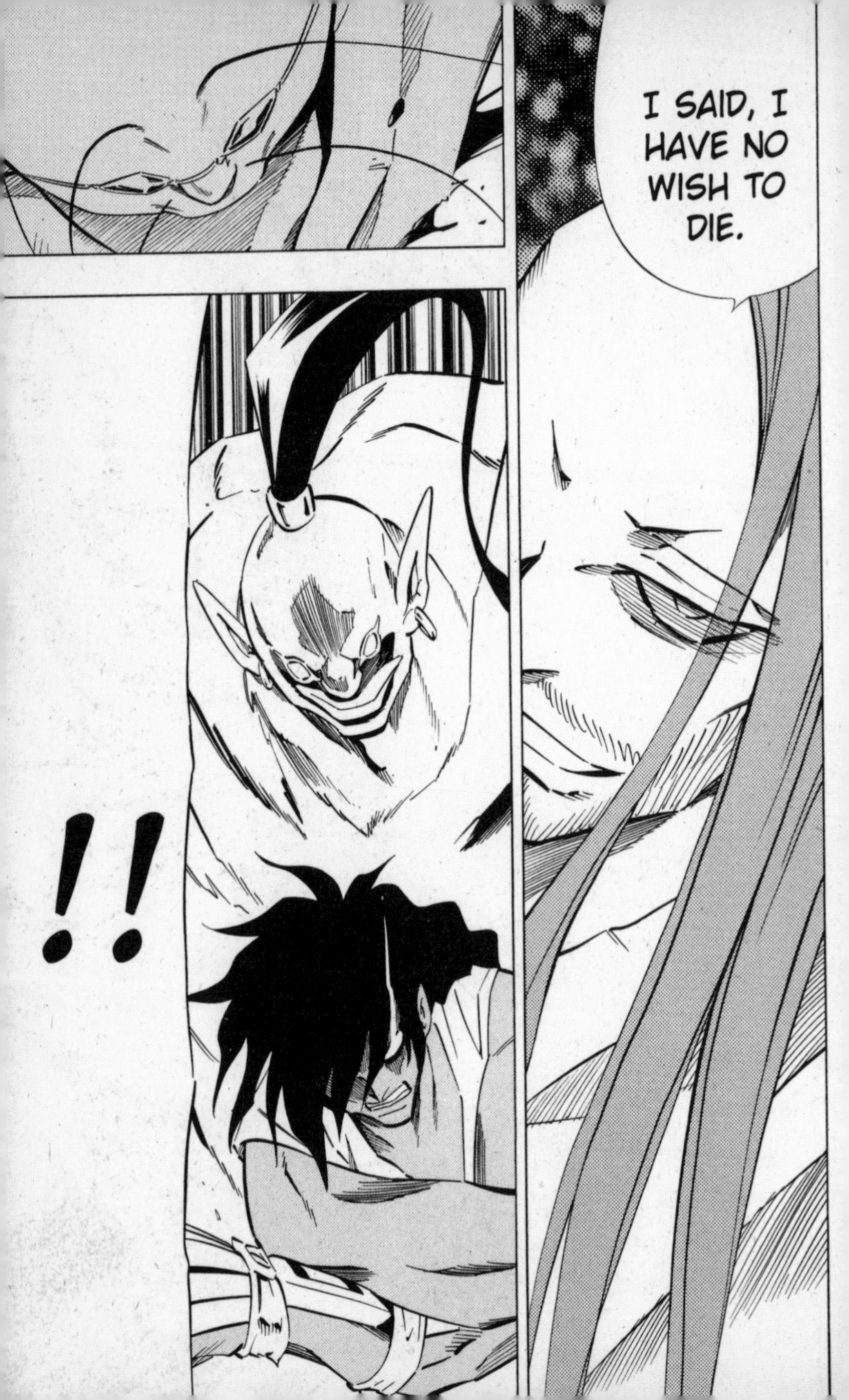
I SAID, I HAVE NO WISH TO DIE.
!!

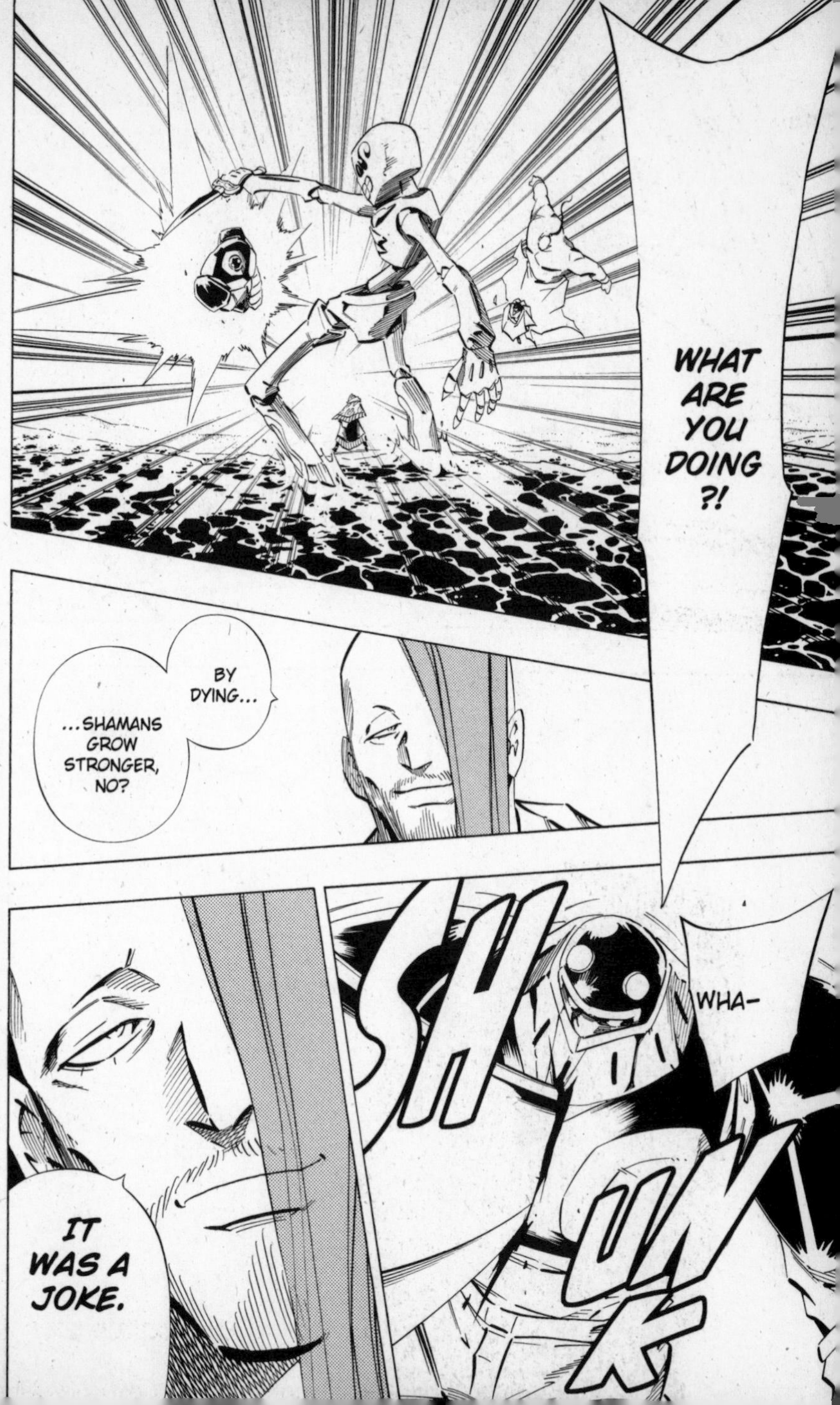
WHAT ARE YOU DOING?!
BY DYING...
...SHAMANS GROW STRONGER, NO?
WHA-
IT WAS A JOKE.

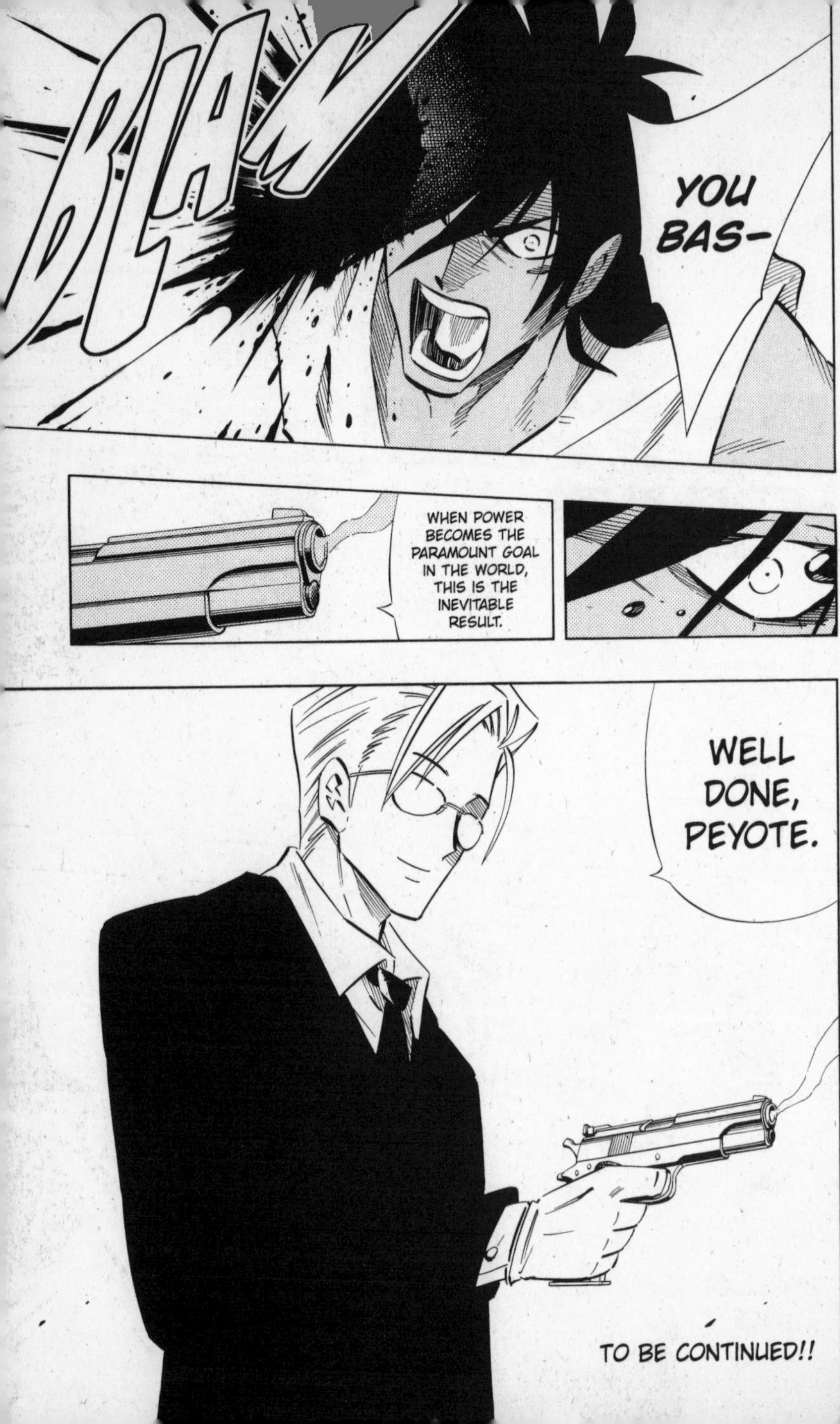
BLAM
YOU BAS-
WHEN POWER BECOMES THE PARAMOUNT GOAL IN THE WORLD, THIS IS THE INEVITABLE RESULT.
WELL DONE, PEYOTE.
TO BE CONTINUED!!

SHAMAN KING CHARACTER FILE No.147

ロータス エリーゼ

LOTUS ELISE

2001
(JAN)

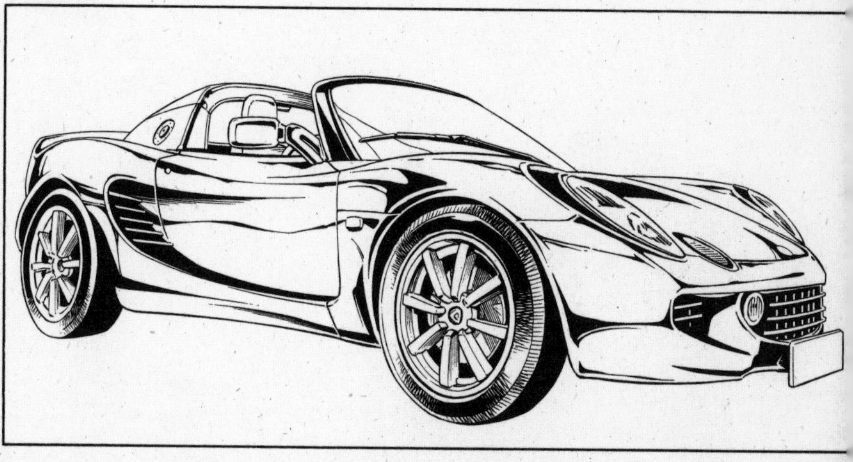

HAUNTED HOUSE

APPEARED IN *WEEKLY SHONEN JUMP* DOUBLE ISSUE 37/38, 2003.

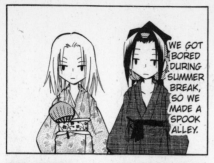

WE GOT BORED DURING SUMMER BREAK, SO WE MADE A SPOOK ALLEY.
THE "SPOOKS" WAITED IN THE SHADOWS TO POUNCE.
SW
F
VEEN
HUFF HUFF
HUFF HUFF
IT WAS MORE OF A TEST OF COURAGE FOR AMIDAMARU.
HUFF HUFF
BUT IF I JUMP OUT AND SCARE HER, ANNA WILL KILL ME!

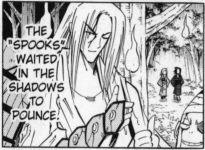

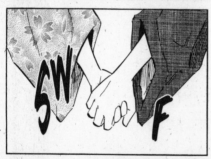

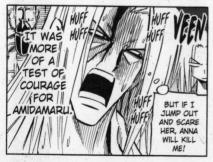

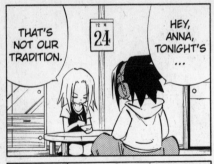

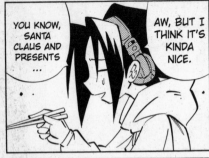

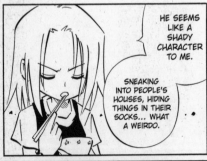

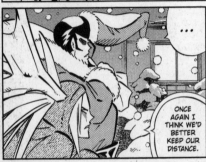

HAUNTED HOUSE

APPEARED IN WEEKLY *SHONEN JUMP* DOUBLE ISSUE 4/5, 2004.

HEY, ANNA, TONIGHT'S ...
12 月
24
THAT'S NOT OUR TRADITION.
AW, BUT I THINK IT'S KINDA NICE.
YOU KNOW, SANTA CLAUS AND PRESENTS ...
HE SEEMS LIKE A SHADY CHARACTER TO ME.
SNEAKING INTO PEOPLE'S HOUSES, HIDING THINGS IN THEIR SOCKS... WHAT A WEIRDO.
...
ONCE AGAIN I THINK WE'D BETTER KEEP OUR DISTANCE.

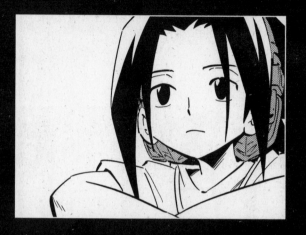

IN THE NEXT VOLUME...

Finally, the shaman slugfest we've all been waiting for: Yoh Asakura vs. Tao Ren! Yoh wants to keep the contest clean, but Ren has other plans. His crew strikes hard and fast and has Team Yoh on the ropes. Get ready for the biggest *Shaman King* shocker of them all!

AVAILABLE JULY 2010!